Lecture Notes in Artificial Intelligence 13251

Subseries of Lecture Notes in Computer Science

Series Editors

Randy Goebel
University of Alberta, Edmonton, Canada

Wolfgang Wahlster
DFKI, Berlin, Germany

Zhi-Hua Zhou
Nanjing University, Nanjing, China

Founding Editor

Jörg Siekmann
DFKI and Saarland University, Saarbrücken, Germany

More information about this subseries at https://link.springer.com/bookseries/1244

Ana Paula Rocha · Luc Steels ·
Jaap van den Herik (Eds.)

Agents and Artificial Intelligence

13th International Conference, ICAART 2021
Virtual Event, February 4–6, 2021
Revised Selected Papers

Springer

Editors
Ana Paula Rocha
LIACC, University of Porto
Porto, Portugal

Luc Steels
ICREA, Institute of Evolutionary Biology
Barcelona, Spain

Jaap van den Herik
Leiden University
Leiden, The Netherlands

ISSN 0302-9743 ISSN 1611-3349 (electronic)
Lecture Notes in Artificial Intelligence
ISBN 978-3-031-10160-1 ISBN 978-3-031-10161-8 (eBook)
https://doi.org/10.1007/978-3-031-10161-8

LNCS Sublibrary: SL7 – Artificial Intelligence

This Springer imprint is published by the registered company Springer Nature Switzerland AG
The registered company address is: Gewerbestrasse 11, 6330 Cham, Switzerland

Preface

The present book includes extended and revised versions of a set of selected papers from the 13th International Conference on Agents and Artificial Intelligence (ICAART 2021), held as an online event due to the COVID-19 pandemic, during February 4–6, 2021.

ICAART 2021 received 298 paper submissions from authors in 53 countries, of which some 6% were included in this book. The papers were selected by the event chairs and their selection is based on a number of criteria that include the classifications and comments provided by the Program Committee members, the session chairs' assessment, and also the program chairs' global view of all papers included in the technical program. Authors of selected papers were then invited to submit revised and extended versions of their papers having at least 30% innovative material.

The purpose of the ICAART 2021 was to bring together researchers, engineers, and practitioners interested in the theory and applications in the areas of agents and artificial intelligence. Two simultaneous related tracks were held, covering both applications and current research work.

The papers selected to be included in this book contribute to the understanding of relevant trends of current research on agents and artificial intelligence.

We would like to thank all authors for their contributions. Moreover, we are grateful to the reviewers who have helped ensure the quality of this publication.

February 2021

Ana Paula Rocha
Luc Steels
Jaap van den Herik

Organization

Conference Chair

Jaap van den Herik   Leiden University, The Netherlands

Program Co-chairs

Ana Paula Rocha   University of Porto, Portugal
Luc Steels   Institute of Evolutionary Biology, Spain

Program Committee

Maysam Abbod   Brunel University London, UK
Varol Akman   Bilkent University, Turkey
Isabel Alexandre   ISCTE – Instituto Universitário de Lisboa and
                                    Instituto de Telecomunicações, Portugal
Vicki Allan   Utah State University, USA
Klaus-Dieter Althoff   German Research Center for Artificial
                                    Intelligence and University of Hildesheim,
                                    Germany
Frédéric Amblard   IRIT - Université Toulouse 1 Capitole, France
Ilze Andersone   Riga Technical University, Latvia
Alla Anohina-Naumeca   Riga Technical University, Latvia
Marcelo Armentano   ISISTAN Research Institute, Argentina
Jean-Michel Auberlet   Université Gustave Eiffel, France
Farshad Badie   Aalborg University, Denmark
Irene Barba Rodriguez   Universidad de Sevilla, Spain
Montserrat Batet   Universitat Rovira i Virgili, Spain
Carole Bernon   Université Toulouse III Paul Sabatier, France
Carlos Bobed Lisbona   University of Zaragoza, Spain
Lars Braubach   City University of Hamburg, Germany
Joerg Bremer   University of Oldenburg, Germany
Paolo Bresciani   Fondazione Bruno Kessler, Italy
Daniela Briola   Università degli Studi di Milano-Bicocca, Italy
Aleksander Byrski   AGH University of Science and Technology,
                                    Poland
Giacomo Cabri   Università degli Studi di Modena e Reggio
                                    Emilia, Italy
Patrice Caire   Stanford University, USA

Valérie Camps	IRIT - Université Toulouse III Paul Sabatier, France
Nicola Capodieci	Università degli Studi di Modena e Reggio Emilia, Italy
Javier Carbó Rubiera	Universidad Carlos III de Madrid, Spain
Amilcar Cardoso	University of Coimbra, Portugal
Henrique Lopes Cardoso	Universidade do Porto, Portugal
Wen-Chung Chang	National Taipei University of Technology, Taiwan, Republic of China
Davide Ciucci	Università degli Studi di Milano-Biocca, Italy
Flavio Correa da Silva	University of Sao Paulo, Brazil
Paulo Cortez	University of Minho, Portugal
Erzsébet Csuhaj-varjú	Eötvös Loránd University, Hungary
Fernando da Souza	Universidade Federal de Pernambuco, Brazil
Riccardo De Benedictis	Italian National Research Council (CNR), Italy
Daniele De Martini	University of Oxford, UK
Guy De Tré	Ghent University, Belgium
Bruno Di Stefano	Nuptek Systems Ltd., Canada
Dragan Doder	Utrecht University, The Netherlands
Michel Dojat	Université Grenoble Alpes, France
Francisco Domínguez Mayo	University of Seville, Spain
Viktor Eisenstadt	University of Hildesheim, Germany
Thomas Eiter	Technische Universität Wien, Austria
Fabrizio Falchi	ISTI-CNR, Italy
Nader Fallah	University of British Columbia, Canada
Christophe Feltus	Luxembourg Institute of Science and Technology, Belgium
Edilson Ferneda	Catholic University of Brasilia, Brazil
Vladimir Filipovic	Belgrade University, Serbia
Roberto Flores	Christopher Newport University, USA
Agostino Forestiero	ICAR-CNR, Italy
Claude Frasson	University of Montreal, Canada
Katsuhide Fujita	Tokyo University of Agriculture and Technology, Japan
Leonardo Garrido	Tecnológico de Monterrey, Mexico
Alfredo Garro	Università della Calabria, Italy
Emmanuelle Grislin-Le Strugeon	LAMIH, France
Luciano H. Tamargo	Universidad Nacional del Sur, Argentina
James Harland	RMIT University, Australia
Hisashi Hayashi	Advanced Institute of Industrial Technology, Japan
Samedi Heng	Université de Liège, Belgium

Lluís Ribas-Xirgo	Universitat Autònoma de Barcelona, Spain
Patrizia Ribino	ICAR-CNR, Italy
Fátima Rodrigues	Interdisciplinary Studies Research Center, Portugal
Daniel Rodriguez	University of Alcalá, Spain
Juha Röning	University of Oulu, Finland
Ruben Ruiz	Universidad Politécnica de Valencia, Spain
Luca Sabatucci	ICAR-CNR, Italy
Francesco Santini	Università di Perugia, Italy
Fabio Sartori	University of Milano-Bicocca, Italy
Jurek Sasiadek	Carleton University, Canada
Domenico Fabio Savo	Università degli Studi di Bergamo, Italy
Stefan Schiffer	RWTH Aachen University, Germany
Frank Schweitzer	ETH Zurich, Switzerland
Emilio Serrano	Universidad Politécnica de Madrid, Spain
Denis Shikhalev	State Fire Service Academy of EMERCOM of Russia, Russia
Marius Silaghi	Florida Institute of Technology, USA
Gerardo Simari	Universidad Nacional del Sur, Argentina
Guillermo Simari	Universidad Nacional del Sur in Bahia Blanca, Argentina
David Sislak	Czech Technical University in Prague, Czech Republic
Armando Sousa	INESC TEC and University of Porto, Portugal
Gerasimos Spanakis	Maastricht University, The Netherlands
Efstathios Stamatatos	University of the Aegean, Greece
Bernd Steinbach	Freiberg University of Mining and Technology, Germany
Kathleen Steinhofel	King's College London, UK
Zhaohao Sun	Federation University Australia, Australia, and PNG University of Technology, Papua New Guinea
Yasuhiro Suzuki	Nagoya University, Japan
Karim Tabia	CRIL, France
Ryszard Tadeusiewicz	AGH University Science Technology, Poland
Nick Taylor	Heriot-Watt University, UK
Patrícia Tedesco	Fade-UFPE, Brazil
Andrea Tettamanzi	Inria, I3S, Université Côte d'Aazur, France
Satoshi Tojo	Japan Advanced Institute of Science and Technology, Japan
Michele Tomaiuolo	University of Parma, Italy
José Torres	Universidade Fernando Pessoa, Portugal
Chittaranjan Tripathy	Walmart Labs, USA

Paulo Urbano	Universidade de Lisboa, Portugal
Marina V. Sokolova	Aristos Secondary School, Spain
Marco Valtorta	University of South Carolina, USA
Leo van Moergestel	HU University of Applied Sciences Utrecht, The Netherlands
Harko Verhagen	Stockholm University, Sweden
Renata Vieira	Pontifícia Universidade Católica do Rio Grande do Sul, Brazil
Jørgen Villadsen	Technical University of Denmark, Denmark
Emilio Vivancos	Universitat Politecnica de Valencia, Spain
Marin Vlada	University of Bucharest, Romania
Wojciech Waloszek	Gdansk University of Technology, Poland
Frank Wang	University of Kent, UK
Yves Wautelet	KU Leuven, Belgium
Jianshu Weng	AI Singapore, Singapore
Bozena Wozna-Szczesniak	Jan Dlugosz University in Czestochowa, Poland
Fusun Yaman	Raytheon BBN Technologies, USA
Kristina Yordanova	University of Rostock, Germany
Hua Zuo	University of Technology Sydney, Australia

Additional Reviewers

Jhonatan Alves	UFSC, Brazil
Remis Balaniuk	Catholic University of Brasilia, Brazil
Thales Bertaglia	Maastricht University, The Netherlands
Maria G. Buey	Universidad de Zaragoza, Spain
Andrea Campagner	University of Milano-Bicocca, Italy
Leonardo Cañete-Sifuentes	Tecnologico de Monterrey, Mexico
José Cruz	University of Porto, Portugal
Hércules do Prado	Catholic University of Brasília, Brazil
Viktor Eisenstadt	German Research Center for Artificial Intelligence and University of Hildesheim, Germany
Alberto Falcone	University of Calabria, Italy
Christoph Gote	ETH Zurich, Switzerland
Corrado Mio	Khalifa University of Science and Technology, UAE
Naveen Nair	Amazon, USA
Andreas Niskanen	University of Helsinki, Finland
Alison Panisson	Pontifical Catholic University of Rio Grande do Sul, Brazil
Otto Pires	Brazil
Giuseppe Russo	ETH Zurich, Switzerland

Vageesh Saxena   Maastricht University, The Netherlands
Jakob Schoenborn   University of Hildesheim and German Research
                                 Center for Artificial Intelligence, Germany
Joaquin Taverner   Universitat Politècnica de València, Spain

Invited Speakers

Gerhard Widmer   Johannes Kepler University and LIT—AI Lab,
                                 Linz Institute of Technology, Austria
Barbara Mazzolai   Istituto Italiano di Tecnologia, Italy
Guy Van den Broeck   UCLA, USA
Fosca Giannotti   ISTI-CNR, Italy

Contents

Agents

Specification Aware Multi-Agent Reinforcement Learning

Fabian Ritz[1]([✉])[iD], Thomy Phan[1], Robert Müller[1][iD], Thomas Gabor[1],
Andreas Sedlmeier[1], Marc Zeller[2], Jan Wieghardt[2], Reiner Schmid[2], Horst Sauer[2],
Cornel Klein[2], and Claudia Linnhoff-Popien[1]

[1] Mobile and Distributed Systems Group, LMU Munich, Munich, Germany
fabian.ritz@ifi.lmu.de
[2] Corporate Technology (CT), Siemens AG, Munich, Germany

Abstract. Engineering intelligent industrial systems is challenging due to high complexity and uncertainty with respect to domain dynamics and multiple agents. If industrial systems act autonomously, their choices and results must be within specified bounds to satisfy these requirements. Reinforcement learning (RL) is promising to find solutions that outperform known or handcrafted heuristics. However in industrial scenarios, it also is crucial to prevent RL from inducing potentially undesired or even dangerous behavior. This paper considers specification alignment in industrial scenarios with multi-agent reinforcement learning (MARL). We propose to embed functional and non-functional requirements into the reward function, enabling the agents to learn to align with the specification. We evaluate our approach in a smart factory simulation representing an industrial lot-size-one production facility, where we train up to eight agents using DQN, VDN, and QMIX. Our results show that the proposed approach enables agents to satisfy a given set of requirements.

Keywords: Multi-agent · Reinforcement learning · Specification compliance · AI safety

1 Introduction

In complex problem domains, humans do not always have optimal solution strategies at hand. In such situations, autonomous agents are still able to adapt and optimize their behavior via *Reinforcement learning (RL)* [36]. They sometimes even surpass human performance [33]. But RL systems need a well-defined goal such as "win the game of chess". Formulating such a goal in real-world problems, e.g. industrial applications, is difficult and a field of ongoing research [14,18]. In this paper, we consider an adaptive production line that could be part of the factory of the near future [38].

Typically, a *smart factory* is given orders of items. These can be broken down into series of tasks for the available machines [27]. The goal is to produce all ordered items within a certain time frame. In software engineering, this is a *functional requirement*. Usually, there are also *non-functional requirements*: for example, the system shall prefer faster production over exhausting the available time; it shall avoid damaging machines;

A. P. Rocha et al. (Eds.): ICAART 2021, LNAI 13251, pp. 3–21, 2022.
https://doi.org/10.1007/978-3-031-10161-8_1

it shall be resilient to (human) intervention and unexpected events [2,4,6]. We refer to the full set of functional and non-functional requirements as the *specification* of a system.

We could set aligning with a given specification as the direct goal for an RL agent. Each requirement could represent a boolean function which yields a binary reward of, e.g., +1 if satisfied or −1 if violated. But a solution involves an intricate balance of satisfying the convoluted requirements. If positive feedback is sparse and delayed, RL learns slowly (it at all). In multi-agent systems, emergent behavior is an additional source of unpredictability. E.g., consider multiple agents competing for the same machine. Approaches such as restricting single actions might prevent collisions. But it does not provide incentives for the agents to adjust their behavior and learn coordination, eventually resulting in a deadlock.

To address these challenges, we propose to translate the specification into a shaped reward function and adjust the weightning of its components during training. Contrary to existing approaches that only maximize performance, we also consider the fulfillment non-functional requirements. In Sect. 4, we introduce a multi-agent domain and adjust it to benchmark typical non-functional requirements. In Sect. 5, we demonstrate how a specification with functional and non-functional requirements can be transferred into different shaped reward functions for RL. We evaluate these reward schemes with different multi-agent RL algorithms in Sect. 6. We find some non-functional requirements (partially) subsumed by overarching functional requirements, i.e. they are learned easily. We find other requirements to affect convergence and propose countermeasures.

Our main contributions are the application of specification-driven reward engineering to a multi-agent domain adapted to industrial requirements and a thorough evaluation of the impact of typical secondary reward terms on the multi-agent RL algorithms DQN, VDN, and QMIX. This paper extends a previous version [31] by additionally contributing an unique case study that demonstrates how training with secondary reward terms impacts run-time behavior. To provide in-depth information, we visualize examples of pro-actively safe strategies and discuss alternatives.

2   Foundations

2.1   Problem Formulation

Single-agent problems can be formulated as *Markov Decision Process (MDP)* $M_{MDP} = \langle \mathcal{S}, \mathcal{A}, \mathcal{P}, \mathcal{R} \rangle$, where $\mathcal{S}$ is a set of states s_t, $\mathcal{A}$ is the set of actions a_t, $\mathcal{P}(s_{t+1}|s_t, a_t)$ is the transition probability, and $r_t = \mathcal{R}(s_t, a_t)$ is a scalar reward at time t. MDPs can be extended to multiple agents by formulating a *stochastic game (SG)* M_{SG}, where $\mathcal{S}$ and $\mathcal{P}$ remain the same. In addition, M_{SG} defines $\mathcal{D} = \{1, ..., N\}$ as a set of agents, $\mathcal{A} = \mathcal{A}_1 \times ... \times \mathcal{A}_N$ as the set of *joint actions* a_t, $r_{t,i} = \mathcal{R}_i(s_t, a_t)$ as the local reward of agent $i \in \mathcal{D}$, $\mathcal{Z}$ as a set of local observations $z_{t,i}$ for each agent i, and $\Omega(s_t, a_t) = z_{t+1} = \langle z_{t,1}, ..., z_{t,N} \rangle \in \mathcal{Z}^N$ as the joint observation function. For cooperative MAS, we assume a common reward function $r_t = \mathcal{R}(s_t, a_t)$ for all agents.

The goal of each agent i is to find a *local policy* $\pi_i(a_{t,i}|z_{t,i})$ as probability distribution over $\mathcal{A}_i$ which maximizes the expected discounted local return or local action value function $Q_i(s_t, a_t) = \mathbb{E}_\pi[\sum_{k=0}^{T} \gamma^k \mathcal{R}_i(s_{t+k}, a_{t+k}) \mid s_t, a_t]$, where T is a finite horizon, $\pi = \langle \pi_1, ..., \pi_N \rangle$ is the *joint policy* of all agents and $\gamma \in [0, 1]$ is the discount factor. A best response π_i^* of agent i depends on the local policies π_j of all other agents $j \neq i$ and maximizes Q_i for each s_t and a_t.

2.2 Reinforcement Learning

Reinforcement Learning (RL) searches for an (near-)optimal policy in an unknown environment M_{MDP} without knowing the effect of executing $a_t \in \mathcal{A}$ in $s_t \in \mathcal{S}$ [36]. RL agents obtain experience samples $E = \{e_1, ..., e_t\}$ with $e_t = \langle s_t, a_t, s_{t+1}, r_t \rangle$ by interacting with M_{MDP}. Deep RL is the current state-of-the-art approach to realize RL agents with deep neural networks in order to solve complex tasks [23,24,33]. In this paper, we focus on value-based RL, which aims to approximate the $Q^*(s_t, a_t) = max_\pi Q(s_t, a_t)$. *Deep Q-Networks (DQN)* is a well-known deep learning variant of Q-Learning [39] used to approximate $Q^*(s_t, a_t)$ for single agents. DQN uses experience replay and target networks to ensure stable learning [24].

2.3 Multi-Agent Reinforcement Learning

In *Multi-Agent Reinforcement Learning (MARL)*, each agent i searches for an (near-)optimal local policy $\pi_i^*(a_{t,i}|z_{t,i})$. DQN can be applied to MARL by training an DQN independently per agent [17,37]. One way is to share a single DQN's parameters among all agents, which offers high scalability with respect to the number of agents. However, the adaptive behavior of each agent renders the system non-stationary, thus independant learning lacks convergence guarantees [16].

Other recent approaches to MARL adopt the paradigm of *centralized training and decentralized execution (CTDE)* to alleviate the non-stationarity problem [9,22,30,34, 35]. During centralized training, global information about the state and the actions of all other agents are integrated into the learning process in order to stably learn local policies. The global information is assumed to be available, since training usually takes place in a laboratory or in a simulated environment.

Value decomposition or factorization is a common approach to CTDE for value-based MARL in cooperative MAS. *Value Decomposition Networks (VDN)* are the most simple approach, where a linear decomposition of the global function for $Q^*(s_t, a_t)$ is learned to derive individual value functions for each agent [35]. Alternatively, the individual value functions can be mixed with a non-linear function approximator to learn the $Q^*(s_t, a_t)$-function [30,34]. *QMIX* is an example for learning non-linear decompositions using a monotonicity constraint which ensures that the maximization of the global $Q^*(s_t, a_t)$-function is equivalent to the maximization of each individual value function [30].

2.4 Reward Shaping in RL

To influence an RL agent's behavior, altering the reward function is an evident approach. Potential based reward shaping (PBRS) [25] was proven to neither alter the optimal policy in single-agent systems, nor introduce side-effects that would allow reward hacking.

The concept is to provide intermediate feedback for the agent in case of sparse environmental rewards. Per step, PBRS adds an additional reward F which is the difference between the prior and the posterior state's potential:

$$F(s_t, s_{t+1}) = \gamma \cdot \Phi(s_{t+1}) - \Phi(s_t) \tag{1}$$

The potential function usually employs additional domain- or expert knowledge. Initially, PBRS required a static potential function. Later, the properties of PRBS were shown to hold for dynamic potential functions as well [7]. PBRS has further been theoretically analyzed and practically applied to episodic RL and MAS [8, 12]. As a fundamental insight, PBRS does not alter the Nash equilibria of MAS but may increase or decrease performance, depending on scenario and heuristics. In this paper, reward shaping differs from PBRS: We use $\gamma = 1.0$ when calculating F while the learning algorithms use $\gamma = 0.95$ in most experiments. But for the theoretic guarantees of PBRS to hold, the same value of γ must be used. We address this by configuring the experiments in Sect. 6 accordingly and the results indicate that the practical impact is negligible in our case. Ultimately, there is currently no proven optimality guarantee for DQN-based algorithms that use deep neural networks for function approximation, anyway.

3   Related Work

Related work [1] contains a list of challenges for learning to respect safety requirements. In [19], a set of gridworld domains is proposed that allow to test safety aspects of single RL agents. The alignment problem, i.e. agents not aligning with the designer's intentions, is unsolved [14]. A comprehensive overview of safe RL approaches is given in [11] that divides existing approaches into modeling either safety or risk. These information can then be used to constrain the MDP to prevent certain actions. Contrary, we do not model risk or safety explicitly. Instead, we aim for agents to learn to align to a given specification as we argue that constraining the MDP is unfeasible in complex multi-agent systems.

Considering learned safety in RL, [32] proposed to extend the MDP by a function that maps states and actions to a binary feedback signal that indicates the validity of the taken action. To predict this validity, an additional neural network is trained. The training objective of the DQN is augmented to push Q-values of forbidden actions below those of valid actions by an auxiliary loss. Similarly, [41] proposed to use an Action Elimination Network (AEN) that is trained to predict the feedback signal. A linear contextual bandit alters the action set by facilitating the features of the penultimate layer of the AEN to eliminate irrelevant actions. Both approaches were shown to minimize unsafe actions and improve performance. Yet, they were evaluated in single agent domains only and augmenting the reward was not considered.

Regarding training in MARL, population-based approaches as in [15] complement a sparse, global reward with dense, individual rewards. The individual rewards consist of additional domain information transferred into rewards which are used during training of the agents. An evolutionary process facilitates those agents whose internal rewards lead to behavior also maximizing the global reward. Similarly, [20] proposed to use separate, individual discounts to adjust the agents' dense, internal rewards such that they align with a global goal. These approaches demonstrated the impact of shaped, dense rewards during training and that automatically evolved rewards can outperform hand-crafted ones. By aiming only at improving MARL performance, these approaches do not consider optimizing multiple convoluted, eventually conflicting goals. In (video) games, finding innovative strategies of which humans were unaware before [33] does not come at any risk and may be desirable. But in industrial domains [2,4], aligning with multiple aspects of given specification including behavioral constraints to avoid unintended side-effects is required.

Reward shaping has previously been used in MAS to improve cooperation. To address the credit assignment problem, i.e. all agents observing the same reward signal, [5] proposed to use Kalman filtering to extract individual reward signals. [40] use the difference between the original reward and an alternative reward derive an individual reward for each agent. The alternative reward is computed by the agent choosing a default action. Ultimately, [10] proposed to use baselines to improve credit-assignment in policy gradient algorithms. These approaches improve cooperation, which is assumed to be important in our scenario, but they do not explicitly consider non-functional requirements to avoid unintended side-effects.

4   Smart Factory Domain

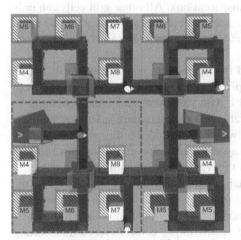

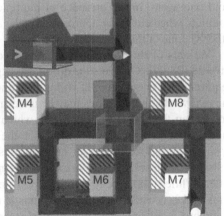

(a) smart factory overview   (b) zoom-in on bottom left

Fig. 1. 3D visualization of the discrete domain used in this paper. Contrary to a fully connected grid world, the agents can only move to adjacent cells via a connecting path and can only dodge each other via on one of the 4 capacitive grid cells (rendered with transparent boxes). Agents spawn on the entry position on the left and finish on the exit position on the right (both rendered with blue boxes). Figure taken from [31]. (Color figure online)

The *smart factory* presented in this paper is inspired by the domain proposed in [27] regarding the simulation of components and production processes in an adaptive facility. We use the layout shown in Fig. 1 which consists of a 5×5 grid of *machines* with different types. Every agent i carries an *item* that needs to be processed at various machines according to its randomly assigned processing tasks $tasks_i = [\{a_{i,1}, b_{i,1}\}, \{a_{i,2}, b_{i,2}\}, ...]$. Each task $a_{i,j}, b_{i,j}$ is contained in a *bucket*. Tasks in the same bucket can be processed in any order but the buckets have to be processed in a specific order. Figure 1b exemplary shows an agent i, rendered as a green cylinder, with $tasks_i = [\{5, 6\}]$, rendered as green boxes. Here, i can choose between different machines to process the tasks $a_{i,1} = 5$ and $b_{i,2} = 6$. All agents spawn on an entrance on the left side of the grid, thus the initial position is fixed. Agents can stay put (*no-op*), can move along the machine grid (*left, right, up, down*) or *enqueue* at the current position. A machine processes only one defined type of item once per time step. If an item is enqueued correctly, the corresponding task is processed and removed from its bucket. If a bucket is empty, it is removed from the item's tasks list. An item is *complete* if its tasks list is empty. The final task always is to move to the exit, which is the mirror position of the entry (on the right). The domain is discrete in all aspects including agent motion.

Contrary to fully-connected grid worlds, every grid cell in the smart factory has defined connections (paths) to the surrounding grid cells and an agent capacity limit. An agent may only move to another grid cell if the target grid cell's maximum capacity is not exceeded and a connecting paths exists. Entry and exit can hold all agents simultaneously. The smart factory contains four *capacitative* grid cells that fully connected to their neighbors that can each hold half of the agents. In Fig. 1b, one capacitive cell is located south to agent i, rendered with a transparent box. All other grid cells can only hold one agent. In the presence of multiple agents, coordination is required to avoid conflicts when choosing appropriate paths and machines: agents can only dodge each other via one of the capacitative grid cells.

Variants of this domain were published during parallel research on resilience in MARL [28,29]. Our version differs by explicitly considering typical non-functional requirements: enqueueing at wrong machines, path violations, and agent collisions. In the real world, these actions may be undesirable and would require safety mechanisms preventing the agents from doing so which we aim to avoid. Further, we additionally model (emergency) situations in which the agents shall either freeze or move to safe positions in limited time. Our motivation is that (partially) autonomous systems typically have fallback routines in case of internal or external failure. Here, we assume the latter. While stopping any activity (freezing) models kill-switches found in many systems and is considered in Sect. 6.4, this is not always desirable solution. Our favorite metaphor is a fire(alarm). For example, the agents might control AGVs transporting either valuable or dangerous, e.g. flammable, items. Maybe, the AGVs and items are expandable, but it may still be important that they neither hinder the evacuation of other high priority entities, e.g. humans, nor block the fire-extinguishing works. In any case, we assume that moving to defined *safe positions* in limited time might be more desirable than just freezing during such an emergency. This scenario is considered in Sect. 6.5.

5 Specification Transfer

To enable the agents to learn to align with a given specification, we propose to transfer functional and non-functional requirements into rewards. Inspired by PBRS, we define

Table 1. Reward overview, taken from [31].

(a) reward components

reward component	variable	sign
item completion rew.	α	+
single task reward	β	+
step cost	δ	-
machine operation cost	ζ	-
path violation penalty	η	-
agent collision penalty	θ	-
emergency violat. pen.	ι	-

(b) reward schemes

scheme	α	β	δ	ζ	η	θ	ι
$r0$	5.0		0.1				
$r1$		1.0	0.1				
$r2$		1.0	0.1	0.2			
$r3$		1.0	0.1		0.1		
$r4$		1.0	0.1			0.4	
$r5$		1.0	0.1	0.2	0.1	0.4	1.0
rx		1.0	0.1	$0-0.2$	0.1	$0-0.4$	$0-1.0$

a potential function and use the potential difference as reward. Differing from PBRS, we completely omit other (primary) rewards. Starting simple, we assume that a typical functional requirement of a production facility is completing items as fast as possible. Thus, our first reward scheme $r0$ increases the potential by α once an agent completes its item and decreases the potential by δ per step. Positive feedback in $r0$ is sparse and delayed, thus a decomposition into more dense parts may improve learnability. This is implemented by reward scheme $r1$ by adding a positive term β whenever a single task is finished.

Industrial scenarios typically also have a number of non-functional requirements that require autonomous agents to comply with certain behavioral constraints. We consider two types of constraints in this paper. We refer to the first type as *soft constraints*. These include to only use the machine type required by the task, to stay on the defined paths and not to collide with other agents. In the simulation, agents trying to move to a grid cell without sufficient capacity or path connection stay put and items processed by wrong machines remain unaltered. Also, soft constraints do not oppose the goal of completing items (fast) as agents would not benefit from violations anyway. The second type of constraints is referred to as *hard constraints*. This includes the agents either freezing or moving to safe positions when an emergency signal is active. The agents can ignore the emergency signal in order to finish their tasks faster in the simulation. Therefore, the hard constraint introduces a goal conflict. As constraint violations generally shall be minimized, they are transferred into negative terms ζ (machine operation cost), η (path violation penalty), θ (agent collision penalty) and ι (emergency violation penalty) of different quantity, considered in the reward schemes $r2$, $r3$, $r4$ and $r5$.

Inspired by curriculum learning [3], reward scheme rx only contains β, δ and η in the first part of the training process in order to learn the basic task. ζ, θ and ι are added later during training, so that some behavioral constraints are introduced to the agents gradually. A summary of reward schemes, reward components and component values is given in Table 1. To actually employ the reward schemes, we implemented a corresponding interface for each component, e.g. the number of *completed items*, at any time step. Depending on the learning algorithm, the potential function is evaluated either per agent (DQN) or globally (VDN, QMIX). Bringing all together:

$$\Phi(s) = \alpha \cdot itemCompleted(s) + \beta \cdot tasksFinished(s)$$
$$+ \delta \cdot stepCount(s) \qquad + \zeta \cdot machinesUsed(s)$$
$$+ \eta \cdot pathViolations(s) + \theta \cdot agentCollisions(s)$$
$$+ \iota \cdot emergencyViolations(s)$$

6 Evaluation

6.1 Experimental Setup

While testing the reward schemes listed in Table 1b on different layouts of the smart factory domain, the reported layout (see Fig. 1a) turned out to be most challenging. After spawning at an entry (on the left), agents must process two buckets of two random tasks each. Finally, the agents must move to the exit (the mirror position to the entry). Unlike a real world setting, machines are not grouped by type but distributed equally to maintain solvability in the presence of up to 8 agents which may cause congestion during exploration. Training is carried out episode-wise, each limited to 50 steps, for up to 6000 episodes.

Independent DQN agents are trained as a *white-box* test: the agents can directly associate the feedback signals, which are individual rewards, with their actions. Our DQN neural network uses two hidden layers of 64 and 32 units with ELU activation, followed by an output dense layer of $|\mathcal{A}_i| = 6$ linear units. We use parameter sharing, i.e. all agents share the weights of the neural network. ADAM for optimization. Q-values are discounted with $\gamma = 0.95$ except the experiments in Sect. 6.4. We further use ϵ-greedy exploration with linear decay for $\sim$1000 episodes. Our DQN implementation uses experience replay and a target network. Per training step, a batch of 64 elements is sampled via prioritized experience replay. The buffer holds up to 20000 elements and after each 4000 training steps, the target network is updated.

VDN and QMIX agents are trained as a *black-box* test: the agents cannot directly associate the feedback signal, which is the sum of the local rewards, with their individual actions (at least in the beginning of the training). For their local Q-networks, VDN and QMIX use the same architecture as DQN and the same hyperparameters. For non-linear decomposition, QMIX uses a mixing network with one hidden layer of 64 units, ELU activation and an dense output layer with a single linear unit.

The components of the reward schemes r0 to r5 remain fixed during training. Contrary, rx alters ζ, θ and ι at particular steps during training. After adding or altering components of the reward function, the exploration rate is set to 0.25 and the optimizer momentum is reset. For any combination of reward scheme and learning algorithm presented in the results, mean and 95% confidence interval of at least 10 independently trained neural networks are reported.

6.2 Analysis of Separate Reward Components

Due to the variety of components to build reward functions upon in our domain, we start with experimentally quantifying how separate components affect the training of the RL agents. Thus, we apply the reward schemes r2, r3 and r4 on 4 DQN agents with

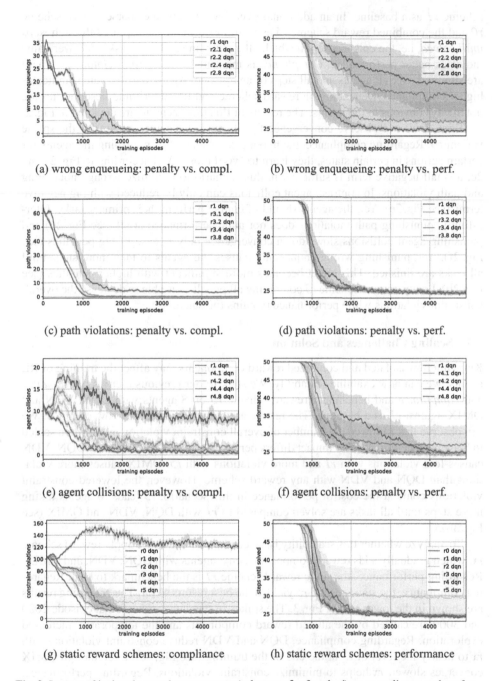

(a) wrong enqueueing: penalty vs. compl.

(b) wrong enqueueing: penalty vs. perf.

(c) path violations: penalty vs. compl.

(d) path violations: penalty vs. perf.

(e) agent collisions: penalty vs. compl.

(f) agent collisions: penalty vs. perf.

(g) static reward schemes: compliance

(h) static reward schemes: performance

Fig. 2. Impact of isolated reward components (schemes $r2$, $r3$ and $r4$) on compliance and performance during training of 4 DQN agents. $r0$ is a sparse reward scheme with only functional components, $r1$ its dense counterpart. $r5$ contains all components of $r1-r4$. Figures taken from [31].

scheme *r1* as a baseline. In an additional overview, we test the sparse reward scheme *r0* and the combined reward scheme *r5* as well. *Performance* is captured through *steps until solved*, i.e. the episode step in which all agents finished their tasks. A lower value indicates better performance. *Compliance* is measured in *constraint violations*. These are summed over all agents and all steps of an episode. Again, a lower values indicates higher compliance. Depending on reward scheme and RL algorithm, these metrics are not always obvious to the agents. The results of this first scenario are depicted in Fig. 2.

First of all, we observe convergence for all reward schemes except for the sparse variant *r0*. Regarding compliance, the hypothesis is that when punishing the agents for certain actions in certain states, they learn to avoid those. And according to Fig. 2a and 2c, a small negative term is sufficient in this scenario to minimize wrong enqueueing and path violations. In contrast, agent collisions can only be reduced with big negative terms (see Fig. 2e). Yet, the agents should of course perform their primary tasks. Interestingly, punishing path violations does not alter performance at all (see Fig. 2d) and punishing agent collisions slows down convergence only in case of big penalties (see Fig. 2f). Yet, punishing wrong enqueueing causes the agents to take more steps until all tasks are finished. This effect becomes more significant with higher penalties (see Fig. 2b). Lastly, reward scheme *r5* combining all penalties is able to decrease the overall constraint violations while performance remains the same.

6.3   Scaling Challenges and Solutions

Knowing how isolated and combined reward components may affect the training of RL agents, we can now examine scalability. We stick to our previous metrics *performance* and *compliance* and benchmark reward scheme *r5* on 8 agents with DQN, VDN and QMIX against *r1* as a baseline. The results are shown in the upper row of Fig. 3. We can observe that *r5* lowers the number of overall constraint violations even when scaled to 8 agents (see Fig. 3b. The impact differs per RL algorithm. Compared to DQN, VDN causes less violations with *r1* and more violations with *r5*. QMIX causes more violations than DQN and VDN with any reward scheme. However, the lowered constraint violations come at the cost of performance in this scenario: *r5* leads to agents taking more steps until all tasks are solved compared to *r1* with DQN, VDN and QMIX (see Fig. 3b).

To analyze whether this scalability issue can be overcome, we apply reward scheme *rx*, which gradually adds reward components, on 8 agents with DQN, VDN, and QMIX. Regarding performance, the static reward scheme *r1* is the benchmark to beat. Regarding compliance, the static reward *r5* yielded the best results so far. The according results are shown in the lower row of Fig. 3. The spikes in the data series of *rx* at episode 2000 and 3000 are caused by the altered reward components and the temporarily increased exploration. Regarding compliance, DQN and VDN reduce constraint violations with *rx* to nearly the level of *r5* at the end of the training (see Fig. 3c). Even though QMIX converges slower, *rx* helps to minimize constraint violations. Regarding performance, DQN with *rx* approaches the level of *r1* step-wise (see Fig. 3d). In contrast to that, *rx* disrupts the convergence of VDN which is not able to reach the performance level of *r1*. QMIX with *rx* shows the same phenomenon. Still, *rx* leads to better performance than *r5*.

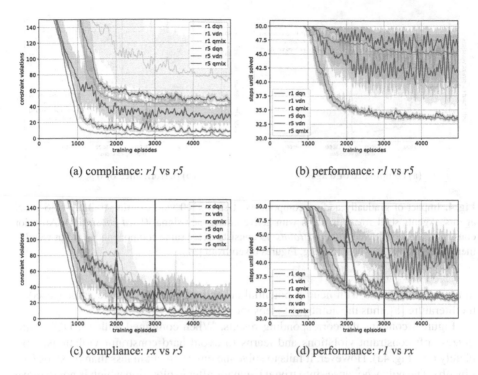

(a) compliance: *r1* vs *r5*   (b) performance: *r1* vs *r5*

(c) compliance: *rx* vs *r5*   (d) performance: *r1* vs *rx*

Fig. 3. Training progress of DQN, VDN and QMIX with 8 agents. *r1* is a static scheme with only functional reward components, *r5* is a static scheme with all reward components. Upper row: compared to *r1*, the reward components of *r5* lead to fewer constraint violations but more steps until the environment is solved. Lower row: adding reward components at steps 2000 and 3000 via *rx* nearly achieves the compliance of *r5* and the performance of *r1*. These results were originally presented in [31] and have been re-arranged for this paper.

As the main insight here, the dynamic reward scheme *rx* partially mitigates the scalability issues of the static reward scheme *r5*. The level of compliance is on par with that of *r5* and, depending on the RL algorithm, performance can be as good as with *r1*.

6.4   Safety Constraints as Reward Components

The *soft constraints* considered in the reward schemes so far are suspected to be subsumed by the agents' functional goal. For example, the agents can not navigate to the required machines any faster by colliding with each other. Complying with these constraints may be difficult to learn but does not involve any trade-offs from a decision making point of view. Thus, we now introduce an actual goal conflict: In case that an emergency signal is activated (randomly for single steps), the agents shall freeze as a *hard* constraint which opposes finishing their tasks as fast as possible. We benchmark the reward schemes *r5* and *rx*, both penalizing the according violations, during the training of 6 DQN agents. To ensure that theoretical guarantees of PBRS hold in this particular scenario, future rewards are discounted with $\gamma = 1.0$ and agents are moved

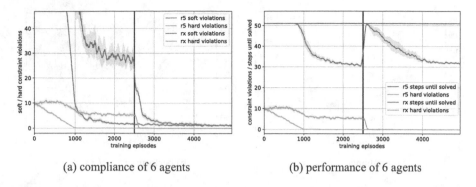

(a) compliance of 6 agents   (b) performance of 6 agents

Fig. 4. Impact of gradually adding components at step 2500 via *rx* during training of 6 DQN agents. Agents shall freeze in steps with active emergency signal (*hard constraint*). All prior constraints are considered *soft constraints*. *r5* consists of the same components as *rx* but weights them fully during the whole training. Figures taken from [31].

to an absorbing state with neutral potential at the end of each episode as proposed in the literature [8], thus the number of steps increases to 51.

Figure 4 contains the corresponding results. When combined with *r5*, DQN minimizes soft constraint violations and learns to avoid hard constraint violations completely (see Fig. 4a). However, it fails to solve the environment in less than 50 steps (see Fig. 4b). The policy collapses into trivial behavior after exploration which is not to move at all. Switching to *rx*, one characteristic spike can be observed during at episode 2500 due to the reward adjustment. At this point, *rx* adds punishment for hard constraint violations. This enables *rx* to resolve the goal conflict: It maintains the performance level but learns to avoid hard constraint violations by not moving when the emergency signal is active.

6.5 Case Study: Specification Compliant Run-Time Behavior

Building upon the goal conflicts introduced in the previous section, we now train the agents for the most complex scenario so far: Instead of freezing, the agents shall move to defined positions within limited time (the emergency signal remains active an according number of steps). In this scenario, we add an additional channel to the agents' observation revealing the emergency positions at any time. This is necessary as we randomize the emergency positions during training and want the agents to take that information into account. As before, active emergencies are signaled via a separate layer. Again, the agents may decide to ignore the emergency signal. First, there may be situations in which an agents would be faster finishing the final task (leaving the smart factory) than moving to an emergency exit. It would not make sense forcing it to navigate back to an emergency position. Second, we are curious if the agents learn to align this scenario's functional and non-functional aspects on their own. During training, the agents are confronted with random combinations of at most 4 possible safe positions (depicted in Fig. 6a) per episode. Thus, not all safe positions are present at all times. The capacity of the safe positions is adjusted to ensure that they can hold all agents. When there's no

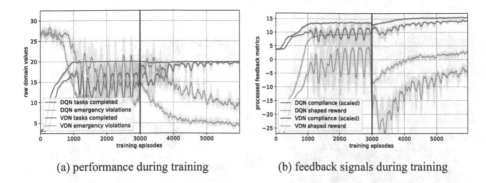

(a) performance during training   (b) feedback signals during training

Fig. 5. Training progress of 4 DQN and VDN agents on the smart factory layout depicted in Fig. 6a. At episode 3000, punishment for emergency violations is added. The left subfigure shows how emergency violations, i.e. steps with ongoing emergency but the agent not being safe positions, are lowered with ongoing training without negatively impacting the number of finished tasks. The right subfigure shows how the shaped reward, i.e. the feedback signal visible the agents, dips when adding the safety related component aspects. In parallel, the agents' compliance, i.e. the degree of fulfilling the requirements, increases steadily. This is a strong indicator that in this scenario, the shaped reward effectively guides the agents towards the intended behavior.

emergency, the safe positions behave as the capacitative grids. Yet, if a safe position is absent, the agents cannot use it to dodge each other, making routing in this layout more difficult than before.

Figure 5 shows the training progress of 4 DQN and VDN agents with reward scheme *rx*, adding punishment for emergency violations at episode 3000. In the left subfigure, we measure the raw domain values, i.e. the agents' *completed tasks* (more is better) and *emergency violations* (less is better). In accordance to previous results, the number of emergency violations can be lowered while the number of completed tasks is not affected negatively. VDN struggles to keep up with DQN, presumably due to the ambiguity of the global reward. We assume that local rewards per agents actually provide feedback that is easier to learn. The right subfigure shows how *shaped rewards*, i.e. the feedback signal for the agents, become more difficult to maximize after the punishment for emergency violations is added. Here, *compliance* is a metric equally weightning the functional goal (all agents shall finish all tasks within 50 time steps) and the non-functional goal (all agents shall be at a safe position within 4 time steps when the emergency signal is active). Thus, compliance represents the degree of alignment with the specification which would be too difficult to learn directly (see results of *r0* in Sect. 6.2). We observe that compliance increases steadily. This is a strong indicator that in this scenario, the shaped rewards effectively guide the agents towards the intended, specification compliant behavior.

Moving on to run-time behavior, we compare the agents behavior in two domain layouts containing two safe positions either in the lower half or the upper half of the machine grid. We track the agent positions of 10 independently trained policies during 100 evaluation episodes per policy and layout. Figure 6b shows the delta of the average agent positions between the two safe position layouts. We observe that agents

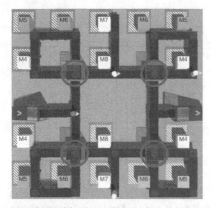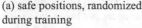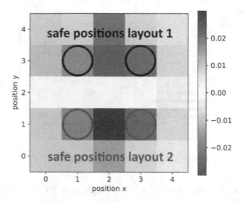

(a) safe positions, randomized during training

(b) agent position delta between two safe position layouts during evaluation

Fig. 6. The domain layouts used for the analysis of specification compliance run-time behavior. During training, the agents are confronted with random combinations of at most four possible safe-room locations depicted on the left. On the right, we compare the average positions of 10 DQN policies controlling 4 agents during 100 evaluation episodes on two layouts. Each layout has two safe-rooms, either in the upper or the lower half of the machine grid. It is important to note that there were no emergencies during the evaluation. The delta in the average agent positions thus indicates that the agents learned a form of proactively safe behavior by finishing their tasks near the safe positions more frequently even in absence of emergencies.

route through the half of the factory that contains the respective safe positions more frequently. This is a very interesting finding since we deactivated emergencies during evaluation. Thus, the agents learned a form of proactively safe behavior: Finishing tasks nearby safe positions more frequently lowers the average time to move to safe positions in case of an emergency.

Yet, the agent still use machines further away from safe positions from time to time, eventually violating our examplary non-functional requirement if an emergency would occur. We assume that this is due to the agents weighing the expected task rewards against the expected violation penalties w.r.t. to the current distribution of tasks, machines and safe positions. This may or may not be desirable. In this case study, we did not aim to enforce that agents stay within a certain distance from the safe positions. Instead, we were interested if such spatial effects would occur at all. We are confident that if a more strict spatial effect was desired, the punishment for violating emergencies could be increased accordingly with ongoing training. Naturally, such an iterative approach requires rigorous testing and is only feasible if a safe training environment (e.g. a simulation) is available where constraint violations do not have any impact.

7   Discussion

The results support our claim that the smart factory domain is suitable to benchmark practically relevant properties of a MAS. The layout used in the experiments could be solved straightforwardly with 4 agents but naive approaches struggled to finish their tasks with 6 and 8 agents. Even if the layout was solved, more steps were required and more constraint violations arose. Thus, we suspect agents to compete for path segments to navigate to the machines and for machines to process items, leading to conflicts in such settings. Consequently, cooperative behavior between agents to is required to perform well. To solve such scenarios, techniques restricting the action space alone are not sufficient: they would not necessarily resolve deadlocks.

Unsurprisingly, sparse reward schemes such as $r0$ did not lead to convergence and its decomposed counterpart $r1$ achieved solid performance throughout all scenarios. However, $r1$ fails to minimize *soft specification violations* in limited training time although they are caused by actions not solving the environment any faster. Instead, reward schemes such as $r5$ that contain more specification components increased compliance throughout all scenarios, which we consider a valuable insight: if we have preferences or even strict requirements on an agent's behavior, we should not rely on the agents to coincidentally employ this behavior but make our preferences accessible, e.g. via the feedback signal, so that the agents are able to learn how to align with them.

Yet, the dense feedback signal has another effect: depending the number of agents and the learning algorithm, $r5$ increased the time until the environment was solved, especially with 8 agents. Further, $r5$ could not resolve the goal conflict introduced by the hard constraints in Sect. 6.3. Obviously, giving the agents access to the whole specification from the beginning on does not necessarily lead to optimal behavior. However, the experiments with adaptive reward schemes such as rx demonstrate that compliance with the whole specification can nevertheless be achieved when starting with a basic reward scheme and gradually adding more components once the learner started to converge. Thus, some reward components seem to negatively affect exploration and may simple be unsuited to begin the training with. Comparable side-effects of reward shaping have been reported in the literature [8]. Another important aspect is the choice of algorithm: Our CTDE algorithms, VDN and QMIX, did not perform as well as independent DQN. Actually, we would have expected the CTDE approaches to benefit from coordinated learning. Instead, the difficulties of assigning which part of the joint action contributed to the joint reward in which way seem to prevail here. In some cases, rx even disrupted convergence of the CDTE algorithms. Hence, the timing when to add reward components also seems to play an important role.

The additional case study of Sect. 6.5 contributes experimental evidence that RL agents are able to learn even complex non-functional parts of a specification such as safety-aspects. Naturally, there are other approaches to such problems. For example, a fall-back controller with hard-coded or heuristic routing could be used and situationally take over control [26]. We argue that this may be problematic depending on the degrees of freedom in the problem domain. Taking the smart factory as an example, routing arbitrarily positioned agents to the nearest safe positions with respect to capacity limits is not trivial. Further, a safety requirement may become unfulfillable if the agents do not act proactively during normal operation: Even an optimal fallback controller could not navigate the agents to safe positions fast enough if the agents were too far away. Thus, the policy of the RL agents would have to be restricted accordingly. But such a restriction would have to take the distribution of tasks, machines and other agents into account: a congestion would oppose any estimation on escape time based on distance alone.

However, in the smart factory, routing while considering the distribution of machines, tasks and other agents is part of the problem the RL agents (are supposed to) learn anyway. Thus, regarding the fundamental problem, the functional and the non-functional requirements can in fact be orthogonal. We argue that in such cases, it might be easier to use the m capabilities also to fulfill the safety-related requirements than finding a heuristic that does so. Vice versa, if we had a good heuristic or a set of constraints solving the safety related aspects, we could simply use them for the functional aspects as well and solve the problem without RL. Summing up, we believe that our approach helps to alleviate the alignment problem [14]. Ideally, it may help to make hand-crafted safety layers around intelligent agents obsolete at some point in the future.

8   Conclusion and Future Work

In this paper, we considered the problem of specification compliance in MARL and adapted a multi-agent domain based on a smart factory setting. We translated a full specification into a shaped reward function and analyzed how functional and non-functional requirements can be modeled by adding terms to that reward function. Besides raw performance, we also evaluated specification compliance in a MARL setting.

Weightning only functional requirements, e.g. tasks or time steps, lead to agents that were able to achieve the functional goal. But these agents still had a high tendency to violate non-functional requirements, e.g. colliding with other agents. This can be harmful in industrial domains. Translating the full set of requirements into a shaped reward function still lead to agents solving the functional goal. Additionally, the agents were able to comply with non-functional requirements. It even allowed the agents to solve goal-conflicts introduced by complex safety-requirements. We observed a form of pro-actively safe behavior, enabling the agents to align with the specification during run-time. Where reward function and scenario became complicated, we found an inherent benefit due to gradually applied rewards. This is in accordance with other work [3,13].

The logical next step is to replace the hand crafted shaping and scheduling with auto-curriculum mechanisms. This should allow the reward functions to adjust in direct response to the agents' learning progress as in [15,20] but focusing on fulfilling the full set of requirements. Considering adversarial learning [21], our results sketch a path on how to implement reward engineering as an adversary given a fixed specification.

In this paper, we only considered a cooperative setting. Thus, it seems natural to expand our approach to groups of self-interested agents with (partially) opposing goals. We assume that deriving reward functions from a shared specification for the whole systems would become significantly more difficult due to the goals having separate reward signals. Yet, ensuring safety between parties with different interests could be a key factor. Ensuring "fair play" by formulating secondary reward terms might allow for even greater improvement in the whole system's performance than it does for the cooperative setting.

Ultimately, we would suspect that results from the evaluation can be translated back of the original specification. Components in the reward function without any impact might indicate that the respective requirements do not rightfully belong in the specification. This way, a human-made specification could be improved via translation into a reward function and execution of RL test runs.

References

1. Amodei, D., Olah, C., Steinhardt, J., Christiano, P.F., Schulman, J., Mané, D.: Concrete problems in AI safety. arXiv:1606.06565 (2016)
2. Belzner, L., Beck, M.T., Gabor, T., Roelle, H., Sauer, H.: Software engineering for distributed autonomous real-time systems. In: 2016 IEEE/ACM 2nd International Workshop on Software Engineering for Smart Cyber-Physical Systems (SEsCPS), pp. 54–57. IEEE (2016)
3. Bengio, Y., Louradour, J., Collobert, R., Weston, J.: Curriculum learning. In: Proceedings of the 26th Annual International Conference on Machine Learning, ICML 2009, pp. 41–48 (2009)
4. Bures, T., et al.: Software engineering for smart cyber-physical systems: challenges and promising solutions. ACM SIGSOFT Softw. Eng. Notes 42(2), 19–24 (2017)
5. Chang, Y.H., Ho, T., Kaelbling, L.P.: All learning is local: multi-agent learning in global reward games. In: Advances in Neural Information Processing Systems, pp. 807–814 (2004)
6. Cheng, B.H.C., et al.: Software engineering for self-adaptive systems: a research roadmap. In: Cheng, B.H.C., de Lemos, R., Giese, H., Inverardi, P., Magee, J. (eds.) Software Engineering for Self-Adaptive Systems. LNCS, vol. 5525, pp. 1–26. Springer, Heidelberg (2009). https://doi.org/10.1007/978-3-642-02161-9_1
7. Devlin, S., Kudenko, D.: Dynamic potential-based reward shaping. In: Proceedings of the 11th International Conference on Autonomous Agents and Multiagent Systems, AAMAS 2012, vol. 1, pp. 433–440 (2012)
8. Devlin, S., Yliniemi, L., Kudenko, D., Tumer, K.: Potential-based difference rewards for multiagent reinforcement learning. In: Proceedings of the 2014 International Conference on Autonomous Agents and Multi-agent Systems, AAMAS 2014, pp. 165–172 (2014)
9. Foerster, J., Assael, I.A., de Freitas, N., Whiteson, S.: Learning to communicate with deep multi-agent reinforcement learning. In: Advances in Neural Information Processing Systems, pp. 2137–2145 (2016)
10. Foerster, J.N., Farquhar, G., Afouras, T., Nardelli, N., Whiteson, S.: Counterfactual multi-agent policy gradients. In: Thirty-Second AAAI Conference on Artificial Intelligence (2018)
11. García, J., Fernández, F.: A comprehensive survey on safe reinforcement learning. J. Mach. Learn. Res. 16(42), 1437–1480 (2015)
12. Grześ, M.: Reward shaping in episodic reinforcement learning. In: Proceedings of the 16th Conference on Autonomous Agents and MultiAgent Systems, AAMAS 2017, pp. 565–573 (2017)
13. Gupta, J.K., Egorov, M., Kochenderfer, M.: Cooperative multi-agent control using deep reinforcement learning. In: Sukthankar, G., Rodriguez-Aguilar, J.A. (eds.) AAMAS 2017. LNCS (LNAI), vol. 10642, pp. 66–83. Springer, Cham (2017). https://doi.org/10.1007/978-3-319-71682-4_5
14. Hendrycks, D., Carlini, N., Schulman, J., Steinhardt, J.: Unsolved problems in ML safety (2021)
15. Jaderberg, M., et al.: Human-level performance in 3D multiplayer games with population-based reinforcement learning. Science 364(6443), 859–865 (2019)
16. Laurent, G.J., Matignon, L., Fort-Piat, L., et al.: The world of Independent Learners is not Markovian. J. Knowl.-Based Intell. Eng. Syst. 15, 55–64 (2011)
17. Leibo, J.Z., Zambaldi, V., Lanctot, M., Marecki, J., Graepel, T.: Multi-agent reinforcement learning in sequential social dilemmas. In: Proceedings of the 16th Conference on Autonomous Agents and Multiagent Systems, pp. 464–473 (2017)
18. Leike, J., Krueger, D., Everitt, T., Martic, M., Maini, V., Legg, S.: Scalable agent alignment via reward modeling: a research direction (2018)
19. Leike, J., et al.: AI safety gridworlds. arXiv:1711.09883 (2017)

20. Liu, S., Lever, G., Merel, J., Tunyasuvunakool, S., Heess, N., Graepel, T.: Emergent coordination through competition. In: 7th International Conference on Learning Representations, ICLR 2019, New Orleans, LA, USA (2019)

21. Lowd, D., Meek, C.: Adversarial learning. In: Proceedings of the Eleventh ACM SIGKDD International Conference on Knowledge Discovery in Data Mining, pp. 641–647. ACM (2005)

22. Lowe, R., Wu, Y., Tamar, A., Harb, J., Abbeel, P., Mordatch, I.: Multi-agent actor-critic for mixed cooperative-competitive environments. In: Advances in Neural Information Processing Systems, pp. 6379–6390 (2017)

23. Mnih, V., et al.: Asynchronous methods for deep reinforcement learning. In: International Conference on Machine Learning (2016)

24. Mnih, V., et al.: Human-level control through deep reinforcement learning. Nature **518**, 529–533 (2015)

25. Ng, A.Y., Harada, D., Russell, S.J.: Policy invariance under reward transformations: theory and application to reward shaping. In: Proceedings of the Sixteenth International Conference on Machine Learning, ICML 1999, pp. 278–287 (1999)

26. Phan, D.T., Grosu, R., Jansen, N., Paoletti, N., Smolka, S.A., Stoller, S.D.: Neural simplex architecture. In: Lee, R., Jha, S., Mavridou, A., Giannakopoulou, D. (eds.) NFM 2020. LNCS, vol. 12229, pp. 97–114. Springer, Cham (2020). https://doi.org/10.1007/978-3-030-55754-6_6

27. Phan, T., Belzner, L., Gabor, T., Schmid, K.: Leveraging statistical multi-agent online planning with emergent value function approximation. In: Proceedings of the 17th International Conference on Autonomous Agents and MultiAgent Systems, AAMAS, pp. 730–738 (2018)

28. Phan, T., Belzner, L., Gabor, T., Sedlmeier, A., Ritz, F., Linnhoff-Popien, C.: Resilient multi-agent reinforcement learning with adversarial value decomposition. In: Proceedings of the AAAI Conference on Artificial Intelligence, vol. 35, no. 13, pp. 11308–11316 (2021)

29. Phan, T., et al.: Learning and testing resilience in cooperative multi-agent systems. In: Proceedings of the 19th Conference on Autonomous Agents and MultiAgent Systems, AAMAS 2020 (2020)

30. Rashid, T., Samvelyan, M., de Witt, C.S., Farquhar, G., Foerster, J., Whiteson, S.: QMIX: monotonic value function factorisation for deep multi-agent reinforcement learning. In: International Conference on Machine Learning, pp. 4292–4301 (2018)

31. Ritz, F., et al.: SAT-MARL: specification aware training in multi-agent reinforcement learning. In: Proceedings of the 13th International Conference on Agents and Artificial Intelligence, Volume 1: ICAART, pp. 28–37. SciTePress (2021). https://doi.org/10.5220/0010189500280037

32. Seurin, M., Preux, P., Pietquin, O.: "I'm sorry Dave, I'm afraid I can't do that" deep q-learning from forbidden action. arXiv:1910.02078 (2019)

33. Silver, D., et al.: A general reinforcement learning algorithm that masters chess, shogi, and go through self-play. Science **362**(6419), 1140–1144 (2018). https://doi.org/10.1126/science.aar6404

34. Son, K., Kim, D., Kang, W.J., Hostallero, D.E., Yi, Y.: QTRAN: learning to factorize with transformation for cooperative multi-agent reinforcement learning. In: International Conference on Machine Learning, pp. 5887–5896 (2019)

35. Sunehag, P., et al.: Value-decomposition networks for cooperative multi-agent learning based on team reward. In: Proceedings of the 17th International Conference on Autonomous Agents and Multiagent Systems (Extended Abstract), IFAAMAS, pp. 2085–2087 (2018)

36. Sutton, R.S., Barto, A.G.: Reinforcement Learning: An Introduction. A Bradford Book, Cambridge (2018)

37. Tampuu, A., et al.: Multiagent cooperation and competition with deep reinforcement learning. PLoS ONE **12**(4), e0172395 (2017)

38. Wang, S., Wan, J., Zhang, D., Li, D., Zhang, C.: Towards smart factory for industry 4.0: a self-organized multi-agent system with big data based feedback and coordination. Comput. Netw. **101**, 158–168 (2016)
39. Watkins, C.J., Dayan, P.: Q-learning. Mach. Learn. **8**(3–4), 279–292 (1992)
40. Wolpert, D.H., Tumer, K.: Optimal payoff functions for members of collectives. In: Modeling Complexity in Economic and Social Systems, pp. 355–369. World Scientific (2002)
41. Zahavy, T., Haroush, M., Merlis, N., Mankowitz, D.J., Mannor, S.: Learn what not to learn: action elimination with deep reinforcement learning. In: Bengio, S., Wallach, H., Larochelle, H., Grauman, K., Cesa-Bianchi, N., Garnett, R. (eds.) Advances in Neural Information Processing Systems, vol. 31, pp. 3562–3573. Curran Associates, Inc. (2018)

Task Bundle Delegation for Reducing the Flowtime

Ellie Beauprez[✉], Anne Cécile Caron, Maxime Morge, and Jean-Christophe Routier

Univ. Lille, CNRS, Centrale Lille, UMR 9189 CRIStAL, 59000 Lille, France
{ellie.beauprez,anne-cecile.caron,maxime.morge,
jean-christophe.routier}@univ-lille.fr

Abstract. In this paper, we study the problem of task reallocation for load-balancing in distributed data processing models that tackle vast amount of data. We propose a strategy based on cooperative agents used to optimize the rescheduling of tasks in multiple jobs which must be executed as soon as possible. It allows agents to determine locally the next tasks to process, to delegate, possibly to swap according to their knowledge, their own belief base and their peer modelling. The novelty lies in the ability of agents to identify opportunities and bottleneck agents, and afterwards to reassign some bundles of tasks thanks to concurrent bilateral negotiations. The strategy adopted by the agents allows to warrant a continuous improvement of the flowtime. Our experimentation reveals that our strategy reaches a flowtime which is better than the one reached by a DCOP resolution, close to the one reached by the classical heuristic approach, and significantly reduces the rescheduling time.

Keywords: Multi-agents systems · Distributed problem solving · Agent-based negotiation

1 Introduction

The problem of efficient task assignment among executing entities is common to many real-world applications for logistics [13, 15], collective robotics [7, 22], distributed systems [12, 20], or more recently Big Data [1]. In particular, Data Science, which involves the processing of large volumes of data which requires distributed file systems and parallel programming, challenges distributed computing with regard to task allocation and load-balancing. This paper is concerned with a class of practical applications where (a) some concurrent jobs (sets of tasks) must be performed as soon as possible, (b) the resources (e.g. data) required to successfully execute a task are distributed among nodes. Here we consider the most prominent distributed data processing model for tackling vast amount of data on commodity clusters, i.e. the MapReduce design pattern [24]. Jobs are composed of tasks executed by the different nodes where the resources are distributed. Since several resources are necessary to perform a task, its execution requires fetching some of these resources from other nodes, thus incurring an extra time cost for its execution.

Many works adopt the multi-agent paradigm to address the problem of task reallocation and load-balancing in distributed systems [12]. The individual-based approach

© Springer Nature Switzerland AG 2022
A. P. Rocha et al. (Eds.): ICAART 2021, LNAI 13251, pp. 22–45, 2022.
https://doi.org/10.1007/978-3-031-10161-8_2

allows the decentralization of heuristics to scale-up the resolution of scheduling problem despite of the combinatory explosion. Furthermore, due to their inherent reactive nature, the multi-agent methods for task reallocation are adaptive to the inaccurate estimation of task execution time and some disruptive phenomena (task consumption, job release, slowing down nodes, etc.). Most of these works adopt the market-oriented approach which models problems as non-cooperative games [7,23], eventually with machine learning techniques which assume past experiences [20,22]. By contrast, we suppose as [1] that: (a) the agents are cooperative, i.e. they have a partial and local perception of the task allocation but they share the same goal, and (b) neither generalizable predictive patterns nor prior model of the data/environment are available since it is not the case for the class of practical applications we are concerned with. We go further here by considering several concurrent jobs composed of tasks. Each task can be executed by a single agent, all of them are competent. Agents want to minimize the mean flowtime of jobs. The main difficulty lies in the formulation of complex systems for the reassignment of tasks-workers which are decentralized and adaptive, i.e. the design of individual and asynchronous behaviours that lead to the emergence of feasible allocations combining the objectives of the task requesters.

We propose a strategy that decides which bilateral reallocation is suggested or accepted. Based on peer modelling, the strategy determines the agent behaviour in the negotiation protocol. The offer strategy selects a potential delegation, i.e. an offer bundle and a respondant. The acceptability rule determines whether the agent accepts or rejects all or part of this delegation. Specifically, our contributions are as follows:

1. We formalize the multi-agent task allocation problem where concurrent jobs are composed of situated tasks with different costs depending on the location of the resources.
2. We propose a strategy that continuously identifies bottleneck agents and opportunities within unbalanced allocations to trigger concurrent and bilateral negotiations in order to delegate or swap tasks.
3. We conduct extensive experiments that show that our method reaches a flowtime close to the one reached by the classical heuristic and significantly reduces the rescheduling time.

This paper is a extended version of [2].

1. We generalize the notion of delegation to consider any bilateral reallocation (delegation or swap of several tasks).
2. We redefine the acceptability criterion of the bilateral reallocations in order to reduce the rescheduling time and the mean flowtime reached by our strategy.
3. We quantitatively compare the performance of our strategy with the performance of a DCOP resolution method.

After an overview of related works in Sect. 2, we formalize the multi-agent situated task allocation problem in Sect. 3. Section 4 describes the consumption/delegation operations and the negotiation process. Section 5 specifies how agents choose which tasks to negotiate and with whom. Our empirical evaluation is described in Sect. 6. Section 7 summarizes our contribution and future work.

Table 1. Analysis grid of methods for task assignment (at top) or reassignment (at bottom).

	Resources	Tasks	Workers	Objective	Dynamics	Decentralized	Approach/Technique
(Kuhn-Munkres, 1955) [13]	—	n single-worker	R_n single-task	W($\vec{A}$)	✗	✗	LP
(SPT, 1967) [8]	—	n single-worker	P_m multi-task	C($\vec{A}$)	✗	✗	Heuristic
(Bruno et al., 1974) [5]	—	n single-worker	R_m multi-task	C($\vec{A}$)	✗	✗	LP
(Shehory et Krause, 1998) [21]	—	n multi-worker	R_m single-task	W($\vec{A}$)	✓	✓	Coalition
(GPGP, 2004) [14]	consumables or not	n single-worker	R_m multi-task	W($\vec{A}$)	✓	✓	Team
(Turner et al., 2018) [22]	scarce	n single-worker	R_m online multi-task	W($\vec{A}$)	✓	✓	CBBA + ML
(Li et al., 2014) [15]	—	n single-worker	P_m multi-task	C($\vec{A}$) $\oplus$W($\vec{A}$)	✓	✓	DCOP
(Schaerf et al., 1995) [20]	—	n single-worker	P_m multi-task	W($\vec{A}$)	✓	✓	MARL
(MASTA, 2021) [1]	transferables duplicables	n single-worker	R_m multi-task	$C_{max}(\vec{A})$	✓	✓	Team
(SMASTA+, 2021) [2]	transferables duplicables	n multi-worker	R_m multi-task	C($\vec{A}$)	✓	✓	Team

2 Related Work

Table 1 summarizes all the works discussed here according to our analysis grid. The left-hand side of the table shows the problems which are addressed, i.e. their ingredients (resources, tasks, workers and objectives). The right-hand side reveals the features of these methods and the techniques used. While the upper part of the table contains some classical task assignment methods, the lower part presents some dynamic and decentralized reassignment methods.

Scheduling theory [6] includes off-line methods for solving various problems of task assignment among workers. For instance, the Kuhn-Munkres algorithm, also called the Hungarian method, minimizes the total cost (denoted W($\vec{A}$)) for n tasks and n workers [13]. *Shortest processing time first* (SPT) is a very simple method that minimizes the flowtime of n single-worker tasks with one multi-task worker [8]. This result generalizes to the problem with m multi-task workers if the cost of tasks is identical from one worker to another (denoted P_m). The scheduling problem, which consists in minimizing the total delay (denoted C($\vec{A}$)) with m multi-task workers and n single-worker tasks whose costs depend on the worker (denoted R_m), can be formalized by a linear-program (LP). This problem reduces to a weighted matching problem in a bipartite graph with n tasks and $n \times m$ positions. This problem is polynomial [11]. Based on the Ford-Fulkerson algorithm, the complexity of the algorithm described by [5] is $\mathcal{O}(max(mn^2, n^3))$. These approaches are not suitable for task reassignment in distributed systems where decentralization and adaptability are required. Indeed, global control is a performance bottleneck, since it must constantly collect information about the state of the system. By contrast, our agents make local decisions on an existing allocation with the aim to improve the load-balancing. Moreover, classical scheduling problems are static. The inaccurate estimation of the task execution time and some disruptive phenomena (task consumption, job release, slowing down nodes, etc.) may require major modifications in the existing allocation to stay optimal. Furthermore, agents can operate in dynamic environments that change over time.

The multi-agent paradigm is particularly suitable for the design and implementation of distributed and adaptive mechanisms for the reassignment of tasks-workers [12]. The existing models differ due to the nature of the tasks and the agents, whether they represent workers or task requesters. Coalition formation is justified if a task requires more than one worker or if its cost decreases with the number of assigned workers. For instance, Shehory and Kraus propose decentralized, greedy and anytime algorithms for assigning multi-worker tasks with precedence constraints to some workers with heterogeneous capabilities/efficiencies [21]. Similarly to a coalition, a team aims at maximizing an overall objective function rather than the individual welfares. However, a team performs single-worker tasks. For instance, Lesser et al. propose a domain-independent coordination framework with a hierarchical task network representation for resource allocation and task assignment/scheduling [14]. The main objective of *Generalized Partial Global Planning* (GPGP) is the maximization of the combined utility accrued by the group of agents as a result of successful completion of its high-level goals. GPGP adopts a planning-oriented approach of coordination which assumes that the effort required for coordination (reasoning and communication) is negligible compared to the tasks execution time. Inspired by economic theories, the market-oriented approach models distributed planning problems as the search of an equilibrium for a non-cooperative game [23]. The agents delegate/swap tasks. Contrary to a team, a marketplace assumes that the constraints and objectives are fully distributed. Among the market-oriented methods, we distinguish three families.

DCOP. The reassignment problems can be formalized as *Distributed Constraint Optimization Problems* (DCOP). Many resolution methods have been developed for finding an optimal solution to a DCOP which is an NP-hard problem (see a recent survey [9]). The main difficulty in applying these methods for task reassignment lies in the representation of a real-world problem as a DCOP, or even several COP sub-problems, since it requires expertise in the resolution method (e.g. [15]).

CBBA. *Consensus Based Bundle Algorithm* [7] is a multi-agent assignment method that consists of: (a) selecting the negotiated tasks; (b) determining the winner of these negotiations. In the same line, Turner et al. study the continuous task assignment for a multi-robot team in order to maximise the throughput before running out of fuel [22]. Thanks to machine learning (ML), they propose a prediction mechanism that uses past experience to select which task allocation strategy yields the optimal global task allocation.

MARL. The reassignment problems can also be formalized as Markov decision processes [4], in particular Decentralized Partially Observed Markov Decision Process (Dec-POMDP). The optimization of a Dec-POMDP with a finite horizon is a NEXP-

TIME problem. Approximate resolution methods can only be applied to small problem instances, they do not scale up. Beyond these off-line planning methods, *Multi-Agent Reinforcement Learning* (MARL) requires a perfect knowledge of the environment and a learning phase [20].

Conversely, we consider neither generalizable predictive patterns nor prior model of the data/environment are available since it is not the case for the class of practical applications we are concerned with. For instance, Baert et al. have in [1] an egalitarian objective which is the minimization of the makespan (denoted $C_{max}(\overrightarrow{A})$). We consider here the problem of coordinating decisions between agents to find a globally optimal solution for a multi-objective function. Agents want to minimize the mean flowtime of several concurrent jobs, each consisting of several tasks.

This paper is a extended version of [2].

1. While our previous work only considers delegations of single task, we here generalize our formal framework to consider any bilateral reallocation (delegation or swap of several tasks) in order to reduce not only the mean flowtime but also the rescheduling time.
2. We here redefine the acceptability criterion of the bilateral reallocations by the agents. Previously, this criterion was based on the local flowtime, i.e. the flowtime restricted to the two contractors. Since this criterion does not guarantee the termination of the multi-agent reallocation algorithm, it was combined with the *makespan*, the maximum completion of all the jobs. In this paper, a bilateral reallocation is acceptable for an agent if, according to its beliefs, it reduces the global flowtime. This acceptability criterion is sufficient to guarantee the convergence of the reallocation process. Moreover, it allows to reduce the rescheduling time and the mean flowtime reached by our strategy.
3. We quantitatively compare the performance of our strategy with the performance of a DCOP resolution method.

3   Multi-agent Situated Task Allocation

In this section, we formalize the multi-agent situated task allocation problem with concurrent jobs.

We consider distributed jobs, each job being a set of independent, non divisible tasks without precedence order. Tasks are non preemptive, and the execution of each task requires resources which are distributed across different nodes. These resources are transferable and non consumable.

Definition 1 (Distributed System). *A system is a triple $\mathcal{D} = \langle \mathcal{N}, \mathcal{E}, \mathcal{R} \rangle$ where:*

- $\mathcal{N} = \{\nu_1, \ldots, \nu_m\}$ *is a set of m nodes;*
- $\mathcal{E}$ *is an acquaintance relation, i.e. a binary and symmetric relation over $\mathcal{N}$;*
- $\mathcal{R} = \{\rho_1, \ldots, \rho_k\}$ *is a set of k resources, each resource ρ_i having a size $|\rho_i|$. The locations of the resources, which are possibly replicated, are determined by the function:*

$$l : \mathcal{R} \to 2^{\mathcal{N}} \tag{1}$$

For simplicity, we assume exactly one agent per node (the set of agents is $\mathcal{N}$), and any agent can access any resource.

Running a job (without a deadline) consists in a set of independent tasks which require resources to produce an outcome.

Definition 2 (Job/Task). *Let $\mathcal{D}$ be a distributed system and Res be the space of outcomes. We consider the set of ℓ jobs $\mathcal{J} = \{J_1, \ldots, J_\ell\}$. Each job J_i is a set of k_i tasks $J_i = \{\tau_1, \ldots, \tau_{k_i}\}$ where each task τ is a function which links a set of resources to an outcome: $\tau : 2^{\mathcal{R}} \mapsto Res$.*

It is worth noticing that we consider in this paper a set of jobs having the same release date. $\mathcal{J} = \bigcup_{1 \leq i \leq \ell} J_i$ denotes the set of the n tasks of $\mathcal{J}$ and $\mathcal{R}_\tau \subseteq \mathcal{R}$ is the set of the resources required for the task τ. The job containing the task τ is written job(τ).

Each task has a cost for a node, which is its estimated execution time by this node. As the fetching time of resources is supposed to be significant, the cost function must verify that the task τ is cheaper for ν_i than for ν_j if the required resources are "more local" to ν_i than to ν_j:

Property 1 (Cost). Let $\mathcal{D}$ a distributed system and $\mathcal{J}$ a set of tasks. The cost function $c : \mathcal{J} \times \mathcal{N} \mapsto \mathbb{R}_+^*$ is such that:

$$c(\tau, \nu_i) \leq c(\tau, \nu_j) \Leftrightarrow \tag{2}$$
$$\Sigma_{\rho \in \mathcal{R}_\tau, \nu_i \in l(\rho)} |\rho| > \Sigma_{\rho \in \mathcal{R}_\tau, \nu_j \in l(\rho)} |\rho|$$

The cost function can be extended to a set of tasks:

$$\forall T \subseteq \mathcal{J}, \quad c(T, \nu_i) = \Sigma_{\tau \in T} c(\tau, \nu_i) \tag{3}$$

Note that in practice, it is difficult to design this function with a good estimation of the runtime. However the adaptability of our multi-agent system compensates for a poor estimation of the cost function. It is one of the benefits of our approach.

A multi-agent situated task allocation problem with concurrent jobs consists in assigning several jobs to some nodes according to their costs.

Definition 3 (MASTA+). *A multi-agent situated task allocation problem with concurrent jobs is a quadruple MASTA+ $= \langle \mathcal{D}, \mathcal{J}, \mathcal{J}, c \rangle$ where:*

- *$\mathcal{D}$ is a distributed system with m nodes;*
- *$\mathcal{J} = \{\tau_1, \ldots, \tau_n\}$ is a set of n tasks;*
- *$\mathcal{J} = \{J_1, \ldots, J_\ell\}$ is a partition of $\mathcal{J}$ into ℓ jobs;*
- *$c : \mathcal{J} \times \mathcal{N} \mapsto \mathbb{R}_+^*$ is the cost function.*

A task allocation is an assignation of sorted bundles to different nodes.

Definition 4 (Allocation). *Let MASTA+ be a task allocation problem. An allocation $\overrightarrow{A}$ is a vector of m sorted task bundles $((B_1, \prec_1), \ldots, (B_m, \prec_m))$. Each bundle $(B_i, \prec_i)$ is the set of tasks $(B_i \subseteq \mathcal{J})$ assigned to the node ν_i associated with a scheduling order, i.e. a strict and total order $(\prec_i \subseteq \mathcal{J} \times \mathcal{J})$ such that $\tau_j \prec_i \tau_k$ means that if $\tau_j, \tau_k \in B_i$ then τ_j is performed before τ_k by ν_i.*

The allocation $\overrightarrow{A}$ is such that:

$$\forall \tau \in \mathcal{T}, \exists \nu_i \in \mathcal{N}, \tau \in B_i \tag{4}$$

$$\forall \nu_i \in \mathcal{N}, \forall \nu_j \in \mathcal{N} \setminus \{\nu_i\}, B_i \cap B_j = \varnothing \tag{5}$$

The set $\mathcal{T}$ is partitioned by an allocation: all the tasks are assigned (Eq. 4) and each task is assigned to a single node (Eq. 5). To simplify, we use the following notations:

- $\overrightarrow{B}_i = (B_i, \prec_i)$, the sorted bundle of ν_i;
- $\min_{\prec_i} B_i$, the next task to perform by ν_i:
- $\text{jobs}(B_i)$, the set of jobs assigned to ν_i, i.e. such that at least one task is in B_i;
- $\text{node}(\tau, \overrightarrow{A})$, the node whose bundle contains τ in $\overrightarrow{A}$;
- $w_i(\overrightarrow{A}) = c(B_i, \nu_i) = \Sigma_{\tau \in B_i} c(\tau, \nu_i)$, the workload of ν_i for $\overrightarrow{A}$.

We assume that nodes are never idle, so the completion time of a task is its delay before the task is started, plus its estimated execution time:

$$C_\tau(\overrightarrow{A}) = t(\tau, \text{node}(\tau, \overrightarrow{A})) + c(\tau, \text{node}(\tau, \overrightarrow{A})) \tag{6}$$

$$\text{with } t(\tau, \nu_i) = \Sigma_{\tau' \in B_i | \tau' \prec_i \tau} c(\tau', \nu_i)$$

Unlike the cost, the delay (so the completion time) depends on the scheduling order over the bundle.

The quality of an allocation is measured by the mean flowtime for all the jobs, where the flowtime of one job is its completion time. The makespan is the time necessary to perform all the jobs. Then, the makespan is the maximum completion time of the jobs and also the maximum workload of the nodes.

Definition 5 (Flowtime/Makespan). *Let MASTA+ a task allocation problem and $\overrightarrow{A}$ an allocation. We define:*

- *the completion time of $J \in \mathcal{J}$ for $\overrightarrow{A}$,*

$$C_J(\overrightarrow{A}) = \max_{\tau \in J}\{C_\tau(\overrightarrow{A})\} \tag{7}$$

- *the (mean) flowtime of $\mathcal{J}$ for $\overrightarrow{A}$,*

$$C_{mean}(\overrightarrow{A}) = \frac{1}{\ell}C(\overrightarrow{A}) \text{ with } C(\overrightarrow{A}) = \Sigma_{J \in \mathcal{J}} C_J(\overrightarrow{A}) \tag{8}$$

- *the makespan of $\mathcal{J}$ for $\overrightarrow{A}$,*

$$C_{max}(\overrightarrow{A}) = \max_{\nu_i \in \mathcal{N}}\{w_i(\overrightarrow{A})\} \tag{9}$$

- *the local availability ratio of $\overrightarrow{A}$,*

$$L(\overrightarrow{A}) = \Sigma_{\tau \in \mathcal{T}} \frac{\Sigma_{\rho \in \mathcal{R}_\tau, \, \text{node}(\tau, \overrightarrow{A}) \in l(\rho)} |\rho|}{\Sigma_{\rho \in \mathcal{R}_\tau} |\rho|} \tag{10}$$

Unlike the makespan, the flowtime depends on the scheduling order. The local availability ratio of $\overrightarrow{A}$ measures the proportion of locally processed resources (Eq. 10).

Example 1 (MASTA+).   From the distributed system $\mathcal{D} = \langle \mathcal{N}, \mathcal{E}, \mathcal{R} \rangle$ with $\mathcal{N} = \{\nu_1, \nu_2, \nu_3\}$, $\mathcal{E} = \{(\nu_1, \nu_2), (\nu_1, \nu_3), (\nu_2, \nu_3)\}$ and $\mathcal{R} = \{\rho_1, \ldots, \rho_9\}$ where resources are replicated on 2 nodes (cf. Fig. 1a), we consider MASTA+ $= \langle \mathcal{D}, \mathcal{T}, \mathcal{J}, c \rangle$ with $\mathcal{T} = \{\tau_1, \ldots, \tau_9\}$ where each task τ_i needs resource ρ_i, $\mathcal{J} = \{J_1, J_2, J_3\}$ such that $J_1 = \{\tau_1, \tau_2, \tau_3\}$, $J_2 = \{\tau_4, \tau_5, \tau_6\}$ and $J_3 = \{\tau_7, \tau_8, \tau_9\}$ and c is the cost function given in Table 2. We assume the cost of a task is proportional to the resources size, and two times greater if the resource is distant. We consider here the allocation $\overrightarrow{A}$ (see Fig. 1b) with $\overrightarrow{B}_1 = (\tau_5, \tau_8, \tau_3, \tau_2)$, $\overrightarrow{B}_2 = (\tau_4, \tau_9)$ and $\overrightarrow{B}_3 = (\tau_7, \tau_1, \tau_6)$. The makespan and the flowtime are $C_{max}(\overrightarrow{A}) = 12$ and $C(\overrightarrow{A}) = 8 + 12 + 12 = 32$.

Table 2. Cost function.

	τ_1	τ_2	τ_3	τ_4	τ_5	τ_6	τ_7	τ_8	τ_9
$c(\tau, \nu_1)$	5	3	1	8	2	10	4	2	4
$c(\tau, \nu_2)$	10	3	2	4	2	5	2	2	8
$c(\tau, \nu_3)$	5	6	1	4	4	5	2	4	4

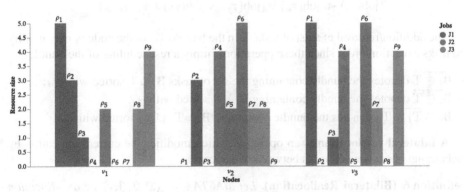

(a) Resource distribution

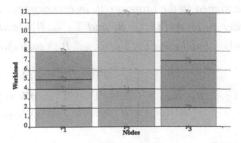

(b) Task allocation

Fig. 1. Resource distribution and task allocation for Example 1.

To conclude this section, due to the locality of resources, a task has not the same cost for every nodes. In this paper, our objective is to minimize the mean flowtime, for a set of concurrent jobs composed of many tasks.

4   Consumption and Reallocation

We describe in this section the operations of consumption and reallocation as well as the negotiation protocol.

A task **consumption** is the removal by a node of a task from its bundle in order to process it. This operation modifies not only the current allocation but also the underlying MASTA+ problem since the consumed task is no longer present. The consumption strategy adopted by an agent specifies the tasks scheduling for the node it is in charge of. Since we aim at minimizing the mean flowtime of the jobs, we consider here a job-oriented strategy which sorts first jobs and then the tasks inside the same job (the tasks of a same job are consecutive in the bundle). More precisely, the less expensive jobs are prior on the most expensive ones in order to minimize locally the completion time of the jobs. Thereafter, $J_1 \blacktriangleleft_i J_2$ means that the tasks in J_1 are prior to the tasks in J_2. $\tau_1 \lhd_i \tau_2$ means that the task τ_1 is prior to the task τ_2. Formally,

$$
\begin{aligned}
&\forall \tau_j, \tau_k \in B_i \ \tau_j \prec_i \tau_k \Leftrightarrow \\
&\mathrm{job}(\tau_j) \blacktriangleleft_i \mathrm{job}(\tau_k) \vee (\mathrm{job}(\tau_j) = \mathrm{job}(\tau_k) \wedge \tau_j \lhd_i \tau_k)
\end{aligned}
\tag{11}
$$

The addition/removal of a list of tasks T in the bundle $\overrightarrow{B}_i$ of the node ν_i may modify the tasks execution order since these operations imply a rescheduling of the bundle:

- $\overrightarrow{B_i \oplus T}$ denotes the bundle containing the set of tasks $B_i \cup T$ sorted with $\prec_i$;
- $\overrightarrow{B_i \ominus T}$ denotes the bundle containing $B_i \setminus T$ sorted with $\prec_i$.
- $\overrightarrow{B_i \ominus T_1 \oplus T_2}$ denotes the bundle containing $B_i \setminus T_1 \cup T_2$ sorted with $\prec_i$.

A **bilateral reallocation** is an operation which modifies the current allocation by exchanging one or several tasks between two agents.

Definition 6 (Bilateral Reallocation). *Let MASTA+ $= \langle \mathcal{D}, \mathcal{T}, \mathcal{J}, c \rangle$ be an allocation problem and $\overrightarrow{A} = (\overrightarrow{B}_1, \ldots, \overrightarrow{B}_m)$ an allocation. The bilateral reallocation of the non-empty list of tasks T_1 assigned to the proposer ν_i in exchange for the list of tasks T_2 assigned to the responder ν_j in $\overrightarrow{A}$ ($T_1 \subseteq B_i$ and $T_2 \subseteq B_j$) leads to the allocation $\gamma(T_1, T_2, \nu_i, \nu_j, \overrightarrow{A})$ with m bundles $\gamma(T_1, T_2, \nu_i, \nu_j, \overrightarrow{B}_k)$ such that:*

$$
\gamma(T_1, T_2, \nu_i, \nu_j, \overrightarrow{B}_k) = \begin{cases} \overrightarrow{B_i \ominus T_1 \oplus T_2} & \text{if } k = i, \\ \overrightarrow{B_j \ominus T_2 \oplus T_1} & \text{if } k = j, \\ \overrightarrow{B}_k & \text{otherwise} \end{cases}
\tag{12}
$$

We distinguish two cases:

- a **swap** where the two lists of tasks are non-empty ($T_1 \neq \varnothing \wedge T_2 \neq \varnothing$), denoted $\sigma(T_1, T_2, \nu_i, \nu_j, \overrightarrow{A})$;

– a **delegation** where an agent gives a part of its tasks to one of its peers without counterpart ($T_2 = \varnothing$), denoted $\delta(T_1, \nu_i, \nu_j, \overrightarrow{A})$. If $|T_1| = 1$, this is an **unary delegation**. Otherwise, this is an n-**ary delegation**.

We will see later that the bilateral reallocation of lists of tasks rather than sets allows to specify the order in which the tasks should be evaluated to validate the interest of all or part of the transaction.

In order to improve an allocation, we introduce the notion of socially rational bilateral reallocation which verifies if a reallocation reduces the global flowtime, i.e. the completion time of the jobs for all nodes.

Definition 7 (Socially Rational Bilateral Reallocation). *Let MASTA+* $=$ $\langle \mathcal{D}, \mathcal{T}, \mathcal{J}, c \rangle$ *be an allocation problem,* $\overrightarrow{A}$ *an allocation. The bilateral reallocation* $\gamma(T_1, T_2, \nu_i, \nu_j, \overrightarrow{A})$ *is socially rational with respect to the flowtime if and only if the global flowtime decreases,*

$$C(\gamma(T_1, T_2, \nu_i, \nu_j, \overrightarrow{A})) < C(\overrightarrow{A}) \tag{13}$$

An allocation is **stable** if there is no socially rational bilateral delegation.

Contrary to [2], we do not consider as socially rational the reallocations reducing the local flowtime (the completion time of jobs restricted to the nodes implied in the reallocation) which does not guarantee the convergence of the reallocation process, nor even the reallocations reducing the local flowtime and the makespan (the maximum workload of the agents). The reduction of the global flowtime guarantees the termination of the process. Hereafter, when it comes to flowtime, it will be, unless specified, the global flowtime (denoted $C(\overrightarrow{A})$ defined in Eq. 8).

Property 2 (Termination). Let MASTA+ $= \langle \mathcal{D}, \mathcal{T}, \mathcal{J}, c \rangle$ be an allocation problem and $\overrightarrow{A}$ a non-stable allocation with respect to the flowtime. There exists a finite path of socially rational bilateral reallocations with respect to the flowtime which leads to a stable allocation for this criterion.

Proof. Let MASTA+ $= \langle \mathcal{D}, \mathcal{T}, \mathcal{J}, c \rangle$ be an allocation problem and $\overrightarrow{A}$ a non-stable allocation with respect to the flowtime. Let γ be a socially rational reallocation which leads to the allocation $\overrightarrow{A'}$ from $\overrightarrow{A}$. Since γ is socially rational with respect to the flowtime, the flowtime strictly decreases. Formally, $\Sigma_{J \in \mathcal{J}} C_J(\overrightarrow{A'}) < \Sigma_{J \in \mathcal{J}} C_J(\overrightarrow{A})$. Since there is a finite number of allocations and $\Sigma_{J \in \mathcal{J}} C_J(\overrightarrow{A})$ strictly decreases at each step, there can only be a finite number of such allocations.

For tasks reallocation, the agents are involved in multiple bilateral single-round negotiation. Each negotiation is based on the alternating offers protocol [18] and includes three decision steps: (a) the offer strategy of the proposer which selects a delegation, i.e. a list of tasks in its bundle and a responder, (b) the counter-offer strategy which allows the responder to determine whether it declines, accepts or makes a counter-offer to the delegation, and (c) the eventual reallocation is confirmed or withdrawn by the proposer according to the consumptions that happen concurrently (cf. Fig. 2).

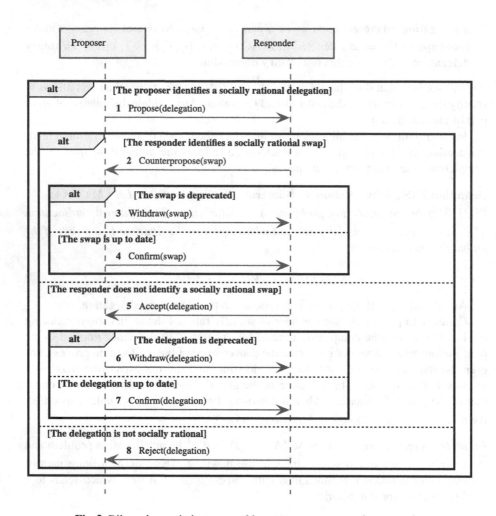

Fig. 2. Bilateral negotiation protocol between a proposer and a responder.

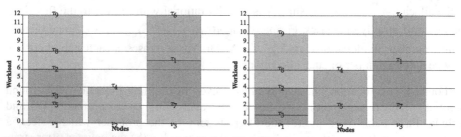

(a) Allocation after the delegation of τ_9 from ν_2 **(b)** Allocation after the swap of τ_9 and τ_5 be-
to ν_1 tween ν_2 and ν_1

Fig. 3. Allocations of the first example resulting from bilateral reallocations.

Example 2 (Consumption and Reallocation). Let us consider the problem MASTA+ from the Example 1 and the allocation $\overrightarrow{A}$ in Fig. 1b. According to the consumption strategy adopted by the agents, each bundle is sorted. The less expensive jobs are prior (e.g. $J_3 \blacktriangleleft_3 J_1 \blacktriangleleft_3 J_2$). In case of a tie, the natural order over the identifiers ensures a strict and total order (e.g. $J_2 \blacktriangleleft_1 J_3$). The tasks among a same job are sorted by increasing cost ($\tau_3 \lhd_1 \tau_2$). The delegation of the task τ_9 by the node ν_2 to the node ν_1 leads to the allocation $\overrightarrow{A}' = \delta([\tau_9], \nu_2, \nu_1, \overrightarrow{A})$. This delegation (cf. Fig. 3a) is socially rational since it decreases the flowtime from 32 to 31. The swap of $\tau_9 \in B_2$ and $\tau_5 \in B_1$ between the nodes ν_2 and ν_1 leads to the allocation $\overrightarrow{A}'' = \sigma([\tau_9], [\tau_5], \nu_2, \nu_1, \overrightarrow{A})$. This swap (cf. Fig. 3b) decreases the flowtime from 32 to 29.

5 Negotiation Strategy

We describe in this section the different parts of the negotiation strategy and we sketch the agent behaviour in the negotiation process.

5.1 Peer Modelling

The peer modelling is built upon exchanged information through messages between the agents. Before the negotiation process and between each bilateral reallocation it is implied in, the agent ν_i informs its peers about the cost of each job J for it ($c(J, \nu_i)$). Since the number of jobs is negligible compared to the number of tasks, the messages size is insignificant compared to the bundle descriptions. The modelling for the target ν_k by the subject ν_i is based on:

1. the belief base of the subject, possibly partial or obsolete, which contains the beliefs about the costs of the jobs for ν_k ($c^i(J, \nu_k), \forall J \in \mathcal{J}$) and so the beliefs about the workload of ν_k ($w_k^i(\overrightarrow{A}) = \Sigma_{J \in \mathcal{J}} c^i(J, \nu_k)$);
2. the consumption strategy of the target assumed by the subject, written ($\mathcal{J}, \blacktriangleleft_k^i$).

The subject can then deduce:

- the completion time ($C_J^i(\overrightarrow{B}_k)$) of the job J for a target k, possibly itself ($\nu_k = \nu_i$), after the addition ($C_J^i(B_k \oplus T)$), the removal ($C_J^i(B_k \ominus T)$) and the replacing of tasks ($C_J^i(\overrightarrow{B_k \ominus T_1 \oplus T_2})$);
- the completion time of a job J for the allocation,

$$C_J^i(\overrightarrow{A}) = \max_{\nu_k \in \mathcal{N}} C_J^i(\overrightarrow{B}_k) \text{ où } C_J^i(\overrightarrow{B}_i) = C_J(\overrightarrow{B}_i) \tag{14}$$

- the **bottleneck node** for each job J, denoted $\nu_{max}^i(\overrightarrow{A}, J)$, i.e. the node ν_k for which the completion time of this job is the maximum completion time in the allocation,

$$C_J^i(\overrightarrow{B}_k) = C_J^i(\overrightarrow{A}) \tag{15}$$

- the flowtime of the allocation $\overrightarrow{A}$

$$C^i(\overrightarrow{A}) = \Sigma_{J \in \mathcal{J}} C_J^i(\overrightarrow{A}) \tag{16}$$

5.2 Acceptability Rule

The **acceptability rule** is a local decision made by an agent which is implied in a bilateral reallocation. This rule, which is based on the agent knowledge and the peer modelling, decides to accept or decline a reallocation.

Definition 8 (Acceptability). *Let MASTA+ = $\langle \mathcal{D}, \mathcal{T}, \mathcal{J}, c \rangle$ be a problem and $\overrightarrow{A}$ an allocation. The bilateral reallocation $\gamma(T_1, T_2, \nu_i, \nu_j, \overrightarrow{A})$ is acceptable by the agent $\nu_k \in \mathcal{N}$ with respect to the flowtime if an only if the agent believes that the flowtime decreases,*

$$\Sigma_{J \in \mathcal{J}} \max_{\forall \nu_o \in \mathcal{N} \setminus \{\nu_i, \nu_j\}} (C_J^k(\overrightarrow{B_i \ominus T_1 \oplus T_2}), C_J^k(\overrightarrow{B_j \ominus T_2 \oplus T_1}), C_J^k(B_o)) < C^k(\overrightarrow{A})$$

(17)

The acceptability with respect to the flowtime is based on the beliefs about the completion time of the jobs for all the nodes before and after the reallocation (Eq. 17).

We propose in this paper a process where the agents trigger concurrent bilateral negotiations leading to socially rational reallocations.

5.3 Offer Strategy

The **offer strategy** of an agent, which is based on its knowledge, its beliefs and its peer modelling, identifies a delegation in three steps. An agent ν_i selects an offer bundle, i.e. a list of tasks to delegate to a responder in a set $\mathcal{N}'$ in order to reduce the completion time of a job in a set $\mathcal{J}'$ for which it is a bottleneck. Initially, $\mathcal{J}' = \mathcal{J}, \mathcal{N}' = \mathcal{N}$.

1. Job Selection. In order to reduce not only the completion time of a job but also the completion time of the next jobs in its bundle, our heuristic selects the most prior job J_* for which it is a bottleneck,

$$J_* = \min_{\blacktriangleleft_i} \{J \in \text{jobs}(B_i) \cap \mathcal{J}' \mid \nu_{\max}^i(\overrightarrow{A}, J = \nu_i)\}$$

(18)

2. Responder Selection. The jobs of a responder that are impacted by the delegation are those after J_* according to $\blacktriangleleft_j^i$. Not to increase the completion time of these jobs, our heuristic selects a responder ν_* for whom the sum of the differences between the completion time for the allocation and the completion time for the agent is the greatest one,

$$\nu_* = random\{\arg\max_{\nu_j \in \mathcal{N}'} \Sigma_{J_* \blacktriangleleft_j^i J}(C_J^i(\overrightarrow{A}) - C_J^i(\overrightarrow{B}_j))\}$$

(19)

where $random$ is a random choice function which selects a node from any set of nodes.

3. Offer Bundle Selection. To determine the offer bundle, we distinguish a strategy which selects a single task as in [2] and a strategy which selects several tasks.

3.a. Unary Delegation Selection. In order to reduce the completion time of J_*, the proposer selects a distant task, i.e. a task whose delegation will reduce its cost. Our heuristic selects the task in the job J_* or in the prior jobs in $\overrightarrow{B}_i$ with the best payoff in terms of cost. In case of a tie, the prior task is chosen,

$$\forall \mathcal{J}' \subseteq \mathcal{J}, \tau_* = \min_{\vartriangleleft_i} \{ \operatorname*{argmax}_{\tau \in \mathcal{J}' \cap B_i \cap \{ J | J = J_* \vee (J \vartriangleleft_i J_*) \}} c(\tau, \nu_i) - c(\tau, \nu_*) \}$$

The delegation $\delta([\tau_*], \nu_i, \nu_*, \overrightarrow{A})$ is triggered if it is acceptable for the proposer (cf Definition 8).

Algorithm 1. Building of the offer bundle by the proposer ν_i.

    Data: J_* the job selected in step #1;
    ν_* the responder selected in step #2;
1 $T_* \leftarrow$ empty_stack ;
2 $T = \{ \tau \mid \text{job}(\tau) = J_* \vee (\text{job}(\tau) \vartriangleleft_i J_*) \}$;
3 $T' \leftarrow (\dots, \tau^k, \dots, \tau^l, \dots) \mid \tau^i \in T \wedge (k < l \Leftrightarrow c(\tau^k, \nu_i) - c(\tau^k, \nu_*) >$
      $c(\tau^l, \nu_i) - c(\tau^l, \nu_*))$ /* the list of tasks by decreasing payoff
      */
4 $bestFlowtime = C^i(\overrightarrow{A})$;
5 **while** $T' \neq \varnothing$ **do**
6     $\tau_* \leftarrow \text{head}(T')$;
7     $T' \leftarrow \text{tail}(T')$;
8   **if** $C^i(\delta(T_* \cup \{\tau_*\}, \nu_i, \nu_*, \overrightarrow{A})) < bestFlowtime$ **then**
9        $T_*.\text{push}(\tau_*)$;
10       $bestFlowtime \leftarrow C^i(\delta(T_*, \nu_i, \nu_*, \overrightarrow{A}))$;
11   **end**
12   **else**
13      $\lfloor$ Return T_* ;
14   **end**
15 **end**
16 Return T_* ;

3.b. N-ary Delegation Selection. The proposer iteratively builds an offer bundle T_*. This bundle is a stack of tasks that will be evaluated by the acceptability strategy of the responder in order to accept all or part of this bundle by unstacking it (cf. Sect. 5.4). As illustrated in Algorithm 1, our heuristic considers the tasks in J_* or in the prior jobs in $\overrightarrow{B}_i$ (line 2). The proposer ν_i selects in priority the distant tasks, i.e. the tasks whose delegation will reduce at most the processing time (lines 3 and 6). According to this ratchet algorithm, the flowtime strictly decreases during the building of the offer bundle (line 8). Moreover, the algorithm stops as soon as a task does not improve the flowtime. If the offer bundle T_* is non-empty, the delegation $\delta(T_*, \nu_i, \nu_*, \overrightarrow{A})$, which is acceptable for the initiator, is triggered.

Whatever the offer bundle selection strategy is (3.a or 3.b), if no delegation is triggered, the offer strategy returns to step #2 to choose another responder ($\mathcal{N}' \leftarrow \mathcal{N}' \setminus \{\nu_*\}$). Otherwise, the offer strategy returns to step #1 to choose another job ($\mathcal{J}' \leftarrow \mathcal{J}' \setminus \{J_*\}$). In case of failure, no delegation is proposed and the agent goes into pause state until its belief base is updated and a new opportunity (i.e. a delegation) is found.

5.4 Acceptation Strategy

Algorithm 2. Selection by the responder ν_* of a sub-bundle among the received offer bundle

---

Data: T_* the received offer bundle

1 $T_{acc} \leftarrow T_*$;
2 **while** $\delta(T_{acc}, \nu_i, \nu_*, \overrightarrow{A})$ *is not acceptable for the agent* ν_* **do**
3 $\quad|\quad T_{acc}.\text{pop}$;
4 **end**
5 Return T_{acc} ;

According to the **acceptation strategy**, the responder accepts a delegation which is acceptable for it. Otherwise, it unstacks one by one the tasks in the offer bundle T_* (cf. Algorithm 2) for possibly accepting a part of it. When the sub-bundle T_{acc} is empty, the responder declines the offer.

5.5 Agent Behaviour

In our approach, a reallocation is the outcome of the negotiation process between agents adopting the same behaviour. The agent behaviour is specified in [3] by a deterministic finite state automaton[1]. An agent executes its behaviour according to its knowledge and its beliefs. In order to avoid deadlock, the proposals are associated with deadlines. The agent's belief base is updated by the reception of messages. None proposal is sent if the agent believes that the allocation is stable.

Example 3 (Negotiation Strategy). Let us consider the MASTA+ problem from Example 1 and the initial allocation $\overrightarrow{A}$ (cf. Fig. 4a) such that $\overrightarrow{B}_1 = (\tau_5, \tau_1)$, $\overrightarrow{B}_2 = (\tau_3, \tau_2, \tau_7, \tau_8, \tau_9)$ and $\overrightarrow{B}_3 = (\tau_4, \tau_6)$. The flowtime is $C(\overrightarrow{A}) = 7 + 9 + 17 = 33$. We consider that the belief bases are up-to-date. The offer strategy of the agent ν_2 selects a delegation as follows:

1. it selects the most prior job for which it is a bottleneck (cf. Eq. 18), $J_* = J_3$;
2. it selects an agent which is the least bottleneck for the job J_3 (cf. Eq. 19). As neither ν_1 nor ν_3 have tasks from J_3, the agent ν_2 randomly chooses, $\nu_* = \nu_1$;
3. The Algorithm 1 allows the agent ν_2 to select its offer bundle:
   (a) the candidate tasks, i.e. the tasks in J_3 or the previous ones in its bundle, are sorted by decreasing payoff, $T' = [\tau_9, \tau_3, \tau_2, \tau_8, \tau_7]$;
   (b) the delegation of the task τ_9 improves the flowtime (cf. Fig. 4b),

$$C^2(\delta([\tau_9], \nu_2, \nu_1, \overrightarrow{A})) = 11 + 9 + 9 = 29 < 33 \tag{20}$$

   The task τ_9 is added to the offer bundle, $T_* = [\tau_9]$,

---

[1] https://gitlab.univ-lille.fr/maxime.morge/smastaplus/-/tree/master/doc/specification.

(c) the delegation of the tasks τ_3 and τ_9 improves the flowtime (cf. Fig. 4c),

$$C^2(\delta([\tau_9, \tau_3], \nu_2, \nu_1, \overrightarrow{A})) = 12 + 9 + 7 = 28 < 29 \tag{21}$$

The task τ_3 is added to the offer bundle, $T_* = [\tau_9, \tau_3]$,

(d) The delegation of the tasks τ_2, τ_3 and τ_9 does not improve the flowtime (cf. Fig. 4c),

$$C^2(\delta([\tau_9, \tau_3, \tau_2], \nu_2, \nu_1, \overrightarrow{A})) = 15 + 9 + 6 = 30 > 28 \tag{22}$$

The selected offer bundle is $T_* = [\tau_9, \tau_3]$.

In summary, the agent ν_2 proposes the delegation $\delta([\tau_9, \tau_3], \nu_2, \nu_1, \overrightarrow{A})$ to the agent ν_1.

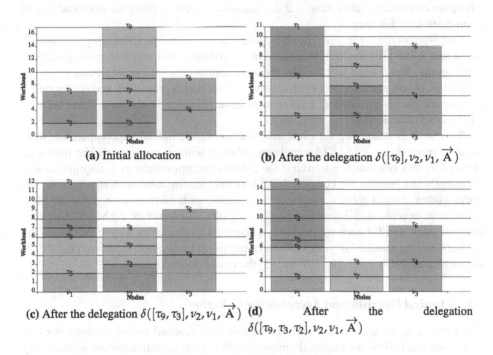

(a) Initial allocation   (b) After the delegation $\delta([\tau_9], \nu_2, \nu_1, \overrightarrow{A})$

(c) After the delegation $\delta([\tau_9, \tau_3], \nu_2, \nu_1, \overrightarrow{A})$ (d) After the delegation $\delta([\tau_9, \tau_3, \tau_2], \nu_2, \nu_1, \overrightarrow{A})$

Fig. 4. Allocations from Example 3.

6 Results and Discussion

After having presented the experimental context, we empirically compare our approach with a classic heuristic and with a distributed constraint optimization (DCOP) resolution method. Moreover, we consider our new acceptability criterion and n-ary delegation.

6.1   Context of Experiments

The practical application we consider is the distributed deployment of the MapReduce design pattern in order to process large datasets on a cluster, as with Spark [24]. We focus here on the *Reduce* stage of MapReduce jobs. This can be formalized by a MASTA+ problem where several jobs are concurrently submitted and the cost function is s.t.:

$$c_i(\tau, \nu_j) = \sum_{\rho_j \in \mathcal{R}_\tau} c_i(\rho_j, \nu_j)$$

$$\text{with } c_i(\rho_j, \nu_i) = \begin{cases} |\rho_j| \text{ if } \nu_i \in l(\rho_j) \\ \kappa \times |\rho_j| \text{ else} \end{cases} \tag{23}$$

where we empirically calibrate $\kappa = 2$ as a realistic value to capture the overhead due to remote resource fetching.

Our prototype [3] is implemented with the programming language Scala and Akka [16] for highly concurrent, distributed, and resilient message-driven applications. We assume that: (a) the message transmission delay is arbitrary but not negligible, (b) the message order per sender-receiver pair is preserved, and (c) the delivery of messages is guaranteed. Experiments have been conducted on a blade with 20 CPUs and 512Go RAM.

This work is a first step for evaluating our strategies. Indeed we compare the reallocation process, i.e. a MASTA+ problem solving, without considering the iterations induced by task consumptions, even if the task consumption strategy is required to sort the agent's task bundle. We consider MASTA+ problem instance such that $m \in [2; 16]$ nodes/agents, $\ell = 4$ jobs, $n = 3 \times \ell \times m$ tasks, with one resource per task. Each resource ρ_i is replicated 3 times and $|\rho_i| \in [0; 100]$. We generate 10 MASTA+ problem instances, and for each we randomly generate 10 initial allocations. We assess the medians and the standard deviations of three metrics: (1) the mean flowtime (Eq. 8), (2) the local availability ratio (Eq. 10), and (3) the rescheduling time.

6.2   Classical Heuristic and Acceptability Criterion

The hypothesis we want to test are: (1) the flowtime reached by our strategy is close to the one reached by the classical approach and (2) the decentralization significantly reduces the scheduling time. Moreover, unlike our previous work [2] where we used the local flowtime and the makespan in our acceptability criterion, here, we only consider the global flowtime which is sufficient to ensure the negotiation process convergence. We also want to verify that the acceptability criterion allows to significantly improve the quality of the outcome.

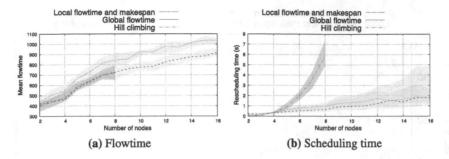

(a) Flowtime   (b) Scheduling time

Fig. 5. The flowtime and the rescheduling time of our strategy, the strategy in [2] and an hill climbing algorithm.

Figures 5a and 5b respectively compare the flowtime and rescheduling time of our unary delegation strategy with the strategy presented in [2] and an hill climbing algorithm. These three algorithms start with the same random initial allocation. At each step, the hill climbing algorithm selects among all the possible delegations, the one which minimizes the flowtime.

In Fig. 5a, we observe that, while the quality of the solution reached by the strategy proposed in [2] is slightly lower than the one reached with the hill climbing algorithm, our strategy now reaches similar solutions. This is due to the fact that a socially rational reallocation according to the global flowtime can only decrease the flowtime, while it is not the case when the local flowtime is used. Moreover, since the acceptability criterion is no more based on the makespan, the number of possible delegations, which can improve the flowtime, increases.

Figure 5b shows that the rescheduling time of our new strategy remains approximately the same as the former one. Then, it is much better than the rescheduling time of the hill climbing algorithm which exponentially grows with the number of nodes. Thus, the acceptability criterion we proposed in this article significantly improves the flowtime with a similar rescheduling time. It is worth noticing that the hill climbing algorithm has been used with small MASTA+ instances due to its prohibitive scheduling time. One can expect to obtain a greater rescheduling time with a local search method, such as simulated annealing, with no guarantee to have a more qualitative outcome. As a result, even if the number of agents is small, the gain realized on the flowtime by the hill climbing algorithm will be penalized and cancelled by the overhead of its scheduling time. This overhead penalized the time-extented assignment in a distributed system which should be adaptive to disruptive phenomena (task consumption, job release, slowing down nodes).

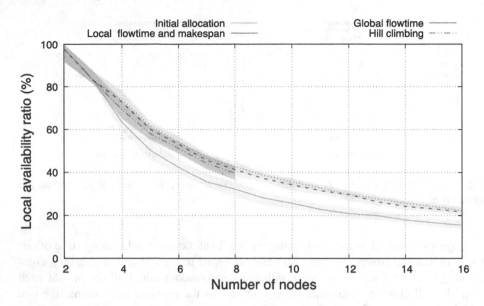

Fig. 6. Local availability ratio of the initial allocation, the allocations reached by our strategy, by the strategy proposed in [2], and by the hill climbing algorithm.

Figure 6 compares the local availability ratio of the initial allocation, the allocations reached by our strategy, by the strategy proposed in [2] and by the hill climbing algorithm. We observe that the availability ratios obtained with our strategies or with the hill climbing algorithm are close. Even if, unlike the latter, our strategy does not consider all the possible unary delegations, it turns out to be efficient by selecting the remote tasks whose delegation decreases the cost.

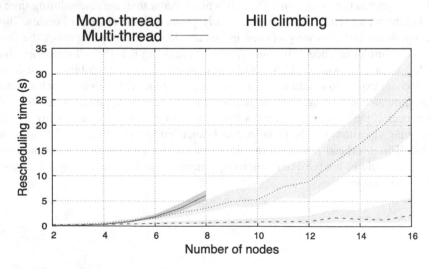

Fig. 7. Rescheduling time of our strategy with one or more threads compared with the rescheduling time of the hill climbing algorithm

Figure 7 compares the rescheduling time of our strategy with one or more threads and the rescheduling time of the hill climbing algorithm. Since our multi-thread strategy run on several cores, we observe that the speedup increases with the number of agents. By example, with a similar flowtime (if the observable non determinism of the executions is neglected), the multi-thread version is 10 times faster than the mono-thread version for 16 agents.

6.3 N-Ary Delegation

Here, we want to verify that the n-ary delegations allow to reduce the flowtime.

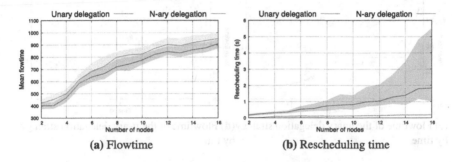

(a) Flowtime   (b) Rescheduling time

Fig. 8. Flowtime and rescheduling time for our unary strategy and our n-ary strategy.

Figures 8a and 8b respectively compare the flowtime and rescheduling time for our unary strategy with our n-ary strategy. We observe that, if the flowtime of our n-ary delegation is slightly not as good as than the one of the unary delegation strategy, the gain in terms of rescheduling time gain is much more beneficial.

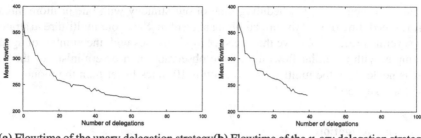

(a) Flowtime of the unary delegation strategy by number of delegations

(b) Flowtime of the n-ary delegation strategy by number of delegations

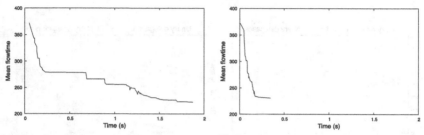

(c) Flowtime of the unary delegation strategy by time

(d) Flowtime of the n-ary delegation strategy by time

Fig. 9. Flowtime of the unary (left) and n-ary (right) delegation strategies by number of delegations (top) and by time (bottom).

Figure 9 shows the evolution of the flowtime for both offer strategies for a particular reallocation problem. We observe that the n-ary strategy reduces the number of delegations (40 versus 66) required to reach a stable allocation with similar flowtime. Therefore, the n-ary strategy reduces the rescheduling time (0, 35 s versus 1, 8 s).

6.4   Distributed Constraint Optimization Problem (DCOP)

We want to compare our strategy with a DCOP resolution method to show that: (a) our rescheduling time is much lower, (b) our flowtime is better.

Finding the optimal allocation for a MASTA+ problem with n tasks, m nodes and ℓ jobs (cf. Sect. 3) can be formalized with:

1. n decision variables x_i such that,

$$x_i = (o - 1) \times n + k \text{ if } \tau_i \text{ is the } k^{th} \text{ task starting from the end on } \nu_o \qquad (24)$$

2. n^2 constraints ensuring that each task is assigned to a single position

$$\forall i \in [1, n] \forall j \in [1, n] \setminus \{i\} \ x_i \neq x_j; \qquad (25)$$

3. the objective function to minimize is $C(\overrightarrow{A})$.

We consider here the MGM2 algorithm [17] – Maximum Gain Message – as the most suitable DCOP resolution method, since it is a distributed local search algorithm which is approximate and asynchronous. We used the pyDCOP library [19]. We consider 100 MASTA+ problems with $m = 2$ nodes, $\ell = 4$ jobs and $n = \ell \times m = 8$ tasks.

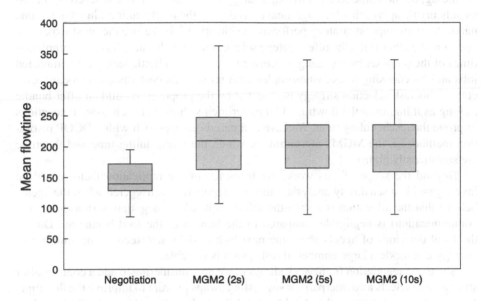

Fig. 10. Box plot of flowtimes reached by our strategy in 55 ms (mean value) and by the MGM2 algorithm with a timeout of 2, 5 and 10 s, respectively.

Figure 10 compares the flowtimes reached by our strategy in 55 ms (mean value) and by the MGM2 algorithm with a timeout of 2, 5 and 10 s, respectively. It is worth noticing that MGM2 never returns a solution when the timeout is 2 s. In this case, we consider that the random initial allocation is returned. Beyond the fact that the rescheduling time can be explained because MGM2 is implemented in Python whereas our strategy runs on a Java Virtual Machine [10], our experiments show that even if the timeout is set to 5 s, MGM2 provides an allocation whose flowtime is greater than the one reached by our strategy. Increasing the timeout does not allow to improve the flowtime of the allocation returned by MGM2. We can notice that MGM2 never returns an allocation with $m = 3$ nodes, $\ell = 5$ jobs and $n = 3 \times \ell \times m = 45$ tasks even with a timeout of 15 minutes. This algorithm does not scale for this kind of problems.

7   Conclusion

In this paper, we have proposed a multi-agent strategy for the reassignment of tasks-nodes based on the location of the required resources in order to minimize the mean flowtime of concurrent jobs. We generalized the notion of delegation to consider any bilateral reallocation (delegation or swap of several tasks) and we defined an acceptability criterion of the bilateral reallocations in order to reduce the rescheduling time and the mean flowtime reached by our strategy.

Since our negotiation process continuously adapts the allocation by reducing the completion time of the jobs for the bottleneck agents in order to improve the load-balancing, the flowtime reached by our strategy is similar to the one reached by a classical heuristic approach while significantly reducing the rescheduling time. On the one hand, the consumption strategy performs the cheapest jobs before the most expensive ones. On the other hand, the offer strategy selects a job which can reduce the completion times of the proposer by choosing a receiver which is not a bottleneck for the impacted jobs and by choosing a task whose delegation reduces its cost since it is locally executed. This task selection strategy is repeated by the proposer to build an offer bundle as long as it improves the flowtime. Our experiments show that such n-ary delegations improve the rescheduling time. We have compared our approach with a DCOP resolution method, i.e. the MGM2 algorithm for which the rescheduling time and flowtime are significantly higher.

Beyond the scope of this work, the influence of the replication factor could be investigated in a sensitivity analysis. Since no negotiation is triggered when the agents believe that the allocation is stable, the effort required for negotiation (reasoning and communication) is negligible compared to the benefit of the load-balancing. Due to the local decisions of agents about the next task to delegate/execute, our multi-agent strategy can tackle a large number of tasks, so it is scalable.

Since our negotiation framework allows it, we are considering to add a counter-offer strategy that selects a counterpart for suggesting swaps in order to improve the flowtime. More generally, future works should extend the task reallocation process toward an iterated, dynamic and on-going process, which takes place concurrently with the task execution, allowing the distributed system to be adaptive to disruptive phenomena (task consumption, job release, slowing down nodes).

References

1. Baert, Q., Caron, A.C., Morge, M., Routier, J.C., Stathis, K.: An adaptive multi-agent system for task reallocation in a MapReduce job. J. Parallel Distrib. Comput. **153**, 75–88 (2021). https://doi.org/10.1016/j.jpdc.2021.03.008
2. Beauprez, E., Caron, A.C., Morge, M., Routier, J.C.: A multi-agent negotiation strategy for reducing the flowtime. In: Proceedings of 13th International Conference on Agents and Artificial Intelligence (ICAART), vol. 1, pp. 58–68, February 2021
3. Beauprez, E., Morge, M.: Scala implementation of the extended multi-agents situated task allocation (2020). https://gitlab.univ-lille.fr/maxime.morge/smastaplus
4. Beynier, A., Charpillet, F., Szer, D., Mouaddib, A.I.: DEC-MDP / DEC-POMDP. In: Olivier Buffet, O.S. (ed.) Markov Decision Processes in Artificial Intelligence, pp. 277–313. Wiley-ISTE (2010)
5. Bruno, J., Coffman, E.G., Jr., Sethi, R.: Scheduling independent tasks to reduce mean finishing time. Commun. ACM **17**(7), 382–387 (1974)

6. Chen, B., Potts, C.N., Woeginger, G.J.: A review of machine scheduling: complexity, algorithms and approximability. In: Du, D.Z., Pardalos, P.M. (eds.) Handbook of Combinatorial Optimization, pp. 1493–1641. Springer, Boston (1998). https://doi.org/10.1007/978-1-4613-0303-9_25

7. Choi, H.L., Brunet, L., How, J.P.: Consensus-based decentralized auctions for robust task allocation. IEEE Trans. Rob. **25**(4), 912–926 (2009)

8. Conway, R., Maxwell, W., Miller, L.: Theory of Scheduling. Addison- Wesley, Reading (1967)

9. Fioretto, F., Pontelli, E., Yeoh, W.: Distributed constraint optimization problems and applications: a survey. J. Artif. Intell. Res. **61**, 623–698 (2018)

10. Fulgham, B., Gouy, I.: The Computer Language Benchmarks Game (2021). https://benchmarksgame-team.pages.debian.net/benchmarksgame/index.html

11. Horn, W.: Minimizing average flow time with parallel machines. Oper. Res. **21**(3), 846–847 (1973)

12. Jiang, Y.: A survey of task allocation and load balancing in distributed systems. IEEE Trans. Parallel Distrib. Syst. **27**(2), 585–599 (2016)

13. Kuhn, H.W.: The Hungarian method for the assignment problem. Naval Res. Logistics Q. **2**(1–2), 83–97 (1955)

14. Lesser, V., et al.: Evolution of the GPGP/TAEMS domain-independent coordination framework. Auton. Agent. Multi-Agent Syst. **9**(1–2), 87–143 (2004)

15. Li, S., Negenborn, R.R., Lodewijks, G.: A distributed constraint optimization approach for vessel rotation planning. In: González-Ramírez, R.G., Schulte, F., Voß, S., Ceroni Díaz, J.A. (eds.) ICCL 2014. LNCS, vol. 8760, pp. 61–80. Springer, Cham (2014). https://doi.org/10.1007/978-3-319-11421-7_5

16. Lightbend: Akka is the implementation of the actor model on the JVM (2020). http://akka.io

17. Maheswaran, R.T., Pearce, J.P., Tambe, M.: Distributed algorithms for DCOP: a graphical-game-based approach. In: Bader, D.A., Khokhar, A.A. (eds.) Proceedings of the ISCA 17th International Conference on Parallel and Distributed Computing Systems, The Canterbury Hotel, San Francisco, California, USA, 15–17 September 2004, pp. 432–439. ISCA (2004)

18. Rubinstein, A.: Perfect equilibrium in a bargaining model. Econometrica **50**(1), 97–102 (1982)

19. Rust, P., Picard, G.: pyDCOP is a python library for Distributed Constraints Optimization (2021). https://github.com/Orange-OpenSource/pyDcop

20. Schaerf, A., Shoham, Y., Tennenholtz, M.: Adaptive load balancing: a study in multi-agent learning. J. Artif. Intell. Res. **2**, 475–500 (1995)

21. Shehory, O., Kraus, S.: Methods for task allocation via agent coalition formation. Artif. Intell. **101**(1–2), 165–200 (1998)

22. Turner, J., Meng, Q., Schaefer, G., Soltoggio, A.: Distributed strategy adaptation with a prediction function in multi-agent task allocation. In: Proceedings of the 17th International Conference on Autonomous Agents and MultiAgent Systems (AAMAS), pp. 739–747 (2018)

23. Wellman, M.P.: A market-oriented programming environment and its application to distributed multicommodity flow problems. J. Artif. Intell. Res. **1**, 1–23 (1993)

24. Zaharia, M., et al.: Resilient distributed datasets: a fault-tolerant abstraction for in-memory cluster computing. In: Proceedings of the 9th USENIX Symposium on Networked Systems Design and Implementation (NSDI), San Jose, CA, USA, pp. 15–28 (2012)

A Detailed Analysis of a Systematic Review About Requirements Engineering Processes for Multi-agent Systems

Giovane D'Avila Mendonça$^{(\boxtimes)}$ (ID), Iderli Pereira de Souza Filho (ID),
and Gilleanes Thorwald Araujo Guedes (ID)

Pampa Federal University, Av. Tiaraju, 810, Alegrete, Brazil
{giovanemendonca,iderlisouza.aluno,
gilleanesguedes}@unipampa.edu.br

Abstract. Requirements Engineering is a crucial area of Software Engineering, as it is through it that what a system should actually do is established, what are its functionalities and what is the expected behavior for the software. It is also through the requirements definition that the basic criteria to determine the software quality are established. All this is equally true for multiagent systems, systems composed of autonomous agents that can work together to solve complex problems. Nevertheless, requirements engineering for this kind of system presents its own challenges, as this type of system has specific requirements that are not normally found in other types of software. Taking this into account, we first performed a systematic literature review in order to determine the current state of the development processes that support requirements engineering for multiagent systems, classifying their coverage regarding the requirements engineering subareas and their support to the BDI model - a widely used model for the cognitive agents development. However, due to the lack of space, in the original publication we were only able to discuss the retrieved studies in a general way. Therefore, in this new work, we discuss the studies of the first review in more depth, emphasizing mainly the methodologies that support the BDI model and the gaps found after analysing them. Furthermore, we highlight the possibilities for further research based on the study of the recovered works.

Keywords: Requirements engineering · Multi-Agent Systems · BDI model · Systematic review

1 Introduction

Agents are intelligent entities that act in a flexible and autonomous way in decision making. A multiagent system (MAS) contains several agents acting in a system to solve problems beyond the capability of just one agent [56]. Multiagent systems have been shown to be good alternatives to deal with complex systems, since the complexity can be divided and assigned to several agents specialized in a given facet of the problem [31].

However, developing this kind of system also proved to be complex and generated new challenges for software engineering, which led to the emergence of AOSE -

© Springer Nature Switzerland AG 2022
A. P. Rocha et al. (Eds.): ICAART 2021, LNAI 13251, pp. 46–69, 2022.
https://doi.org/10.1007/978-3-031-10161-8_3

Agent-Oriented Software Engineering, an area that mixes features from both software engineering and Artificial Intelligence [36].

One of the several software engineering subareas is requirements engeineering, which aims to elicit, analyze, specify, and validate system requirements, in order to ensure the correct understanding about what a system really should do. According [73], requirements engineering is one of the most vital activities in the entire software development lifecycle, as the success of a software project depends much of how well users requirements have been understood and converted into proper functionalities.

Thus, several requirements engineering processes for multiagent systems have been proposed over the years. These processes aim to offer techniques, methods, and models adapted for this type of system, since multiagent systems present their own complexity, challenges, and particular requirements which differentiate them from other kinds of systems.

In SWEBOK [15] - a reference book in the field of software engineering - requirements engineering is divided into four subareas, Requirements Elicitation, Requirements Analysis, Requirements Specification, and Requirements Validation. We emphasize that each one of these subareas plays an essential role to Requirements Engineering.

This way, in order to understand the state-of-art of requirements engineering processes for multiagent systems, we carried out a literature systematic review [59]. This review analysed the processes mainly regarding the coverage of requirements engineering subareas defined in SWEBOK and its support to the BDI model, one of the most recognized approaches to integrate desired cognitive skills in autonomous agents and which facilitates the description of the relation cause-effect needed to an agent to achieve its goals [5]. Furthermore, this model proved to be one of the most suitable for the development of agents with flexible behavior [4].

However, this systematic review only presented the support for the BDI model and the coverage regarding SWEBOK requirements engineering of the analysed processes in a general way, without discussing these works in more depth. Therefore, this current paper aims to extend the analysis performed in the previous review, describing in detail the support of the processes regarding the BDI model and the gaps found in these processes, both in the BDI model support as in the processes coverage regarding the requirements engineering subareas as defined in SWEBOK.

This work is organized as follows. Section 2 contains the background. Section 3 presents the related works. The research method is described in Sect. 4. In Sect. 5, the results are presented and discussed. Threats to the validity are described in Sect. 6. Next, we present some insights that we gained from this research and, finally, the conclusion and future works.

2 Background

2.1 Requirements Engineering

According to [9], the RE goals are: (I) to identify software requirements, (II) to analyse requirements in order to classify them and to derive additional requirements, as well as to solve conflicts among them (III) to document requirements, and (IV) to validate the documented requirements.

In SWEBOK [15] - a reference book in the area - it is stated that the RE process cover four main subareas: (I) Requirements Elicitation; (II) Requirements Analysis; (III) Requirements Specification; and (IV) Requirements Validation.

Requirements elicitation investigates how to extract requirements and which are its origins. Requirements analysis aims to detect and solve conflicts among the requirements and to discover the system boundaries. Requirements specification, by its turn, produce requirements documents that can be systematically reviewed, evaluated, and approved. Finally, requirements validation evaluates requirements documents to ensure that the requirements be understandable, consistent, and complete.

2.2 Belief-Desire-Intention Model

The Belief-Desire-Intention (BDI) model is a software model developed to programming intelligent agents. It includes beliefs, desires, and intentions in the agent architecture [17], and that, according to [75] has been widely used in MAS development. Moreover, in the last 30 years this model has been the basis for much research on autonomous agents architectures [28].

In this model, Beliefs represent the information state the agent owns, i.e., what he believes to be true about the environment, about itself, and about other agents. Desires represent the agents motivational state. They represent the goals or situations the agent would like to achieve. Finally, the intentions represent desires the agent believes he can achieve and take actions to achieve them [67].

This model allows to the agents a more complex behavior than the reactive models, without the computational overload of the cognitive architectures. Moreover, it is easier to specify knowledge by means of this model [49].

According to [41], concepts of belief and goal perform a central role in the conception and implementation of autonomous agents. The concept of BDI, consider mental attitudes to be fundamental to the agents, where the beliefs are adapted to the environment truths, while in the intentions, the agents try to make the environment to correspond to its goals.

3 Related Works

We discovered some studies that aimed to identify and to evaluate methodologies/processes in the AOSE area. However, these studies do not follow a systematic vision, they are informal literature reviews with subjective comparison criteria.

The study of [40] discusses the state of AOSE methodologies and how to turn them into acceptable products for the industry. This study also presents a methodology classification, dividing them in (I) independent of goal-oriented methodologies and (II) extensions of goal-oriented methodologies to give support to the agent concepts. The study of [76] evaluates agent-oriented software methodologies. The work proposes a comparison frame with four selection groups: concepts, notations, process, and pragmatics. This proposal was evaluated comparing the methodology adequation and its development capacity. For this comparison, were used three methodologies, MaSE (an old version of O-MaSE), Tropos, and Prometheus. Finally, the work of [22] investigates the AOSE methodologies coverage regarding software engineering concepts. However, besides this work not following a systematic vision, it does not present several method-ologies and does not have a wide coverage of requirements engineering.

Regarding systematic reviews, we found the study of [11] that developed a review about requirements engineering in multi-agent systems development. Nevertheless, this study tried to verify which modeling techniques were applied in the requirements engi-neering for MAS. On the other hand, our work has as its goal to identify the coverage of the requirements engineering process regarding the SWEBOK stages and its adequation to the BDI model.

The Table 1, presents a comparison of the studies related to our work, having as a comparison point the main features of this work. As can be noticed our work covers some characteristics that are different from the previous ones.

Table 1. Comparison of studies related to this work.

Study	Multi-Agent Systems	Focus on Methodologies	Systematic review	Requirements Engineering	BDI Model
[40]	✓	✓			
[76]	✓	✓			
[22]	✓	✓			
[11]	✓		✓	✓	
This Work	✓	✓	✓	✓	✓

4 Research Method

A systematic literature review (SLR) is a research technique whose purpose is iden-tifying, selecting, evaluating, interpreting, and summarizing the available studies con-sidered relevant to the research theme or phenomenon of interest [47]. This technique searches for primary studies related to the theme and provides a deeper synthesis about the data obtained from these studies [48].

A SLR has as its basis a protocol previously defined, that formalizes its execution, beginning by the stipulation of the research questions, passing by establishing the stud-ies inclusion and exclusion criteria, selecting the digital basis for the extraction of works related with the keywords applied during the search in these basis, and concluding with the definition of how the results will be presented [10].

Our review has as its goal to establish the state-of-art of the process/methodo- logies for MAS development that support in somehow requirements engineering for this kind of system. Our main interest is about how these processes identify and specify the BDI model features in the requirements engineering phase.

4.1 The Research Questions

We defined four research questions for this review. The first research question (RQ1) aims to identify which methodologies/processes support RE for MAS.

The second research question (RQ2) was defined to identify the coverage of the RE by these methodologies. We believe that with this question we can discover possible gaps in the area and that this will allow for future research.

The third research question (RQ3) aims to verify which methodologies support the BDI model. As we stated before, this is a consolidated model in the MAS development and we believe it aggregates better reliability in using the methodologies that support it.

Finally, the fourth question (RQ4) has as its goal to show a wider view of the area needs and to focus on the points that can be approached in future works.

The four research questions are listed below:

- **RQ1:** Which methodologies for the MAS development support a specific requirements engineering (RE) life cycle to this kind of system?
- **RQ2:** Which is the coverage of the requirements engineering by these methodologies taking as a basis the subareas defined by SWEBOK [15]?
- **RQ3:** Which of these methodologies focus on the BDI model during the requirements engineering?
- **RQ4:** Which are the existing gaps in the methodologies that support RE for MAS?

4.2 Identifying and Selecting Primary Studies

To recover relevant works for this study, we built a String containing a set of keywords based on the research questions. This String was adapted to the particularities of each bibliographic basis.

To perform this review, we used bibliographic bases which (I) have a search mechanism based on web; (II) have a mechanism able to use keywords; (III) contain documents from the computer science area; and (IV) their data bases are updated regularly. It is important to highlight that we do not limited the period in which the studies were published

In addition, we have included a book [26] about methodologies for MAS, as well as other classical and known studies. These studies were manually selected by a specialist in the area because we considered that they would not be selected in the search String as they do not present in its title, abstract, and keywords topics related to the requirements engineering, since they are not processes focused on RE, though their life cycles encompass the RE area.

In Table 2 we show the generic String used in the basis. In addition to the search String, we used manual filters in the bibliographic bases. We considered necessary to apply these manual filters because, in some bases, the results obtained were high and many of the studies returned were outside the scope.

For ACM library it was used the filter "Title/Abstract/keywords"; for Engineering Village, "Subject/Title/Abstract"; for IEEE Xplore, All metadata, filters suggested by the base software "agents and multi-agent systems"; for Science Direct, "Subject/Title/Abstract" and "Title/Abstract/keywords" and commands "multiagent OR multi-agent OR agent-based"; for Scopus, "Title/Abstract/key- words"; and for Springer Link it were applied the filters "Filter of the area: Computer science", "Filter of the subarea: Software Engineering and Artificial intelligence".

4.3 Inclusion and Exclusion Criteria

The selection criteria have as its objective to identify the primary studies that provide contents to answer the research questions. Thus, firstly the studies were analysed with

Table 2. String generic [58].

String	Conector
("multiagent" OR "multi-agent" OR "multi agent" OR "agent-based" OR "agent society")	AND
("methodology" OR "method" OR "process")	AND
("requirements engineering" OR "requirements elicitation" OR "requirements modeling" OR "requirements analysis" OR "requirements specification")	

basis on the title, abstract, and keywords. If there were still doubts about the final classification of a study in relation to the inclusion or exclusion criteria, a specialist would be consulted. These criteria are described in the Table 3.

Table 3. Inclusion and Exclusion Criteria [58].

Criterion	ID	Description
Inclusion	IC1	Does the study presents a methodology or an extension of a methodology for multi-agent systems that contemplates at least one of the requirements engineering subareas defined in the SWEBOK?
Exclusion	EC1	Studies that cover a methodology already included in more recent work
	EC2	Studies that are not a paper or a chapter of book
	EC3	Studies with less than 6 pages
	EC4	Studies that boils down to a case study or methodology evaluation
	EC5	Studies that boils down to a comparison of methodologies
	EC6	Studies that do not present a methodology (or extension of a methodology) for multi-agent systems that contemplate at least one of requirements engineering subareas from SWEBOK
	EC7	Studies that concentrate in other areas of Software Engineering
	EC8	Studies that boils down to the development of a system
	EC9	Studies that present a methodology or extension of a methodology created only to a kind of specific application

4.4 Studies Quality Assessment

We defined two quality criteria to evaluate the relevance of the studies to the scope of this research. These criteria were not used to the exclusion of studies, only for the ranking of studies more relevant. Next we described the two qualitative criteria and the score attributed for each criterion defined.

1. **QC1:** The work supports the BDI model?
   Yes (Y): the work fully supports the BDI model;
   Partly (P): the work supports at least one of the features of the BDI model;
   Not (N): the work does not support the BDI model.
2. **QC2:** the work applies some empirical study (experiment, case study, etc.)?
   Yes (Y): the study applies some empirical study;
   Not (N): the study does not apply some empirical study.

To establish a quality general index of the selected studies, we attributed scores to each criterion defined, where Yes (Y) corresponds to 1 score, Partly (P) 0.5 score and Not (N) 0 score.

The Table 4, shows the score of each selected study. We noticed that only three studies ([46, 60, 62]) reached the maximum ranking of 2 scores.

On the other hand, some studies got 0 score ([2, 13, 35, 38]), though these studies did not achieve any score, they were kept because the qualitative criteria were used only for ranking the studies, not for eliminate them.

Table 4. Quality Indexes of the Studies [58].

Study	QC1	QC2	Total	Study	QC1	QC2	Total
[78]	0.50	0.00	0.50	[77]	0.50	1.00	0.00
[1]	0.50	1.00	1.50	[71]	0.50	1.00	1.50
[65]	1.00	0.00	1.00	[39]	0.50	1.00	1.50
[53]	0.00	1.00	1.00	[55]	0.50	1.00	1.50
[6]	0.50	0.00	0.50	[80]	0.50	0.00	0.50
[70]	0.50	1.00	1.50	[81]	0.50	1.00	1.50
[12]	0.50	1.00	1.50	[54]	0.00	1.00	1.00
[44]	0.50	0.00	0.50	[38]	0.00	0.00	0.00
[32]	0.50	1.00	1.50	[7]	0.50	1.00	1.50
[68]	0.50	1.00	1.50	[13]	0.00	0.00	0.00
[42]	0.50	0.00	0.50	[43]	0.00	1.00	1.00
[19]	0.50	0.00	0.50	[33]	0.50	1.00	1.50
[50]	0.50	1.00	1.50	[64]	0.50	1.00	1.50
[66]	0.50	0.00	0.50	[79]	0.50	1.00	1.50
[52]	0.50	0.00	0.50	[69]	0.50	1.00	1.50
[74]	0.50	0.00	0.50	[30]	0.00	1.00	1.00
[2]	0.00	0.00	0.00	[23]	0.50	0.00	0.50
[46]	1.00	1.00	2.00	[27]	0.00	1.00	1.00
[62]	1.00	1.00	2.00	[35]	0.00	0.00	0.00
[57]	1.00	0.00	1.00	[14]	0.00	1.00	1.00
[24]	0.50	0.00	0.50	[29]	0.50	0.00	0.50
[8]	0.50	0.00	0.50	[63]	1.00	0.00	1.00
[60]	1.00	1.00	2.00	[20]	0.50	1.00	1.50
[61]	0.00	1.00	1.00	[21]	0.50	0.00	0.50
[25]	0.50	0.00	0.50	[34]	1.00	0.00	1.00
[18]	0.50	1.00	1.50	[45]	1.00	0.00	1.00
[72]	0.50	1.00	1.50	[51]	0.00	1.00	1.00

4.5   Data Extraction Strategy

When the studies selection process was concluded, the basic information of each paper was registered for data extraction. The extraction was performed using the Google Spreadsheet to capture all the information of each work included, allowing the posterior synthesis.

The data extracted from the included works were analysed in order to answer the research questions. In Sect. 5, these results were exposed and discussed.

4.6   Conducting the Review

The conduction of this systematic review was performed between the months of February and May of 2020. We defined four stages for the studies selection: (I) executing the search String in the bibliographic bases; (II) removing the duplicated studies; (III) applying the inclusion and exclusion criteria to the works; and (IV) reading and extracting the information of the remaining studies of the Stage (III). The studies were read by two reviewers in consultation with a specialist in the area.

In Stage 1, the search String was executed in the bibliographic bases selected for this review. The overview of this stage can be observed in Fig. 1. The conduction began analysing the 1060 works imported from the selected bibliographic bases.

In Stage 2, a total of 247 duplicated studies were removed. In Stage 3, there were applied the inclusion and exclusion criteria based on the reading of the title, abstract, and keywords, resulting in the selection of 53 studies considered promising.

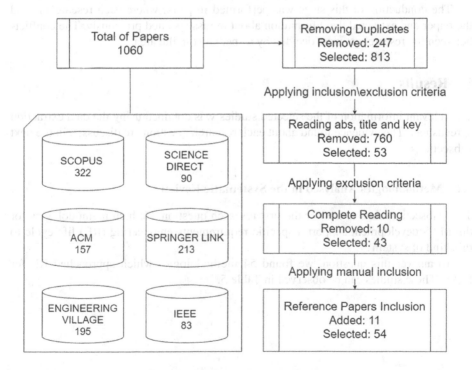

Fig. 1. Search process [58].

To avoid the selection of works that are not fitted in the scope of this review, the 53 studies, selected in the third stage, were completely read, what resulted in the exclusion of 10 works, totalling 43 selected works. The rejected works in this stage were inside of two exclusion criteria:

1. Works that concentrate in other Software Engineering areas: the works excluded that were inside on this criterion were methodologies that worked with MAS only in posterior stages to the requirements engineering. The requirements engineering was performed in a traditional way, not focusing on any particular feature of MAS.
2. Works that cover a methodology already included in a work: for this criterion we selected the most recent work in such a way we can understand the current state of the methodology.

At the end of the conduction Stage, the manually selected studies ([14,20,21,23,27, 29,34,35,45,51,63]) were added to the set of papers searched in the bases, according with defined in Sect. 4.2. This resulted in a total of 54 accepted studies.

4.7   Data Extraction

For data extracting in the accepted works, we read them all and tried to identify which SWEBOK RE subareas each work covers, whether the methodology proposed in the study has a well-defined life cycle, whether the RE presented in the study is adequate for MAS, and whether the study supports the BDI model.

The conduction of this stage was performed in pairs, where each researcher read the paper and extracted the information about the issues cited previously. The conflicts between the researchers were decided by a specialist in the area.

5   Results

The relevant information of the selected studies was obtained using the data extraction spreadsheet. The evidence found about each research question are discussed in the next subsections.

5.1   Methodologies Analysed in the Systematic Review

This subsection aims to answer the first research question: "Which methodologies for the MAS development support a specific requirements engineering (RE) life cycle to this kind of system?"

To answer this question, we found 54 methodologies which approached RE for MAS. These studies can be observed in Table 5.

Table 5. Methodologies/Processes that support RE for MAS and its coverage with relation to the SWEBOK subareas [58].

Methodology	Elicitation	Analysis	Specification	Validation
KAOS Extension [78]		✓	✓	
JAAMAS [1]		✓		
Patrizia Ribino [65]		✓		
AGSIRA [53]	✓	✓	✓	
GORMAS [6]		✓		
ATABGE [70]	✓			
RE4Gaia [12]			✓	
Xu Huiying [44]		✓	✓	
REG for AOSE [32]	✓	✓		
Extension GAIA [68]		✓		
B-Tropos [19]	✓	✓	✓	
JONGWON LEE [50]		✓	✓	
Prabhat Ranjan [66]	✓	✓	✓	
SRAMO [52]			✓	
Zhiqi Shen [74]		✓		
SONIA [2]		✓	✓	
BDI ASP [46]		✓	✓	
Tropos [62]	✓	✓	✓	
Cysneiros [57]		✓	✓	✓
Chiung-Hui [24]		✓		
KAOS [8]		✓	✓	
PRACTIONIST [60]		✓	✓	
Murray [61]		✓		
ASPECS [25]		✓	✓	
REF [18]		✓	✓	
Sen and Jain [72]	✓			
Hsieh et al. [43]		✓	✓	
Sutcliffe [77]		✓	✓	
Agile Sen and Jain [71]	✓	✓		
CREWS-EVE [39]	✓		✓	✓
Cao et al. [55]		✓	✓	
HOMER [80]	✓			
Wu et al. [81]	✓			
Liu and Li [54]		✓		
Mahmoud et al. [38]		✓		
Ashamalla et al. [7]		✓		
Consensus [13]		✓		
Hilaire et al. [42]		✓		
Gaur and Soni [33]		✓		
Passos et al. [64]	✓	✓		
PLANT [79]		✓	✓	
Ronald et al. [69]		✓	✓	
aMIAC [30]		✓		
GAIA [23]		✓	✓	
PASSI [27]	✓	✓	✓	
INGENIAS-SCRUM [35]	✓	✓	✓	
ADELFE [14]	✓	✓	✓	✓
O-MaSE [29]		✓	✓	
PROMETHEUS [63]		✓	✓	
MESSAGE [20]		✓	✓	
OSOAD [21]		✓	✓	
COMOMAS [34]			✓	
MAS-COMMONKADS [45]		✓		
MASSIVE [51]	✓	✓	✓	
Total	16	46	31	3

5.2   Coverage in Relation to the Requirements Engineering Subareas Defined in SWEBOK

This subsection aims to answer the second research question: "Which is the coverage of the requirements engineering by these methodologies taking as a basis the subareas defined by SWEBOK [15]?"

From the 54 selected studies we observed that all of them present Requirements Engineering fit for multi-agent systems. Thus, we extracted which RE sub-areas defined in SWEBOK [15] are supported by these studies.

Table 5 shows the 54 studies and the sub-areas that they support. Great part of these studies, 46 in the total, support the sub-area of requirements analysis. While 31 of them support the sub-area of requirements specification.

The sub-area of requirements elicitation, by its turn, is supported by 16 studies.

From these methodologies, Homer methodology (Human Oriented Method for Eliciting Requirements) [80], stood out for being the only one that presented a way to elicit requirements from direct contact with the stakeholders.

Homer operation can be described as the use of organizational metaphors. In these metaphors, during the interview, the Stakeholder must simulate that the system is a company that is hiring new employees to work on a certain problem. This elicitation style aims to more easily discover the agent roles and their goals inside the system. In its execution, Homer presents a series of questions that should be asked to the Stakeholders.

However, Homer methodology presents problems in its application. In addition to not supporting requirements related to the BDI model, there is not a way to easily elicit the agents perceptions and plans. Moreover, this methodology does not provide support for eliciting requirements about external agents, being focused on the system's internal functions.

Another important point is that no methodology contains a way to elicit requirements related to the BDI model. Although Tropos methodology [62] supports the BDI model and has a elicitation phase, Tropos does not detail how its elicitation should be done, differently from Homer.

We also noticed that several of the methodologies do not seek to determine whether the use of multiagent systems is valid, being uncommon a methodology that contains a viability study to establish the need for a multiagent system. Most of the time, methodologies assume that the system under analysis is a multiagent system.

Finally, concerning the sub-area of requirements validation, it is the area that have the lower number of studies, with only 3 of the total supporting validation.

We also noticed that, from these studies, only ADELFE methodology [14] supports the four RE sub-areas (elicitation, analysis, specification, and validation). However, the elicitation in the ADELFE methodology is not suitable for MAS, being applied a traditional elicitation. The features suitable for a MAS began to be presented in the analysis stage. However, this stage does not present the means for validating the documents specific for MAS. ADELFE validates only documents produced by a traditional requirements engineering.

Another important fact that we noticed in the extraction is that only 30 studies presented some empirical experiments for the validation of the methodology.

5.3 Methodologies Supporting the BDI Model

In this subsection we aim to answer the third research question: "Which of these methodologies focus on the BDI model during the requirements engineering?"

We tried to identify which methodologies support the BDI model. We observed that most part of the studies, 43 in the total, support partially the BDI model, i.e., they identify at least one of the features of this model.

These features are: agent beliefs; agent goals/desires; and agent intentions. However, it is necessary to state that the majority of these works do not cite explicitly the BDI model, most of them are goal-oriented methodologies, i.e., they focus on just in one feature of the BDI model and they do not necessarily use this model, but the fact that these studies identify one of the features is useful for our research.

Agents goals were the most identified feature, in most cases in isolation. There are studies that identify intentions, however we noticed that beliefs and intentions are not identified in isolation, they are always accompanied by the identification of their goals.

Another issue to be highlighted is that 11 studies do not present support to the BDI model and only 8 present support for all these features in at least one stage of their requirements engineering. Table 6 presents the methodologies coverage regarding their support to the BDI model.

Next we will present how the 8 methodologies that support totally the BDI model, in some requirements engineering phase, are structured.

The study of Ribino [65], supports the BDI model in the phase related to the requirements analysis. This methodology proposes a modeling of BDI organization for requirements analysis. This analysis is performed through an ontology that aims to represent the problem domain reality and the problem specification incompleteness.

The ontology describes the environment, its main states, and what can be done to achieve/modify these states. This ontology is composed of the Action (specialized in intentional and unintentional action), Concept (specialized in position and object) and Predicate metaclasses. In this ontology, the "predicates" represent the beliefs and states that influence a concept that, in turn, works as a scenario related to the environment.

We understand that this way of representing beliefs weakens a view of BDI agents since, for this kind of agents, beliefs represent the knowledge that an agent or agent role has about the environment, and delimiting the knowledge related only to the environment can result in conflicts in the analysis, since all beliefs are related to the environment and not to a particular agent or agent role.

This methodology allows the identification of goals from patterns discovered by the requirements analysis described textually. There is a set of guidelines that establish how to identify positions, actions, and predicates. However, it is not possible to identify the perceptions associated with a goal or how that goal becomes an intention.

The BDI ASP process [46] appeared to be promissor in its preliminary reading. This process is entirely turned to BDI agents development, besides using as its basis the use-cases production, a technique widely used both in the industry and academia.

Nevertheless, after an analysis of the process, we found errors that could compromise this proposal. The first point is the use of the term intention as a synonym of plan. We believe that this could compromise the support of the BDI model, since an intention is usually related to one or more plans, but intentions and plans are not synonymous. In

Table 6. Coverage of methodologies/processes regarding the BDI model support [58].

Methodology	Belief	Desire (Goal)	Intention	Not support
KAOS Extension [78]		✓	✓	
JAAMAS [1]		✓		
Patrizia Ribino [65]	✓	✓	✓	
AGSIRA [53]		✓		
GORMAS [6]		✓		
ATABGE [70]		✓		
RE4Gaia [12]		✓		
Xu Huiying [44]		✓	✓	
REG for AOSE [32]		✓		
Extension GAIA [68]		✓		
B-Tropos [19]		✓		
JONGWON LEE [50]		✓		
Prabhat Ranjan [66]		✓		
SRAMO [52]		✓		
Zhiqi Shen [74]		✓		
SONIA [2]				✓
BDI ASP [46]	✓	✓	✓	
Tropos [62]	✓	✓	✓	
Cysneiros [57]	✓	✓	✓	
Chiung-Hui [24]		✓		
KAOS [8]		✓		
PRACTIONIST [60]	✓	✓	✓	
Murray [61]				✓
ASPECS [25]		✓		
REF [18]		✓		
Sen and Jain [72]		✓		
Hsieh et al. [43]				✓
Sutcliffe [77]		✓		
Agile Sen and Jain [71]		✓		
CREWS-EVE [39]		✓		
Cao et al. [55]		✓		
HOMER [80]		✓		
Wu et al. [81]		✓		
Liu and Li [54]				✓
Mahmoud et al. [38]				✓
Ashamalla et al. [7]		✓		
Consensus [13]				✓
Hilaire et al. [42]		✓		
Gaur and Soni [33]		✓		
Passos et al. [64]		✓		
PLANT [79]		✓		
Ronald et al. [69]		✓		
aMIAC [30]				✓
GAIA [23]		✓		
PASSI [27]				✓
INGENIAS-SCRUM [35]				✓
ADELFE [14]				✓
O-MaSE [29]		✓	✓	
PROMETHEUS [63]	✓	✓	✓	
MESSAGE [20]		✓		
OSOAD [21]		✓		
COMOMAS [34]	✓	✓	✓	
MAS-COMMONKADS [45]	✓	✓	✓	
MASSIVE [51]				✓
Total	8	43	11	11

addition, the methodology uses what has been called "internal use cases" to represent plans, desires, and beliefs, however, no adaptation of the use-cases diagram to represent these concepts is presented, and this approach contains conceptual errors, such as the representation of agents as use-cases.

Tropos [62] supports the BDI model through the i* framework. However, this framework presents limitations in the coverage of this model. These limitations can be perceived by the lack of a way to visualize when a goal becomes an intention and how the beliefs affect the agents' goals. In addition to the support provided by i*, Tropos dedicates, in the design phase, a stage to BDI agents, however we have not analysed this stage in depth because it belongs to the design phase and not to the requirements engineering phase.

Cysneiros methodology [57], theoritically supports the BDI model since it uses the i* framework. However, although it uses a framework containing concepts of BDI agents, the work of Cysneiros does not state at any moment that it works with the BDI model.

PRACTIONIST [60] is a goal-oriented methodology. However, unlike the other goal-oriented methodologies found in this review, the authors of PRACTIONIST describe its goals as goals of BDI agents.

PRACTIONIST is based on the BDI model, presenting total support for its use. As an overview of the support to this model, we can highlight that the methodology cover the following concepts: a set of perceptors that hear some relevant external stimuli (perceptions); a set of beliefs that represent information the agent got about its internal state and the external environment; a set of goals that the agent desire to achieve, representing the states or activities the agent would like to perform in the system, related to the agent desires or intentions; a set of goals relation that the agent uses during the deliberation and reasoning means-end process; a set of plans that are the means to achieve the intentions; a set of actions the agent can execute to act in the environment; and a set of effectors that really execute the actions.

However, although PRACTIONIST structure is adequate to the BDI model use, the methodology has structural problems for its application. The main issue is that the methodology seems to be more suitable for the design area, the only point that contributed to include this methodology as suitable for requirements engineering is that the authors understand that the methodology is useful for requirements analysis. Even so, PRACTIONIST does not porvide a lifecycle for its requirements engineering and does not detail how should be done the requirements analysis for BDI agents.

Prometheus [63] states to have full support for the BDI model, however, it does not present in its models examples or explanations of how to apply the BDI model, leaving open for interpretation by whoever applies the methodology. We considered it a risk, as it can generate inconsistencies and even errors during the system development.

Even so, some concepts can be understood through Prometheus models, such as the use of "data" to represent the beliefs. However, only data repositories are identified and not the beliefs. Belief repositories are linked to the goals, which may result in conflict since in a BDI agent view, beliefs contain the knowledge of an agent. Furthermore, although goals are represented in the Prometheus models, it is not clear how they change in intentions.

Lastly, regarding CoMoMAS [34] and MAS-CommonKADS [45] methodologies, we believe that they work with the same notation to represent the BDI model, since both methodologies have their models derived from the CommonKADS language, a conceptual language for modeling.

However, the MAS-CommonKADS methodology does not detail the use of the BDI model, it only states that they support this model. Regarding the CoMoMAS methodology, it uses the BDI model to represent the system internal structure, using the concepts of belief, goal, and intention (described through the plan model). Nevertheless, in spite of the concepts seeming to follow a logic line of BDI agents, there are conceptual errors in its approach. In this view, intentions do not appear to be originated from goals, being represented practically as new goals. Furthermore, the example presented does not detail how beliefs influence a goal to become an intention.

5.4   Gaps Found in This Review

In this subsection we will detail the gaps found in this review, aiming to answer the fourth research question: "Which are the existing gaps in the methodologies that support RE for MAS?"

We noticed that only three studies cover the validation sub-area in their RE cycle. It demonstrates that the majority of the methodologies do not care with this phase that is so important to the systems quality.

We also noticed that just one study covers the four sub-areas of RE in its cycle [14]. On the other hand, this study does not support the BDI model, what demonstrates a gap and the need of the proposition of a methodology containing a requirements engineering phase that supports the BDI model.

Regarding the BDI model coverage, we understand that the support to just 8 studies from a total of 54 is a low number. Moreover, just two methodologies have as their focus to cover this model ([46,65]) and none of them cover elicitation and validation, what highlights a gap in the RE for MAS area.

Other point that we could identify as a neglect is that, among the methodologies that support BDI, only the Tropos methodology [62] covers the requirements elicitation and just the methodology proposed by Cysneiros [57] includes requirements validation. It demonstrates that most of the methodologies that support BDI focus on the requirements analysis and specification and that, besides these areas, there is space to be explored in the elicitation and validation areas.

We highlight in Table 7, which are the gaps of each study that fully supports the BDI model. Although some studies partially support this model, such as allowing the goals representation, they do not refer to the BDI model explicitly and we are only interested in studies that fully support the features needed for the BDI model.

As can be seen in Table 7, of all the studies fully supporting the BDI model, only the work of Cysneiros [57] covers the validation subarea, however it does not present any specific technique for check the requirements. In this methodology it is mentioned only that the artifacts should be validated, but without defining how this should be done. It demonstrates that the validation subarea, so important for quality control, is being neglected by the current methodologies.

Table 7. Studies that fully support the BDI model and its gaps.

Methodology	Gaps
Patrizia Ribino [65]	• Does not cover the Elicitation, Analysis, and Validation subareas
	• Does not allow specifying a communication pattern
	• Does not allow specifying communication between agents or agents and external users
	• Does not allow specifying in a clear way the goals associated with the agents
	• Does not allows identifying when a goal becomes an intention
	• Does not use a requirements specification standard
BDI ASP [46]	• Does not cover the Elicitation, Specification, and Validation subareas
	• Does not allow specifying when a goal becomes an intention
	• The UML adaptation contains conceptual errors, such as applying use cases to represent agents
	• Represents intentions and plans as synonyms
Tropos [62]	• Does not cover the validation subarea
	• Does not present any elicitation technique
	• Does not allow specifying a communication pattern
	• Does not allow specifying the kind of message sent between agents or agents and external users
	• Does not provide resources to identify and model perceptions associated with agents
	• Does not present any requirements elicitation technique
	• Does not use any requirements specification standard
	• Does not allow specifying when a goal becomes an intention
Cysneiros and Yu [57]	• Does not present any requirements validation technique
	• Does not allow specifying a communication pattern
	• Does not allow specifying communication between agents or agents and external users
	• Does not cover the elicitation subarea
	• Does not use any requirements specification standard
PRACTIONIST [60]	• Does not cover the Elicitation and Validation subareas
	• Does not allow specifying a communication pattern
	• Does not allow specifying communication between agents or agents and external users
	• Does not use any requirements specification standard
	• Does not concretely present the requirements engineering subareas.
Prometheus [63]	• Does not cover the Elicitation, Specification, and Validation subareas
	• Does not show how to apply the BDI model in its structure
	• Does not allow specifying when a goal becomes an intention
CoMoMAS [34]	• Does not cover the Elicitation, Specification, and Validation subareas
	• Does not allow specifying when a goal becomes an intention
MAS-CommonKADS [45]	• Does not cover the Elicitation and Validation subareas
	• Does not allow specifying a communication pattern
	• Does not allow specifying communication between agents or agents and external users
	• Does not provide resources to identify and model perceptions associated with agents
	• Does not use any requirements specification standard
	• Does not allow specifying when a goal becomes an intention

Another point that can be highlighted is that from these studies only the Tropos [62] methodology covers the requirements elicitation subarea, however, Tropos does not present any technique for capturing specific requirements for multiagent systems, such as those necessary to apply the BDI model.

Furthermore, the studies presented by Ribino [65], Tropos [62], Cysneiros [57], PRACTIONIST [60], and MAS-CommonKADS [45] despite covering the requirements specification subarea, they do not adopt a specification standard. Whereas, according Alsanad [3] due to the general complexity of requirements specification documents, software stakeholders tend not to use them efficiently, therefore, according to Boyarchuk [16], during requirements formation and formulation, it is important to follow the standards that rule the software development process. Moreover, the adoption of a specification standard establishes what information about requirements must be collected and how this information must be organized and structured in documents.

6 Threats to Validity

During the planning and execution of this review, some factors were characterized as threats to the research validity. The potential threats are discussed to orient the interpretation of this work:

1. **Construct Validity:** The reliability of the search string defined to select relevant works can be a threat to the construct. To minimize this threat the string was calibrated with the execution of several tests and the area expert was consulted about the most used terms.
2. **Internal Validity:** A possible threat could have arisen from the individual interpretation of each researcher, something that could have led to the exclusion of relevant studies. To minimize this threat, the protocol of this review was strictly followed, considering mainly the inclusion and exclusion criteria. When necessary, a researcher with experience in this area was consulted to reach a consensus about the acceptance of the identified studies.
3. **External Validity:** Another possible threat is that some studies could not have been found because it does not contain keywords defined in the search string. To minimize this threat, the book "Handbook on Agent-Oriented Design Processes" [26] was used as research source and some classical papers were manually selected by a specialist in the area. To complement the research we performed a manual search in the methodologies found aiming to ensure the use of studies with the most recent version.
4. **Coverage Validity:** Regarding the possible papers that were not captured by our String, we intend, as a future work, to apply the snowballing technique trying to find more relevant papers. Another issue is that the snowballing technique can allow us to find more papers about the analysed methodologies, since in this analysis we focused only on the last paper of each methodology and this practice may not fully guarantee a complete coverage of the methodology.
5. **Conclusion Validity:** In spite of following a systematic protocol, systematic reviews are subject to human error, especially in the data extraction from papers. To mitigate this threat, the data extraction was performed by two independent researchers following the strategy defined in Subsect. 4.7 and, in case of divergences, a specialist in the area was consulted.

7 Insights for Future Works

Based on this systematic literature review, we found some gaps that could become future research. Among these gaps, we highlight two of them that are already being addressed in our research group: I) the need to propose requirements engineering processes for the context of multi-agent systems that cover the four sub-areas of requirements engineering and support the resources needed to the BDI model, as none of the 54 processes analyzed in this review actually support these characteristics, which shows a good research opportunity; and II) the need to propose techniques related to the four sub-areas of requirements engineering, especially where the main gaps were found, such as requirements elicitation, specification and validation.

Thus, in the elicitation subarea, we believe it is necessary to develop techniques to obtain requirements related to the BDI model which we have not found. Regarding direct contact with the stakeholders, we found only Homer [80] technique addressing this issue, however Homer presents limitations that need to be addressed in future works.

Regarding the studies that support the specification subarea, none of them adopt a specification standard that establishes how the requirements needed for the BDI model must be organized and documented. Therefore, it is necessary to propose or adopt a standard to document the collected and analysed requirements. Furthermore, this standard should allow describing not only the requirements associated with agents, but also the requirements describing functionalites accessed by normal users.

Finally, these documents must be verified using appropriate techniques to ensure their quality. However, none of the studies returned in our systematic review presented a validation subarea in a consistent way and none of them presented a specific technique for verifying the documented requirements.

8   Conclusions and Future Works

Our original systematic review published in [58], aimed to answer research questions about which methodologies for multiagent systems support the requirements engineering lifecycle, what is the level of coverage of the requirements engineering subareas of these methodologies and which of them have focus on the BDI model. Our study has categorized the studies directly related to the research theme and revealed new possibilities of scientific research in this area.

In that work, we presented 54 studies that support at least one of the subareas of requirements engineering, somehow adapted or applied in the multiagent systems context. Among these studies we noticed that only 8 methodologies support the features needed to the BDI model. However, we have not discussed in depth these methodologies due to lack of space.

Thus, this new study aimed to detail the support of these methodologies regarding the BDI model, as well as to discuss the gaps found in these studies. Regarding the elicitation subarea, we noticed that only the Homer methodology [80] presented a new way to elicit requirements from the direct contact with the stakeholders. However Homer does not support requirements related to the BDI model. Therefore, we realized the need of proposing a technique to elicit requirements related to systems based on the BDI model.

Another gap found is related to the requirements specification subarea, considering that no study uses a specification standard. Lastly, analysing the studies supporting the BDI model, we noticed that only the work of Cysneiros [57] covers the validation subarea, but it does not present any specific technique for requirements verification. Thus, we concluded that further studies are need to create a requirements specification standard for multi-agent systems, as well as, to develop a verification technique to ensure that the requirements documented in this standard are correct, consistent and non-ambiguous.

Based on the data synthesis from the retrieved studies and their gaps, we are currently proposing a requirements engineering process for multiagent systems covering the subareas of elicitation, analysis, specification, and validation. Furthermore, this process is based on the notation proposed in the Multi-Agent Systems Requirements Modeling Language (MASRML) [37] that aims to support the BDI model.

This requirement engineering process will contain a elicitation technique and a verification technique both specific for multiagent systems based on the BDI model. Moreover, the requirements specification will follow an internationally recognized standard extended to the multiagent systems context. All these works are already in development in our research group.

References

1. Abushark, Y., Miller, T., Thangarajah, J., Winikoff, M., Harland, J.: Requirements specification via activity diagrams for agent-based systems. Auton. Agents Multi-Agent Syst. **31**(3), 423–468 (2016). https://doi.org/10.1007/s10458-016-9327-7
2. Alonso, F., Frutos, S., Martínez, L., Montes, C.: SONIA: a methodology for natural agent development. In: Gleizes, M.-P., Omicini, A., Zambonelli, F. (eds.) ESAW 2004. LNCS (LNAI), vol. 3451, pp. 245–260. Springer, Heidelberg (2005). https://doi.org/10.1007/11423355_18
3. AlSanad, A., Chikh, A.: Reengineering of software requirement specification. In: Rocha, Á., Correia, A.M., Tan, F.B., Stroetmann, K.A. (eds.) New Perspectives in Information Systems and Technologies, Volume 2. AISC, vol. 276, pp. 95–111. Springer, Cham (2014). https://doi.org/10.1007/978-3-319-05948-8_10
4. Alzetta, F., Giorgini, P., Marinoni, M., Calvaresi, D.: RT-BDI: a real-time BDI model. In: Demazeau, Y., Holvoet, T., Corchado, J.M., Costantini, S. (eds.) PAAMS 2020. LNCS (LNAI), vol. 12092, pp. 16–29. Springer, Cham (2020). https://doi.org/10.1007/978-3-030-49778-1_2
5. Alzetta, F., Giorgini, P., Najjar, A., Schumacher, M.I., Calvaresi, D.: In-Time explainability in multi-agent systems: challenges, opportunities, and roadmap. In: Calvaresi, D., Najjar, A., Winikoff, M., Främling, K. (eds.) EXTRAAMAS 2020. LNCS (LNAI), vol. 12175, pp. 39–53. Springer, Cham (2020). https://doi.org/10.1007/978-3-030-51924-7_3
6. Argente, E., Botti, V., Julian, V.: GORMAS: an organizational-oriented methodological guideline for open MAS. In: Gleizes, M.-P., Gomez-Sanz, J.J. (eds.) AOSE 2009. LNCS, vol. 6038, pp. 32–47. Springer, Heidelberg (2011). https://doi.org/10.1007/978-3-642-19208-1_3
7. Ashamalla, A., Beydoun, G., Low, G.: Model driven approach for real-time requirement analysis of multi-agent systems. Comput. Lang. Syst. Struct. **50**, 127–139 (2017)
8. Banach, R.: A deidealisation semantics for KAOS. In: Proceedings of the 2010 ACM Symposium on Applied Computing, SAC '10, pp. 267–274. Association for Computing Machinery, New York, NY, USA (2010). https://doi.org/10.1145/1774088.1774146
9. Berenbach, B., Paulish, D., Kazmeier, J., Rudorfer, A.: Software & Systems Requirements Engineering: In Practice. McGraw-Hill Inc, New York (2009). 978-0-07-160548-9
10. Biolchini, J., Mian, P.G., Natali, A.C.C., Travassos, G.H.: Systematic review in software engineering (2005)
11. Blanes, D., Insfran, E., Abrahão, S.: Requirements engineering in the development of multi-agent systems: a systematic review. In: Corchado, E., Yin, H. (eds.) IDEAL 2009. LNCS, vol. 5788, pp. 510–517. Springer, Heidelberg (2009). https://doi.org/10.1007/978-3-642-04394-9_62

12. Blanes, D., Insfran, E., Abrahão, S.: RE4Gaia: a requirements modeling approach for the development of multi-agent systems. In: Ślęzak, D., Kim, T., Kiumi, A., Jiang, T., Verner, J., Abrahão, S. (eds.) ASEA 2009. CCIS, vol. 59, pp. 245–252. Springer, Heidelberg (2009). https://doi.org/10.1007/978-3-642-10619-4_30

13. Bokma, A., Slade, A., Kerridge, S., Johnson, K.: Engineering large-scale agent-based systems with consensus. Robot. Comput. Integr. Manuf. 11(2), 81–90 (1994)

14. Bonjean, N., Mefteh, W., Gleizes, M.P., Maurel, C., Migeon, F.: ADELFE 2.0. In: Cossentino, M., Hilaire, V., Molesini, A., Seidita, V. (eds.) Handbook on Agent-Oriented Design Processes, pp. 19–63. Springer, Heidelberg (2014). https://doi.org/10.1007/978-3-642-39975-6_3

15. Bourque, P., Fairley, R.E., et al.: Guide to the software engineering body of knowledge (SWEBOK (R)): Version 3.0. IEEE Computer Society Press (2014). 978-0-7695-5166-1

16. Boyarchuk, A., Pavlova, O., Bodnar, M., Lopatto, I.: Approach to the analysis of software requirements specification on its structure correctness. In: CEUR Workshop Proceedings 2623, pp. 85–95 (2020). http://ceur-ws.org/Vol-2623/paper9.pdf

17. Bratman, M., et al.: Intention, Plans, and Practical Reason, vol. 10. Harvard University Press Cambridge, MA (1987). 1–57586-192-5

18. Bresciani, P., Donzelli, P.: REF: a practical agent-based requirement engineering framework. In: Jeusfeld, M.A., Pastor, Ó. (eds.) ER 2003. LNCS, vol. 2814, pp. 217–228. Springer, Heidelberg (2003). https://doi.org/10.1007/978-3-540-39597-3_21

19. Bryl, V., Mello, P., Montali, M., Torroni, P., Zannone, N.: B-tropos: agent-oriented requirements engineering meets computational logic for declarative business process modeling and verification. In: Lecture Notes in Computer Science (including subseries Lecture Notes in Artificial Intelligence and Lecture Notes in Bioinformatics), vol. 5056, pp. 157–176 (2008). http://dx.doi.org/10.1007/978-3-540-88833-8-9

20. Caire, G., Coulier, W., Garijo, F., Gómez-Sanz, J., Pavón, J., Kearney, P., Massonet, P.: The Message Methodology, In: Bergenti, F., Gleizes, MP., Zambonelli, F. (eds) Methodologies and Software Engineering for Agent Systems. Multiagent Systems, Artificial Societies, and Simulated Organizations, vol. 11, pp. 177–194. Springer, US, Boston, MA (2004). https://doi.org/10.1007/1-4020-8058-1_12

21. Cao, L.: OSOAD methodology. In: Metasynthetic Computing and Engineering of Complex Systems. AIKP, pp. 111–129. Springer, London (2015). https://doi.org/10.1007/978-1-4471-6551-4_6

22. Cernuzzi, L., Cossentino, M., Zambonelli, F.: Process models for agent-based development. Eng. Appl. Artif. Intell. 18(2), 205–222 (2005)

23. Cernuzzi, L., Molesini, A., Omicini, A.: The gaia methodology process. In: Cossentino, M., Hilaire, V., Molesini, A., Seidita, V. (eds.) Handbook on Agent-Oriented Design Processes, pp. 141–172. Springer, Heidelberg (2014). https://doi.org/10.1007/978-3-642-39975-6_6

24. Lee, C.H.L., Liu, A.: A method for agent-based system requirements analysis. In: 2002 Proceedings of the Fourth International Symposium on Multimedia Software Engineering, pp. 214–221. IEEE (2002). https://doi.org/10.1109/MMSE.2002.1181615

25. Cossentino, M., Galland, S., Gaud, N., Hilaire, V., Koukam, A.: A glimpse of the ASPECS process documented with the FIPA DPDF template. In: Proceedings of The Multi-Agent Logics, Languages, and Organisations Federated Workshops (MALLOW 2010), vol. 627 (2010)

26. Cossentino, M., Hilaire, V., Molesini, A., Seidita, V. (eds.): Handbook on Agent-Oriented Design Processes. Springer, Heidelberg (2014). https://doi.org/10.1007/978-3-642-39975-6

27. Cossentino, M., Seidita, V.: PASSI: process for agent societies specification and implementation. In: Cossentino, M., Hilaire, V., Molesini, A., Seidita, V. (eds.) Handbook on Agent-Oriented Design Processes, pp. 287–329. Springer, Heidelberg (2014). https://doi.org/10.1007/978-3-642-39975-6_10

28. De Silva, L., Meneguzzi, F., Logan, B.: BDI agent architectures: a survey. In: IJCAI International Joint Conference on Artificial Intelligence (2020)

29. DeLoach, S.A., Garcia-Ojeda, J.C.: The o-mase methodology. In: Cossentino, M., Hilaire, V., Molesini, A., Seidita, V. (eds.) Handbook on Agent-Oriented Design Processes, pp. 253–285. Springer, Heidelberg (2014). https://doi.org/10.1007/978-3-642-39975-6_9

30. Domann, J., Hartmann, S., Burkhardt, M., Barge, A., Albayrak, S.: An agile method for multiagent software engineering. Procedia Computer Science, vol. 32, pp. 928–934 (2014). https://doi.org/10.1016/j.procs.2014.05.513, http://www.sciencedirect.com/science/article/pii/S1877050914007133. In: The 5th International Conference on Ambient Systems, Networks and Technologies (ANT-2014), the 4th International Conference on Sustainable Energy Information Technology (SEIT-2014), Elsevier

31. Dorri, A., Kanhere, S.S., Jurdak, R.: Multi-agent systems: a survey. IEEE Access, vol. 6, pp. 28573–28593. Institute of Electrical and Electronics Engineers Inc (2018)

32. Fuentes-Fernández, R., Gómez-Sanz, J., Pavón, J.: Requirements elicitation and analysis of multiagent systems using activity theory. Systems, Man and Cybernetics, Part A: Systems and Humans, IEEE Transactions on vol. 39, pp. 282–298. IEEE (2009). https://doi.org/10.1109/TSMCA.2008.2010747

33. Gaur, V., Soni, A.: A novel approach to explore inter agent dependencies from user requirements. Procedia Technology, vol. 1, pp. 412–419. Elsevier (2012). https://doi.org/10.1016/j.protcy.2012.02.093

34. Glaser, N.: The CoMoMAS methodology and environment for multi-agent system development. In: Zhang, C., Lukose, D. (eds.) DAI 1996. LNCS, vol. 1286, pp. 1–16. Springer, Heidelberg (1997). https://doi.org/10.1007/BFb0030078

35. González-Moreno, J.C., Gómez-Rodríguez, A., Fuentes-Fernández, R., Ramos-Valcárcel, D.: Ingenias-scrum. In: Cossentino, M., Hilaire, V., Molesini, A., Seidita, V. (eds.) Handbook on Agent-Oriented Design Processes, pp. 219–251. Springer, Heidelberg (2014). https://doi.org/10.1007/978-3-642-39975-6_8

36. Guedes, G.T.A., Vicari, R.M.: A UML profile oriented to the requirements modeling in intelligent tutoring systems projects. In: Bramer, M. (ed.) IFIP AI 2010. IAICT, vol. 331, pp. 133–142. Springer, Heidelberg (2010). https://doi.org/10.1007/978-3-642-15286-3_13

37. Guedes, G., Souza Filho, I., Gaedicke, L., Mendonça, G., Vicari, R., Brusius, C.: Masrml - a domain-specific modeling language for multi-agent systems requirements. Int. J. Soft. Eng. Appl. (IJSEA) 11(5) (2020)

38. Hajer, B.M., Taieb, B.R., Raouf, K.: A new mas based approach modeling the QMS continual improvement. In: 2009 IEEE International Conference on Systems, Man and Cybernetics, pp. 4734–4739. IEEE (2009)

39. Haumer, P., Heymans, P., Jarke, M., Pohl, K.: Bridging the gap between past and future in re: a scenario-based approach. In: Proceedings IEEE International Symposium on Requirements Engineering (Cat. No.PR00188). pp. 66–73. IEEE (1999)

40. Henderson-Sellers, B., Gorton, I.: Agent-based software development methodologies. In: White Paper, Summary of Workshop at the OOPSLA, vol. 2003 (2002)

41. Herzig, A., Lorini, E., Perrussel, L., Xiao, Z.: BDI logics for BDI Architectures: old problems, new perspectives. KI - Künstliche Intelligenz 31(1), 73–83 (2016). https://doi.org/10.1007/s13218-016-0457-5

42. Hilaire, V., Cossentino, M., Gechter, F., Rodriguez, S., Koukam, A.: An approach for the integration of swarm intelligence in mas: an engineering perspective. Expert Systems with Applications, vol. 40, pp. 1–24. Elsevier (2012). https://doi.org/10.1016/j.eswa.2012.08.058

43. Hsieh, M., Hung, W., Shin, S., Lin, S., Huang, T.: Spoken dialogue agent interface requirements modeling based on PASSI methodology. In: 2008 Eighth International Conference on Intelligent Systems Design and Applications, vol. 1, pp. 339–342. IEEE (2008)

44. Huiying, X., Zhi, J.: An agent-oriented requirement graphic symbol representation and formalization modeling method. In: SETN 2002: Methods and Applications of Artificial Intelligence, vol. 4, pp. 569–574. IEEE Computer Society (2009). https://doi.org/10.1109/CSIE.2009.923

45. Iglesias, C.A., Garijo, M., González, J.C., Velasco, J.R.: Analysis and design of multiagent systems using MAS-CommonKADS. In: Singh, M.P., Rao, A., Wooldridge, M.J. (eds.) ATAL 1997. LNCS, vol. 1365, pp. 313–327. Springer, Heidelberg (1998). https://doi.org/10.1007/BFb0026768

46. Jo, C.H., Einhorn, J.: A BDI agent-based software process. J. Object Technol. **4**, 101–121 (2005). https://doi.org/10.5381/jot.2005.4.9.a3

47. Kitchenham, B., Charters, S.: Guidelines for performing systematic literature reviews in software engineering (2007)

48. Kitchenham, B., Brereton, P.: A systematic review of systematic review process research in software engineering. Inf. Softw. Technol. **55**(12), 2049–2075 (2013)

49. Larsen, J.B.: Agent programming languages and logics in agent-based simulation. In: Sieminski, A., Kozierkiewicz, A., Nunez, M., Ha, Q.T. (eds.) Modern Approaches for Intelligent Information and Database Systems. SCI, vol. 769, pp. 517–526. Springer, Cham (2018). https://doi.org/10.1007/978-3-319-76081-0_44

50. Lee, J., Lee, H.: Strategic agent based web system development methodology. Int. J. Inf. Technol. Decis. Making **7**, 309–337. World Scientific (2008). https://doi.org/10.1142/S02196220080029837,

51. Lind, J. (ed.): MASSIVE views. In: Iterative Software Engineering for Multiagent Systems. LNCS (LNAI), vol. 1994, pp. 121–204. Springer, Heidelberg (2001). https://doi.org/10.1007/3-540-45162-5_5

52. Lindoso, A., Girardi, R.: The SRAMO technique for analysis and reuse of requirements in multi-agent application engineering. In: 9th Workshop on Requirements Engineering, pp. 41–50. Workshop on Requirements Engineering (2006)

53. Liu, L., Jin, Z., Lu, R., Yang, H.: Agent-oriented requirements analysis from scenarios. In: O'Shea, J., Nguyen, N.T., Crockett, K., Howlett, R.J., Jain, L.C. (eds.) KES-AMSTA 2011. LNCS (LNAI), vol. 6682, pp. 394–405. Springer, Heidelberg (2011). https://doi.org/10.1007/978-3-642-22000-5_41

54. Liu, W., Li, M.: Requirements planning with event calculus for runtime self-adaptive system. In: 2015 IEEE 39th Annual Computer Software and Applications Conference, vol. 2, pp. 77–82. IEEE (2015)

55. Cao, L., Zhang, C., Luo, D., Chen, W., Zamani, N.: Integrative early requirements analysis for agent-based systems. In: Fourth International Conference on Hybrid Intelligent Systems (HIS'04), pp. 118–123. IEEE (2004)

56. Mahela, O.P., et al.: Comprehensive overview of multi-agent systems for controlling smart grids. CSEE J. Power Energy Syst. **8**(1), 115–131 (2020)

57. Marcio Cysneiros, L., Yu, E.: Requirements engineering for large-scale multi-agent systems. In: Garcia, A., Lucena, C., Zambonelli, F., Omicini, A., Castro, J. (eds.) SELMAS 2002. LNCS, vol. 2603, pp. 39–56. Springer, Heidelberg (2003). https://doi.org/10.1007/3-540-35828-5_3

58. Mendonça, G., Souza, Filho, I., Guedes, G.: A systematic review about requirements engineering processes for multi-agent systems. In: 13th International Conference on Agents and Artificial Intelligence (ICAART 2021), vol. 1, pp. 69–79 (2021)

59. Mendonça, G.D., de Souza Filho, I.P., Guedes, G.T.A.: A systematic review about requirements engineering processes for multi-agent systems. In: ICAART, vol. 1, pp. 69–79 (2021)

60. Morreale, V., Bonura, S., Francaviglia, G., Centineo, F., Cossentino, M., Gaglio, S.: Goal-oriented development of bdi agents: the practionist approach. In: Proceedings of the 2006

IEEE/WIC/ACM International Conference on Intelligent Agent Technology, pp. 66–72. IEEE (2006). https://doi.org/10.1109/IAT.2006.71

61. Murray, J.: Specifying agent behaviors with UML statecharts and statedit. In: Polani, D., Browning, B., Bonarini, A., Yoshida, K. (eds.) RoboCup 2003. LNCS (LNAI), vol. 3020, pp. 145–156. Springer, Heidelberg (2004). https://doi.org/10.1007/978-3-540-25940-4_13

62. Mylopoulos, J., Castro, J., Kolp, M.: The evolution of tropos. In: Seminal Contributions to Information Systems Engineering, pp. 281–287. Springer, Heidelberg (2013). https://doi.org/10.1007/978-3-642-36926-1_22

63. Padgham, L., Thangarajah, J., Winikoff, M.: Prometheus research directions. In: Shehory, O., Sturm, A. (eds.) Agent-Oriented Software Engineering, pp. 155–171. Springer, Heidelberg (2014). https://doi.org/10.1007/978-3-642-54432-3_8

64. Passos, L.S., Rossetti, R.J., Gabriel, J.: An agent methodology for processes, the environment, and services. In: Rossetti, R.J., Liu, R. (eds.) Advances in Artificial Transportation Systems and Simulation, pp. 37–53. Academic Press, Boston (2015). https://doi.org/10.1016/B978-0-12-397041-1.00003-0, http://www.sciencedirect.com/science/article/pii/B9780123970411000030

65. Patrizia, R., Lodato, C., Sabatucci, L.: Ontology and goal model in designing BDI multi-agent systems. In: CEUR Workshop Proceedings, vol. 1099 (2013)

66. Ranjan, P., Misra, A.: A novel approach of requirements analysis for agent based system. In: Seventh ACIS International Conference on Software Engineering, Artificial Intelligence, Networking, and Parallel/Distributed Computing (SNPD'06), pp. 299–304. IEEE (2006). https://doi.org/10.1109/SNPD-SAWN.2006.5

67. Rao, A.S., Georgeff, M.P.: Bdi agents: From theory to practice. In: Proceedings of the First International Conference on Multi-Agent Systems (ICMAS-95). pp. 312–319 (1995)

68. Rodriguez, L., Hume, A., Cernuzzi, L., Insfran, E.: Improving the quality of agent-based systems: integration of requirements modeling into gaia. In: 2009 Ninth International Conference on Quality Software, pp. 278–283. IEEE Computer Society (08 2009). https://doi.org/10.1109/QSIC.2009.43

69. Ronald, N., Dignum, V., Jonker, C., Arentze, T., Timmermans, H.: On the engineering of agent-based simulations of social activities with social networks. Information and Software Technology, **54**(6), 625–638 (2012). https://doi.org/10.1016/j.infsof.2011.12.004, http://www.sciencedirect.com/science/article/pii/S0950584911002485. Special Section: Engineering Complex Software Systems through Multi-Agent Systems and Simulation, Elsevier

70. Sen, A., Hemachandran, K.: Elicitation of goals in requirements engineering using agile methods. In: 2010 IEEE 34th Annual Computer Software and Applications Conference Workshops, pp. 263–268. IEEE (2010). https://doi.org/10.1109/COMPSACW.2010.53

71. Sen, A.M., Jain, S.K.: An agile technique for agent based goal refinement to elicit soft goals in goal oriented requirements engineering. In: 15th International Conference on Advanced Computing and Communications (ADCOM 2007), pp. 41–47. IEEE (2007)

72. Sen, A.M., Jain, S.K.: A visualization technique for agent based goal refinement to elicit soft goals in goal oriented requirements engineering. In: Second International Workshop on Requirements Engineering Visualization (REV 2007), pp. 2–2. IEEE (2007). https://doi.org/10.1109/REV.2007.1

73. Shah, U.S., Jinwala, D.C.: Resolving ambiguities in natural language software requirements: a comprehensive survey. ACM SIGSOFT Softw. Eng. Notes **40**(5), 1–7 (2015)

74. Shen, Z., Li, D., Miao, C., Gay, R., Miao, Y.: Goal-oriented methodology for agent system development. In: IEICE TRANSACTIONS on Information and Systems, vol. 89, pp. 95–101. The Institute of Electronics, Information and Communication Engineers (2005). https://doi.org/10.1109/IAT.2005.80

75. Singh, D., Padgham, L., Logan, B.: Integrating BDI agents with agent-based simulation platforms. Autonomous Agents and Multi-Agent Systems **30**(6), 1050–1071 (2016). https://doi.org/10.1007/s10458-016-9332-x
76. Sudeikat, J., Braubach, L., Pokahr, A., Lamersdorf, W.: Evaluation of agent–oriented software methodologies – examination of the Gap between modeling and platform. In: Odell, J., Giorgini, P., Müller, J.P. (eds.) AOSE 2004. LNCS, vol. 3382, pp. 126–141. Springer, Heidelberg (2005). https://doi.org/10.1007/978-3-540-30578-1_9
77. Sutcliffe, A.: Requirements engineering for complex collaborative systems. In: Proceedings Fifth IEEE International Symposium on Requirements Engineering, pp. 110–117. IEEE (2001). https://doi.org/10.1109/ISRE.2001.948550
78. Ulfat-Bunyadi, N., Mohammadi, N., Heisel, M.: Supporting the systematic goal refinement in kaos using the six-variable model. In: 13th International Conference on Software Technologies, pp. 102–111. SciTePress (2018). https://doi.org/10.5220/0006850701020111
79. Wang, Y., Zhao, L., Wang, X., Yang, X., Supakkul, S.: Plant: A pattern language for transforming scenarios into requirements models. Int. J. Hum. Comput. Stud. **71**, 1026–1043. Elsevier (2013). https://doi.org/10.1016/j.ijhcs.2013.08.001
80. Wilmann, D., Sterling, L.: Guiding agent-oriented requirements elicitation: Homer. In: Fifth International Conference on Quality Software (QSIC'05), pp. 419–424. IEEE (2005)
81. Wu, H., Liu, L., Ma, W.: Optimizing requirements elicitation with an i* and bayesian network integrated modelling approach. In: IEEE 34th Annual Computer Software and Applications Conference Workshops, pp. 182–188. IEEE (2010)

Automatically-Generated Agent Organizations for Flexible Workflow Enactment

Massimo Cossentino(iD), Salvatore Lopes(iD), and Luca Sabatucci(✉)(iD)

National Research Council of Italy (CNR), ICAR, Palermo, Italy
{massimo.cossentino,salvatore.lopes,luca.sabatucci}@icar.cnr.it

Abstract. The use of multi-agent systems for the implementation and management of data-intensive workflows is generally considered a particularly interesting solution. We propose an approach that exploits the definition of processes described with the BPMN language for the automatic generation of agent organisations. To demonstrate the use of our approach, we chose the JaCaMo agent framework for its inherent support of agent organisations described with the MOISE meta-model. The resulting agent organization is built for adapting to different execution context, by self-modifying its structural and functional specification for continuing to fulfil the BP goal.

Keywords: Multi-agent organization · Business process · Dynamic workflow

1 Introduction

Traditionally, Business Process (BP) languages are defined to describe static processes as composition of atomic services that may be enacted in centralized or distributed environment [22]. Recently, enterprises yield to redesign their information and process management systems to implement advanced features such as adaptation ability [10, 13]. When exceptions may be anticipated, instruments like BPMN allows catching them as special events leading to pre-defined deviations. Other exceptions cannot be anticipated, and therefore it is difficult to incorporate their management inside the specification. These situations fall apart in a mismatch between the real processes and the software counterpart [16]. A taxonomy of motivations for facing dynamic workflows is provided in [11].

This work aims to increase the agility and flexibility of workflow enactment. A promising direction is to use multiagent systems [3,4,23]. This is an alliance, very frequent in literature, in which the enactment of workflows takes great benefits from distinctive agent features like distribution, adaptation, and smartness. The proposed approach consists in providing an automated and flexible support based on agent organizations. The challenge is that of coordinating heterogeneous, autonomous agents, whose internal designs could not be fully known a-priori.

In [20] we already presented an automatic support to goal extraction from BPs, in [6] we illustrated how to map agent-based adaptive workflow to business process goals. The current paper is an extension of these couple of previous works by entering into the details of the algorithm to automatically generate the agent organization.

© Springer Nature Switzerland AG 2022
A. P. Rocha et al. (Eds.): ICAART 2021, LNAI 13251, pp. 70–84, 2022.
https://doi.org/10.1007/978-3-031-10161-8_4

To this aim, we selected JaCaMo [1] as an agent framework for implementing our ideas. It is composed of three different components: Jason [2] (a BDI [15] agent language), CArtAgo [17] (a Java-based language for describing the environment), and MOISE [12] (an XML language for describing agent organizations).

In our approach we suppose the process is specified via BPMN [5], a de-facto standard for specifying workflows. More in details, we specify the workflow together with all the artifacts used and exchanged during the process. We use theories from [20] for automatically translating BPMN specifications into a list of goals. The advantage is that goals allow for breaking the rules: whereas sequence flows specify the precise order in which services are invoked, goals can relax strict constraints, widening the space for adaptation [19]. In addition, we propose the use of workflow enactment as a tool for cooperative problem-solving. To this aim we suppose to have a multiagent systems in which agents are service providers whose contribution to the goal is orchestrated by the workflow itself [8].

This paper builds over the previous work [8] adding some novelties. The main contribution is to tie up business goals [20] to the automatic definition of social organisations for agents. Here we give the complete framework to automatically generate social organisations for enacting the workflow. Generated workflows have self-adaptation abilities, i.e., if the system owns many alternative services, then the organization is able to switch among several alternate solutions to address the same set of goals.

The paper is structured as follows: Sect. 2 presents a running example that motivates the remaining sections. Section 3 presents an overview of the approach by describing its components. Section 4 enters into the details of the transformation algorithm. Finally, conclusions and future works are sketched in Sect. 5.

2   A Running Example

The *Business Process Model and Notation* (BPMN) [5] is a de-facto standard for business analysts to model a process. It contains a very metamodel-model and an expressive notation for representing business processes of diverse nature. The graphical notation allows several modelling perspectives [5]; this paper focuses on the collaboration diagram (similar to an activity diagram), in which a process is described by means of five categories of objects: activities, events, messages, data objects, and many kinds of gateways. Every participant (each one depicted in a different Swimlane) owns a different flow of activities. Coordination among participant occurs via message flows.

This paper uses the email-voting business process, available in [14] as running example. It is a good choice because it is an articulated process which aim is mediating and coordinating remote voting members in resolving issues. Moreover, in this process, data and messages are explicitly represented, that is a necessary requirement for obtaining significant result with the presented approach. The original process is represented with more than 20 tasks, organized in several subprocesses; for reasons of readability, a compact version of the workflow is shown in Fig. 1). Its functioning is briefly summarized as follows: a manager prepares the issue list for a discussion; all participants propose solutions via email. After one week, the discussion is closed with a voting session and the manager communicates results. If the issue has not been solved, then a new discussion cycle starts.

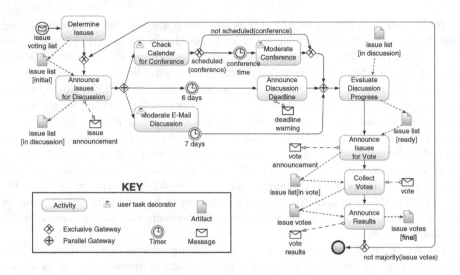

Fig. 1. A compact version of the voting-by-email process, modified from [14].

Let us suppose that, given this high-level specification of the process, developers have created a set of web services for enacting the corresponding workflow. The execution involves several automatic and manual tasks. Automatic tasks should be performed through the invocation of web services, whereas manual tasks must be designed for supporting humans with appropriate automations. An example of a service task is the *Check Calendar for Conference* that accesses the user's digital agenda for discovering free time slots for allocating a meeting. Conversely, *Moderate Conference* is a manual task in which the issue manager uses digital instruments for conducting a conference meeting. According to available services, different workflows could address the business process of Fig. 1. We can classify these concrete workflows in two categories: 1) same workflow structure but employing services from different providers, 2) different workflow structure where differences reflect the use of diverse services (e.g., smaller services that must be composed, or a similar service with a different set of output conditions).

In any case, the workflow management must be ready to deal with potential points of failure: a web-service could be temporarily unavailable, or it may produce wrong/incomplete results. Moreover, given the presence of humans in the loop, a process may fail because of a human's delay/failure. To cope with situations like these, agent organizations represent a promising approach for dynamic workflow management because they are able to adapt their behaviour at run-time. In the worst cases, the use of a dynamic workflow management could modify the whole workflow structure at run-time to continue to pursue business goals.

In this paper we exploit automatically extracted goals and awareness of available resources in order to automatically generate an agent organization for workflow management. The three ingredients of the proposed approach are agents, organizations, and goals. Agents encapsulate workflow tasks, providing the advantage of autonomous decision-making, easiness in distribution, and, optionally, the ability to maintain a state and learn from previous cases. Organizations represent the interaction mechanism for composing the workflow as a sum of services, with the additional advantage of acting under a customizable normative background. Goals are the instrument for binding organizational rules (for formation and adaptation) to the initial BP definition. These goals are automatically derived from the BPMN specification and capture the nature of dependencies between states of the system. Providing the workflow as goals (rather than as BPMN specification) allows relaxing some strong relationships imposed by sequence-flows, and providing the workflow management engine with a higher degree of freedom in defining (at run-time) the flow of activities.

3   From Business Process Models to Agent Organizations

This section provides the basis for automatically generating the specification of an agent organization that is suitable for the workflow management. The first step is giving an intuition of how to extract goals from BPMN specifications. The second step is mapping extracted goals to an agent organization. Additional details on this latter part are in Sect. 4.

3.1   Ontology and Goals from a Business Process

Extracting goals from the BPMN specification is a two-step process. First an ontology is defined to represent conditions on the state of the world that constitute the basis for goal expressions, finally goals are extracted from the business process.

Ontology Extraction. A semantic approach requires a vocabulary of terms that may be usefully employed to specify a part of the world where the agents live (typically expressed as fluents in a predicate logic), and the actions that can be done in it (that implement BPMN tasks). The ontology extraction automatically generates a primordial ontology that is implicitly embedded in a workflow structure.

As an example we could consider picking ontological concepts from Data Object labels, whereas Data Object's states could generate predicates. Similarly, a Data type (associated to a work-item) could produce a IS-A relationship.

- $available(\langle Data \rangle)$ describes the availability of a given input/output artifact;
- $received(\langle Message \rangle, \langle Actor \rangle)$ when a message incomes from a participant;
- $done(\langle Activity \rangle)$ when an activity has been completed with success.

Goal Extraction. The preliminary ontological base makes us ready for identifying the goals that are hidden in a BPMN process. Goal extraction relies on [20] that provides the theoretical background we assume in this work.

It is worth noting the goals we are looking at, are actually *implicit goals*, that means they are operative elements describing functional aspects of a traditional workflow definition in terms of conditions and desired states of the world. The key of the approach is to consider the elements of a BP as 'transition enablers' that produce changes in the current state of the world. In other words, every element in a BP (activities, events, and gateways) contributes to the state evolution desired by the workflow enactment.

The goal extraction grounds on the assumption that a goal change is due to the balance of two forces: internal factors (what is the intended contribution of the element?) and external relationships (how is the element connected to other ones?).

Leaving apart the raw theory, the interested reader may read in [20], here we limit ourself to show and discuss an example.

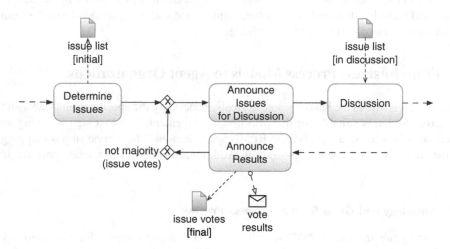

Fig. 2. Predecessors and successors of the Announce Issues for Discussion task, revised from [8].

Figure 2 shows an excerpt from a complex email-voting process. In particular, we focus on the Announce Issues for Discussion task and its relationships with predecessors and successors (two predecessors tasks are joined through an exclusive gateway). Looking only at the target task (as it was isolated from the diagram), we observe that the expected input/output conditions related to the input data are issue_list[initial], and the output data issue_list[in_discussion], while the outgoing message is: issue_management. The results are summarized in the following:

$$\begin{cases} data\_in(e) & = initial(issue\_list) \\ data\_out(e) & = in\_discussion(issue\_votes) \\ mess\_in(e) & = sent(issue\_announc, member) \end{cases}$$

However, reconnecting the element into the diagram, we discover that Announce Issues for Discussion is ready for execution when the following condition holds:

$$initial(issue\_list) \oplus (sent(vote\_results) \wedge final(issue\_votes) \wedge \neg majority(issue\_votes))$$

where the $\oplus$ derives from the exclusive gateways. Finally, after its execution, for the workflow to proceed, the state must include $in\_discussion(issue\_list)$.

Therefore, combining internal and external factors, this analysis makes an implicit goal emerging:

```
GOAL: Announce Issues for Discussion

WHEN:
(((final(issue_votes) and sent(vote_results))
and not majority(issue_votes))
xor initial(issue_list))

THE SYSTEM SHALL:
in_discussion(issue_list)
and sent(issue_announcement)
```

In the subsection, we will discuss how to map goals to the agents that will pursue them and how to build the proper organization for agents.

3.2 Mapping Goals to Agents via Organization

There is a huge literature about the use of agents for implementing flexible workflows. The use of agents allows for modularizing tasks spread over different software components that are opaque and independent of each other. One of the most interesting challenges in this area is the relationship between agent autonomy and the constraints of the rigid rules of a workflow. It may result that an agent, employed into workflow enactment, looses some degree of freedom, with a negative impact over the whole agent paradigm.

The organization metaphor has been introduced in MAS research to face the inherent need of coordination among autonomous agents. Agent organizations represent a natural way of decomposing complex business goals into simpler sub-tasks and allocating them to agents. By entering an organization, agents acquire responsibilities and operate in a distributed, coordinated and regulated fashion.

In our work, the organization is viewed as a normative set of rules that constrains the agents' behaviour while preserving their autonomy. When an agent enters an organization, it becomes part of a network of delegation and mutual obligations. Looking at the single agent, it is the concept of role that mediates about agent autonomy and constrain their possibilities. The agent autonomy is preserved, since they can even decide not to satisfy an obligation.

For realizing our agent organizations, we adopted the MOISE [12] model prescribing an organization must encompass a functional, a structural, and a normative perspective. We selected MOISE because of its well-defined metamodel, grounding on a sound theory; moreover, it is fully integrated with a framework for BDI agents (JaCaMo) that amplifies its usability in many real contexts.

Part of the contribution of this work is mapping BPMN and implicit goals (as they appear in [20]) into concepts of the MOISE metamodel. For building the basis of this task, the most significant MOISE elements are briefly described below:

- Organization: cooperative collection of agents' roles described through structural, functional and normative perspectives.
- Role/Group: a role is a holder of responsibility whereas a group is the structural definition of the organization in terms of roles and links among roles. In practice, a group defines a cluster of related responsibilities (links specify how roles interact).

– Goal/Plan: in MOISE, goals are the means for decomposing group responsibilities into affordable pieces of work. Goal specification uses plans to decompose the effort into sub-goals. Plans are decomposition operators (sequence, parallel, choice). We specialize the concept of goal in two directions: a *Collective Goal* addresses a goal associated to a group of distinct roles, besides an *Individual Goal* is individually assigned to a single agent's role.
– Scheme: it provides the functional specification of a group's objective. It is further refined into sub-goals, and sub-plans down to the level of granularity of implicit goals.
– Mission: links implicit goals to the roles that are responsible for their fulfilment.
– Norms: obligations and permissions that hold in the organization.

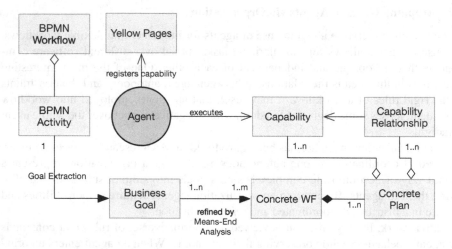

Fig. 3. The metamodel implicitly adopted in extracting goal-oriented solutions from BPMN work-flows, revised from [8].

Figure 3 shows the metamodel implicitly adopted in [20] that combines elements of BPMN and elements of a goal-oriented self-adaptive framework. In the following, we describe these elements and how they map into MOISE concepts (see Fig. 3):

– BPMN Workflow: this is the BPMN representation of the target workflow, composed by activities, events, gateways and flow relationships. In this work we are omitting a few advanced elements such as swimlanes and sub-processes. A workflow natu-rally maps to an agent organization. In the mapping, each group is responsible for enacting a process (or even a sub-process). Each group is connected to a scheme describing the overall process goal.
– BPMN Activity: a portion of work to be done. Each workflow activity directly maps into the role that will perform that. However, the same role may gather more activi-ties.

- Implicit Goal: defined as <tc, fs> where *tc* is a triggering condition and *fs* is a final state. They are automatically extracted by the workflow, according to the generated ontology. Individual goals directly map into the generated implicit goals.
- Agent's Capability and Yellow Pages: a capability represents the agent's awareness about its available skills for solving concrete problems. In some cases, it represents a wrapper to an external service. By looking at its own capabilities, the agent may decide if entering the organization for playing a specific role or not (a match between the agent's capabilities and the tasks assigned to the role is required). Yellow pages are a public directory of the available capabilities provided by the agents populating the system. The directory may be dynamically updated, and it is consulted when generating new plans.
- Concrete Plan: often single capabilities are not enough to address complex distributed problems. To this aim, we adopt the Proactive Means-eng Reasoning (PMR) algorithm [18] to produce plans that can address the desired states of the world. In this approach, plans are cooperation protocols provided as flows of capabilities, decision points and loops. Given a goal, zero-to-many plans may exist, each one with different performances and quality of service according to the capabilities employed in that. In the mapping, a concrete plan is rendered as a MOISE Schema (Fig. 4).

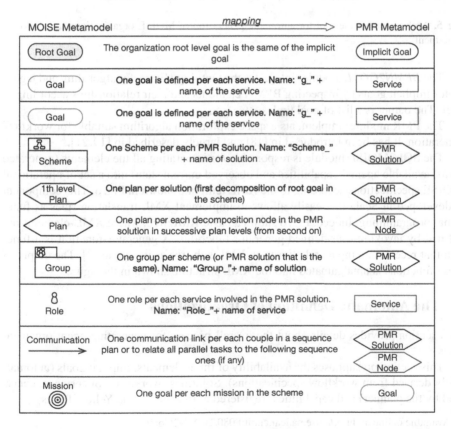

Fig. 4. The proposed mapping among Solutions and MOISE organisation metamodel elements, revised from [8].

3.3   The BPMN2MOISE Tool

We developed a tool, BPMN2MOISE, for generating the organization starting from the BPMN specification of a workflow. Coherently with the above reported discussion, the tool has been designed for supporting the MOISE specifications (Fig. 5).

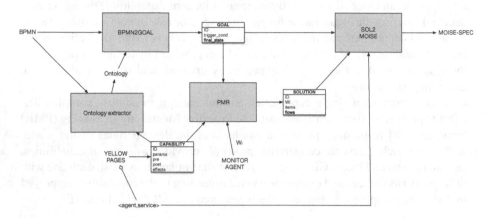

Fig. 5. Architecture of the tool for automatic generation of MOISE organizations for workflow enactment.

The *BPMN2GOAL* module[1] integrates the Ontology Extractor algorithm, and it generates implicit goals by inspecting BPMN elements and their relationships according to [20]. The output is a list of goal tuples <tc, fs>.

The PMR module[2] implements a space exploration algorithm suitable for workflow generation. It has been introduced in [18] and largely described in [19,21].

The SOL2MOISE module is responsible for integrating all the elements (generated goals, available agents' capabilities and observed current state) into a set of operational MOISE specifications according to the XML template shown in Fig. 6. This component is developed in Scala that easily allows to implement XML translation rules as functional programming. Indeed, Fig. 6 shows a basic XML tree, where XML-elements are defined by invoking user-defined generator functions. A generator-function is a function that receives an input and returns an XML sub-tree as its output [7]. The output of these functions is amalgamated into the XML structure shown in the figure.

4   The Automatic Definition of Organizations

This section provides details about the overall process for generating agent organizations.

This section presupposes the availability of three elements: implicit goals (automatically derived from workflow specifications), Solutions (workflows of services, generated by the planner) and capabilities (registered at run-time in the Yellow Pages).

---

[1] Available online at: http://aose.pa.icar.cnr.it:8080/BPMN2Goal/.
[2] Source code is available online at: https://github.com/icar-aose/musa_2_scala.

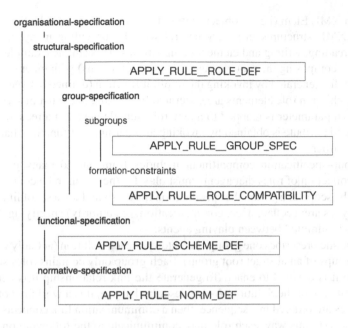

Fig. 6. Tree decomposition of the algorithm for generating the MOISE organization.

4.1 Heuristic for the Structural Specification: Roles and Groups

MOISE structural-specification includes two compartments: role-definition and group-specification.

The role-definition compartment describes roles (with the meaning of holders of responsibility) and inheritance relationships among them. The semantic of inheritance is quite straightforward: when a sub-role is a specialization of a super-role, it owns all the responsibilities of the super-role while adding other specific ones. In our implementation, we set a default abstract Worker role. All the other roles are a specialization of the Worker role. Therefore, the heuristic grounds on the idea that roles of these organizations are responsible for providing services embedded in the various Solutions. This implies generating one **role** for each service in one of the Solutions.

The "role definition rule" is shown in the following Scala function:

```scala
def apply_rule__role_def(yp:List[ServiceDescr]): Elem = {
<role-definitions>
  {yp.map(service =>         // implicit function
    <role id={service.id + "_role"}>
        <extends role="worker"/>
    </role>
    )}
</role-definitions>
}
```

This excerpt of code is a procedure (it starts with a def keyword) that receives a list of ServiceDescr (agent capabilities registered in the system Yellow Pages) as an input;

it returns an XML Elem (i.e. an object representing an XML tree). The Scala language deals with XML structures in a very natural way, by providing many operators for facilitating reading, writing and element compositions. This simple example defines an XML tree by composing the root element (i.e. role-definitions) with inner elements that are dynamically generated by invoking the implicit function (defined between brackets). In this case, children role elements are generated by looking at the list of services (each item in the yp parameter is mapped to a new role sub-element). In a recursive fashion, here the role id attribute is obtained by invoking another implicit function that generates a unique identifier.

The group-specification compartment includes from one to many groups. Each group is a collection of roles that agents must play for the group to be considered well-formed. In the scope of a group, the specification may also include a set of links between roles (link types are: acquaintance, communication, or authority) specifying the kind of relationship is admitted between playing agents.

The heuristic prescribes one **group** is created per each Solution (actually we are talking of subgroups of an abstract root group). Each group only contains roles suitable for the Solution it is devoted to enact. To generate the link relationship it is necessary to study the structure of the Solution. As we described above, it is a workflow of services: when services are ordered in a sequence, then a communication link connects the corresponding roles (in this way, each role may communicate to the following one when its work is done, together with any relevant data). When services are in parallel, a special role for synchronization is necessary (we associate this special role to the Join element).

The following procedure generates the group specification corresponding to a Solution.

```
def apply_rule__group_specification(sol: Solution): Elem = {
  <group-specification id={get_group_id} min="0">
  {apply_rule__group_roles(sol) ++ apply_rule__group_links(sol)}
  </group-specification>
}
def apply_rule__group_roles(s: Solution): Elem = {
  <roles>
    <role id="manager" min="1" max="1"/>
    {solution.wftasks.map(capability =>
      <role id={capability.id + "_role"} min="1" max="1"/>
    )}
  </roles>
}
def apply_rule__group_links(s: Solution): Elem = {
  <links>
    <link from="manager" to="worker" type="authority"
    extends-subgroups="false" bi-dir="false"
    scope="intra-group"/>
    <link from="worker" to="manager" type="acquaintance"
    extends-subgroups="false" bi-dir="false"
    scope="intra-group"/>
    ++ apply_rule__dynamic_link_generator(s)
  </links>
}
```

The first procedure returns a 'group-specification' by concatenating (the ++ operator) the results of two sub-procedures. The first one is for generating roles admitted to the group; it maps services of the target Solutions to a corresponding role. The second procedure generates links among the roles; the first couple of links is static (from manager to worker and vice versa), whereas the second part id dynamically generated by appending the result of a sub-procedures that inspects the structure of the Solution.

4.2 Heuristic for the Functional Specification: Goals and Plans

MOISE functional-specification is done by specifying a set of schemes. Each scheme includes missions, a root goal and its decomposition in sub-plans. Moreover, a goal is specified by an id, a type (either achievement or maintenance), a cardinality and a time to fulfil. A plan is specified for decomposing a goal into sub-goals; a plan is declared with a type (sequence, choice, or parallel) that specifies how the super-goal relates to its sub-goals.

One **scheme** is defined per each Solution. The overall business goal of the workflow is the root goal. Being generally abstract and collective, this goal requires a decomposition. The heuristic for deriving the decomposition tree is the core of the functional specification. It works by looking at the Solution and implicit goals. The structure of the Solution provides three workflow patterns (respectively sequence, exclusive choice and structured cycle) that map to the three types of plan. Finally, implicit goals represent the exit cases of the goal decomposition, being mapped one-to-one with the Individual Goals that are leaf goals of the schema. **Individual goals** are always marked as *achievement* goals and their final state derives from the corresponding implicit goal. This procedure is shown in the following Scala code:

```scala
def apply_rule__scheme(s: Solution): Elem = {
  val sol_tree = new SolutionPattern(s)
  val opt_tree: Option[WorkflowPattern] = sol_tree.get_tree

  if (opt_tree.isDefined) {
    val tree : WorkflowPattern = opt_tree.get
    val capabilities = get_solution_capabilities(s)
    val scheme_id = get_scheme_id

    <scheme id={scheme_id}>
    {
    apply_rule__plan(tree)++
    capabilities.map(c=>apply_rule__mission(c))
    }
    </scheme>
  } else {
    <scheme id={get_scheme_id}>
    </scheme>
  }
}
```

The procedure translates the workflow graph into a tree structure (that we call Solu-tionPattern tree), i.e. a decomposition tree ruled by basic workflow patterns [9]. In the specific, the algorithm exploits the control-flow perspective of the solution in order to identify three basic constructs: Sequence patterns, Choice patterns, Loop patterns.

Sequence Pattern: a 'sequence' models consecutive steps in a workflow. Activities A, B, C represent a sequence if the execution of B is enabled after the completion of A, and, the execution of C is enabled after the completion of B. Identification: the translation algorithm supposes the sequence is the default strategy for implementing a workflow when gateways are not present.

Exclusive Choice Pattern: a point in the workflow where the control may pass to one among several branches, depending on the evaluation of a condition. Identification: the translation algorithm supposes a split exclusive gateway starts an Exclusive Choice pattern. Branches are identified as possible sequences that terminates either with the same join exclusive gateway (Simple Merge pattern) or an end event.

Structured Cycle Pattern: a point in the workflow where one or more activities can be executed repeatedly. Identification: the translation algorithm supposes a join exclusive gateway possibly begins a loop, whereas it contains a 'before check' sequence of activi-ties until a split exclusive gateway that provides at least one exit condition, and a loop condition that begins one or more 'after check' sequences that rolling back to the first split gateway.

If the conversion towards a SolutionPattern tree successes, then the schema XML element is built by adding the goal tree element (apply_rule_plan sub-procedure).

In MOISE, each **Mission** cluster several goals, therefore the agent adopting that mission must commit to all of them. We do not have any specific constraint on how roles and goals relates, so we prefer to adopt a one-to-one mapping: one mission for each individual goal. In the previous source code, this mapping appears in the apply_rule_mission sub-procedure.

4.3   Heuristic for the Normative Specification

In MOISE, the agent playing a role must explicitly commit to a mission before starting to address the corresponding goals. Commitment is ruled by the normative specifica-tion. When a role is tie up to a mission, the designer specifies a norm (either obligation or permission) plus a temporal deadline. A permission link states that the involved role is allowed to commit itself to the related mission and to complete the task within a time constraint. Conversely, an obligation states the role ought to commit itself to the related mission with the specified temporal constraint.

So far, the heuristic simply produces a norm for each couple (role-mission) that derives from the same capability. This way, roles are related to their corresponding mission by means of an obligation norm.

Figure 7 summarizes the three perspectives of a MOISE specification for the pro-posed case study. At the bottom, a package describes the structural specification (related to one possible Solution). Above, another package shows a MOISE functional schema representing how the root goal is decomposed in a goal hierarchy. Norms connect the structural and the functional views, by adding obligations between roles and missions.

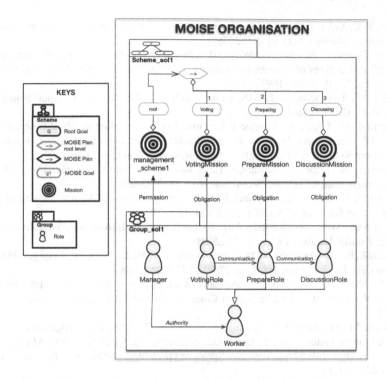

Fig. 7. MOISE organisation schemes and groups for the proposed case study.

5   Conclusions

This paper has presented an automated approach for generating agent organizations for enabling the adaptive execution of a business process. The main steps of the approach are: 1) the automatic generation of goals from the BPMN process, 2) the mapping of goals and service-oriented solutions into schemes of the agent organization, 3) the runtime schema selection according to performance criteria or to overcome a failure (future work). The use of goals relaxes the strict BPMN constraints, thus finding many possible executable workflow for the same business process. This has the advantage of automatically switching among alternative organizational solutions for pursuing the business goal. Therefore, the availability of different organization's schemes allows selecting alternate goal decomposition trees and set of missions that better suite for the problem at hand.

References

1. Boissier, O., Bordini, R.H., Hübner, J.F., Ricci, A., Santi, A.: Multi-agent oriented programming with JaCaMo. Sci. Comput. Program. **78**(6), 747–761 (2013)
2. Bordini, R.H., Hübner, J.F., Wooldridge, M.: Programming Multi-agent Systems in AgentSpeak Using Jason, vol. 8. Wiley, Hoboken (2007)

3. Buhler, P.A., Vidal, J.M.: Towards adaptive workflow enactment using multiagent systems. Inf. Technol. Manage. **6**(1), 61–87 (2005)
4. Ceri, S., Grefen, P., Sanchez, G.: Wide-a distributed architecture for workflow management. In: 1997 Proceedings of Seventh International Workshop on Research Issues in Data Engineering, pp. 76–79. IEEE (1997)
5. Chinosi, M., Trombetta, A.: BPMN: an introduction to the standard. Comput. Stand. Interfaces **34**(1), 124–134 (2012)
6. Cossentino, M., Lopes, S., Sabatucci, L.: Goal-driven adaptation of MOISE organizations for workflow enactment. In: Proceedings of the 8th International Workshop on Engineering Multi-agent Systems (EMAS 2020). National Research Council of Italy (2020)
7. Cossentino, M., Lopes, S., Sabatucci, L.: A tool for the automatic generation of MOISE organisations from BPMN. In: WOA, vol. 1613, p. 69 (2020)
8. Cossentino, M., Lopes, S., Sabatucci, L.: Automatic definition of MOISE organizations for adaptive workflows. In: ICAART (1), pp. 125–136 (2021)
9. van Der Aalst, W.M., Ter Hofstede, A.H., Kiepuszewski, B., Barros, A.P.: Workflow patterns. Distrib. Parallel Databases **14**(1), 5–51 (2003)
10. Gottschalk, F., Van Der Aalst, W.M., Jansen-Vullers, M.H., La Rosa, M.: Configurable workflow models. Int. J. Cooper. Inf. Syst. **17**(02), 177–221 (2008)
11. Han, Y., Sheth, A., Bussler, C.: A taxonomy of adaptive workflow management. In: Workshop of the 1998 ACM Conference on Computer Supported Cooperative Work, pp. 1–11 (1998)
12. Hannoun, M., Boissier, O., Sichman, J.S., Sayettat, C.: MOISE: an organizational model for multi-agent systems. In: Monard, M.C., Sichman, J.S. (eds.) IBERAMIA/SBIA -2000. LNCS (LNAI), vol. 1952, pp. 156–165. Springer, Heidelberg (2000). https://doi.org/10.1007/3-540-44399-1_17
13. Laukkanen, M., Helin, H.: Composing workflows of semantic web services. In: Cavedon, L., Maamar, Z., Martin, D., Benatallah, B. (eds.) Extending Web Services Technologies, pp. 209–228. Springer, Boston (2004). https://doi.org/10.1007/0-387-23344-X_10
14. Object Management Group (OMG): Business Process Model and Notation (BPMN 2.0) by Example (2010). https://www.omg.org/cgi-bin/doc?dtc/10-06-02.pdf
15. Rao, A.S., Georgeff, M.P., et al.: BDI agents: from theory to practice. In: ICMAS, vol. 95, pp. 312–319 (1995)
16. Reichert, M., Dadam, P.: Adept flex–supporting dynamic changes of workflows without losing control. J. Intell. Inf. Syst. **10**(2), 93–129 (1998)
17. Ricci, A., Viroli, M., Omicini, A.: Programming MAS with artifacts. In: Bordini, R.H., Dastani, M.M., Dix, J., El Fallah Seghrouchni, A. (eds.) ProMAS 2005. LNCS (LNAI), vol. 3862, pp. 206–221. Springer, Heidelberg (2006). https://doi.org/10.1007/11678823_13
18. Sabatucci, L., Cossentino, M.: From means-end analysis to proactive means-end reasoning. In: Proceedings of the 10th International Symposium on Software Engineering for Adaptive and Self-Managing Systems, pp. 2–12. IEEE Press (2015)
19. Sabatucci, L., Cossentino, M.: Self-adaptive smart spaces by proactive means-end reasoning. J. Reliable Intell. Environ. **3**(3), 159–175 (2017)
20. Sabatucci, L., Cossentino, M.: Supporting dynamic workflows with automatic extraction of goals from BPMN. ACM Trans. Auton. Adapt. Syst. (TAAS) **14**(2), 1–38 (2019)
21. Sabatucci, L., Lopes, S., Cossentino, M.: Self-configuring cloud application mashup with goals and capabilities. Clust. Comput. **20**(3), 2047–2063 (2017). https://doi.org/10.1007/s10586-017-0911-7
22. Sawhney, M., Zabin, J.: The Seven Steps to Nirvana: Strategic Insights into Ebusiness Transformation. McGraw-Hill, Inc. (2002)
23. Singh, M.P., Huhns, M.N.: Multiagent systems for workflow. Intell. Syst. Account. Financ. Manag. **8**(2), 105–117 (1999)

Negotiation Considering Privacy Loss on Asymmetric Multi-objective Decentralized Constraint Optimization Problem

Toshihiro Matsui[✉][iD]

Nagoya Institute of Technology, Gokiso-cho, Showa-ku,
Nagoya, Aichi 466-8555, Japan
matsui.t@nitech.ac.jp

Abstract. Reducing the information revealed by agents is an important requirement in multiagent systems. Privacy preservation has been studied in several research areas including automated negotiating agents and Distributed Constraint Optimization Problems (DCOPs). Although one of recent approaches for privacy preservation is applying secure computation to negotiation process, publishing some information during the negotiation is necessary in the cases where agents should evaluate the reason of their agreement. We propose a negotiation framework consisting of two types of Asymmetric Multi-Objective DCOPs that are repeatedly solved to gradually publish the utility values of agents until an agreement is reached. One problem defines the selection of utility values that are gradually published by agents while another is the problem consist of the published utility values and related assignments to variables. With the general formalization of DCOPs, there are opportunities to represent several classes of negotiation problems. We define several constraints for heuristic strategies that choose the utility values to be published in the next negotiation step. The criterion of social welfare to consider the multiple objectives among individual agents are also introduced. Moreover, we apply two additional preprocessing methods to adjust the utilities among agents by transferring some amount of utility values and to reduce the complexity of the original problem by approximating several relationships of agent pairs. We experimentally evaluate the effect and influence of our proposed approaches including the heuristics to select the published utility information and the additional preprocessing methods.

Keywords: Privacy · Decentralized problem solving · Asymmetric constraint optimization · Multi-objective · Social welfare · Negotiation · Multiagent system

1 Introduction

Information revealed by agents is critical in cooperative problem solving and negotiation in multi-agent systems. Research in automated negotiation agents [5] and distributed constraint optimization problems [2, 20] addresses the privacy of

© Springer Nature Switzerland AG 2022
A. P. Rocha et al. (Eds.): ICAART 2021, LNAI 13251, pp. 85–110, 2022.
https://doi.org/10.1007/978-3-031-10161-8_5

agents. Although several studies employ secure computation that completely restricts access to the information in solution processes [4,6,17,18], a part of the information is necessary so that agents can understand the situation of an agreement.

We focus on a cooperation approach based on a class of asymmetric constraint optimization problems [3] that represents the situation where agents have different individual utility functions [10,11,15]. This problem can be extended as the basis of a negotiation framework that publishes/reveals the selected partial information of constraints and solves problems with published information. An advantage of the approach, which is based on constraint optimization problems, is its ability to formalize general problems.

In a previous work [8], we presented a solution framework that consists of asymmetric constraint optimization problems with the publication of private utility values and a centralized local search method as a mediator. With the approach, agents gradually reveal their information until they agree on the first globally consistent solution. Although the agents locally select utility values to be published by considering the information from the mediator, the published utility values of individual agents are globally aggregated with a traditional summation operator in the optimization process based on the published information.

However, there are opportunities for designing decentralized frameworks without central nodes. In addition, for the problems that consider the utilities and the cost values of the published information for individual agents, the criteria of multiple objectives should be employed. For this class of negotiation, we address to apply decentralized constraint optimization with multiple objectives for individual agents [10].

For problem settings that resemble the previous study, we apply a decentralized framework where agents iteratively negotiate and gradually publish the information of their utilities that are employed to determine a solution of a constraint optimization problem among the agents. The proposed framework incrementally publishes the utility values in constraints for agents to restrict the revealed information and solves the problems with only the published information until a termination condition of the negotiation process.

In recent study, distributed constraint optimization problems with cost values to obtain the information of objective functions was proposed [19]. The study addresses an extended class of fundamental distributed constraint optimization problems and assumes that the cost values to retrieve the information can be directly evaluated in the solution process. We focus on the formalization and solution methods based on asymmetric multi-objective constraint optimization approach for preferences of individual agents to design a negotiation framework.

In our framework, we represent two problems to select the newly published information of utility values and to find the optimal solution based on the published utility values as decentralized asymmetric multi-objective constraint optimization problems. We investigate opportunities to design constraints that define the simple strategies of agents to determine the utility values to be published. For the objectives of individual agents, we also apply several social welfare functions. In addition, we apply several preprocessing methods to reduce complexity of problems and to trade utility between agents. Our experimental results

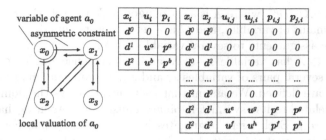

x_i	u_i	p_i	x_i	x_j	$u_{i,j}$	$u_{j,i}$	$p_{i,j}$	$p_{j,i}$
d^0	0	0	d^0	d^0	0	0	0	0
d^1	u^a	p^a	d^0	d^1	0	0	0	0
d^2	u^b	p^b	d^0	d^2	0	0	0	0
...	...		...	...	...	...	...	...
			d^2	d^0	0	0	0	0
			d^2	d^1	u^e	u^g	p^e	p^g
			d^2	d^2	u^f	u^h	p^f	p^h

Fig. 1. Asymmetric multi-objective DCOP with publication cost [8,9].

demonstrate the influence and effect of criteria to select published information of constraint.

The following are our contributions: (1) the fundamental design of a negotiation framework that applies a decentralized constraint optimization approach with criteria for multiple objectives among individual agents; (2) an investigation of the composite constraints of the fundamental strategies to determine newly published utility values; (3) application of several preprocessing techniques, including the approximation of problems to reduce the combination of assignments; and (4) an experimental investigation on the influences different settings of utility and corresponding cost valuers for published information.

This paper is an extended version of a previous work [9]. We improved its description, applied several preprocessing methods to modify the original problem, and presented additional experimental results.

The rest of the paper is organized as follows. In the next section, we present the background of our study, including the problem definitions, the optimization criteria, and the basis of the solution methods by referring previous studies. Then we present a framework with complete decentralized constraint optimization methods that iterates the rounds of the negotiation process to gradually publish utility values by considering the publication cost in Sect. 3. We also present several additional preprocessing methods to modify the original problem for approximation and trade among agents in Sect. 4. We experimentally investigate the proposed approach in Sect. 5, address discussions in Sect. 6, and conclude in Sect. 7.

2 Background

2.1 Asymmetric Constraint Optimization Problem with Cost of Private Information to Be Published

In our previous study, we presented a fundamental solution framework based on an asymmetric constraint optimization problem with the publication of constraints and a central processing that performs a local search [8]. Here we address a similar problem with a decentralized solution framework.

In an asymmetric constraint optimization problem with the publication of constraints, agents select the publicity of each utility value in the constraints by considering their privacy cost values. This problem is defined by

$\langle A, X, D, C, P, X^p, D^p \rangle$, where A is a set of agents, X is a set of variables, D is a set of the domains of variables, and C is a set of constraints defining the utility values for the assignments to several variables in X.

Agent $a_i \in A$ has variable $x_i \in X$ and unary constraint $u_i \in C$ for the variable. For several pairs of variables x_i and x_j, asymmetric binary constraints $u_{i,j}, u_{j,i} \in C$ are defined. We assum that each agent knows the domains of the peer agents related to its asymmetric binary constraints. Agent a_i has $u_{i,j}$, and agent a_j has $u_{j,i}$. Each agent aggregates its own utility value for unary and binary constraints that are related to the agent. The utility values are defined as $u_i : D_i \to \mathbb{N}_0$ and $u_{i,j} : D_i \times D_j \to \mathbb{N}_0$. The functions are also denoted by $u_i(d)$ and $u_{i,j}(d_i, d_j)$.

P is a set of privacy cost values for the utility values in the constraints. $p_i \in P$ corresponds to u_i, and $p_{i,j} \in P$ corresponds to $u_{i,j}$. The privacy cost values are individually evaluated by each agent to select its related utility value to be published. The cost values of the constraints are defined as $p_i : D_i \to \mathbb{N}_0$ and $p_{i,j} : D_i \times D_j \to \mathbb{N}_0$. The functions are also denoted by $p_i(d)$ and $p_{i,j}(d_i, d_j)$.

Figure 1 shows an example of a directed constraint graph and related function tables for the part of a problem.

X^p and D^p are a set of binary variables and a set of the domains of the variables that represent the publication of the utility values. When a utility value in a constraint is published, its corresponding variable takes 1. Otherwise, it takes 0. Variable $x^p_{i,(d)} \in X^p$ corresponds to utility value $u_i(d)$ in unary constraint u_i. Similarly, variable $x^p_{i,j,(d,d')} \in X^p$ corresponds to utility value $u_{i,j}(d, d')$ of assignments $d \in D_i$ and $d' \in D_j$ in asymmetric binary constraint $u_{i,j}$. If at least one of $x^p_{i,j,(d,d')}$ takes 1, $x^p_{i,(d)}$ is set to 1.

For each variable $x_i \in X$, value $d^0 \in D_i$ represents a special case where an agent does not cooperate with any other agents. Value d^0 is selected by several agents when no solution can be globally evaluated with utility functions whose utility values have been partially published. For assignment d^0 to variable x_i, corresponding utility value $u_i(d^0)$ and privacy cost value $p_i(d^0)$ take zero. Similarly, $u_{i,j}(d^0, d)$, $u_{i,j}(d, d^0)$, and the corresponding privacy cost values take zero. Value d^0 is given as a common value in the domains of all the variables, and the corresponding zero utility/privacy cost values are also commonly defined for all the functions. Unpublished utility values related to assignment d^0 are defined as $-\infty$. Evaluations $v_i(d)$ and $v_{i,j}(d, d')$ for a unary constraint and an asymmetric binary constraint are represented by the following:

$$v_i(d) = \begin{cases} u_i(d) & \text{if } x^p_{i,(d)} = 1 \\ -\infty & \text{otherwise,} \end{cases} \tag{1}$$

$$v_{i,j}(d, d') = \begin{cases} u_{i,j}(d, d') & \text{if } x^p_{i,j,(d,d')} = 1 \\ -\infty & \text{otherwise.} \end{cases} \tag{2}$$

With an assignment to the related variables in X^p, local valuation $f_i(\mathcal{D}_i)$ for agent a_i and assignment $\mathcal{D}_i$ to the related variables in X is defined as the summation of the evaluations for its own unary constraint and the asymmetric binary constraints for the neighborhood agents in Nbr_i that are related to i by constraints:

$$f_i(\mathcal{D}_i) = v_i(d_i) + \sum_{j \in Nbr_i} v_{i,j}(d_i, d_j) , \qquad (3)$$

where d_i and d_j are the values of x_i and x_j in assignment $\mathcal{D}_i$.

The problem's goal is the maximization of the globally aggregated valuations for all f_i.

$$\text{maximize} \quad \oplus_{a_i \in A} f_i(\mathcal{D}_i) \qquad (4)$$

Altough a typical aggregation operator of the valuations is the summation of the values, different operators can be applied in the case of multi-objective problems among the individual utilities of the agents (Sect. 2.2).

To avoid the utility value of $-\infty$ in Eqs. (1) and (2), value d^0 can be assigned to several agents' variables if no other solutions can be evaluated with the published part of the utility functions. However, such a situation can also be avoided, since the utility value that corresponds to value d^0 is zero.

The agent can partially publish the utility values of its own utility functions. The total published cost of agent a_i is defined:

$$\sum_{d \in D_i \text{ s.t. } x^P_{i,(d)}=1} p_i(d) + \sum_{j \in Nbr_i, d \in D_i, d' \in D_j \text{ s.t. } x^P_{i,j,(d,d')}=1} p_{i,j}(d, d'). \qquad (5)$$

One problem is how to determine the utility values to be published within a budget. We consider a scheme of a negotiation process where agents iteratively publish their utility values based on the situations in each round of the process.

2.2 Criteria and Measurement of Social Welfare

When we consider the objectives of individual agents, several operators $\oplus$ and corresponding criteria aggregate/compare the objectives, as shown in Eq. (4). For multi-objective problems, several types of social welfare [16] and scalarization methods [7] are employed to handle the objectives. In addition to the traditional summation operator and the comparison on scalar values, we employ leximin and maximin with a tie-break by a summation value; they are also employed in a solution method [10]. We solve our problem employing a solution method in the previous study and also inherit these operators and criteria. Although these operators and criteria are designed for the maximization problems of utilities, they can be easily modified for minimization problems.

Summation $\sum_{a_i \in A} f_i$ only considers the total utilities. Even though maximin $\max \min_{a_i \in A} f_i$ improves the worst case utility value, it fails to consider the whole utilities and is not Pareto optimal. Therefore, ties are additionally broken by comparing summation values. Leximin can be considered an extension of maximin where the objective values are represented as a vector whose values are sorted in ascending order, and the comparison of two vectors is based on a dictionary order of their values. Maximization with leximin is Pareto optimal and improves the fairness among objectives. See the literature for details [7, 10, 16].

To measure the degree of unfairness among agents in a resulting solution, we also employ the Theil index, which is based on entropy: $T = \frac{1}{N} \sum_{i=1}^{N} \left(\frac{x_i}{\bar{x}} \ln \frac{x_i}{\bar{x}} \right)$, where $\bar{x}$ denotes the average value for all x_i. T increases with the unfairness among the value of x_i and takes zero if all x_i are equal.

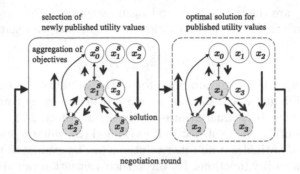

Fig. 2. A negotiation framework [9].

2.3 Decentralized Complete Solution Method for Asymmetric Multi-objective Constraint Optimization Problems Based on Pseudo-trees and Dynamic Programming

A class of asymmetric constraint optimization problems with individual objectives of agents and decentralized complete solution methods was proposed [10]. Its' goal was the application of a social welfare criterion called leximin to pseudo-tree-based solution methods to improve the fairness among agents. As mentioned above, with leximin, the individual objectives of agents are aggregated and optimized improving the worst case and fairness among the objectives. In addition to leximin, several social welfare criteria were compared, including summation and maximin.

The solution methods are extended versions of dynamic programming and tree-search based on the pseudo-trees of constraint graphs. A pseudo-tree is a structure on a constraint graph that decomposes problems [12,14]. A pseudo-tree is based on a depth-first search tree on a constraint graph. The edges of the original graph are categorized into tree edges of the depth-first search tree and other back edges. Several optimization methods are performed along the spanning tree considering back edges. For asymmetric problems, the pseudo-tree and solution methods are modified so that both agents, which are related to each other by a pair of asymmetric constraints, can evaluate the assignments to the opposite agent's variable. By this modification, the value of each variable is determined by an agent in the higher level of a pseudo-tree that is related to the variable by a constraint. Figure 2 shows a simple example of the modified pseudo-trees in part of the proposed framework.

In this study, we employ a variant of a pseudo-tree-based dynamic programming method called DPOP [14], which was extended in the previous study [10], because it is a relatively simple basis of our extension. The main part of the solution method consists of two phases. In the first phase, each agent aggregates the optimal utility/cost values for the assignments to the related variables whose values are determined by the agents in the higher level of a pseudo-tree in a bottom-up manner. After the optimal utility value is computed at the root agent, in the second phase, the optimal assignment to the variable is deter mined in a top-down manner. See the literature for details [10].

Note that its scalability is limited for complex problems. When problems are densely constrained, the tree width of pseudo-trees, corresponding to the maximum number of combinations of variables in partial problems for agents, grows and causes a combinational explosion. However, for a fundamental investigation, we concentrate on the problems that can be addressed with this class of simple and complete solution methods. We employ two variants of the solution method for our problem definitions.

3 Decentralized Solution Framework for Selection of Utility Values to Be Published and Solution of Published Problems

3.1 Basic Design of Proposed Framework

We propose a framework that alternates two optimization methods to select the utility values to be published and solve the current problem with published utilities. For both optimization methods, we employ a decentralized dynamic programming method based on pseudo-trees as mentioned above. For simplicity, both methods employ a common pseudo-tree. For the first investigation, we focus on the process that incrementally publishes the utility values of the constraints/functions. While arbitrary conditions and parameters to control and stop the publication process can be defined, we evaluate relatively fundamental ones.

The framework iterates negotiation rounds among agents, and utility values are incrementally published. In each round, the utility values to be published are selected, and the next problem with the published utility values is solved. Similar to the previous methods, in the optimization for the problem with published utility values, the globally aggregated utility is maximized under an criterion.

3.2 Selection of Newly Published Utility Values

In the phase of the selecting utility values to be published, agents iteratively publish a part of the utility values of their own constraints in each negotiation round. As defined in Sect. 2.1, the decision variables of agent a_i in this problem are originally $x_i^p, x_{i,j}^p \in X^p$ for Nbr_i. In the initial state, all the variables in X^p are initialized by zero and set to one when their corresponding utility values are published. However, the solution space for the variables in X^p is too huge to explore especially for the complete solution method that is employed in this study. Therefore, we define another problem for this negotiation to restrict the number of solutions.

The problem is defined by $\langle A, X^s, D, C^s \rangle$. Here we introduce new decision variables X^s. For agent a_i, a decision variable $x_i^s \in X^s$ is defined. Variable x_i^s takes a value from $D_i \in D$ that is identical as a part of the decision variables in the original problem. Assigning d and d' to x_i^s and x_j^s denotes that utility values $u_i(d)$ and $u_{i,j}(d, d')$ are published in the next round of negotiation. When x_i^s takes special variable value d^0, it means that no utility values related to x_i are newly published. In addition, if a utility value corresponding to d and d' have already been published, the published utility value does not change the current situation. At the end of each round, several original variables in X^p are set to one by translating the solution for X^s. If an assignment to variable $x_i^p \in X^p$ or $x_{i,j}^p \in X^p$ is changed from zero to one, its corresponding utility value is newly published.

The structure of this problem that determines the utility values to be published for the next problem resembles the maximization problem with published utility values. The variables and their domains are identical to the maximization problem for the utility values. However, it is defined as a minimization problem with cost values for the published utility values. Constraints $c_i \in C^s$ are asymmetrically defined for each agent a_i. Here the cost values related to a constraint can take a real number to represent ratio values. Several cost values for the constraints can be defined based on different publication strategies and integrated as vectors with a structure. We investigate the fundamental strategies in Sects. 3.3 and 3.4.

3.3   Evaluation Criteria for Utility Values to Be Published

We use the following criteria to evaluate the situation of the newly published utility values that are represented by an assignment to variables in X^s. We assume that some information about the status of the published utility values is available in the evaluation. Such information can be collected by simple additional protocols.

R) Ratio of Revealed Privacy Cost. We assume that the information of the published cost values can be employed in the negotiation of agents by modifying them to the ratio values of the locally aggregated cost values so that the ratio values only represent a normalized degree of dissatisfaction. For each agent, the ratio of the privacy cost values between the total values for the published utilities and for all the constraints is defined as a criterion:

$$c_i^R(\mathcal{D}_i^s) = (x_{i,(d_i)}^{p+} * p_i(d_i) + \sum_{j \in Nbr_i} x_{i,j,(d_i,d_j)}^{p+} * p_{i,j}(d_i, d_j))/ \qquad (6)$$

$$(\sum_{d \in D_i} p_i(d) + \sum_{j \in Nbr_j, d \in D_i, d' \in D_j} p_{i,j}(d, d')) ,$$

where d_i is the value of x_i^s in assignment $\mathcal{D}_i^s$. The values of variables $x_{i,(d)}^{p+}$ and $x_{i,j,(d,d')}^{p+}$ equal $x_{i,(d)}^p$ and $x_{i,j,(d,d')}^p$, respectively if x_i^s and x_j^s do not represent the publication of the corresponding utility values. Otherwise, $x_{i,(d)}^{p+}$ and $x_{i,j,(d,d')}^{p+}$ are set to one.

Since agents might relate different numbers of constraints and utility values, the above ratio value is also considered.

A) Agreement Opportunity Estimated by Degree of Unpublished Utility Values. For each value d of each agent's variable x_i^s, the number of unpublished utility values that are related to the variable's value is considered as a criterion. For $x_i^s = d_i$,

$$c_i^A(d_i) = 2|\{(d_i, d_j)|j \in Nbr_i, d_j \in D_j, d_i = d^0 \vee d_j = d^0\}| \qquad (7)$$
$$+ |\{x_{i,j,(d_i,d_j)}^p|j \in Nbr_i, d_j \in D_j, d_i \neq d^0 \wedge d_j \neq d^0, x_{i,j,(d_i,d_j)}^p = 0\}|$$

We employ this criterion by considering that when the number of unpublished utilities that relates the assignment for newly published utility values is relatively large, the opportunity is relatively small for agreement among agents with the assignment. For the assignment of d^0 that represents no publication for a pair of variables' values, the count of an unpublished utility for the assignment is doubled for emphasis.

U) Utility Publication Progress. Since the cost values for the revealed information restrict the publishing of utility values, a counterpart of the cost values is necessary to continue the publication process. Here we employ a ratio of the published utility values:

$$c_i^U(\mathcal{D}_i^s) = |\{x_{i,j,(d_i,d_j)}^p|j \in Nbr_i, x_{i,j,(d_i,d_j)}^p = 1\}|/ \sum_{j \in Nbr_i} |D_i| \times |D_j|. \qquad (8)$$

As addressed below, this cost value is combined with other criteria so that it has a higher priority than the others.

T) Trade-Off Measurement for Publication Cost and Utility. The above criteria do not employ the information of utility value. To address the expected gain of the utility by publishing utility values, the information of utility values should be considered. However, the utility values are originally hidden until their publication. As abstract information, we employ the ratio of the trade-off values, which are locally aggregated, as difference values between the expected utility values and the cost values of the published utility values.

Since the optimal utility value is unknown, each agent employs rough upper and lower bound values of the trade-off:

$$trd_i(\mathcal{D}_i^s)^\top = u_i(d_i) + \sum_{j \in Nbr_i} u_{i,j}(d_i, d_j) - rvl_i(\mathcal{D}_i^s), \qquad (9)$$

$$trd_i(\mathcal{D}_i^s)^\perp = u_i(d_i) - rvl_i(\mathcal{D}_i^s), \qquad (10)$$

$$rvl_i(\mathcal{D}_i^s) = x_{i,(d_i)}^{p+} * p_i(d_i) + \sum_{j \in Nbr_i} x_{i,j,(d_i,d_j)}^{p+} * p_{i,j}(d_i, d_j). \qquad (11)$$

Although arbitrary estimation values between the bounds can be employed, we investigate simple cases for a fundamental analysis. Estimation trade-off value $trd_i(\mathcal{D}_i^s)$ is set to $trd_i(\mathcal{D}_i^s)^\perp$, $(trd_i(\mathcal{D}_i^s)^\top + trd_i(\mathcal{D}_i^s)^\perp)/2$ or $trd_i(\mathcal{D}_i^s)^\top$. Then the ratio of the trade-off value is employed as a criterion:

$$c_i^T(\mathcal{D}_i^s) = 1 - (trd_i(\mathcal{D}_i^s) - trd_i^\perp)/(trd_i^\top - trd_i^\perp), \tag{12}$$

$$trd_i^\top = u_i(d_i) + \sum_{j \in Nbr_i} \max_{d_i \in D_i, d_j \in D_j} u_{i,j}(d_i, d_j), \tag{13}$$

$$trd_i^\perp = -(\sum_{d \in D_i} p_i(d) + \sum_{j \in Nbr_j, d \in D_i, d' \in D_j} p_{i,j}(d, d')). \tag{14}$$

S) Switching Trade-Off Measurement Based on Degree of Newly Published Utility Values. The above cost values except U need energy to continue the publication process. We modified previous criteria T to conditionally continue the publication process. Modified cost $c_i^S(\mathcal{D}_i^s)$ is defined as follows. First, we evaluate the cost value for the newly published utility values:

$$rvl_i^{new}(\mathcal{D}_i^s) = (x_{i,(d_i)}^{p+} - x_{i,(d_i)}^p) * p_i(d_i) \tag{15}$$

$$+ \sum_{j \in Nbr_i} (x_{i,j,(d_i,d_j)}^{p+} - x_{i,j,(d_i,d_j)}^p) * p_{i,j}(d_i, d_j)$$

$$c_i^S(\mathcal{D}_i^s) = \begin{cases} 0 & rvl^{new} = 0 \\ -(trd_i(\mathcal{D}_i^s) - trd_i^\perp)/(trd_i^\top - trd_i^\perp) & rvl^{new} \neq 0 \wedge trd_i(\mathcal{D}_i^s) > 0 \\ c_i^T(\mathcal{D}_i^s) & \text{otherwise} \end{cases}$$
$$\tag{16}$$

With this criterion, the publication is preferred by a negative cost value when $trd_i(\mathcal{D}_i^s) > 0$.

H) Hard Constraint for Termination. We also introduce cost value $c^H(\mathcal{D}_i^s)$ of a hard constraint for the assignments that should be avoided. The value of $c^H(\mathcal{D}_i^s)$ is one or zero and represents violation or satisfaction. This cost value have the first priority in all types of cost values. We employ $c^H(\mathcal{D}_i^s)$ for a termination condition based on above the trade-off value. $c^H(\mathcal{D}_i^s) = 1$ if $rvl_i^{new}(\mathcal{D}_i^s) > 0 \wedge trd_i(\mathcal{D}_i^s) < 0$. Otherwise, $c^H(\mathcal{D}_i^s) = 0$. This constraint inhibits the publication with a negative trade-off value where an estimated utility value is less than the total publish cost.

3.4   Hierarchically Structured Cost Vector Integrating Criteria for Publication of Utility Values

The above criteria can be combined as hierarchically structured cost vectors, and the optimization method solves a minimization problem on them to determine the utility values to be newly published. Hard constraint H is most prioritized. Since criteria R, A and T with higher priorities will cause quicker convergence without publication of sufficient utility values, cost U should be secondarily prioritized. S can be used without U. T and S consider a trade-off between estimation utility and total publish cost, while R and A do not evaluate the utility values. Considering these properties, we investigate the following combinations of criteria:

- S: $c^H \gg c^S$
- UAR: $c^H \gg c^U \gg c^A \gg c^R$
- URA: $c^H \gg c^U \gg c^R \gg c^A$
- UT: $c^H \gg c^U \gg c^T$.

Here no aggregated cost values exceed a cost value with a higher priority.

For two hierarchically structured cost vectors $\boldsymbol{v} = [v_1, \cdots, v_k]$ and $\boldsymbol{v}' = [v'_1, \cdots, v'_k]$, the aggregation of the vectors is defined as $\boldsymbol{v} \oplus \boldsymbol{v}' = [v_1 \oplus v'_1, \cdots, v_k \oplus v'_k]$. Comparison $\boldsymbol{v} < \boldsymbol{v}'$ is defined as $\exists t, \forall t' < t, v_{t'} = v'_{t'} \wedge v_t < v'_t$.

We also investigate the cases where the elements of the vectors are aggregated/compared using several criteria for multiple objectives for individual agents, including summation, lexicographic augmented weighted Tchebycheff function [7], and leximax. The lexicographic augmented weighted Tchebycheff function is a criterion that minimizes the maximum value. The ties of maximum values are broken by the summation values. Leximax is a modified leximin for the minimization problems.

3.5 Solving Problems with Published Utility Values

After the newly published utility values are determined in each negotiation round, agents can solve a problem with the currently published utility values, as shown in Sect. 2.1. We only evaluate the anytime property for the rounds of negotiation as our first study, while this result might be employed as feedback to the agents' strategies.

4 Additional Preprocessing Methods

4.1 Trading Utility Between Neighborhood Agents

Although the main part of our proposed solution framework does not modify the utility values between agents, there are opportunities to trade utility with incentives. We focus on the case where agents consider their degree (i.e., the number of neighborhood agents) and export a part of their utility to their neighborhood agents. In particular, we investigate the influence in two simple cases where the partial utility values are exported from agents of higher or lower degree to their neighborhood agents.

Utility value $u'_{i \to j}(d_j)$ transfered from agent a_i to a_j is aggregated for unary and binary constraints related to source agent a_i:

$$u'_{i \to j}(d_j) = \begin{cases} 0 & \text{if } d_j = d^0 \\ w^{trd} \times \max_{d_i \in D_i \setminus \{d^0\}} (u_i(d_i) + u_{i,j}(d_i, d_j) + & \text{otherwise} \\ \quad \sum_{j' \in Nbr_i \setminus \{j\}} \min_{d'_j \in D'_j \setminus \{d^0\}} u_{i,j'}(d_i, d'_j)) & \end{cases} \quad (17)$$

where w^{trd} is a weight parameter in $[0,1]$. In the above equation, value d^0 of the variables is excluded from the aggregation. Although the transfered utility is optimistically maximized for the assignments to the variables of source agent

a_i and destination agent a_j, it is pessimistically minimized for the assignments to the variables of other neighborhood agents. We chose a relatively small w^{trd} in comparison to the utility values.

Then $u'_{i \to j}(d_j)$ is added to unary utility function $u_j(d_j)$ of destination agent j. Finally, the value of $u'_{i \to j}(d_j)$ is subtracted from the values of the utility functions related to source agent i. We evenly subtract the exported value from the values of the utility functions for the assignment corresponding to $u'_{i \to j}(d_j)$ as much as possible.

4.2   Approximation of Binary Functions

For a fundamental investigation, we employ an exact solution method based on dynamic programming that is performed according to pseudo-trees on constraint graphs. However, such an exact algorithm cannot be applied to densely constrained problems due to the large tree width of pseudo-trees. In the case of our asymmetric settings, the assignment of both variables related to each binary constraint must be managed by the agent in the higher level of a pseudo-tree as shown in Fig. 2. This doubles the size of the combination of variables contained in the local problems of the agents. Therefore, the limitation of tree width is a serious issue even though the constraint density is not so large. Similar to several approximation methods for fundamental solvers based on pseudo-trees [11, 13], we apply an approximation method to reduce the tree width by eliminating their back edges.

After a pseudo-tree is generated, its tree width is reduced. First, the agent with the maximum induced width, which corresponds the number of back edges plus one tree edge at the agent, is selected. Then a back edge that relates the selected agent is chosen. We consider the following ordering rule of edges. (1) The edge with the maximum band width (i.e., the number of nodes/agents between the end nodes of a back edge) has the first priority to be eliminated. (2) The edge with the endpoint of the highest degree (i.e., the number of connected edges) has the second priority for a tie-break. The selected back edge is eliminated, and the related functions of the asymmetric binary constraints are approximated to the unary constraints of the related agents.

Note that we address the case of asymmetric binary constraints. Therefore, one of the two functions for each edge is owned by an agent and approximated to a unary function for the owner agent. On the other hand, we have to approximate both the utility and publication cost values. Generally, a pessimistic approximation is reasonable, since it assures a lower bound evaluation value when the agents that are related to an eliminated binary constraint do not consider the consistency between their assignments. Here we employ the following approximation.

For the utility values of a binary constraint, the minimum utility value is selected

$$u'_i(d_i) = \begin{cases} 0 & \text{if } d_i = d^0 \\ \min_{d_j \in D_j \setminus \{d^0\}} u_{i,j}(d_i, d_j) & \text{otherwise.} \end{cases} \tag{18}$$

Then the publish cost value corresponding to the minimum utility value is selected:

$$p'_i(d_i) = \begin{cases} 0 & \text{if } d_i = d^0 \\ \max_{d'_j \in \{d|d=\text{argmin}_{d_j} u_{i,j}(d_i,d_j)\}} p_{i,j}(d_i, d'_j) & \text{otherwise.} \end{cases} \quad (19)$$

For the same value of minimum $u_{i,j}(d_i, d_j)$, the maximum publish cost value is selected.

Finally, the approximated unary functions are aggregated with the original unary functions, and the related binary functions are removed.

5   Evaluation

5.1   Settings of Experiment

We empirically evaluated our proposed approach. As motioned above, we employed relatively small scale and sparse problems due to the limitations of dynamic programming on a pseudo-tree. A problem consists of n variables/agents/unary-constraints and c pairs of asymmetric binary constraints. For a pair of variables, we defined a pair of asymmetric constraints. The size of the variables' domain including d^0 was commonly set to four. The utility values of the constraints were randomly set to integer values in $[10, 50]$ based on uniform distribution. The privacy cost values were set as follows:

- equ: A privacy cost value for utility value u is integer value $\lfloor \max(1, u/10) \rfloor$, and there is a positive correlation between the utility and privacy cost values.
- inv: A privacy cost value for utility value u is integer value $\lfloor \max(1, (50 - u + 1)/10) \rfloor$, and there is a negative correlation for the values.
- rnd: Random integer values in $[1, 5]$ are based on uniform distribution.

We also evaluated the cases of different asymmetry of constraints as shown in following Sect. 5.2.

As shown in Sect. 3.4, we compared the influence of several combinations of criteria for selecting published utility values that are denoted by S, UAR, URA and UT. In addition, as shown in Sect. 3.3, the estimated trade-off values for criterion T, S, and H are set to the minimum/average/maximum values of the lower and upper bounds denoted by tmin/tave/tmax.

We also applied different aggregation/comparison operators of objectives, including summation, the maximum/minimum value with tie-break by summation, and leximin/leximax on utility/privacy-cost values/vectors:

- sum: summation for both minimization problems determining the published utility values and the maximization problems of the utilities under published utility values.
- ms: the maximum/minimum value with a tie-break by summation for the minimization/maximization problems for publication/utility.
- lxm: leximax/leximin for the minimization/maximization problems for publication/utility.

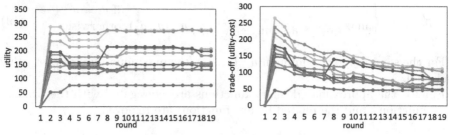

Each curve corresponds to an agent.

Fig. 3. Utility and trade-off of agents ($n = 10$, $c = 20$, equ, S, lxm) [9].

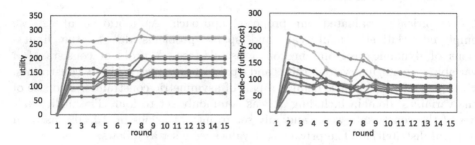

Fig. 4. Utility and trade-off of agents ($n = 10$, $c = 20$, equ, URA, lxm) [9].

– summs: summation value for the minimization problems for publication and the minimum value with tie-break by summation for the maximization problem for utility.
– sumlxm: summation value for the minimization problems for publication and leximin for the maximization problem for utility.

Two preprocessing methods shown in Sect. 4 to transfer utility values among agents and to limit the tree width of pseudo-trees are also evaluated with the optimization criteria above.

We assumed a simple termination condition where an accumulated publish cost exceeds the estimated utility for next publication. In this case, such an agent does not select a corresponding assignment. When no agents do select a new publication, the negotiation process terminates.

For each setting, the results are averaged over ten instances.

5.2   Experimental Results

Anytime Curve of Resulting Utility and Trade-Off Values for Agents.
Figures 3 and 4 show the typical anytime-curves of utility and trade-off. Each curve in the graphs corresponds to an agent. While the utility values almost converge in earlier rounds, the trade-off values decrease until a termination. Therefore, an issue is the selection of the published utility values within a budget;

Table 1. Influence of priorities on criteria for utility values to be published ($n = 10$, $c = 20$, equ, sum) [9].

(a) Termination round, utility and trade-off

alg.	term.	utiliy				trade-off		
	round	sum.	min.	ave.	max	min.	ave.	max.
sum, S, tmin	6.7	1620.9	97.4	162.1	225.0	**76.9**	**134.1**	**194.2**
sum, S, tave	21.2	1763.2	**110.2**	176.3	248.8	46.7	88.3	127.9
sum, S, tmax	21.8	**1773.1**	103.0	**177.3**	**254.3**	30.9	77.3	115.4
sum, UAR, tmin	6.1	1560.6	95.6	156.1	223.4	72.8	124.2	187.3
sum, UAR, tave	13.9	1770.1	106.3	177.0	251.9	39.2	84.4	123.0
sum, UAR, tmax	11.9	**1773.1**	103.0	**177.3**	**254.3**	30.9	77.3	115.4
sum, URA, tmin	6.0	1526.6	90.2	152.7	219.0	64.7	121.1	181.9
sum, URA, tave	14.8	1762.1	107.1	176.2	253.1	38.5	83.0	124.3
sum, URA, tmax	13.7	**1773.1**	103.0	177.3	**254.3**	30.9	77.3	115.4
sum, UT, tmin	5.5	1598.4	97.6	159.8	225.4	76.2	130.5	190.5
sum, UT, tave	16.3	1764.2	103.2	176.4	251.9	41.3	86.8	129.4
sum, UT, tmax	13.4	**1773.1**	103.0	**177.3**	**254.3**	30.9	77.3	115.4

(b) Ratio of revealed information

alg.	ratio. rvl. num.			ratio. rvl. cost		
	min.	ave.	max.	min.	ave.	max.
sum, S, tmin	**0.181**	**0.291**	**0.429**	**0.178**	**0.292**	**0.435**
sum, S, tave	0.763	0.856	0.934	0.805	0.884	0.961
sum, S, tmax	1	1	1	1	1	1
sum, UAR, tmin	0.245	0.357	0.482	0.211	0.330	0.478
sum, UAR, tave	0.859	0.929	0.985	0.854	0.929	0.988
sum, UAR, tmax	1	1	1	1	1	1
sum, URA, tmin	0.248	0.359	0.488	0.212	0.328	0.472
sum, URA, tave	0.881	0.938	0.991	0.865	0.934	0.987
sum, URA, tmax	1	1	1	1	1	1
sum, UT, tmin	0.193	0.307	0.438	0.191	0.305	**0.453**
sum, UT, tave	0.754	0.873	0.950	0.800	0.898	0.964
sum, UT, tmax	1	1	1	1	1	1

we investigate such opportunities. In these problem settings, the trade-off values are better in the earlier steps for most agents. A major reason is the effect of solution method for the publication of utility values that intends to maximize the estimated utility as much as possible. While there is another reason is that the scale of the accumulated publication cost values are relatively greater than that of utility values, the results resemble even in other cases with different scales of utility and publish cost values. We do not focus on this issue because more

Table 2. Influence of social-welfare criteria for two phases in framework ($n = 10$, $c = 20$, equ, S, same criterion of social welfare) [9].

(a) Termination round, utility and trade-off

alg.	term.	utiliy					trade-off			
	round	sum.	min.	ave.	max	theil	min.	ave.	max.	theil
sum, tmin	6.7	1620.9	97.4	162.1	225	0.032	76.9	**134.1**	194.2	0.039
sum, tave	21.2	1763.2	110.2	176.3	248.8	0.031	46.7	88.3	127.9	0.041
sum, tmax	21.8	**1773.1**	103	**177.3**	**254.3**	0.035	30.9	77.3	115.4	0.061
ms, tmin	6.6	1617.9	110.5	161.8	226.9	0.026	**86.9**	133.3	**194.5**	0.031
ms, tave	20.7	1704.4	126.5	170.4	231.3	0.019	56.9	82.2	118.3	**0.025**
ms, tmax	19.7	1710.2	**126.6**	171.0	232.5	0.020	44.9	71.0	102.8	0.033
lxm, tmin	6.5	1600.3	109.2	160.0	218.9	0.025	84.4	131.5	185.8	0.031
lxm, tave	20	1657.2	125.4	165.7	224	0.020	51.5	78.1	113.1	0.032
lxm, tmax	19.8	1653.8	**126.6**	165.4	219.4	**0.015**	38.6	65.4	90.3	0.033

(b) Ratio of revealed information

alg.	ratio. rvl. num.				ratio. rvl. cost			
	min.	ave.	max.	theil	min.	ave.	max.	theil
sum, tmin	**0.181**	**0.291**	**0.429**	0.032	**0.178**	**0.292**	**0.435**	0.035
sum, tave	0.763	0.856	0.934	0.002	0.805	0.884	0.961	0.002
sum, tmax	1	1	1	**0**	1	1	1	**0**
ms, tmin	0.185	0.298	0.434	0.034	0.184	0.299	0.457	0.037
ms, tave	0.755	0.853	0.940	0.002	0.807	0.885	0.955	0.001
ms, tmax	1	1	1	**0**	1	1	1	**0**
lxm, tmin	0.183	0.295	0.439	0.036	0.181	0.301	0.471	0.040
lxm, tave	0.741	0.849	0.935	0.002	0.784	0.879	0.957	0.002
lxm, tmax	1	1	1	**0**	1	1	1	**0**

sophisticated strategies of agents to terminate the publication will be included our future work based on the investigation in the current study.

Influence of Criteria for Publication of Utility Values. Table 1 shows the results in the final round of the publication process in the case of $n = 10$ variables/agents, the number of pairs of asymmetric binary constraints $c = 20$, equ, and sum. We evaluated the minimum/average/maximum values for the agents:

- utility: the optimal utility value of the problem with published utility values.
- trade-off: the trade-off values, which are the difference values between the utility and the total privacy cost value for the published utility values.
- ratio. rvl. num.: the ratio of revealed number of utility values.

Table 3. Influence of social-welfare criteria for two phases in framework ($n = 10$, $c = 20$, equ, S, combination with summation criterion for first phase) [9].

(a) Termination round, utility and trade-off

alg.	term.	utiliy					trade-off			
	round	sum.	min.	ave.	max	theil	min.	ave.	max.	theil
sum, tmin	6.7	1620.9	97.4	162.1	225	0.032	76.9	**134.1**	**194.2**	0.039
sum, tave	21.2	1763.2	110.2	176.3	248.8	0.031	46.7	88.3	127.9	0.041
sum, tmax	21.8	**1773.1**	103	**177.3**	**254.3**	0.035	30.9	77.3	115.4	0.061
summs, tmin	6.7	1576.5	99.8	157.7	216.4	0.029	**79.1**	129.6	184.4	0.036
summs, tave	21.2	1697.5	**126.6**	169.8	227	0.019	54.7	81.7	114.3	0.026
summs, tmax	21.8	1710.2	**126.6**	171.0	232.5	0.020	44.9	71.0	102.8	0.033
sumlxm, tmin	6.7	1573.4	99.8	157.3	214.6	0.028	**79.1**	129.3	182.6	0.034
sumlxm, tave	21.2	1673.8	**126.6**	167.4	216.8	0.016	53.7	79.3	106.9	**0.022**
sumlxm, tmax	21.8	1653.8	**126.6**	165.4	219.4	**0.015**	38.6	65.4	90.3	0.033

(b) Ratio of revealed information

alg.	ratio. rvl. num.				ratio. rvl. cost			
	min.	ave.	max.	theil	min.	ave.	max.	theil
sum, tmin	**0.181**	**0.291**	**0.429**	0.032	**0.178**	**0.292**	**0.435**	0.035
sum, tave	0.763	0.856	0.934	0.002	0.805	0.884	0.961	0.002
sum, tmax	1	1	1	**0**	1	1	1	**0**
summs, tmin	**0.181**	**0.291**	**0.429**	0.032	**0.178**	**0.292**	**0.435**	0.035
summs, tave	0.763	0.856	0.934	0.002	0.805	0.884	0.961	0.002
summs, tmax	1	1	1	**0**	1	1	1	**0**
sumlxm, tmin	**0.181**	**0.291**	**0.429**	0.032	**0.178**	**0.292**	**0.435**	0.035
sumlxm, tave	0.763	0.856	0.934	0.002	0.805	0.884	0.961	0.002
sumlxm, tmax	1	1	1	**0**	1	1	1	**0**

- ratio. rvl. cost.: the ratio of total privacy cost values for the revealed utility values.

The result shows that the publication process continued until all the utility values are published for the case of estimation trade-off tmax, since this estimation value is too optimistic. In this problem setting, a quicker termination of publication process is relatively better to reduce the privacy cost for obtaining some utility. The trade-off values of criteria S and UT that consider the trade-off between the estimation utility and the total cost of the published utility values are relatively greater than those of the other criteria for tmin that terminates in rather earlier rounds. In the case of tmin, the utility values of UAR are relatively better than URA, since UAR gives priority to consider the opportunities of aggregation. Basically, U enforces publication and dominates other criteria. As a result, the total publication cost is relatively greater than S. In the following, we concentrate on the cases of S for different settings.

Table 4. Influence of social-welfare criteria for two phases in framework ($n = 10$, $c = 20$, inv, S) [9].

(a) Termination round, utility and trade-off

alg.	term.	utiliy					trade-off			
	round	sum.	min.	ave.	max	theil	min.	ave.	max.	theil
sum, tmin	8.6	1703.0	107.2	170.3	235.4	0.029	87.1	**145.6**	**205.4**	0.034
sum, tave	22.6	**1773.1**	103	**177.3**	**254.3**	0.035	50.8	105.4	159.6	0.052
sum, tmax	21.8	**1773.1**	103	**177.3**	**254.3**	0.035	49.2	104.3	159	0.054
ms, tmin	8.5	1668.5	114.5	166.9	233.2	0.027	94.4	141.7	202.5	0.031
ms, tave	21.7	1711.7	**126.6**	171.2	232.5	0.020	69.2	99.2	142.1	0.024
ms, tmax	19.6	1710.2	**126.6**	171.0	232.5	0.020	68.1	98.0	141.3	0.025
lxm, tmin	8.3	1656.8	116.3	165.7	228.7	0.023	**96**	140.9	199.5	0.027
lxm, tave	21.4	1653.8	**126.6**	165.4	219.4	**0.015**	64	93.4	129.5	**0.021**
lxm, tmax	19.8	1653.8	**126.6**	165.4	219.4	**0.015**	63.3	92.4	128.7	0.022

(b) Ratio of revealed information

alg.	ratio. rvl. num.				ratio. rvl. cost			
	min.	ave.	max.	theil	min.	ave.	max.	theil
sum, tmin	0.218	**0.381**	**0.540**	0.037	**0.206**	**0.356**	0.541	0.041
sum, tave	0.962	0.990	1	0.0001	0.940	0.986	1	0.0003
sum, tmax	1	1	1	0	1	1	1	0
ms, tmin	0.217	0.387	0.546	0.036	0.208	0.363	0.548	0.040
ms, tave	0.963	0.991	1	0.0001	0.942	0.987	1	0.0003
ms, tmax	1	1	1	0	1	1	1	0
lxm, tmin	**0.216**	0.386	0.556	0.037	**0.206**	0.357	**0.537**	0.039
lxm, tave	0.965	0.990	1	0.0001	0.945	0.987	1	0.0003
lxm, tmax	1	1	1	0	1	1	1	0

Influence of Social Welfare Criteria for Solution Methods. Table 2 shows the results in the final round of publication process in the case of $n = 10$, $c = 20$, equ, and S. Here the Theil index, which is a measurement of the inequality among agents, is also evaluated. When all the agents have the same value, the Theil index value is zero. Note inherent trade-off between the summation/average value and fairness, which is often preferred by selfish agents without other mechanisms to transfer their profits. The Theil index values of trade-off in ms and lxm are relatively smaller than that of the sum, since these criteria consider the improvement of the worst case. However, lxm did not overcome ms. Although lxm generally improves the inequality, the result reveals the difficulty of designing appropriate estimations of the trade-off values to be well optimized. Table 3 shows the results of the same problem settings, although the optimization criterion for the publication process is sum. Since the publication process is identical, lxm is the fairest criterion for utility and also affects the trade-off.

Table 5. Influence of social-welfare criteria for two phases in framework ($n = 10$, $c = 20$, rnd, S) [9].

(a) Termination round, utility and trade-off

alg.	term.	utiliy					trade-off			
	round	sum.	min.	ave.	max	theil	min.	ave.	max.	theil
sum, tmin	6.4	1649.5	102.8	165.0	237.5	0.03414	**80.4**	**137.4**	207.2	0.043
sum, tave	18.6	1760.7	105	176.1	250.6	0.03417	46.3	88.1	132	0.052
sum, tmax	22.1	**1770.9**	101.8	**177.1**	**260.7**	0.037	20.6	61.2	100.5	(0.061)
ms, tmin	6.6	1619.2	102.5	161.9	236.5	0.032	75	133.3	203.8	0.042
ms, tave	18.4	1675.8	117.6	167.6	236.9	0.026	46.3	79.5	119.2	**0.040**
ms, tmax	20.4	1673.8	**120.5**	167.4	229	0.0227	14.4	51.5	84.8	(0.048)
lxm, tmin	6.5	1624	101.6	162.4	240.6	0.033	74.3	133.4	**207.6**	0.045
lxm, tave	17.7	1644.5	117.6	164.5	232.7	0.0231	44.6	77.2	117	**0.040**
lxm, tmax	20.8	1642.1	**120.5**	164.2	230.8	**0.020**	11.8	48.2	79.9	(0.043)

(b) Ratio of revealed information

alg.	ratio. rvl. num.				ratio. rvl. cost			
	min.	ave.	max.	theil	min.	ave.	max.	theil
sum, tmin	**0.172**	**0.261**	**0.379**	0.032	**0.158**	**0.249**	**0.364**	0.035
sum, tave	0.660	0.767	0.862	0.003	0.648	0.758	0.862	0.004
sum, tmax	0.962	0.993	1	**0.0001**	0.954	0.992	1	0.00022
ms, tmin	0.184	0.274	0.410	0.034	0.161	0.259	0.388	0.039
ms, tave	0.644	0.772	0.872	0.004	0.641	0.760	0.865	0.004
ms, tmax	0.952	0.992	1	0.0002	0.944	0.991	1	0.0003
lxm, tmin	0.183	0.278	0.419	0.037	0.162	0.262	0.404	0.041
lxm, tave	0.660	0.767	0.859	0.003	0.639	0.752	0.845	0.004
lxm, tmax	0.958	0.993	1	0.0002	0.952	0.992	1	**0.00025**

Results for Different Correlation Between Utility and Privacy Cost Values. Table 4 shows the results in the final round of the publication process in the case of $n = 10$, $c = 20$, inv, and S. The Theil index of lxm for the trade-off was relatively better.

Table 5 shows the results $n = 10$, $c = 20$, rnd, and S. Due to the problem settings, the trade-off values were negative in a few instances in the case of tave and tmax. For such cases, the Theil index of the trade-off was evaluated only for positive values and denoted by parentheses. Here the benefit of lxm seems to small. These results reveal the influence of correlation between the utility values and their publish cost values.

Results for Different Size of Problems. Table 6 shows the results in the case of $n = 20$, $c = 20$, equ, and S. Due to the limitation of the dynamic programming

Table 6. Influence of social-welfare criteria for two phases in framework ($n = 20$, $c = 20$, equ, S) [9].

(a) Termination round, utility and trade-off

alg.	term.	utiliy					trade-off			
	round	sum.	min.	ave.	max	theil	min.	ave.	max.	theil
sum, tmin	7.2	2166.6	54.4	108.3	183.5	0.057	38.3	**84.7**	**150.3**	0.066
sum, tave	15.1	2231.9	57.2	111.60	195.8	0.055	27.8	63.2	104.9	0.053
sum, tmax	17.1	**2232.3**	57	**111.62**	**198**	0.056	24.4	58.3	96.6	0.052
ms, tmin	7.2	2150.1	61.8	107.5	182.7	0.049	46	84.1	150.3	0.055
ms, tave	15.1	2169.6	69.3	108.5	189.8	0.044	27.4	60.2	96.2	0.044
ms, tmax	16.4	2164.6	**69.5**	108.2	190.3	0.044	21	55.0	86.6	0.050
lxm, tmin	7	2108.9	61.8	105.4	171.4	0.040	**46.6**	82.2	139.0	0.045
lxm, tave	14.2	2098.8	68.9	104.9	173.8	0.033	30.3	57.0	88.5	**0.035**
lxm, tmax	15.6	2102.9	**69.5**	105.1	171.8	**0.031**	24.6	51.9	79.5	0.039

(b) Ratio of revealed information

alg.	ratio. rvl. num.				ratio. rvl. cost			
	min.	ave.	max.	theil	min.	ave.	max.	theil
sum, tmin	0.254	0.463	**0.683**	0.031	0.262	0.472	**0.707**	0.032
sum, tave	0.715	0.889	0.992	0.00347	0.771	0.913	0.996	0.0024
sum, tmax	0.940	0.992	1	**0.00024**	0.965	0.995	1	**0.00008**
ms, tmin	**0.251**	0.461	0.692	0.034	0.258	0.470	0.710	0.0331
ms, tave	0.715	0.883	0.995	0.00357	0.771	0.907	0.998	0.00247
ms, tmax	0.924	0.990	1	0.000335	0.956	0.994	1	0.000117
lxm, tmin	0.254	**0.459**	0.692	0.033	**0.256**	**0.468**	0.710	0.0332
lxm, tave	0.707	0.873	0.992	0.00354	0.760	0.900	0.997	0.00255
lxm, tmax	0.925	0.990	1	0.000329	0.957	0.994	1	0.000116

based solution method, we only performed the experiment on sparse problems. The results including other different settings resemble the case of $n = 10$ and $c = 20$.

Different Asymmetry of Constraints. Tables 7 and 8 show the results for different asymmetries on the utility and privacy cost values. In case (a), the utility values of binary functions $u_{i,j}$ and uj, i are identical for each pair of the variable's values. We used constant value 10 for all the values of unary functions, and the random utility values in $[10, 50]$ for each value of the binary functions. On the other hand, in case (b), the utility values of $u_{j,i}$ are set to $\max(0, 50 - u_{i,j} + 1)$, while $u_{j,i}$ is identical to case (a). Here the privacy cost values were 0.1 times corresponding utility values in the case denoted by 'equ', while those were set with negative correlation in the case of 'inv'.

Table 7. Influence of asymmetry on utility and publish cost values to resulting utility and trade-off values ($n = 10$, $c = 20$, S).

(a) Common utility

alg.	equ						inv					
	term.	utility			trade-off			term.	utility			trade-off		
	round	min.	ave.	max	min.	ave.	max.	round	min.	ave.	max	min.	ave.	max.
sum, tmin	6.8	0	69.7	121.8	-7.9	61.0	113	6.5	64.3	140.8	214.4	56.7	132.1	205.4
sum, tave	18.3	97.8	165.4	**248.4**	48.6	89.6	136.8	23.9	95.5	166.6	248	52.6	100.1	152.7
sum, tmax	22	95.2	**166.8**	244.4	36.8	71.2	108.2	21.3	95.3	**166.8**	244.5	47	96.6	145.6
ms, tmin	6.8	0	69.7	121.8	-7.9	61.0	113	6.4	67.7	143.8	224.9	**59.7**	135	**215.9**
ms, tave	16.9	101.6	161.2	239	51.2	86.4	129.9	22	**102.9**	163.4	244.2	59.6	96.9	148
ms, tmax	20	102.8	163.4	244.1	40.9	67.9	102.2	19.6	**102.9**	163.4	244.2	54.7	93.3	144.4
lxm, tmin	6.4	0	71.7	124.3	-8.1	62.9	115.5	6.4	61.5	144.3	220.8	53.4	**135.6**	211.8
lxm, tave	17.1	101.4	157.4	240	51.8	82.1	128.3	21.7	**102.9**	158.0	232.2	59.6	91.7	135.9
lxm, tmax	20	102.8	157.8	233.8	38.1	62.2	92.6	19.6	**102.9**	157.8	233.9	54	87.7	134.1

(b) Competitive utility

alg.	equ						inv					
	term.	utility			trade-off			term.	utility			trade-off		
	round	min.	ave.	max	min.	ave.	max.	round	min.	ave.	max	min.	ave.	max.
sum, tmin	6.7	0	73.5	121	-8.6	64.7	112	7.1	0	66.3	148.7	-8.8	57.8	139.7
sum, tave	15.8	50.6	112	179.1	2.9	48.7	94.8	16.7	46.2	112	175.1	-2.3	52.5	106.8
sum, tmax	23.8	54.3	112	186.8	-13	19.5	60	22.5	54.3	112	186.4	-21.7	23.6	85.5
ms, tmin	6.7	0	73.5	121	-8.6	64.7	112	7.1	0	66.3	148.7	-8.8	57.8	139.7
ms, tave	15.3	73.4	112	172.3	16.9	48	83.2	16.3	76.5	112	168.6	20.9	52.2	98.4
ms, tmax	22.1	83.8	112	156.3	-13.9	19.7	49.2	20.9	81.5	112	155.8	-23.4	23.7	67.9
lxm, tmin	6.3	0	74.5	123.4	-8.6	65.7	114.4	6.8	0	66.3	152.1	-8.1	57.9	143.2
lxm, tave	16.1	75.6	112	159.8	19.3	47.6	74.3	15.6	75.4	112	168.9	18.8	51.8	98.6
lxm, tmax	22.3	83.8	112	150.2	-14.3	19.9	53.7	21	81.1	112	148.7	-17.2	23.9	60

The result shows that relatively higher utility values were obtained in the case of (a) and 'inv', because the agents agree rather easily when selecting higher utility and lower privacy cost values. However, the amount of revealed information was also rather large. In addition, in several settings, the trade-off values were negative. It reveals that the utility and privacy cost values should be set considering appropriate balance and margin.

Trading Utility Values Between Neighborhood Agents. Table 9 shows the influence of trading utility values between pairs of neighborhood agents. We set the ratio of transferred utility w^{trd} to 0.1. In the case of the transfer from larger degree (i.e. larger number of neighborhood nodes) agents to smaller ones, the inequality of the resulting utility and trade-off values were reduced in comparison to the opposite case. The Theil index values were also decreased.

Table 8. Influence of asymmetry on utility and publish cost values to revealed information ($n = 10$, $c = 20$, S).

(a) Common utility

alg.	equ						inv					
	ratio. rvl. num.			ratio. rvl. cost			ratio. rvl. num.			ratio. rvl. cost		
	min.	ave.	max.	min.	ave.	max.	min.	ave.	max.	min.	ave.	max.
sum, tmin	0.095	0.165	0.303	**0.056**	0.101	0.180	0.123	0.195	0.304	0.086	0.134	0.202
sum, tave	0.669	0.753	0.824	0.706	0.799	0.883	0.908	0.966	0.998	0.860	0.949	0.997
sum, tmax	0.983	0.998	1	0.993	0.999	1	1	1	1	1	1	1
ms, tmin	0.095	0.165	0.303	**0.056**	0.101	0.180	0.126	0.193	0.304	0.086	0.137	0.221
ms, tave	0.659	0.742	0.807	0.707	0.788	0.853	0.905	0.966	0.997	0.856	0.948	0.993
ms, tmax	0.983	0.998	1.000	0.993	0.999	1.000	0.988	0.998	1.000	0.982	0.998	1.000
lxm, tmin	0.093	0.159	0.270	0.057	0.101	**0.164**	0.123	0.192	0.299	0.086	0.137	0.221
lxm, tave	0.677	0.751	0.815	0.715	0.793	0.864	0.903	0.963	0.993	0.851	0.946	0.990
lxm, tmax	0.983	0.998	1	0.993	0.999	1	0.988	0.998	1	0.982	0.998	1

(b) Competitive utility

alg.	equ						inv					
	ratio. rvl. num.			ratio. rvl. cost			ratio. rvl. num.			ratio. rvl. cost		
	min.	ave.	max.	min.	ave.	max.	min.	ave.	max.	min.	ave.	max.
sum, tmin	0.092	0.153	0.269	0.063	0.103	0.168	0.079	0.145	0.269	0.057	0.102	0.180
sum, tave	0.560	0.647	0.739	0.589	0.680	0.785	0.540	0.684	0.810	0.483	0.647	0.786
sum, tmax	0.901	0.983	1	0.926	0.987	1	0.851	0.954	0.995	0.808	0.948	0.997
ms, tmin	0.092	0.153	0.269	0.063	0.103	0.168	**0.079**	0.145	0.269	0.057	0.102	0.180
ms, tave	0.540	0.660	0.754	0.580	0.689	0.796	0.544	0.684	0.797	0.493	0.650	0.784
ms, tmax	0.888	0.979	1	0.912	0.983	1	0.850	0.954	0.994	0.806	0.948	0.994
lxm, tmin	0.091	0.149	0.271	0.064	0.103	0.174	0.080	**0.140**	**0.252**	0.058	**0.100**	0.175
lxm, tave	0.541	0.661	0.747	0.588	0.690	0.802	0.558	0.688	0.822	0.509	0.655	0.806
lxm, tmax	0.888	0.977	1	0.909	0.982	1	0.854	0.951	0.995	0.810	0.945	0.997

In this case, published information was relatively increased. It can be considered that the exported utility values to the relatively large number of agents of smaller degree increased the opportunities to publish their information.

Limitation of Tree-Width of Pseudo-trees. Table 10 shows the result when the maximum tree width was limited to two. Since we employed the pessimistic approximation based on lower bound utility values, the true utility and trade-off values are not less than the values for the approximated problems. However, the true values and corresponding termination rounds are different from those for the problems without approximation shown in Table 5. Table 11 shows the result in the case of $n = 20$ and $c = 30$. Several values of the minimum utility/trade-off

Table 9. Influence of trading utility values ($n = 10$, $c = 20$, rnd, S).

(a) Utility and trade-off

alg.	from smaller degree node								from larger degree node							
	utiliy				trade-off				utiliy				trade-off			
	min.	ave.	max.	theil	min.	ave.	max.	theil	min.	ave.	max.	theil	min.	ave.	max.	theil
sum, tmin	85	171	289	0.069	62	**132**	216	0.069	106	164	213	0.030	**76**	127	170	0.026
sum, tave	92	183	304	0.064	30	88	163	0.108	126	186	240	0.018	55	91	134	0.039
sum, tmax	93	184	**314**	0.066	10	68	144	0.079	124	**187**	243	0.019	33	71	119	0.074
ms, tmin	91	165	274	0.062	68	126	208	0.062	106	162	216	0.030	74	125	179	0.024
ms, tave	109	173	290	0.054	42	79	145	0.084	136	180	232	0.017	52	87	125	0.039
ms, tmax	111	176	300	0.055	20	60	130	0.140	**139**	180	227	0.015	17	64	111	0.075
lxm, tmin	94	163	275	0.058	71	124	207	0.058	106	162	204	0.025	71	124	169	**0.020**
lxm, tave	107	169	277	0.047	40	76	134	0.070	137	177	218	0.012	52	83	117	0.032
lxm, tmax	111	171	290	0.048	18	55	122	0.167	139	178	219	**0.010**	15	61	102	0.096

(b) Ratio of revealed information

alg.	from smaller degree node								from larger degree node							
	ratio. rvl. num.				ratio. rvl. cost				ratio. rvl. num.				ratio. rvl. cost			
	min.	ave.	max.	theil	min.	ave.	max.	theil	min.	ave.	max.	theil	min.	ave.	max.	theil
sum, tmin	0.21	**0.34**	**0.48**	0.031	0.20	0.33	**0.46**	0.032	**0.15**	0.36	0.53	0.061	**0.13**	0.35	0.52	0.075
sum, tave	0.69	0.81	0.90	0.003	0.68	0.80	0.90	0.004	0.69	0.84	0.95	0.004	0.70	0.83	0.95	0.004
sum, tmax	0.97	0.99	1	**0.000**	0.97	0.99	1	**0.000**	1.00	1.00	1	0.000	1.00	1.00	1	0.000
ms, tmin	0.22	**0.34**	**0.48**	0.030	0.20	**0.32**	0.46	0.032	0.16	0.36	0.51	0.056	**0.13**	0.35	0.51	0.071
ms, tave	0.68	0.80	0.89	0.003	0.68	0.79	0.90	0.004	0.66	0.83	0.96	0.005	0.66	0.82	0.95	0.006
ms, tmax	0.96	0.99	1	**0.000**	0.95	0.99	1	**0.000**	1.00	1.00	1	0.000	1.00	1.00	1	0.000
lxm, tmin	0.22	0.35	0.51	0.033	0.20	0.33	0.50	0.035	0.17	0.36	0.53	0.057	**0.13**	0.35	0.52	0.078
lxm, tave	0.67	0.80	0.90	0.004	0.66	0.80	0.90	0.004	0.66	0.83	0.96	0.006	0.65	0.82	0.96	0.007
lxm, tmax	0.96	0.99	1	0.000	0.95	0.99	1	0.000	1.00	1.00	1	0.000	1.00	1.00	1	0.000

Table 10. Influence of limitation of tree width ($n = 10$, $c = 20$, rnd, S, max. tree width= 2).

alg.	term. round	approximated						true value					
		utility			trade-off			utility			trade-off		
		min.	ave.	max	min.	ave.	max.	min.	ave.	max	min.	ave.	max.
sum, tmin	8.7	95.5	153.86	216.1	61.3	104.68	158.3	101.6	168.69	240.1	67.5	**119.51**	174.7
sum, tave	15.5	91.3	156.74	228.9	38.2	79.16	124.4	103	**171.9**	253.6	45.4	94.32	146.9
sum, tmax	17	89.8	157.09	230.3	24.5	68.84	113.9	101	171.82	**253.7**	28.8	83.57	137.4
ms, tmin	9.3	97.5	151.78	212.2	62.4	102.41	151	105.4	166.24	238.6	71.1	116.87	174.4
ms, tave	15	103.3	151.73	209.8	41.7	74.33	106.7	109.5	166.84	236.6	53.8	89.44	134.6
ms, tmax	17.2	103.6	152.57	211.8	31.3	64.32	102.3	**110.6**	170.47	244.2	36	82.22	134.4
lxm, tmin	9	101.4	149.34	203.6	63.9	100.13	143.4	109.6	163.67	234.1	**75.5**	114.46	165.5
lxm, tave	14.9	103.3	147.13	191.8	41.7	69.2	90.8	108.4	162.37	231	49.9	84.44	132
lxm, tmax	16.7	103.8	147.03	192.4	31.2	58.74	88.3	108.4	163.77	228.4	36.1	75.48	129.1

for the approximated problems are identical to the corresponding true values in this case.

Table 11. Influence of limitation of tree width ($n = 20$, $c = 30$, rnd, S, max. tree width= 2).

alg.	term. round	approximated						true value					
		utility			trade-off			utility			trade-off		
		min.	ave.	max	min.	ave.	max.	min.	ave.	max	min.	ave.	max.
sum, tmin	7.9	62.5	129.33	221.6	43.6	96.075	169.4	62.5	135.185	240.2	43.8	**101.93**	**181.8**
sum, tave	15.9	61.5	134.55	222.8	25.6	68.73	124.2	61.6	140.7	**248.9**	25.7	74.88	146.7
sum, tmax	18.1	61.6	134.7	222.8	15.5	57.645	108.9	61.7	**140.975**	**248.9**	15.6	63.92	131.9
ms, tmin	7.7	64.3	125.53	211.6	**47.3**	92.53	156.9	64.3	131.89	238.7	**47.3**	98.89	177.3
ms, tave	15.2	**70.4**	132.3	217.2	30	67.11	116.9	**70.4**	138.705	242.9	32.4	73.515	142
ms, tmax	17.4	**70.4**	132.885	217.6	16.7	56.14	102.9	**70.4**	139.585	244.1	19.5	62.84	128.6
lxm, tmin	7.7	62.8	122.47	201	45	89.31	150.2	62.8	128.85	226.3	45.6	95.69	169.7
lxm, tave	15	70	126.155	201.9	32.7	61.48	99.2	70	131.925	221.3	35	67.25	124.6
lxm, tmax	16.9	**70.4**	126.8	200.2	7	50.03	92.3	**70.4**	133.495	236.3	9	56.725	129.9

The average execution time of our experimental implementation on a computer with g++ (GCC) 8.5.0, Linux version 4.18, Intel (R) Core (TM) i7-9700K CPU @ 3.60 GHz and 64 GB memory was 758 s in the case of $n = 10$, $c = 20$, lxm, S, and tave that took the maximum computation time.

6 Discussion

In our previous work [8], a similar problem was solved using a mediator agent that performed a centralized local search. The goal of the study was to find the first solution where all the agents can agree with the published utility values. Therefore, the solution process only finds one combination of parts of the constraints that involves an assignment to all the variables, and no other possible complete solutions were explored. In only employs the summation criterion to aggregate and evaluate the publish cost values and utility values.

Our study investigated the negotiation process on similar problems with a decentralized complete solution method that employed several criteria to consider preferences of individual agents. While most agents find better solution in early steps of the negotiation in general cases, it is possible to continue the search for other solutions with better utility values. On the other hand, due to the limitation of dynamic programming on pseudo-trees, we focused on relatively small scale and sparse problem instances.

We assumed that it is acceptable to reveal some abstract information to determine the utility values to be published as a fundamental investigation. Opportunities exist fro employing a secure computation in part of the negotiation process of publication. In such an approach, one issue will be the information that is finally published so that agents can understand the reasons behind an agreement on a solution.

We employed complete solution methods to solve problems in each negotiation round so that the parts of negotiations are based on optimal solutions. However, incomplete solution methods are necessary for complex and large-scale problems in practical domains. There are opportunities to develop such scalable solution methods for composite criteria based on social welfare among agents. For an initial investigation, we employed fundamental benchmark problems. Applying our proposed approach to practical resource allocation and collaboration problems using scalable solution methods will be included in our future work.

We employed a well known approach to reduce the size of the subproblems in pseudo-tree based solution methods, we eliminated back edges. On the other hand, when a node has a large number of child nodes, that situation also increases the size of the subproblems of agents. For such problems, there are opportunities to employ the mini-bucket algorithm that approximates functions with large arity by decomposing the original function to multiple functions with smaller arities [1]. Another approach is applying inexact methods, although existing solution methods have to be adjusted to this class of problems.

7 Conclusion

We proposed a multiagent negotiation framework based on asymmetric multi objective distributed constraint optimization problems where agents gradually publish their utility information until an agreement is reached. The proposed negotiation framework consists of two types of AMODCOPs including the problem to select the utility information to be published by agents and another decision-making problem based on the published utility values. Agents repeatedly solve both problems using an exact solution method according to pseudo-trees on constraint graphs. We introduced the heuristic constraints to gradually publish utility information of agents and also employed the criterion to evaluate multiple objectives among agents. In addition, we applied preprocessing methods to adjust utility values among agents, and to approximate complex problems. The experimental result revealed the effects and influences of the proposed approaches.

The pricing of individual utility information, more practical strategies and interactive agreement conditions will be future directions of the study. Applying solution methods based on soft computing approaches to large-scale and complex problems will also be included in our future work.

Acknowledgements. This work was supported in part by JSPS KAKENHI Grant Number JP19K12117.

References

1. Dechter, R.: Mini-buckets: a general scheme for generating approximations in automated reasoning. In: 15th International Joint Conference on Artificial Intelligence, vol. 2, pp. 1297–1302 (1997)
2. Fioretto, F., Pontelli, E., Yeoh, W.: Distributed constraint optimization problems and applications: a survey. J. Artif. Intell. Res. **61**, 623–698 (2018)
3. Grinshpoun, T., Grubshtein, A., Zivan, R., Netzer, A., Meisels, A.: Asymmetric distributed constraint optimization problems. J. Artif. Intell. Res. **47**, 613–647 (2013)

 4. Grinshpoun, T., Tassa, T.: P-SyncBB: a privacy preserving branch and bound DCOP algorithm. J. Artif. Int. Res. **57**(1), 621–660 (2016)
 5. Kexing, L.: A survey of agent based automated negotiation. In: 2011 International Conference on Network Computing and Information Security, vol. 2, pp. 24–27, May 2011. https://doi.org/10.1109/NCIS.2011.103
 6. Léauté, T., Faltings, B.: Protecting privacy through distributed computation in multi-agent decision making. J. Artif. Intell. Res. **47**(1), 649–695 (2013)
 7. Marler, R.T., Arora, J.S.: Survey of multi-objective optimization methods for engineering. Struct. Multidiscip. Optimiz. **26**, 369–395 (2004)
 8. Matsui, T.: A study of cooperation with privacy loss based on asymmetric constraint optimization problem among agents. In: 3rd International Conference on Advances in Artificial Intelligence, pp. 127–134 (2019)
 9. Matsui, T.: A study on negotiation for revealed information with decentralized asymmetric multi-objective constraint optimization. In: 13th International Conference on Agents and Artificial Intelligence, pp. 149–159 (2021)
10. Matsui, T., Matsuo, H., Silaghi, M., Hirayama, K., Yokoo, M.: Leximin asymmetric multiple objective distributed constraint optimization problem. Comput. Intell. **34**(1), 49–84 (2018)
11. Matsui, T., Silaghi, M., Okimoto, T., Hirayama, K., Yokoo, M., Matsuo, H.: Leximin multiple objective DCOPs on factor graphs for preferences of agents. Fundam. Inform. **158**(1–3), 63–91 (2018)
12. Modi, P.J., Shen, W., Tambe, M., Yokoo, M.: ADOPT: asynchronous distributed constraint optimization with quality guarantees. Artif. Intell. **161**(1–2), 149–180 (2005)
13. Okimoto, T., Joe, Y., Iwasaki, A., Yokoo, M., Faltings, B.: Pseudo-tree-based incomplete algorithm for distributed constraint optimization with quality bounds. In: Lee, J. (ed.) CP 2011. LNCS, vol. 6876, pp. 660–674. Springer, Heidelberg (2011). https://doi.org/10.1007/978-3-642-23786-7_50
14. Petcu, A., Faltings, B.: A scalable method for multiagent constraint optimization. In: 19th International Joint Conference on Artificial Intelligence, pp. 266–271 (2005)
15. Petcu, A., Faltings, B., Parkes, D.C.: M-DPOP: faithful distributed implementation of efficient social choice problems. J. Artif. Intell. Res. **32**, 705–755 (2008)
16. Sen, A.K.: Choice, Welfare and Measurement. Harvard University Press, Cambridge (1997)
17. Tassa, T., Grinshpoun, T., Yanay, A.: A privacy preserving collusion secure DCOP algorithm. In: 28th International Joint Conference on Artificial Intelligence, pp. 4774–4780 (2019)
18. Tassa, T., Grinshpoun, T., Zivan, R.: Privacy preserving implementation of the max-sum algorithm and its variants. J. Artif. Int. Res. **59**(1), 311–349 (2017)
19. Xiao, Y., Tabakhi, A.M., Yeoh, W.: Embedding preference elicitation within the search for DCOP solutions. In: Proceedings of the 19th International Conference on Autonomous Agents and MultiAgent Systems, pp. 2044–2046 (2020)
20. Yeoh, W., Yokoo, M.: Distributed problem solving. AI Mag. **33**(3), 53–65 (2012)

Artificial Intelligence

Utilizing Out-Domain Datasets to Enhance Multi-task Citation Analysis

Dominique Mercier[1,2]([envelope])[ORCID], Syed Tahseen Raza Rizvi[1,2][ORCID], Vikas Rajashekar[1][ORCID], Sheraz Ahmed[1][ORCID], and Andreas Dengel[1,2][ORCID]

[1] German Research Center for Artificial Intelligence (DFKI) GmbH,
Trippstadter Straße 122, 67663 Kaiserslautern, Germany
{dominique.mercier,syed.rizvi,vikas.rajashekar,sheraz.ahmed,
andreas.dengel}@dfki.de
[2] TU Kaiserslautern, Erwin-Schrödinger-Straße 52, 67663 Kaiserslautern, Germany

Abstract. Citations are generally analyzed using only quantitative measures while excluding qualitative aspects such as sentiment and intent. However, qualitative aspects provide deeper insights into the impact of a scientific research artifact and make it possible to focus on relevant literature free from bias associated with quantitative aspects. Therefore, it is possible to rank and categorize papers based on their sentiment and intent. For this purpose, larger citation sentiment datasets are required. However, from a time and cost perspective, curating a large citation sentiment dataset is a challenging task. Particularly, citation sentiment analysis suffers from both data scarcity and tremendous costs for dataset annotation. To overcome the bottleneck of data scarcity in the citation analysis domain we explore the impact of out-domain data during training to enhance the model performance. Our results emphasize the use of different scheduling methods based on the use case. We empirically found that a model trained using sequential data scheduling is more suitable for domain-specific usecases. Conversely, shuffled data feeding achieves better performance on a cross-domain task. Based on our findings, we propose an end-to-end trainable multi-task model that covers the sentiment and intent analysis that utilizes out-domain datasets to overcome the data scarcity. .

Keywords: Artificial intelligence · Natural language processing · Scientific citation analysis · Multi-task · Transformers · Sentiment analysis · Intent analysis · Multi-domain

1 Introduction

Neural Networks have recently been applied to tasks from a wide range of domains. They are also notorious for their desire for very large amounts of annotated data, one of the key requirements to use neural networks is the availability of annotated data. While the process of data annotation can be automated in some domains to ensure the

D. Mercier, S. T. R. Rizvi and V. Rajashekar—Equal Contribution.

availability of the necessary data. However, it is not always possible and the quality of automatically annotated data can not be ensured as mentioned in [27].

Citations data for sentiment analysis is a particular example of such a scenario where the data is already very scarce and challenging to collect and annotate using automated approaches. While the annotation of product reviews can be automated, the automated annotation of texts without additional features like stars ratings and emojis, etc. is a significantly more complex task [25].

Scientific publications play an important role in the progress of a community. The "Publish or Perish" principle continuously pushes the researchers to periodically publish their scientific contributions which resulted in a boom of publications. This exponential increase in the amount of existing scientific publications has posed a challenge of evaluating the impact of each contribution in this publication outburst. Despite the existence of various metrics, including the h-index, aspects such as sentiment and intent are rarely evaluated. It is a well-established fact that most of the existing metrics heavily rely on citation counts and therefore only take quantitative aspects of a citation into consideration [5]. However, the quality of a scientific contribution should not entirely depend on quantitative aspects rather on the content and the results [12,36].

Such qualitative facet greatly assists in the citation impact measurements by enriching them and therefore resulting in more sophisticated significance rankings [36]. The task of sentiment classification offers contextual insights into a given text corpus and is applied on various domains such as movie review, product reviews, and Twitter data [3,11,16,19,32]. Performing sentiment analysis on objective citation data is still challenging due to the objectivity of the text and the limited amount of annotated data.

The intent of a citation found in scientific literature refers to the purpose of citing the existing scientific artifacts. Citation intent analysis serves a dual purpose. Besides the intention of a citation i.e. approach, dataset, survey, or related work, it also plays a crucial role in identifying the sentiment [20] of that citation based on its occurrence position in the paper. For instance, citations found in the evaluation and discussion section are more likely to be negative, as the citing authors usually compare the results of their approach in evaluation to prove the superiority of their proposed approach.

Despite the recently published approaches [4] there is still a scarcity of methods and datasets for the task of scientific citation analysis. There are a couple of factors that caused this data scarcity. Firstly, the high costs of manual annotation and the highly objective text make it impossible to automatically annotate it with a high quality. Secondly, there is no formal definition of intention used to classify citations properly.

In our previous paper ImpactCite [21], we contributed by releasing a cleaned citation sentiment dataset for the task of citation sentiment analysis. In addition, we proposed a transformer-based approach for classifying the sentiment or intent of a given citation string. Even with our dataset contribution, the scarcity of citation sentiment data was not eliminated. Therefore, in this paper, we further investigated the usage of out-domain sentiment datasets to learn and transfer their knowledge to the citation sentiment task. For this purpose, we utilize the cleaned dataset proposed in ImpactCite [21] and extend its analysis using out-domain data to further improve the performance of the citation analysis model. We also evaluate different scheduling methods to train models on the data and investigate the impact of those strategies concerning the model performance. Furthermore, we investigate the impact of training a single model for two different tasks of the same domain to enhance the accuracy of the task with limited annotated data. It will significantly save both time and computation resources. To our knowledge, it is the first endeavor of investigating sentiment and intent classification on scientific data including out-domain data integration. Citation sentiment analysis would benefit greatly if sentiment datasets from other domains had a positive effect on citation analysis models. The contributions of this publication are as follows:

1. Evaluation of out-domain data usage during training
2. Evaluation of different scheduling methods
3. An end-to-end sentiment and intent citation classification multi-task model.

2   Related Work

This section discusses the literature related to three relevant aspects. Firstly, we will discuss the works related to the sentiment classification followed by the intent classification. Later, we cover literature related to the use of out-domain data, transfer learning, and the possible impact of these approaches concerning data scarcity.

2.1   Sentiment Classification

Sentiment analysis has been a notable task in natural language processing. Several approaches have been proposed in the existing literature which focused on tackling the task of Sentiment classification. The most common use cases for the task of sentiment classification include the sentiment analysis of tweets, movies, and products reviews. Tang et al. [30] proposed a word embeddings-based approach contingent on sentiment present in a tweet. These sentiment-oriented word embeddings make this approach very suitable for the task of sentiment classification. Thongtan et al. [31] took it one step further and applied document embeddings instead of word embeddings. These document embeddings were trained using cosine similarity as the similarity measure. The effectiveness of this approach was demonstrated by applying it to a dataset consisting of movie reviews. Cliche [6] adopted a slightly different path and employed an ensemble of Convolutional Neural Network (CNN) and Long-Short Term Memory (LSTM) models. This approach was trained and fine-tuned on a large corpus of unlabeled tweets for the task of sentiment classification.

BERT [9] is considered as the most popular choice for different natural language processing (NLP) tasks. It was trained on a large corpus of unlabeled data. Owing to its success in resolving other NLP problems, BERT has also been applied to the task of sentiment analysis. Several approaches [23,33,37] took advantage of the baseline BERT model and further tapped the potential of the model by incorporating different modules like pre-processing, attention, and structural features, etc. These modules provided some additional information to the model which in turn helped the model to better predict the resultant label.

Most of the research related to the task of sentiment analysis is performed for the domains of movie/product review or Twitter data sentiment analysis. However, a minor fraction of the literature also targets a different domain for the task of sentiment analysis. Citation sentiment analysis is also of extreme importance as it helps us in understanding the impact of research artifacts in a scientific community. Citation sentiment analysis is vastly different from movie/product review or Twitter sentiment analysis, unlike reviews and tweets, citations appear in the scientific literature which is a quite formal form of text. Esuli and Sebastiani [10] proposed the idea that sentiment classification has striking similarities with opinion and subjectivity mining. They further discussed that an individual can premeditate a seemingly positive or negative citation by only using their inclinations and writing style.

Athar et al. [2] explored the idea of using sets of several features like science lexicon, contextual polarity, dependencies, negation, sentence splitting, and word-level features for citation sentiment classification. They performed several experiments to establish a set of most suitable features which has optimal performance in classifying citation sentiment found in scientific literature. On a similar line, Xu et al. [34] carried out a citation sentiment analysis on the clinical trial literature. For this task, they employed a different set of features like n-grams, sentiment lexicon, and structure information. The task of sentiment classification is particularly hard for citation data due to the inadequate number of datasets available which have a very limited number of samples for sufficiently training a model. Finding a sentiment in a text that is written to be analytical and objective is substantially different from doing so in highly subjective text pieces like Twitter data.

2.2 Intent Classification

Intent classification and sentiment classification seem to be nearly identical tasks. However, both tasks are inherently different as intent classification is more inclined towards motive behind citation which is generally closely related to the section in which the citation string appears. Intent classification has become a more challenging task due to the increasing usage of compound section titles. Cohan et al. [7] employed bi-directional LSTM equipped with an attention mechanism. Additionally, they proposed to use ELMo vectors and structural scaffolds i.e. citation worthiness and section title.

Another interesting work is SciBERT which is a variation of BERT specifically optimized for scientific publications and was proposed by Beltagy et al. [4]. The model was trained on 1.14 million scientific publications containing 3.17 billion tokens. The training data originates from two different domains, namely the computer science and biomedical domain. SciBERT was successfully applied on several NLP tasks including the classification of sections.

Furthermore, Mercier et al. [20] tackled the sentiment and intent classification using a fusion approach of different baseline classifiers such as a Support Vector Machine (SVM) and a perceptron. They used a set of textual features consisting of adjectives, hypernyms, type, length of tokens, capitalization, and synonyms. Closely related to that, Abu-Jabra et al. [1] proposed an SVM-based approach to perform the intent classification of citations. They stated that structural and lexical features in their experiments have shown to be of very high significance when it comes to the intent of a citation.

2.3   Out-Domain Data Utilization

Su et al. [29] presented in their work to study the impact of out-domain data for question answering. They investigated different training schedules and their impact on accuracy. The main focus of their work was a better generalization. Another work that conducted experiments related to the robust training using in-domain and out-domain data was proposed by Li et al. [15]. Their proposed method provides the capabilities to learn domain-specific and general data in conjunction to overcome the convergence towards domain-specific properties. Sajjad et al. [26] proposed an approach that first learns of different out-domain data and finally fine-tunes on in-domain data to achieve the optimal results. This approach intuitively utilizes the data of the different domains and therefore has a much larger training corpus for a better generalization.

Khayrallah et al. [13] addressed the amount of out-domain vocabulary. Their findings showed that with the use of out-domain data and a continuous adaption towards the domain, the number of words not included in the vocabulary can be reduced efficiently. For this purpose, they used an out-domain model and trained it with a modified training objective continuously on the in-domain data. Furthermore, Mrkšić et al. [22] showed that using the out-domain data can yield significant improvements for very small datasets. And therefore makes it possible to train models using these sets when it is not possible to do that without the use of out-domain data.

3   Datasets

This paper mainly focuses on the task of sentiment and intent analysis. Therefore we selected a range of datasets suitable for sentiment classification and also for intent classification.

3.1   Sentiment Datasets

For the task of Sentiment classification, we employed various datasets for our experiments. Our target domain is the scientific literature. However, we selected some out-domain datasets to overcome the data scarcity. Following are the datasets selected for the sentiment classification task:

1. Movie reviews
2. Product reviews
3. Twitter data
4. Scientific data.

To standardize the labels of selected datasets, a preprocessing step was essential. For experiments evaluating out-domain knowledge transfer and sequential training, we preprocessed the selected datasets for binary sentiment classification tasks i.e. positive and negative. It enabled us to train and test models across different datasets. To do so, we excluded the neutral class and grouped different labels if the datasets had multiple classes that correspond to the positive or negative label e.g. 'good' and 'very good' or 4 out of 5 and 5 out of 5 stars. However, we used all three classes i.e. positive, negative, and neutral for the multi-task experiments. The details of the selected sentiment datasets are as follows:

Movie Reviews. From the domain of movie reviews, we decided to use three popular datasets that quantified both positive and negative reviews in the form of a numerical score. The IMDB [17] dataset contains about 25, 000 training and 25, 000 test instances of highly polar reviews. It is the largest dataset by volume in the selected datasets. The second dataset we used in our experiments is the Cornell movie review data [24]. It is a considerably small dataset as compared to IMDB. However, it has an even distribution of 1, 000 samples for each of the positive and negative classes. The last dataset that we selected from movie reviews is the Stanford Sentiment Treebank dataset [28]. For this dataset, we had to discard the samples not related to either negative or positive classes. All three above-mentioned datasets are related to the same task from the same domain and therefore their underlying structure should be rather similar.

Product Reviews. To include a dataset from a different domain than the Movie reviews, we selected the amazon product review dataset [18]. This dataset consists of various product categories. Some of the categories in the amazon data are closely related to the movie reviews such as Books, TV, and Movies. On the other hand, some categories are completely different from movie reviews such as Beauty, Electronic, and Video Games. For our experiments, we selected one category from amazon data that was unrelated to the movie reviews. The chosen category was related to the instrument reviews. The product reviews were quantified in the form of $1 - 5$ stars. For our experiments, we converted the star ratings into positive and negative classes while skipping the neutral class. Product reviews with ratings with 4 and 5 stars were labeled as positive. On the other hand, product reviews with 1 and 2 stars were labeled as negative. However, product reviews with a star rating of 3 were skipped as they belonged to the neutral class and were not relevant for our experiments.

Twitter Data. Sentiment analysis on Twitter data is a quite popular task. For this purpose, we selected a couple of Twitter datasets. Intuitively, we assume that the Twitter datasets are the most subjective ones in our selection as their language style differs significantly from the scientific and other domain datasets. The first dataset is related to airline reviews in form of tweets. The data was taken from Kaggle[1] and contains three classes i.e. positive, negative, and neutral. Similar to other datasets, we removed the neutral class. The same class elimination was performed for the second dataset Sentiment140 dataset[2]. This dataset was composed using 1.6 Million general tweets collected from Twitter along with their sentiment.

Scientific Data. From the scientific domain, we selected a dataset called Citation Sentiment Corpus (CSC-Clean). It was proposed in our previous paper [21]. There have been very limited contributions for the citation sentiment analysis task as the number of available datasets is almost not existent. Although there exist some datasets proposed by Xu et al. [34] and Athar [2] those are either not publicly available or suffer from bad

---

[1] Twitter US Airline Sentiment: https://www.kaggle.com/crowdflower/twitter-airline-senti ment.

[2] Sentiment140: https://www.kaggle.com/kazanova/sentiment140.

Table 1. Comparison of citation sentiment corpus (CSC) and citation sentiment clean (CSC-C) dataset. Taken from [21].

Classes	CSC	CSC-Clean	CSC-Clean Dist.	Removed [%]
Positive	829	728	9.12%	101 (12.18)
Neutral	280	253	87.71%	27 (9.64)
Negative	7,627	6,999	3.17%	629 (8.25)

quality. The reason for this data scarcity is the expensive and complicated labeling process. We decided to use the CSC dataset [2] as a baseline. Upon careful dataset analysis, we found out that there exist duplicate instances with an occasionally same or different label in the CSC dataset. These instances also often exist in different data splits such as training and test set. We identified these quality issues and cleaned the dataset to achieve a better quality throughout the same corpus. Table 1 shows the original sample count, number of removed instances concerning duplicates, and the remaining number of samples. In addition, we show the updated dataset distribution and the percentage of removed instances concerning each class. In total, we removed 757 instances which are 8.67% of the data. For duplicates with two different labels, we removed both the original and the duplicated instances as this is the only appropriate solution to avoid a subjective bias from our side. Including one of the instances would bias the data and results. The resultant dataset is referred to as CSC-Clean and publicly available[3].

Sentiment Dataset Statistics. In Table 2 we show the statistics of each sentiment dataset after pre-processing them to exclude the neutral class and existing duplicates. These statistics include the number of samples used to train, validate, and test our models. In addition, the table also shows the dataset distribution highlighting that datasets such as the Instruments, US Airline, and CSC-Clean are heavily biased towards one of the two classes. Another characteristic is that the collected datasets differ largely in their size. This resulted in the need to upsample or downsample the data for some experiments to make the results comparable.

3.2 Intent Dataset

From the scientific domain, we selected a dataset related to citation intent analysis called SciCite. The SciCite dataset proposed in [7] is a famous benchmark for citation intent classification. It was curated using medical and computer science publications and is publicly available. The size of this dataset is sufficient to train any deep learning model and the existing benchmarks emphasize the high quality of the dataset. However, the dataset has an imbalanced sample distribution in which the vast majority of the samples are assigned to the 'Background' class. Another, important aspect of the dataset is the coarse-grained label process which was applied to create that dataset. According to

---

[3] https://github.com/DominiqueMercier/ImpactCite.

Table 2. Comparison all used datasets. Only including the positive and negative class. Neutral class for CSC-Clean was excluded in this table.

Domain	Dataset	Train	Val	Test	Positive [%]	Negative [%]
	IMDB	19,923	4,981	24,678	50.19	49.81
Movie Reviews	Cornell	6,823	1,706	2,133	50.0	50.0
	Stanford Sent.	6,911	872	1,819	51.64	48.36
Product Reviews	Instruments	6,068	1,507	1,897	95.07	4.93
Twitter Data	US Airline	7,243	1,811	2,264	19.81	80.19
	Sentiment140	10,161	2,541	3,176	49.94	50.06
Scientific Data	CSC-Clean	797	89	95	74.21	25.79

Table 3. SciCite [7]. Number of instances and class distribution. Taken from [21].

Classes	Training	Validation	Test	Total	Percentage
Result	1,109	123	259	1,491	13.53
Method	2,294	255	605	3,154	28.62
Background	4,840	538	997	6,375	57.85

the authors, the distribution follows the real-world distribution and the number of samples is large enough to sufficiently learn the concepts of each class. Detailed information about the dataset can be found in Table 3. We mainly employed SciCite along with the CSC-Clean dataset to demonstrate the capability of training a multi-task model, where tasks are different and yet from the same domain.

4   Contributions

We divided this section into three main parts. The first part discusses the baseline work from our previous paper ImpactCite [21]. Secondly, we will discuss the impact of training a model on out-domain data. And the third part covers a fusion approach to combine sentiment and intent. We further show that both methods rely on different aspects of the task and highlight their advantages.

4.1   ImpactCite

Our previously proposed approach, ImpactCite [21] served as a baseline for this paper. It is an XLNet [35] based approach for analysis of sentiment and intent of citations found in scientific literature. ImpactCite utilizes two separate XLNets to provide a citation sentiment and intent analysis. To the best of our knowledge, there exists only limited work concerning scientific citation analysis.

The task of citation analysis involves two challenging dataset characteristics. First, the dependency on sentences next to the actual citation. Taking into account that most of the citation sentiment origins from neighborhood sentences lead to longer sequences. Secondly, the model needs to cover dependencies in both directions as in the scientific

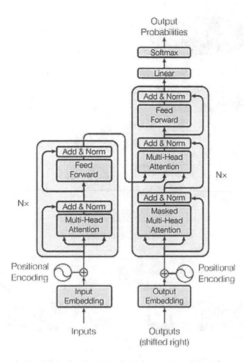

Fig. 1. Transformer-XL architecture [8]. Each of the Multi-Head Attention layers is composed of multiple attention heads that apply a linear transformation and compute the attention.

world the sentiment might be given before or even after the actual citation sentence. Taking into account these essential properties we decided to use XLNet [35] as a model for our experiments. XLNet is a well-known transformer-based network structure that can cover long sequences and bi-directional dependencies. The auto-regressive model is based on a Transformer-XL [8] as the backbone. The Transformer XL architecture is shown in Fig. 1. In addition, there exist many pre-trained XLNet models which is essential for the sentiment classification as the number of datasets for scientific sentiment citation is not sufficient to train such a model from scratch. Precisely, we decided to use the XLNet-Large model to make sure that the model is large enough to cover the whole context. XLNet-Large consists of 24-layers, $1,024$ hidden units, and 16 heads. During our experiments, we only fine-tune the pre-trained model according to the different tasks involving cross-domain sentiment analysis, scientific sentiment classification, and scientific intent classification. As the language of the pre-trained model and the data used to fine-tune it we benefit from the pre-trained weights as the general language structure is similar and only needs small adjustments concerning the domain and task.

Separating these two tasks enables us to fine-tune the corresponding model to each task and achieve the best possible results for that task. This is especially beneficial for the intent as the amount of sentiment citation data is limited. However, the major drawback is that two separate models are required for this purpose and the sentiment does not benefit from the intent model although both tasks are from the same domain.

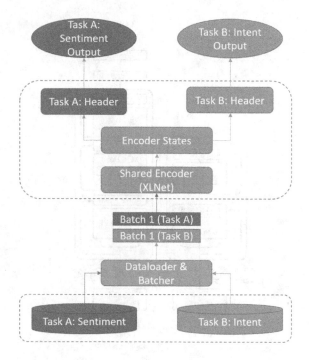

Fig. 2. Mutli-Task setup combining sentiment and intent task. The same encoder is used for both tasks and a task specific head is trained.

4.2 Overcoming Data Scarcity and Data Feeding Techniques

In this paper, we investigated the techniques to overcome the scarcity of data for certain domains. Particularly for sentiment analysis of scientific citations, there are not many datasets available. In this paper, we propose that training on out-domain data and later finetuning on target domain results in better model performance, therefore, bridging the data scarcity gap. Additionally, we experimented with different data feeding methods to analyze their impact on the performance of the final model.

4.3 Fusion Approach

Lastly, in this paper, we propose that although the citation sentiment and intent analysis are different tasks. However, we believe that the underlying text structure concerning the sentiment and intent task on scientific data is similar. Based on the cross-domain sentiment classification we show that the addition of data addressing the same task or the same domain can enhance the scientific sentiment classification. Ultimately, we train a single XLNet model on both the sentiment and intent datasets that performs the complete citation analysis and resolves the dataset size issues. The pipeline is visualized in Fig. 2.

5 Experiments and Analysis

In this section, we will discuss our experiments and their results. All experiments are classified into four sets. The first set discusses the performance benchmark of XLNet [35] for the task of intent classification. The second set discusses the experiments related to the performance benchmark of XLNet for sentiment classification. We performed these benchmarking experiments using several other models ranging from the baseline models i.e. CNN to highly sophisticated language models i.e. BERT [9], ALBERT [14] and XLNet [35]. In the third set of experiments, we will discuss the experiments related to training on out-domain data and testing on several different domains dataset, which also includes finetuning on the target domain dataset. Additionally, a collection of experiments discussing the effects of different data feeding techniques are also discussed in this set of experiments.

Finally, we discuss experiments combining the sentiment and intent modality and serve a single model that processes both tasks. Doing so requires a deep understanding of multiple aspects such as domain dependency, model selection, and task relation. In our case, the first two aspects are covered by benchmarking and the out-domain evaluation. In addition, it has been shown that the tasks are related to each other [20].

5.1 Intent Classification

Experiment1: Performance Benchmarking. To evaluate the performance of different model architectures on the intent classification task we decided to use the SciCite dataset [7]. We used the original train and test splits provided by the dataset and divided our models into two categories. The first category includes all baseline models. We explored different setups of CNNs, LSTMs, and RNNs. These models were trained from scratch using the SciCite dataset. In addition, we also trained BERT [9], ALBERT [14] and ImpactCite (XLNet). The second category of models was pre-trained and is a member of the transformer-based solutions. These models were only fine-tuned on the SciCite dataset. Due to high imbalance data, we employed the micro-f1 and macro-f1 scores for performance comparison. Furthermore, initial experiments using the CNN, LSTM, and RNN approaches have shown that their performance using pre-trained embeddings e.g. GloVe[4] did not improve compared to newly initialized embeddings. We emphasize that one of the reasons for this might be the domain discrepancy between the pre-trained embeddings and the scientific domain.

Results and Discussion. Table 4 shows the performance benchmark results of different selected architectures for the intent classification task. It is evident from the results that both the LSTM and RNN are not able to compete with the CNN. A reason for the inferior performance of the RNN is the length of the sequences resulting in vanishing gradients for the RNN. The LSTM on the other hand suffers from the bi-directional influences between the sentences that are not completely covered by the architecture. We further explored different layer and filter sizes for baseline models. However, there is only an insignificant difference when tuning the parameters. Concerning the time

---

[4] https://nlp.stanford.edu/projects/glove/.

Table 4. Performance evaluation on SciCite [7] (intent) dataset. L = Layer, F = Filter, C = convolution size. Taken from [21].

Topography	Architecture	Class-based accuracy			micro-f1	macro-f1
		Result [%]	Method [%]	Background [%]		
CNN	L 3 F 100 C 3,4,5	79.92	76.53	79.24	78.50	78.56
CNN	L 3 F 100 C 2,4,6	81.85	77.69	81.14	80.12	**80.22**
CNN	L 3 F 100 C 3,3,3	64.09	71.74	85.46	78.05	73.76
CNN	L 3 F 100 C 3,5,7	76.45	74.05	85.46	**80.49**	78.65
CNN	L 3 F 100 C 3,7,9	68.34	70.58	87.26	79.20	75.39
LSTM	L 2 F 512	73.75	73.55	79.54	76.80	75.61
LSTM	L 4 F 512	75.29	69.59	82.95	77.54	75.94
LSTM	L 4 F 1024	68.73	70.91	84.25	77.75	74.63
RNN	L 2 F 512	25.10	56.86	62.19	55.30	48.05
BERT [9]	Base	84.56	75.37	89.47	84.20	83.13
ALBERT [14]	Base	83.78	77.03	87.06	83.34	82.62
ImpactCite [21]	Base	92.67	85.79	88.34	**88.13**	**88.93**
BiLSTM-Att [7]	*	*	*	*	*	82.60
Scaffolds [7]	*	*	*	*	*	84.00
BERT [4,9]	Base	*	*	*	*	84.85
SciBert [4]	*	*	*	*	*	85.49

consumption, the CNN shows superior performance over the other baseline approaches as it can compute things in parallel as compared to LSTMs and RNNs.

The second category presented in Table 4 shows the complex language models. We were able to achieve a new state-of-the-art performance using ImpactCite [21]. It significantly outperformed the other fine-tuned language models by up to 3.9% micro-f1 and 5.8% macro-f1 score. Especially, the increase in the minority classes has shown a significant difference of 10%. Summarizing the findings, we have demonstrated that ImpactCite (XLNet) was able to outperform the CNN by 8.71% and the language models by 3.9% macro-f1 score and significantly increased the performance for the minority class. This highlights the significantly better capabilities of the larger transformer-based model pre-trained on a different domain and later fine-tuned.

5.2 Sentiment Classification

In this section, we will discuss the experiments conducted for the task of scientific sentiment classification. There were two datasets used in these experiments namely Citation Sentiment Corpus (CSC) and our proposed clean version of the dataset called CSC-C.

Experiment 1: Fixed Dataset Split on CSC Sentiment Dataset. For this experiment, we employed a fixed 70/30 data split for the CSC dataset excluding any additional dataset cleansing. We evaluated the performance of each previously used model. Additionally, we employed several sample strategies i.e. focal loss, SMOTE & upsampling, and analyzed their impact concerning the imbalanced data.

Table 5. Performance: Citation Sentiment Corpus (CSC). Taken from [21].

Topography	Modification	Class-based accuracy		
		Positive [%]	Negative [%]	Neutral [%]
CNN	*	28.2	21.3	94.8
CNN	Focal	36.9	16.9	94.3
CNN	SMOTE	39.4	20.2	84.2
CNN	Upsampling	36.1	6.7	92.8
LSTM	*	32.8	12.4	93.9
LSTM	Focal	42.7	19.1	82.8
LSTM	SMOTE	42.3	20.2	83.7
LSTM	Upsampling	26.1	11.2	**97.0**
RNN	*	24.5	21.3	72.7
BERT [9]	*	38.6	20.4	96.4
ALBERT [14]	*	44.3	28.8	95.8
ImpactCite [21]	*	**78.9**	**85.7**	75.4

Results and Discussion. The results of this experiment are shown in Table 5. We observed that all models mainly captured the concept of neutral citations. Additionally, we also observed that the methods like focal loss and SMOTE sampling increased the performance of the CNNs and LSTMs. Furthermore, upsampling does not help to improve the performance of the model. However, ImpactCite [21] effectively learned representations of each class. Especially, the negative class was captured in a much better way by ImpactCite. Although ImpactCite showed slightly worse performance on the neutral class, it performed significantly better for positive and negative classes. We conclude that ImpactCite is able to deal with the large class imbalance and show that the complex language models are superior to the baseline approaches enhanced with sampling and focus strategies for the CSC dataset.

Experiment 2: Cross-Validation on CSC-Clean Sentiment Dataset. In order to compare our proposed ImpactCite with the results of Athar [2] we used a 10-fold-cross validation. However, due to the missing split information and the duplicates that exist in the original CSC dataset, we decided to perform the experiment on the CSC-C dataset. Although the results are not directly comparable, the approach [2] is favored due to the duplicates that appear in the training and test data. For the sake of completion, we included [2] as a reference. During the 10-fold cross-validation, we used nine splits as training and one split as a test dataset for each run and averaged the results at the end. A collection of experiments were performed employing a variety of models ranging from baseline CNN models to complex BERT language models. In order to successfully apply the baseline methods, we used the class weights as they have shown superior performance in previous experiments.

Table 6. Cross validation performance: Sentiment citation corpus (CSC-C). Taken from [21].

Topography	Class-based accuracy			micro-f1	macro-f1
	Positive [%]	Negative [%]	Neutral [%]		
CNN	40.2	24.9	95.0	88.6	43.4
LSTM	34.8	19.0	92.1	84.6	46.1
RNN	20.7	17.9	86.0	77.9	41.5
BERT [9]	72.8	80.2	70.3	74.4	74.4
ALBERT [14]	71.1	72.5	67.6	70.4	70.4
ImpactCite [21]	64.6	86.6	82.0	77.7	**77.7**
SVM [2]^a	*	*	*	**89.9**	76.4

^{a} Trained and tested on CSC

Results and Discussion. The results of this experiment are shown in Table 6. Interestingly, the baseline models were not able to achieve comparable performance even though the class weights were employed. In order to resolve the class imbalance issue, we pre-processed the folds for the baseline approaches such that the number of positive and neutral training samples was decreased to the number of negative samples. Doing so resulted in the performances shown in the table. Additionally, we observed that the complex language models performed much better on the small dataset. They significantly outperformed the baseline methods and achieved good results across all three classes. In addition, ImpactCite~[21] outperformed all other selected models and sets a new state-of-the-art for citation sentiment classification on the CSC-Clean. For the sake of completeness, we included the SVM used by Athar evaluated on the CSC dataset.

5.3   Out-Domain: Evaluating Impact of Additional Data

In this section, we present our results using out-domain data to evaluate its impact on the model performance. We investigate multiple scenarios of cross dataset training and testing on datasets from different domains. Furthermore, we conducted experiments concerning the use of multiple datasets and an optimal schedule strategy to enlarge the corpus size. We also discuss details of some experiments related to different data feeding methods.

Experiment 1: Out-domain Testing. In this experiment, we employed a pre-trained XLNet for each dataset and fine-tune it on one dataset. Once the model is trained, we evaluated its performance across all datasets to find out which datasets are semantically closer to each other. The goal is to better understand the correlation of the dataset and to what extent it is possible to use the model trained on an out-domain dataset for the prediction of sentiment across other domains. In this experiment, we trained each model for 40 epochs with a batch size of 24. In addition, we also used an early stopping mechanism such that if the model converges before 40 epochs then it will stop further training to prevent over-fitting. It has to be mentioned, that in this experiment the datasets had different sizes, as shown in Table 2.

Table 7. Results for testing on out-domain data using XLNets trained on a single dataset. Results are macro f1-scores in percent.

Test Train	Movie			Product	Twitter		Scientific
	IMDB	Cornell	Stanford	Instruments	Us Airline	Sentiment140	CSC-Clean
IMDB	**94.38**	81.58	83.66	70.20	64.53	62.72	54.16
Cornell	92.05	**89.69**	**94.39**	57.46	87.69	69.15	60.28
Stanford	91.71	89.49	92.85	63.68	86.46	68.89	63.76
Instruments	86.51	55.53	57.14	**82.73**	52.63	57.52	49.71
US Airline	56.80	71.45	79.47	43.80	**92.21**	68.39	43.45
Sentiment140	79.28	72.63	76.95	65.13	77.14	**80.57**	62.42
CSC-Clean	85.04	62.91	62.79	64.60	63.88	62.13	**76.67**

Results and Discussion. In Table 7 we show the results when using a single training set and testing across all datasets. Overall the best performance was achieved using the same dataset for training and testing, the only exception is the Stanford dataset. Interestingly, the performance for the Stanford dataset is surprisingly good when the model is trained on the Cornell data. It has to be mentioned, that both datasets are from the same domain. This shows that training on more domain data without fine-tuning on a specific dataset can result in a pretty good model for that dataset which is taken from the same domain. Overall training on the Stanford dataset was not successful. In general training on a dataset of the same domain without fine-tuning the model resulted in a good performance on their own domain however it is not the case when trained on out-domain data. One reason for this is the correlation between the data within the same domain. The results further show that the correlation across domains is in general lower but in the case of the Instruments dataset, the correlation is high enough to achieve superior performance using a dataset that is more balanced from the movie review domain. This suggests that a correlation between movie reviews and instrument reviews (product reviews) exists. Intuitively, this is the case because the understanding of positive and negative in the scientific domain is fundamentally different compared to review data or tweets.

Experiment 2: Sequential Training. In this experiment, we evaluated the impact of a sequential training scheme. The idea is that if a dataset is very small and therefore it is not possible to train only on that dataset, we enhance the data size by using additional datasets. There are two interesting aspects to using additional datasets. One it will increase the amount of data available for training and secondly, we also want to evaluate the impact of the dataset sequence in which data is fed to the network. Intuitively, the last dataset category in the training sequence should be favored with respect to the performance as the gradients are optimized on it. We performed this for a fixed sequence of datasets and categories and used several permutations of the sequence of categories to have comparable results. In addition, we performed these experiments twice, once for the upsampled datasets and once for the downsampled. The reason for this procedure is that it is important to make all datasets the same size such that they can contribute

Table 8. Macro f1-scores for sequential training. Sequence within the categories: [P]roduct (Instruments), [M]ovie (Cornell, IMDB Stanford Sent.), [S]cientific (CSC-Clean), [T]witter (Sentiment140, US Airline). 'Up' corresponds to the upsampled training data and 'Down' to the downsampled training data.

Test	Movie			Product	Twitter		Scientific
Train	IMDB	Cornell	Stanford	Instruments	Us Airline	Sentiment140	CSC-Clean
Up							
S T P M	**93.05**	**88.51**	90.87	80.22	89.69	75.45	**78.18**
M S T P	92.94	86.98	89.35	**80.25**	86.97	**77.16**	69.16
P M S T	91.62	87.81	90.05	74.32	89.84	76.25	70.39
T P M S	92.19	88.19	**91.26**	77.72	**90.04**	76.08	76.97
Down							
S T P M	**92.38**	87.29	**89.98**	80.45	85.93	**76.96**	**75.55**
M S T P	92.26	85.65	88.27	78.69	88.38	76.13	**75.55**
P M S T	90.55	85.94	89.27	65.93	**88.79**	75.33	66.73
T P M S	88.95	83.00	86.98	72.07	87.11	75.18	67.34

the same amount to the training. With the initial dataset sizes, this would not be the case and a few datasets would dominate the training due to their size. In the upsampled version we used $3,000$ samples whereas for the downsampling experiment we used the number of instances of the smallest dataset as a reference number. For some datasets, this means we had to select a subset of the training instances. This means we do not preserve the individual class distribution. The sequence of the datasets is shown in the corresponding results tables.

Results and Discussion. In Table 8 we present the results for sequential training. The upper part of the table covers the training results using the upsampling whereas the lower part covers the downsampling results. Our results for the upsampling showed that putting the movie review data at the end achieved the best scores for three out of the seven datasets. The performances overall were superior to the scores of the downsampling. Using the movie data as the last dataset in the training resulted in a 78.18% macro f1-score for the scientific data which is 1.21% better compared to setting the scientific data at the end of the sequence. The downsampled part shows that the training with the product data, in the end, has shown the best performance for the three datasets. Interestingly, the performance on the scientific data was 8.21% better using the downsampled either the product or movie datasets in the end compared to using its own dataset as last in the downsampled scenario. Except for the testing on Instruments and the CSC-Clean dataset, the performances of the other datasets did not change dramatically based on the feeding sequence. Another interesting finding was that putting the movie reviews in the end for the downsampled experiments did not result in a bad performance for all other dataset categories and led to a maximum drop of 2.86% for the US Airline dataset compared to the best performance for that dataset. In general, it was not the case that the models shows a bias towards the dataset that was used last in the training epoch. It is to be noted that due to the computational effort we did not try every combination but selected a subset that puts every category once at each position.

Table 9. Macro f1-scores for shuffled training. 'Up' corresponds to the upsampled training data and 'Down' to the downsampled training data.

Test / Train	Movie			Product	Twitter		Scientific
	IMDB	Cornell	Stanford	Instruments	Us Airline	Sentiment140	CSC-Clean
Up	93.65	88.04	91.81	88.90	89.99	77.13	74.45
Down	97.80	87.07	88.42	83.40	86.96	76.65	73.73

Furthermore, the general finding of this experiment series is that unexpectedly the network does not work better when trained last on the evaluating dataset. Although most of the achieved accuracies are comparable it is not easy to predict which sequence works best for which testing set. Generally, upsampling was superior for most of the datasets. However, it requires much more training time. In our case, the dataset size is $3,000$ compared to 797 samples for the downsampled version.

Experiment 3: Shuffled Training. In addition to the sequential data feeding experiment, we performed similar experiments by shuffling the data. The major difference compared to the previous experiment was that there is no sequence preserved, neither within the categories nor between the categories. Therefore, the gradients can align to each of the data samples and are not biased towards the last category in the setup.

Results and Discussion. In Table 9 we show the results of the shuffled upsampling and downsampling experiments. Surprisingly, the macro-f1 scores are close to each other. In these experiments, the downsampled data used about 800 instances of each dataset whereas the upsampled $3,000$. Even more interesting is that the shuffled model performed well across all datasets. The largest accuracy drop compared to the single dataset training models was about 3.44% for the Sentiment140 dataset. Comparing the performances of the downsampled model to the models trained exclusively on those datasets, the accuracy of the shuffled model is impressively good. The same holds for the upsampled model. In general, the shuffled model holds a better generalization as it can be applied on all the datasets even without fine-tuning and sticks to good performance.

5.4   Multi-task Model: Fusing Scientific Sentiment and Intent

Experiment 1: Multi-domain Usage. We further experimented with the unified model for the sentiment and intent classification. This experiment combines both tasks into a single model. The motivation behind this experiment is to handle the increased amount of computation resource and inference time when using two separated models as proposed in ImpactCite. However, due to the small size of the CSC-Clean dataset it is not possible to train it directly in conjunction with the intent task. Therefore, we utilized the previous findings and combined the citation sentiment data with the sentiment datasets from other domains to enlarge the training set. Therefore, the sentiment task covers the sentiment classification for all used datasets that included a neutral class.

Table 10. Macro f1-scores sentiment and intent classification. Shows that the single task model is superior for the individual tasks.

Setup Task	Mutli-Task		Single-Task (ImpactCite)	
	All sent. datasets	CSC-Clean + Stanford	CSC-Clean	SciCite
Sentiment	64.00	56.00	**80.41**	*
Intent	78.00	78.00	*	**88.93**

Results and Discussion. Results in Table 10 show that the unified multi-task model has advantages however it is achieved with certain limitations. Firstly, the advantage of the multi-task model is that only a single model is used and two different heads are trained. This makes inference twice as fast as only one forward pass is needed and reduces the required hardware. However, the only impediment is that the model is trained on the conjunction of sentiment data and therefore the bias of the out-domain context can hinder the intent performance. It is to be noted that the model is robust against out-domain data for the sentiment task.

6   Discussion

In our previous paper [21] we have shown that our approach is capable to perform well on both the sentiment and intent classification. The results clearly highlighted the problems with the scientific sentiment domain and the lack of data. Additionally, the unbalanced datasets resulted in difficulties to converge for all evaluated methods except ImpactCite [21]. Neither ALBERT [14] nor BERT [9] were able to converge up to a state that provides a sufficient performance across all tested classes. While an intent classification using those models works well this is not the case for sentiment classification as some classes were not captured by the models. Especially, the negative class was identified as one of the major shortcomings. However, we were able to overcome this data shortcoming up to a certain extent using ImpactCite [20]. We achieved a new state-of-the-art performance for both tasks emphasizing the gains using XLNet [35] when the existing data is limited and unbalanced. In addition, these findings served as a baseline for qualitative citation analysis which is most times not considered due to the lack of available datasets.

In this paper we mainly focused on the utilization of out-domain data to enhance the sentiment classification in the scientific domain which suffers from the lack of existing annotated datasets. Our experiments have shown that without a specific fine-tuning the correlation between in-domain datasets is stronger compared to out-domain datasets and it is possible to achieve surprisingly good results training a classifier on a dataset of the same domain even without fine-tuning. Interestingly, in some cases, the larger quality datasets have shown better performance on some test sets than using the original training set. Going one step ahead, we evaluated different scheduling techniques to better understand the impact of data fusion. First, we tried different sequential concatenations resulting in better-generalized models that we are able to perform well across all datasets. Although the sequence has been shown to bias the performance slightly towards the last category the results showed that the movie data as the last set in the sequence performed best. In addition, the difference between the upsampled and down-sampled training dataset versions highlighted that if the number of datasets concatenated is sufficient then this approach works for very small datasets below 800 samples. Next, we mixed all sentiment training data to avoid preserving sequence to favor any of the domains which resulted in a superior model with respect to the generalization. Shuffling all the data removed the convergence towards a single domain. Although it would be possible to fine-tune the model on a single dataset. We demonstrate that our solution is more robust as it is confronted with out-domain data during the training and further utilizes this data to establish a more general understanding of the underlying language concepts that are not bound towards one domain.

Ultimately, the combination of tasks within a single model can be very complex. During our experiments, we faced several challenges while combining the sentiment and intent tasks. It was not possible to train a model that is capable to converge using only the scientific sentiment and intent data. This is the case as the sentiment data is very small and when combined with the intent task, the network is not able to learn the concept of sentiment, especially negative sentiment, due to a large amount of unrelated data. Although we have shown in our previous work [21] that the use of two separate models is possible this might not be desired as the hardware required to run two models parallel is expensive. Furthermore, a sequential inference suffers from time delay. As a feasibility study, we combined the sentiment data with the out-domain sentiment data and trained the multi-task model. Ultimately, the proposed model is capturing multiple tasks and domains.

7 Conclusion

Utilizing our previous conducted experiments and findings presented in [21] we evaluated the impact of out-domain data usage during the training to enhance datasets and overcome data scarcity in less popular domains. Specifically, the issues faced in the sentiment analysis motivated us to evaluate the combination of different domain sentiment tasks and our results show impressive performances when the training procedure is aligned to work with the multiple concatenated datasets. Our first finding highlights that training using an in-domain dataset can already result in a suitable classifier for the target dataset even without fine-tuning due to the correlation of the data within the same domain. Going one step further we evaluated the impact of mixed datasets across the domains to enlarge the available amount of data. Doing so we found that the results for some datasets could be improved using a sequential approach in which the datasets with higher quality at the end boost the classifier. Furthermore, shuffling the datasets resulted in a powerful cross-domain model showing a good performance across all datasets. In contrast to the sequential scheduling, the performance of the shuffled approach was more balanced and not biased towards a single domain. Ultimately, we have shown in a feasibility study that multi-task models can be enhanced using out-domain data to enlarge the dataset. It was impossible to combine the scientific sentiment and citation data directly using the sentiment data due to the scarcity of the data. However, with out-domain data mixing, and a shuffled schedule we were able to come up with a fully converge sentiment and intent model. One benefit of this model is the shared encoder resulting in much lower hardware requirements, faster training, and inference. In contrast to that, the separately trained models better converge for their specific task resulting in higher accuracies. We aim for the optimization of the dataset combinations and task combinations to achieve a better multi-task model open for future research.

References

1. Abu-Jbara, A., Ezra, J., Radev, D.: Purpose and polarity of citation: towards NLP-based bibliometrics. In: Proceedings of the 2013 Conference of the North American Chapter of the Association for Computational Linguistics: Human Language Technologies, pp. 596–606. Association for Computational Linguistics, Atlanta, June 2013. https://www.aclweb.org/anthology/N13-1067
2. Athar, A.: Sentiment analysis of citations using sentence structure-based features. In: Proceedings of the ACL 2011 Student Session, pp. 81–87. Association for Computational Linguistics, Portland, June 2011. https://www.aclweb.org/anthology/P11-3015
3. Bahrainian, S.A., Dengel, A.: Sentiment analysis and summarization of Twitter data. In: 2013 IEEE 16th International Conference on Computational Science and Engineering, pp. 227–234. IEEE (2013)
4. Beltagy, I., Lo, K., Cohan, A.: SciBERT: a pretrained language model for scientific text. In: Proceedings of the 2019 Conference on Empirical Methods in Natural Language Processing and the 9th International Joint Conference on Natural Language Processing (EMNLP-IJCNLP), pp. 3606–3611 (2019)
5. Bornmann, L., Daniel, H.D.: What do we know about the h index? J. Am. Soc. Inform. Sci. Technol. **58**(9), 1381–1385 (2007)
6. Cliche, M.: BB_twtr at SemEval-2017 task 4: Twitter sentiment analysis with CNNs and LSTMs. In: Proceedings of the 11th International Workshop on Semantic Evaluation (SemEval-2017), pp. 573–580. Association for Computational Linguistics, Vancouver, August 2017. https://doi.org/10.18653/v1/S17-2094, https://www.aclweb.org/anthology/S17-2094
7. Cohan, A., Ammar, W., van Zuylen, M., Cady, F.: Structural scaffolds for citation intent classification in scientific publications. arXiv preprint arXiv:1904.01608 (2019)
8. Dai, Z., Yang, Z., Yang, Y., Carbonell, J., Le, Q.V., Salakhutdinov, R.: Transformer-XL: attentive language models beyond a fixed-length context. arXiv preprint arXiv:1901.02860 (2019)
9. Devlin, J., Chang, M.W., Lee, K., Toutanova, K.: BERT: pre-training of deep bidirectional transformers for language understanding. arXiv preprint arXiv:1810.04805 (2018)
10. Esuli, A., Sebastiani, F.: Determining term subjectivity and term orientation for opinion mining. In: 11th Conference of the European Chapter of the Association for Computational Linguistics (2006)
11. Feldman, R.: Techniques and applications for sentiment analysis. Commun. ACM **56**(4), 82–89 (2013)
12. Garfield, E.: Is citation analysis a legitimate evaluation tool? Scientometrics **1**(4), 359–375 (1979)
13. Khayrallah, H., Thompson, B., Duh, K., Koehn, P.: Regularized training objective for continued training for domain adaptation in neural machine translation. In: Proceedings of the 2nd Workshop on Neural Machine Translation and Generation, pp. 36–44 (2018)
14. Lan, Z., Chen, M., Goodman, S., Gimpel, K., Sharma, P., Soricut, R.: ALBERT: a lite bert for self-supervised learning of language representations. arXiv preprint arXiv:1909.11942 (2019)

15. Li, Y., Baldwin, T., Cohn, T.: What's in a domain? Learning domain-robust text representations using adversarial training. arXiv preprint arXiv:1805.06088 (2018)
16. Lin, C., He, Y.: Joint sentiment/topic model for sentiment analysis. In: Proceedings of the 18th ACM Conference on Information and Knowledge Management, pp. 375–384 (2009)
17. Maas, A.L., Daly, R.E., Pham, P.T., Huang, D., Ng, A.Y., Potts, C.: Learning word vectors for sentiment analysis. In: Proceedings of the 49th Annual Meeting of the Association for Computational Linguistics: Human Language Technologies, pp. 142–150. Association for Computational Linguistics, Portland, June 2011. http://www.aclweb.org/anthology/P11-1015
18. McAuley, J., Targett, C., Shi, Q., Van Den Hengel, A.: Image-based recommendations on styles and substitutes. In: Proceedings of the 38th International ACM SIGIR Conference on Research and Development in Information Retrieval, pp. 43–52 (2015)
19. Medhat, W., Hassan, A., Korashy, H.: Sentiment analysis algorithms and applications: a survey. Ain Shams Eng. J. 5(4), 1093–1113 (2014)
20. Mercier, D., Bhardwaj, A., Dengel, A., Ahmed, S.: SentiCite: an approach for publication sentiment analysis. arXiv preprint arXiv:1910.03498 (2019)
21. Mercier, D., Rizvi, S.T.R., Rajashekar, V., Dengel, A., Ahmed, S.: ImpactCite: an XLNet-based solution enabling qualitative citation impact analysis utilizing sentiment and intent. In: Proceedings of the 13th International Conference on Agents and Artificial Intelligence - Volume 2: ICAART, pp. 159–168. INSTICC, SciTePress (2021). https://doi.org/10.5220/0010235201590168
22. Mrkšić, N., et al.: Multi-domain dialog state tracking using recurrent neural networks. arXiv preprint arXiv:1506.07190 (2015)
23. Munikar, M., Shakya, S., Shrestha, A.: Fine-grained sentiment classification using BERT. In: 2019 Artificial Intelligence for Transforming Business and Society (AITB), vol. 1, pp. 1–5 (2019)
24. Pang, B., Lee, L.: A sentimental education: sentiment analysis using subjectivity. In: Proceedings of ACL, pp. 271–278 (2004)
25. Ranjan, H., Agarwal, S., Prakash, A., Saha, S.K.: Automatic labelling of important terms and phrases from medical discussions. In: 2017 Conference on Information and Communication Technology (CICT), pp. 1–5. IEEE (2017)
26. Sajjad, H., Durrani, N., Dalvi, F., Belinkov, Y., Vogel, S.: Neural machine translation training in a multi-domain scenario. arXiv preprint arXiv:1708.08712 (2017)
27. Snow, R., O'connor, B., Jurafsky, D., Ng, A.Y.: Cheap and fast-but is it good? Evaluating non-expert annotations for natural language tasks. In: Proceedings of the 2008 Conference on Empirical Methods in Natural Language Processing, pp. 254–263 (2008)
28. Socher, R., et al.: Recursive deep models for semantic compositionality over a sentiment treebank. In: Proceedings of the 2013 Conference on Empirical Methods in Natural Language Processing, pp. 1631–1642 (2013)
29. Su, D., et al.: Generalizing question answering system with pre-trained language model fine-tuning. In: Proceedings of the 2nd Workshop on Machine Reading for Question Answering, pp. 203–211 (2019)
30. Tang, D., Wei, F., Yang, N., Zhou, M., Liu, T., Qin, B.: Learning sentiment-specific word embedding for twitter sentiment classification. In: Proceedings of the 52nd Annual Meeting of the Association for Computational Linguistics (Volume 1: Long Papers), pp. 1555–1565 (2014)
31. Thongtan, T., Phienthrakul, T.: Sentiment classification using document embeddings trained with cosine similarity. In: Proceedings of the 57th Annual Meeting of the Association for Computational Linguistics: Student Research Workshop, pp. 407–414. Association for Computational Linguistics, Florence, July 2019. https://doi.org/10.18653/v1/P19-2057, https://www.aclweb.org/anthology/P19-2057

32. Wu, Z., Rao, Y., Li, X., Li, J., Xie, H., Wang, F.L.: Sentiment detection of short text via probabilistic topic modeling. In: Liu, A., Ishikawa, Y., Qian, T., Nutanong, S., Cheema, M.A. (eds.) DASFAA 2015. LNCS, vol. 9052, pp. 76–85. Springer, Cham (2015). https://doi.org/10.1007/978-3-319-22324-7_7

33. Xie, Q., Dai, Z., Hovy, E.H., Luong, M., Le, Q.V.: Unsupervised data augmentation. CoRR abs/1904.12848 (2019). http://arxiv.org/abs/1904.12848

34. Xu, J., Zhang, Y., Wu, Y., Wang, J., Dong, X., Xu, H.: Citation sentiment analysis in clinical trial papers. In: AMIA Annual Symposium Proceedings, vol. 2015, p. 1334. American Medical Informatics Association (2015)

35. Yang, Z., Dai, Z., Yang, Y., Carbonell, J., Salakhutdinov, R.R., Le, Q.V.: XLNet: generalized autoregressive pretraining for language understanding. In: Advances in Neural Information Processing Systems, pp. 5754–5764 (2019)

36. Yousif, A., Niu, Z., Tarus, J.K., Ahmad, A.: A survey on sentiment analysis of scientific citations. Artif. Intell. Rev. **52**(3), 1805–1838 (2017). https://doi.org/10.1007/s10462-017-9597-8

37. Zhou, P., et al.: Attention-based bidirectional long short-term memory networks for relation classification. In: Proceedings of the 54th Annual Meeting of the Association for Computational Linguistics (volume 2: Short Papers), pp. 207–212 (2016)

Using Possibilistic Networks to Compute Learning Course Indicators

Guillaume Petiot$^{(\boxtimes)}$

Catholic Institute of Toulouse, 31 rue de la Fonderie, 31000 Toulouse, France
guillaume.petiot@ict-toulouse.fr

Abstract. E-learning systems generate more and more data that can be used to improve pedagogy. They can also provide a better understanding of a student's learning style. As a result, it is possible to propose a differentiated pedagogy which takes into account learners' needs. The aim of this research is to build course indicators by using expert knowledge in order to provide a synthesis of information about students. As knowledge is often imprecise and uncertain, we used possibility theory to represent knowledge through a possibilistic network. Firstly, we used a message passing algorithm to compute learning course indicators, then we proposed several improvements. Indeed, the use of uncertain gates allows us to generate automatically Conditional Possibility Tables (CPT) instead of eliciting all parameters. Next, we compiled the junction tree of the possibilistic network in order to improve computation time. We compared our compiling approach with message passing inference. A decision support system is generated automatically at the end of the computations. The indicators are presented in a decision support system in which color codes illustrate certainty.

Keywords: Compiling knowledge · Decision Making · Education · Possibilistic networks · Possibility theory · Uncertainty

1 Introduction

E-learning platforms generate a huge amount of data that cannot be fully interpreted by teachers. So researchers have tried to use the AI tools as a solution to this problem [3,6,13,26]. Several applications of AI have already been proposed [1,31] in order to personalize students' learning experience, to develop adaptive learning, model learning behaviour, improve decision-making, analyze the learners' sentiments, give recommendations, perform a classroom monitoring, propose an intelligent tutoring systems, etc. The aforementioned researchers also tried to highlight the students risking dropping out or failing at the examination. They made use of Bayesian networks, neural networks, support vector machines, reinforcement learning, deep learning, and so on.

We propose in this study to compute learning course indicators by using teachers' knowledge. Our previous paper published in [24] presented an overview of our approach. We present here a more detailed description of our research and particularly of the algorithms used to compute indicators. We provide more examples and results obtained by using our solution.

© Springer Nature Switzerland AG 2022
A. P. Rocha et al. (Eds.): ICAART 2021, LNAI 13251, pp. 135–157, 2022.
https://doi.org/10.1007/978-3-031-10161-8_7

Defining indicators by using knowledge leads us to consider several problems. Indeed, expert knowledge is often imprecise, uncertain and sometime incomplete. Possibility theory, proposed by L. A. Zadeh [30] in 1978 after the fuzzy set theory in 1965, can be used to solve this problem. The indicators can be represented by a Directional Acyclic Graph that shows the causal link between the variables. We can use a possibilistic network [4] which is an adaptation of the Bayesian network [18,20] to possibility theory. In the possibilistic network, we need to define for each variable a CPT. After the injection of evidence, which is new information in the network, we can compute its effect on the indicators. The problem however arises when the number of parents of a variable grows because the number of parameters of the CPT grows exponentially. That is why it may be more appropriate to use uncertain logical gates [10]. Moreover, they allow us to represent unknown variables of a complex system by adding a leakage variable. The authors of [10] proposed to encode variables with several ordered states. For example the states low, medium and high of a variable can be encoded into a scale of numerical values, 0, 1 and 2.

Several algorithms of exact inference can be used in a possibilistic network. They are inspired by the algorithms that exist for Bayesian networks (e.g., the message propagation inference algorithm, loop cut-set conditioning proposed by J. Pearl [21,22], arc reversal [27,28], the variable elimination [32], Shenoy-Shafer [29], Hugin [14], etc.). Most of the inference algorithms based on a junction tree share an exponential computation time which is proportional to the largest clique in the junction tree.

In this paper, we would like to perform an experimentation of indicator calculation by using possibilistic networks and uncertain gates. To improve the running time of the inference, we propose to use a new approach based on the compiling of the junction tree. We will compare this solution to the traditional message passing algorithm.

In our experimentation, we will use an existing dataset, fully anonymized, made up of Moodle logs for a course of spreadsheet, and some external information, such as attendance and results at the examination. The knowledge of the course indicators is provided by the teachers and extracted by data mining [23].

To do this, we will first present possibility theory and uncertain gates. Then, we will describe our message passing algorithm and compile our possibilistic networks. Finally, we will discuss our results.

2   Possibility Theory

Possibility theory was proposed in 1978 by L.A. Zadeh [30] as an extension of the fuzzy set theory. Possibility theory, in which imprecise knowledge can be represented by a possibility distribution π, deals with the management of uncertainty and provides two dual operators, the possibility measure Π and the necessity measure N from $P(\Omega)$ in $[0, 1]$, as presented by the authors [11]. Ω is the universe of the discourse and $P(\Omega)$ is the set of all subsets of Ω. The possibility distribution must be normalized ($\exists x \in \Omega$ such as $\pi(x) = 1$). The possibility measure and the necessity measure are defined as follows [24]:

$$\forall A \in P(\Omega), \Pi(A) = \sup_{x \in A} \pi(x) \tag{1}$$

$$\forall A \in P(\Omega), N(A) = 1 - \Pi(\neg A) = \inf_{x \notin A} 1 - \pi(x) \tag{2}$$

Possibility theory is not additive but maxitive. We have the following properties:

$$\forall A, B \in P(\Omega), \Pi(A \cup B) = \max(\Pi(A), \Pi(B)). \tag{3}$$

$$\forall A, B \in P(\Omega), \Pi(A \cap B) \leq \min(\Pi(A), \Pi(B)). \tag{4}$$

We also have the following properties for the dual necessity measure:

$$\forall A, B \in P(\Omega), N(A \cap B) = \min(N(A), N(B)). \tag{5}$$

$$\forall A, B \in P(\Omega), N(A \cup B) \geq \max(N(A), N(B)). \tag{6}$$

E. Hisdal [12] proposed a solution to compute the possibility of a variable A given the variable B, generalized by D. Dubois and H. Prade [11]:

$$\Pi(A|B) = \begin{cases} \Pi(A, B) & \text{if } \Pi(A, B) < \Pi(B), \\ 1 & \text{if } \Pi(A, B) = \Pi(B). \end{cases} \tag{7}$$

Possibilistic networks [4,5] are the counterpart of Bayesian networks in possibility theory and can be defined as follows:

Definition 1. *A possibilistic network (G, Σ) is defined when the following elements are given:*

- *A Directional Acyclic Graph G, $G = (V, E)$, where V is the set of nodes of the graph and E the edges of G;*
- *The set of all conditional possibility distributions noted Σ. All conditional possibility distributions must be normalized;*
- *The factoring property, where the possibility $\Pi(V)$ can be factorized toward the graph G:*

$$\Pi(V) = \bigotimes_{X \in V} \Pi(X/Pa(X)). \tag{8}$$

The function $Pa(X)$ returns the parents of the variable X.

There are two classes of possibilistic networks. Min-based possibilistic networks (qualitative) if $\otimes$ is the minimum and the Product-based possibilistic networks (quantitative) if $\otimes$ is the product. In min-based possibilistic network the possibility distribution is a mapping from Ω to an ordinal scale leading to consider only the ordering of the values. The product-based possibilistic network is very similar to the Bayesian network in the sense that the possibilistic scale is numerical and can be combined by using arithmetic operators. In this case the possibility degree can be interpreted in the ranking scale $[0, 1]$. In this research, we will use a min-based possibilistic network because we have chosen to compare the possibilistic values instead of using an intensity scale in $[0, 1]$.

Uncertain logical gates were proposed for the first time by the authors of [10] to compute automatically the CPTs in a possibilistic network. They are the counterpart of noisy gates in possibility theory. They use the property of the Independence of Causal Influence to provide a model that represents uncertainty between a set of causal variables $X_1, ..., X_n$ and an effect variable Y. This model is built by introducing an intermediate variable Z_i between each causal variable and the effect variable.

This allows us to represent two possible behaviors: inhibition and substitution. The former appears when a cause is met and the effect variable Y is not produced. The latter takes place when a cause is not met and the variable Y is produced. In fact, these behaviours are due to inhibitor parameters κ and substitute parameters noted s.

The possibilistic model with the ICI is summarized in the following Fig. 1:

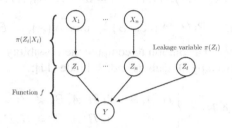

Fig. 1. Possibilistic model with ICI [24].

In this model, there is a deterministic function f that combines the influence of the variables Z_is to compute the variable Y: $Y = f(Z_1, ..., Z_n)$. To represent the unknown knowledge, we can add a leakage variable Z_l. This new variable represents all unknown knowledge and brings forth an uncertain leaky model [10]. For all instantiations y of the variable Y, x_i of the variables X_i, z_i of the variables Z_i and z_l of the variable Z_l, we obtain the following equation for a Min-based possibilistic network [24]:

$$\pi(y|x_1, ..., x_n) = \bigoplus_{z_1, ..., z_n, z_l : y = f(z_1, ..., z_n, z_l)} \bigotimes_{i=1}^{n} \pi(z_i|x_i) \otimes \pi(z_l) \qquad (9)$$

The $\otimes$ is the minimum and $\oplus$ is the maximum. There are several possible functions for f, for example AND, OR, NOT, INV, XOR, MAX, MIN, MEAN, linear combination, etc. To compute the CPT from the equation, we must define $\pi(Z_i|X_i)$, $\pi(Z_l)$, and we must choose a function f. In our experimentation, all variables have three ordered states of intensity: low, medium and high. We propose to encode these states as the authors [10]: 0 for low, 1 for medium and 2 for high. Here is an example of a table for $\pi(Z_i|X_i)$ (Table 1):

Table 1. Possibility table for 3 ordered states [24].

$\pi(Z_i|X_i)$	$x_i = 2$	$x_i = 1$	$x_i = 0$
$z_i = 2$	1	$s_i^{2,1}$	$s_i^{2,0}$
$z_i = 1$	$\kappa_i^{1,2}$	1	$s_i^{1,0}$
$z_i = 0$	$\kappa_i^{0,2}$	$\kappa_i^{0,1}$	1

In the above table, κ_i represents the possibility that an inhibitor exists and s_i the possibility that a substitute exists. If a cause of weak intensity cannot produce a strong effect, then all $s_i = 0$. So in the above example, there are 6 parameters at most per variable and 2 parameters for $\pi(Z_l)$. Another constraint is that $\kappa_i^{1,2} \geq \kappa_i^{0,2}$.

The authors of [10] proposed to use as the function f the function MIN and MAX leading to the connectors uncertain MIN ($\bot$) and uncertain MAX ($\top$). We will use these connectors in our experimentation. We will also use a weighted average function (WAVG) and a MYCIN Like connector ($\hbar$) [23,24]. The result of the function f must be in the domain of Y. We can see that the connectors uncertain MIN and uncertain MAX satisfy this property. Nevertheless, this is not the case for the weighted average function and the MYCIN Like function. Our solution is to use a scaling function f_s, such that $f = f_s \circ g$ where g is the weighted average function or the MYCIN Like function. If we consider the example of the weighted average function, then $g(z_1, ..., z_n) = \omega_1 z_1 + ... + \omega_n z_n$. The parameters ω_i are the weights of the weighted average. If all weights ω_i are equal to $\frac{1}{n}$, then we calculate the average of the intensities. If all weights $\omega_i = 1$, then we make the sum of the intensities (connector $\sum$). If $(\epsilon_0, \epsilon_1, ..., \epsilon_{m-1})$ are the m ordered states of Y, then the function f_s can be as follows:

$$
f_s(x) = \begin{cases} \epsilon_0 & \text{if } x \leq \theta_0 \\ \epsilon_1 & \text{if } \theta_0 < x \leq \theta_1 \\ \vdots & \vdots \\ \epsilon_{m-1} & \text{if } \theta_{m-2} < x \end{cases} \tag{10}
$$

The parameters θ_i allow us to adjust the behaviour of f_s. If the values of θ_i are well defined $\theta_i = i + \frac{1}{2}$, then we perform a rounding to the nearest value.

3 Message Passing Inference

The message passing algorithm for possibilistic networks was inspired by the algorithm proposed for Bayesian networks [18,20]. We used an algorithm of message passing in the junction tree [5,17], which contains two kinds of nodes: cliques and separators. To extract the cliques, we first compute the moral graph, then we compute the triangulated graph by using Kjaerulff's algorithm [15], and finally, we compute the maximal spanning tree by using Kruskal's algorithm [16]. The propagation of evidence is performed by using three phases. The first is the initialization of evidence in the graph, then we perform the phase of collect that consists in propagating evidence from the leaves to the root. The last phase, called distribution, is the propagation from the root to the leaves. Then, we can compute the possibility of the variables. During the initialization, all separators are initialized to 1 and all variables are affected to only one clique. The potential of the cliques can be computed as follows:

$$
w_{C_i}(v) = \bigotimes_{X \in C_i, X \notin C_j, j < i} \pi(X = v_k / pa(X)). \tag{11}
$$

where $v = (v_1, ..., v_{n_i})$ is an instantiation of the variables of the clique C_i, n_i is the size of the clique C_i, $X = v_k$ is the instantiation of the variable X in v, and $pa(X)$ is the instantiation of the parents of the variable X. If C_i is the first clique, all variables of the clique are taken into account to compute $w_{C_i}(v)$. Message passing between the cliques C_i and C_j requires the marginalization of the variables of the clique C_i regarding the variables in the separator $S_{i,j}$ of the two cliques: $w^*_{S_{i,j}}(s) = \bigoplus\limits_{v \in C_i \setminus S_{i,j}} w_{C_i}(s,v)$, where s is an instantiation of the separator $S_{i,j}$ and v is an instantiation of the variables in $C_i \setminus S_{i,j}$. Then, we update the possibility table of the clique C_j: $w^*_{C_j}(s,v) = w_{C_j}(s,v) \otimes w^*_{S_{i,j}}(s)$ where s is an instantiation of the separator $S_{i,j}$ and v is an instantiation of $C_j \setminus S_{i,j}$. To compute the possibility of a variable given evidence ϵ, we compute the combination of the possibility of the variable and the possibility of evidence by using conditioning. When all evidence is injected in the network, we apply the propagation algorithm:

Algorithm 1. Possibilistic message passing.

    Input : The evidence ϵ and a root cluster;

    Output: The conditional possibility of all cluster given ϵ : $\forall_i \, \pi(C_i|\epsilon)$;

1 /* Initialization

2 **forall** $S_{i,j}$ *and* s *instantiation of* $S_{i,j}$ **do**

3     $w^{[0]}_{S_{i,j}}(s) = 1$

4 **forall** C_i *and* $v = (x_1, ..., x_{n_i})$ *instantiation of* C_i **do**

5     $w^{[0]}_{C_i}(v) = \bigotimes\limits_{X \in C_i, X \notin C_j, j < i} \pi(X = x_k / pa(X))$

6 /* Collect

7 **forall** C_i *from the leaves to the root with a unique adjacent clique* C_j *of potential* $w^{[1]}_{C_j}$ *not yet computed* **do**

8   Marginalize C_i on $C_i \setminus S_{i,j}$

9   **forall** s *(instantiation of* $S_{i,j}$*)* **do**

10   Compute $w^{[1]}_{S_{i,j}}(s)$

11   **forall** s *instantiation of* $S_{i,j}$ *and* u *instantiation of* $C_j \setminus S_{i,j}$ **do**

12       $w^{[1]}_{C_j}(s,u) = w^{[0]}_{C_j}(s,u) \otimes w^{[1]}_{S_{i,j}}(s)$

13 /* Distribution

14 **forall** C_i *from the root to the leaves with a unique adjacent clique* C_j *of potential* $w^{[2]}_{C_j}$ *not yet computed* **do**

15   Marginalize C_i on $C_i \setminus S_{i,j}$

16   **forall** s *instantiation of* $S_{i,j}$ **do**

17   Compute $w^{[2]}_{S_{i,j}}(s)$

18   **forall** s *instantiation of* $S_{i,j}$ *and* v *instantiation of* $C_j \setminus S_{i,j}$ **do**

19       $w^{[2]}_{C_j}(s,v) = w^{[1]}_{C_j}(s,v) \otimes w^{[2]}_{S_{i,j}}(s)$

This algorithm allows us to compute the possibility measure of each variable by marginalizing the cluster which contains the variable and its parents. Then, we can deduce the dual necessity measure. This second measure represents certainty.

4   Compiling Possibilistic Networks

In the previous section, we considered the propagation of evidence in a possibilistic network by using a message passing algorithm. Nevertheless, we can also compute possibility and necessity measures by using a different approach. Indeed, the junction tree of a possibilistic network, can be compiled before evaluating the effects of evidence. The same reasoning as in compiling Bayesian networks [8] can be used. The compiling of possibilistic network has been introduced by the authors of [25] but the compiling of the junction tree is not presented. The authors of [19] proposed an algorithm to differentiate the arithmetic circuit of a junction tree. We propose the counterpart of this approach for possibilistic networks.

As for the multilinear function of Bayesian networks, we propose to represent the possibilistic network by using a function f. This function can be defined as follows [24]:

Definition 2. *If P is a possibilistic network, $V = v$ the instantiations of the variables of the possibilistic network and $U = u$ the consistent instantiation of the parents of a variable X with the instantiation $X = x$, then the function f of P is:*

$$f = \bigoplus_{v} \bigotimes_{xu \sim v} \lambda_x \otimes \theta_{x|u} \tag{12}$$

In the above formula, xu denotes the instantiation of the family of X and its parents U compatible with the instantiation v. λ_x are evidence indicators and $\theta_{x|u}$ are the parameters of the CPTs. In fact, for all network CPT parameters of $\pi(X|U)$, we define a parameter $\theta_{x|u}$ where u is an instantiation of U, the parents of the variable X and x an instantiation of the variable X.

The operator $\bigoplus$ can be the function maximum and $\bigotimes$ the function minimum if we consider a qualitative possibilistic network.

We can study, as an example, the following possibilistic network (Table 2):

Table 2. Example of a possibilistic network $A \rightarrow B \rightarrow C$ [24].

A	B			A			B	C	
true	true	$\theta_{b|a}$		A			true	true	$\theta_{c|b}$
true	false	$\theta_{\bar{b}|a}$		true	θ_a		true	false	$\theta_{\bar{c}|b}$
false	true	$\theta_{b|\bar{a}}$		false	$\theta_{\bar{a}}$		false	true	$\theta_{c|\bar{b}}$
false	false	$\theta_{\bar{b}|\bar{a}}$					false	false	$\theta_{\bar{c}|\bar{b}}$

In this case the function f is:

$$
\begin{aligned}
f = {} & \lambda_a \otimes \lambda_b \otimes \lambda_c \otimes \theta_a \otimes \theta_{b|a} \otimes \theta_{c|b} \\
& \oplus \lambda_a \otimes \lambda_b \otimes \lambda_{\bar{c}} \otimes \theta_a \otimes \theta_{b|a} \otimes \theta_{\bar{c}|b} \\
& \vdots \\
& \oplus \lambda_{\bar{a}} \otimes \lambda_{\bar{b}} \otimes \lambda_{\bar{c}} \otimes \theta_{\bar{a}} \otimes \theta_{\bar{b}|\bar{a}} \otimes \theta_{\bar{c}|\bar{b}}
\end{aligned}
\tag{13}
$$

The evidence corresponds to an instantiation of several variables of the possibilistic network. The value of $f(e)$ can be computed by replacing the evidence indicator consistent with the evidence e by 1 or by 0. This assumption leads us to the following definition:

Definition 3. *If the evidence e is an instantiation of several variables, then we have the property $f(e) = \pi(e)$.*

We consider the following example:

Table 3. Example of a possibilistic network $A \to B$ [24].

A	B	
true	true	1
true	false	0.2
false	true	0.1
false	false	1

A	
true	1
false	0.1

If the evidence is $\bar{a}$, then we obtain $\lambda_a = 0$, $\lambda_{\bar{a}} = 1$, $\lambda_b = 1$, $\lambda_{\bar{b}} = 1$ and the computation of $f(e)$ is: $f(\bar{a}) = f(\lambda_a = 0, \lambda_{\bar{a}} = 1, \lambda_b = 1, \lambda_{\bar{b}} = 1) = \theta_{\bar{a}} \otimes \theta_{b|\bar{a}} \oplus \theta_{\bar{a}} \otimes \theta_{\bar{b}|\bar{a}} = 0.1 \otimes 0.1 \oplus 0.1 \otimes 1.0 = 0.1$. The evaluation of f leads us to compute $\pi(e)$.

We can compute the possibility of the variable X given the evidence e by using the conditioning of Eq. 7.

If the variable X has n states and x is one of its states, then we must discuss two cases: if X is not in the evidence e, then $\pi(x|e)$ can be computed by using $\pi(x, e) = f(e, 1_{\lambda_x})$ with $1_{\lambda_x} = (\lambda_{x_1} = 0, ..., \lambda_x = 1, ..., \lambda_{x_n} = 0)$. Otherwise, if X is in e, we have to compute $\pi(x|e - X)$. This leads us to the definition of Evidence Retraction [8] in possibility theory. In fact, $e - X$ denotes the instantiation e without the instantiation of the variable X.

If the operator $\oplus$ is the function maximum and $\otimes$ is the function minimum, then the function f can be transformed into a MIN-MAX circuit. We propose the following definition of a MIN-MAX circuit:

Definition 4. *If we have a min-based possibilistic network $P = (G, \Sigma)$ and its function f, the MIN-MAX circuit of the function f is a directed acyclic graph. The latter is built by considering a root node which is the result of f and the child nodes that are the functions MIN and MAX used in f. The leaf nodes are evidence indicators λ and network parameters θ.*

It is possible to represent a function f of exponential size by a MIN-MAX circuit of linear size [25]. This improvement results in reducing the number of operations to perform to compute f. Moreover, it can also reduce memory used and computation time. We present an example of a MIN-MAX circuit in the following Fig. 2:

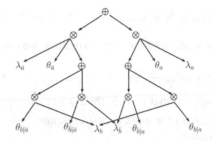

Fig. 2. MIN-MAX circuit of the example [24].

We have chosen to perform the factorization of the function f and then to use the junction tree method. To compile a Bayesian network under evidence, we generate an arithmetic circuit and we differentiate the circuit in order to obtain all posterior probabilities $p(x|e)$. The differentiation is very easy with the arithmetic circuit in probability theory. So we propose to use this advantage to find an algorithm to compute posterior possibilities from the MIN-MAX circuit of a junction tree in possibility theory. Our approach consists of three steps: encoding the MIN-MAX circuit into an arithmetic circuit, differentiating the arithmetic circuit to find an algorithm, and finally performing the inverse encoding of the previous algorithm.

Definition 5. *We obtain the multi-linear function f' of f by applying the Δ operator which replaces the $\otimes$ by multiplications and the $\oplus$ by additions. The circuit generated by applying the same operator to the MIN-MAX circuit is the arithmetic circuit of f'. The operator Δ^{-1} is the inverse operator which replaces the multiplication by $\otimes$ and the addition by $\oplus$.*

The following example summarizes this process (Fig. 3):

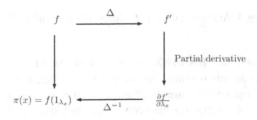

Fig. 3. Use of operators Δ and Δ^{-1}.

We can deduce the proof easily if we consider that the partial derivative way replaces the evidence indicator of x by 1 and substitutes 0 for any other state of this variable. We can verify that the result is the same when we apply Δ^{-1} to $\frac{\partial f'}{\partial \lambda_x}$ and when we compute $f(1_{\lambda_x})$. This leads us to compute $\pi(x)$.

If we consider the example of Table 3, we obtain the following function:

$$f = \lambda_a \otimes \theta_a \otimes (\lambda_b \otimes \theta_{b|a} \oplus \lambda_{\bar{b}} \otimes \theta_{\bar{b}|a}) \oplus \lambda_{\bar{a}} \otimes \theta_{\bar{a}} \otimes (\lambda_b \otimes \theta_{b|\bar{a}} \oplus \lambda_{\bar{b}} \otimes \theta_{\bar{b}|\bar{a}}) \quad (14)$$

We apply the Δ operator and after the transformation, we obtain the following polynomial:

$$f' = \lambda_a \theta_a (\lambda_b \theta_{b|a} + \lambda_{\bar{b}} \theta_{\bar{b}|a}) + \lambda_{\bar{a}} \theta_{\bar{a}} (\lambda_b \theta_{b|\bar{a}} + \lambda_{\bar{b}} \theta_{\bar{b}|\bar{a}}) \quad (15)$$

For example, if we suppose that $e = b$, then $f'(e) = f'(\lambda_b = 1; \lambda_{\bar{b}} = 0; \lambda_a = 1; \lambda_{\bar{a}} = 1)$. To compute $\pi(a, e)$ we must at first compute $\frac{\partial f'(e)}{\partial \lambda_a}$ because a is not in e. We obtain the following result:

$$\frac{\partial f'(e)}{\partial \lambda_a} = \theta_a \theta_{b|a} \quad (16)$$

To obtain $\pi(a, e)$ we apply the inverse operation Δ^{-1} that replaces the additions by $\oplus$ and the multiplications by $\otimes$ in the above equation:

$$\pi(a, e) = \theta_a \otimes \theta_{b|a} \quad (17)$$

We can also encode the MIN-MAX circuit into an arithmetic circuit as follows (Fig. 4):

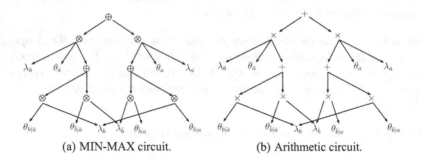

(a) MIN-MAX circuit.   (b) Arithmetic circuit.

Fig. 4. Arithmetic circuit of a MIN-MAX circuit [24].

We propose to build the MIN-MAX circuit of a junction tree obtained from a possibilistic network. To do this we must first select a root node which is the result of f. The children of the output node f are the $\otimes$ nodes of the root cluster. We add a $\oplus$ node for each instantiation of a separator between a current cluster and a child cluster. We add a $\otimes$ node for each instantiation of the variables of a cluster. The children of the $\oplus$ nodes are compatible nodes generated by the child clusters and the children of a $\otimes$ node are compatible nodes generated by the child separators. We have only one node λ_x for each instantiation of a variable X and only one node $\theta_{x|u}$ for each instantiation of a node X and its parents U. Moreover each variable, evidence indicators λ, and network parameters $\theta_{x|u}$ are affected to only one cluster.

We propose now to differentiate the arithmetic circuit of f' generated from the MIN-MAX circuit of f by using the operator Δ. If v is the current node and P represents the parents of v, then we can compute $\frac{\partial f'}{\partial v}$ by using the chain rule [24]:

$$\frac{\partial f'}{\partial v} = \sum_{p \in P} \frac{\partial f'}{\partial p} \frac{\partial p}{\partial v} \tag{18}$$

If one of the parents noted p of P has n other children v_i different from the node v, there are several cases to discuss:

- If v is the root node then $\frac{\partial f'}{\partial v} = 1$;
- If p is an addition node then $\frac{\partial p}{\partial v} = \frac{\partial(v+\sum_{i=1}^{n} v_i)}{\partial v} = 1$;
- If p is a multiplication node then $\frac{\partial p}{\partial v} = \frac{\partial(v \prod_{i=1}^{n} v_i)}{\partial v} = \prod_{i=1}^{n} v_i$.

As a result, by using the operator Δ^{-1} we obtain the following step to evaluate the MIN-MAX circuit of a junction tree [24]. We need two registers for each node to perform the computation noted u and d.

1. Upward: compute the value of the node v and store it in $u(v)$;
2. If v is the root then set $d(v) = 1$ else set $d(v) = 0$;
3. Downward: for each parent p of the node v compute $d(v)$ as follows:
   (a) if p is a node $\oplus$:

$$d(v) = d(v) \bigoplus d(p) \tag{19}$$

   (b) if p is a node $\otimes$:

$$d(v) = d(v) \bigoplus \left[d(p) \otimes \left[\bigotimes_{i=1}^{n} u(v_i^p) \right] \right] \tag{20}$$

The nodes v_i^p are the other children of p;

As a result, we obtain the following algorithm:

Algorithm 2. Junction tree compiling algorithm.

    Input : The MIN-MAX circuit Γ and its root node r
    Output: The computing of u and v for all nodes of Γ
1 Initialize(u)
2 Upward(r)
3 **forall** $v \in \Gamma$ **do**
4   **if** $v == r$ **then**
5   set $d(v) = 1$
6   **else**
7   set $d(v) = 0$
8 Downward(r)

The recursive function Upward is described in the following algorithm:

Algorithm 3. Upward.

Input : node e
Output: The computing of $u(e)$
1 **if** *NumberOfChildren*(e) == 0 **then**
2   **return** $u(e)$

3 **else**
4   **if** *Operator*(e) == $\oplus$ **then**
5      $u(e) = 0$

6   **else**
7      $u(e) = 1$

8   **forall** $c \in$ *ChildrenOf*(e) **do**
9   **if** *Operator*(e) == $\oplus$ **then**
10        $u(e) = u(e) \oplus$ Upward(c)

11   **else**
12        $u(e) = u(e) \otimes$ Upward(c)

13   **return** $u(e)$

In this algorithm, the function NumberOfChildren(e) returns the number of the children of e. The function ChildrenOf(e) returns the set of children of the node e and the function Operator(e) returns the type of the node of e: $\otimes$ or $\oplus$. The recursive function Downward is as follows:

Algorithm 4. Downward.

Input : node e
Output: The computing of $d(c)$ for all children c of e
1 **if** *NumberOfChildren*(e)! = 0 **then**
2   **forall** $c \in$ *ChildrenOf*(e) **do**
3   **if** *Operator*(e) == $\oplus$ **then**
4        $d(c) = d(e) \oplus d(c)$

5   **else**
6        $t = d(e)$
7   **forall** $b \in$ *ChildrenOf*(e) *and* $b! = c$ **do**
8          $t = t \otimes u(b)$
9        $d(c) = t \oplus d(c)$

10   **forall** $c \in$ *ChildrenOf*(e) **do**
11   Downward(c)

---

5   Experimentation

5.1   Presentation

In our experimentation, we used an existing anonymized dataset for a Spreadsheet course at bachelor level proposed in face-to-face learning enriched by an online supplement on Moodle. This dataset was compiled by gathering all data of logs in a table. Then a process of anonymization was performed.

For example, we used the data of Moodle, such as quiz results, sources consulted, wiki consulted, forum participation,... and external data such as attendance, groups, etc. The quiz questions were categorized by skills. When data are missing there are several methods to estimate the missing data in education [2,7,9]. For example one can use mean imputation, regression imputation, Maximum Likelihood Expectation-Maximization (EM) imputation, multiple imputation, hot deck imputation, zero imputation (replace missing values by 0), iterative PCA imputation, ... We chose iterative PCA imputation also called EM-PCA because this method takes into account the profile of the students to provide an estimation of the missing data.

The knowledge about the indicators was provided by the teachers and extracted from the data. We used exploratory statistics approach such as correlation graph, Principal Component Analysis, and Ascending Hierarchical Classification to extract knowledge from the data.

To represent this knowledge we have chosen to use a DAG (Fig. 5):

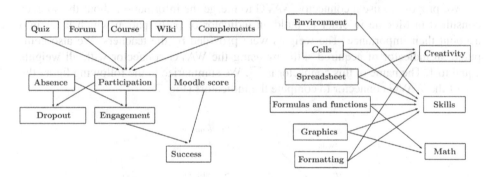

Fig. 5. Modeling of knowledge by a DAG [24].

The variables in the DAG have 3 ordered modalities (low, medium, high) encoded with the numerical values (0,1,2). The description of the indicators by teachers is often imprecise, so we used a possibility distribution to represent each state of a variable. In fact, the variables are linguistic variables and we used the following possibility distributions to compute the evidence from the data (Fig. 6):

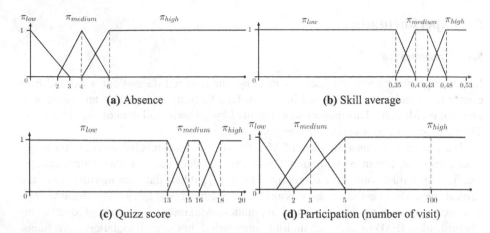

(a) Absence

(b) Skill average

(c) Quizz score

(d) Participation (number of visit)

Fig. 6. Possibility distributions of the variables.

The possibilistic networks require defining all CPTs but if the number of parents of a variable is high, then there are too many parameters to elicit. The use of uncertain gates provides a solution to this problem. Indeed, the CPTs are computed automatically.

We used the uncertain MIN connector ($\perp$) for conjunctive behavior and the uncertain hybrid connector ($\hbar$) for indicators which need a compromise in case of conflict and a reinforcement if the values are concordant.

We propose to use a connector WAVG to merge the information about the sources consulted in Moodle in order to build an indicator of participation which takes into account their importance. The weights were provided by the teachers. We also computed an indicator of acquired skills by using the WAVG connector with all weights equal to 1. The name of this connector is $\sum$. We summarize in the following figure the use of the WAVG connector to compute the indicators (Fig. 7):

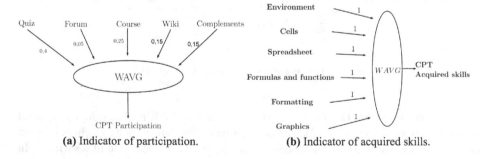

(a) Indicator of participation.

(b) Indicator of acquired skills.

Fig. 7. Weights of the WAVG connectors [24].

As a result, we obtain the following model (Fig. 8):

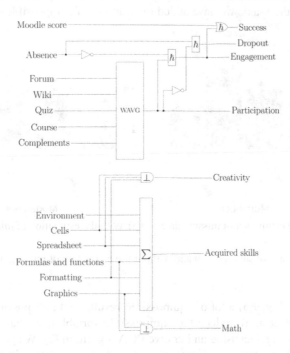

Fig. 8. Knowledge modeling with uncertain connectors [24].

The learning course indicators of our experimentation are computed after several processing operations. Before the propagation of new information, we have to compute the CPTs of all the uncertain gates. Then we compile the junction tree of the possibilistic network and finally we perform the initialization of evidence before applying the upward pass and downward pass. As a result, we obtain for each state of the learning course indicator a possibility measure and a necessity measure. We have compared this approach with the message passing algorithm studied in our previous research [23].

5.2   Results

We have performed several improvements of the initial approach based on a possibilistic network. We have elicited all CPT parameters and performed the computation of the indicators by using the message passing algorithm. The first improvement proposed was to use uncertain gates to avoid the eliciting of all the CPT parameters. Then the computation time was improved by compiling the junction tree of the possibilistic networks. We compared the compilation of the possibilistic networks and the message passing algorithm. As expected, the results of the indicators in both approaches were identical. For example, the indicator of success deals with the prediction of a student's success at the examination. We have computed the percentage of success for each state of the indicator of success. When all states of a variable have a possibility equal to 1 they are equipossible. We obtain the results of Fig. 9 by using the compilation of the possibilistic networks. On the x-axis we have added the number of equipossible results after the modalities.

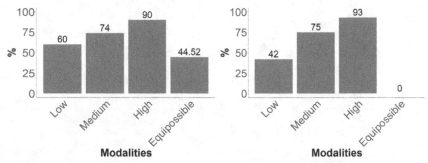

(a) Without the estimation of missing data.   (b) With the estimation of missing data.

Fig. 9. Indicator of success with and without the estimation of missing data [24].

We can see in Fig. 9(a) a lot of equipossible results (with all possibilities equal to 1) due to missing data. To reduce the equipossible variables, we have performed an imputation of missing data using an iterative PCA algorithm [2]. We present the results in Fig. 9(b). Another advantage of our approach is the use of uncertain gates in order to avoid eliciting all parameters of the CPTs. We have compared the result of the indicator of success with and without uncertain gates by compiling the possibilistic networks. The results are the following (Fig. 10):

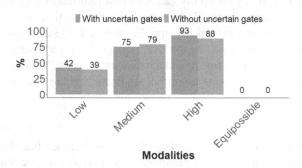

Fig. 10. Comparison of the indicator of success with and without uncertain gates [24].

The results are very close but uncertain gates require fewer parameters than the CPTs elicited by a human expert (Fig. 11).

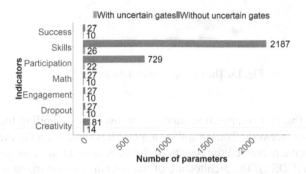

Fig. 11. Comparison of the results with and without uncertain gates by using the compiling of the possibilistic network [24].

The above figure shows that the number of parameters is highly decreased by using uncertain gates for all indicators. We have also compared the running time of the computation of the indicators by using the compiling of the possibilistic networks and the message passing algorithm. The results are the following (Fig. 12):

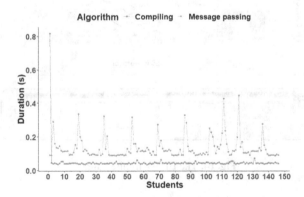

Fig. 12. Comparison of computation time for all students.

We can see in the above figure that the computation time for the indicators of the first student is higher because of the circuit generation. The variation of the computation time between the other students are due to the operating system. Indeed, we used a reinitialization module that allows us to reuse the circuit instead of rebuilding every circuit for each student. The calculation is then faster for the other students because we reuse the first circuit. We have computed the average of the computation time for both methods and we obtain (Fig. 13):

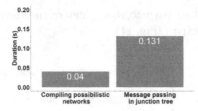

Fig. 13. The average computation time [24].

We can see that the computation time is improved by compiling the junction tree of the possibilistic network. The compiling approach is faster than the message passing algorithm. We have presented the results of the indicators in an Educational Decision Support System (EDSS). The architecture of the system is summarized in the following Fig. 14:

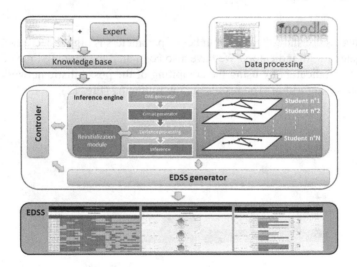

Fig. 14. The EDSS architecture.

This visualization of the indicator is easy to interpret. Indeed, the possibilistic results are transformed to present only the modality of the indicators with the highest necessity. We used a radar graph for the indicator of skills and a horizontal bar graph for the other indicators. We also used a color code to indicate the students with difficulties. The indicators allow us to detect the students at risk. Nevertheless, we must be careful with the interpretation of the results because the indicators are shortcuts of reasoning. Further investigations must be performed by the teachers to confirm the results before taking a decision. We present here two examples of results, the first one concerns successful students:

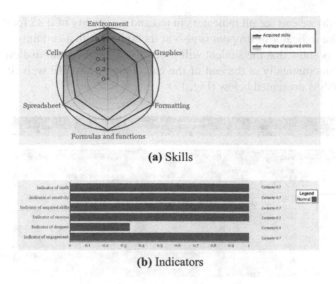

(a) Skills

(b) Indicators

Fig. 15. Student with good results.

In Fig. 15(a) we can see that the curve in blue, representing the score for all skills, has its full value. We have also presented the average skill level in red. In Fig. 15 (b) we can see that all indicators are green and we can see the certainty of the indicators at the right of the graph. Certainty is the necessity measure. The following figures represent a student's disengagement:

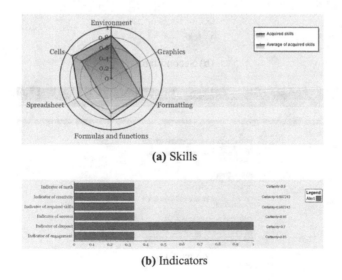

(a) Skills

(b) Indicators

Fig. 16. Dropout student.

In Fig. 16(b) we can see all indicators in red and a certainty of 0.85 for the indicator of success. The indicator of dropout is also at its highest with a certainty of 0.7. All of these indicators show that the student will probably fail at the examination. The EDSS is generated automatically at the end of the calculation as a PHP web site with three tabs. The EDSS is presented below (Fig. 17):

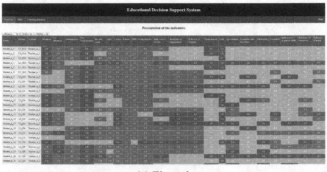

(a) First tab.

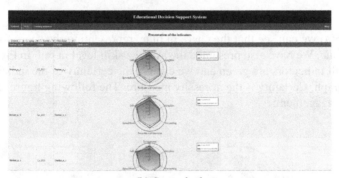

(b) Second tab.

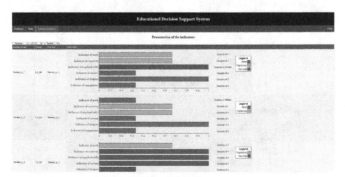

(c) Third tab.

Fig. 17. The tabs of the EDSS.

The first tab is the synthesis of all information with its certainty and it allows us to sort data for all columns. The second tab gathers all skill information in a radar graph. We can compare the skills of a student to the average skills of the year group, the class or the teacher's groups. We can also visualize the certainty for all skills. The last tab concerns all course indicators and uses a color code to highlight the students with difficulties.

6 Conclusion

We proposed to compute learning course indicators for a course of Spreadsheet based on the teachers' knowledge. The indicators were presented in a decision making system for the teachers. To do this we used possibility theory to manage the uncertainties and imprecisions of the teachers' knowledge. As the latter can be represented by a DAG, we used possibilistic networks to compute the indicators by using a message passing algorithm. Then, we performed several improvements, the first of which was using uncertain gates to compute automatically the CPTs. Indeed, uncertain gates allow us to reduce the number of parameters to elicit. Then we proposed a new approach of exact inference based on the compilation of the junction tree. The first step was to generate the MIN-MAX circuit, then we applied an upward pass followed by a downward pass. We compared the performance of both algorithms and highlighted the performance of the compiling approach. The computation time is improved compared to the message passing algorithm.

In future, we would like to perform further experimentations in order to better evaluate the performance of our algorithm proposed for the compilation of the junction tree of a possibilistic network. We would like to compare our approach with approaches based on propositional logic and more especially the deterministic decomposable negation normal form (d-DNNF). We would like to conduct other experiments concerning the computation of learning indicators. Another perspective can be to build a recommendation system based on these indicators and to use a chatbot as a virtual companion to provide advice to students.

References

1. Ahmad, K., et al.: Artificial intelligence in education: a panoramic review (06 2020)
2. Audigier, V., Husson, F., Josse, J.: A principal components method to impute missing values for mixed data. Adv. Data Anal. Classif. **10**(1), 5–26 (2015)
3. Baker, R.S.J.D., Yacef, K.: The state of educational data mining in 2009: a review and future visions. J. Educ. Data Min. **1**(1), 3–17 (2009)
4. Benferhat, S., Dubois, D., Garcia, L., Prade, H.: Possibilistic logic bases and possibilistic graphs. In: the Conference on Uncertainty in Artificial Intelligence, pp. 57–64 (1999)
5. Borgelt, C., Gebhardt, J., Kruse, R.: Possibilistic graphical models. Comput. Intell. Data Min. **26**, 51–68 (2000)
6. Bousbia, N., Labat, J.M., Balla, A., Rebaï, I.: Analyzing learning styles using behavioral indicators in web based learning environments. In: EDM 2010 International Conference on Educational Data Mining, pp. 279–280 (2010)

7. Cheema, J.R.: A review of missing data handling methods in education research. Rev. Educ. Res. **84**, 487–508 (2014)
8. Darwiche, A.: A differential approach to inference in Bayesian networks. J. ACM **50**(3), 280–305 (2003)
9. Dray, S., Josse, J.: Principal component analysis with missing values: a comparative survey of methods. Plant Ecol. **216**(5), 657–667 (2014). https://doi.org/10.1007/s11258-014-0406-z
10. Dubois, D., Fusco, G., Prade, H., Tettamanzi, A.: Uncertain logical gates in possibilistic networks. an application to human geography. In: Beierle, C., Dekhtyar, A. (eds.) SUM 2015. LNCS (LNAI), vol. 9310, pp. 249–263. Springer, Cham (2015). https://doi.org/10.1007/978-3-319-23540-0_17
11. Dubois, D., Prade, H.: Possibility Theory: An Approach to Computerized Processing of Uncertainty. Plenum Press, New York (1988)
12. Hisdal, E.: Conditional possibilities independence and noninteraction. Fuzzy Sets Syst. **1**(4), 283–297 (1978)
13. Huebner, R.A.: A survey of educational data mining research. Res. High. Educ. J. **19**, 13 (2013)
14. Jensen, F.V., Lauritzen, S., Olesen, K.: Bayesian updating in causal probabilistic networks by local computation. Comput. Stat. Q. **4**, 269–282 (1990)
15. Kjaerulff, U.: Reduction of computational complexity in Bayesian networks through removal of week dependences. In: Proceeding of the 10th Conference on Uncertainty in Artificial Intelligence, pp. 374–382. Morgan Kaufmann (1994)
16. Kruskal, J.B.: On the shortest spanning subtree of a graph and the travelling salesman problem. In: Proceedings of the American Mathematical Society, pp. 48–50 (1956)
17. Lauritzen, S., Spiegelhalter, D.: Local computation with probabilities on graphical structures and their application to expert systems. J. R. Stat. Soc. **50**(2), 157–224 (1988)
18. Neapolitan, R.E.: Probabilistic Reasoning in Expert Systems: Theory and Algorithms. Wiley, Hoboken (1990)
19. Park, J.D., Darwiche, A.: A differential semantics for jointree algorithms. In: Advances in Neural Information Processing Systems 15 [Neural Information Processing Systems, NIPS 2002, 9–14 December 2002, Vancouver, British Columbia, Canada], pp. 785–784 (2002)
20. Pearl, J.: Probabilistic Reasoning in Intelligent Systems: Networks of Plausible Inference. Morgan Kaufmann Publishers Inc., San Francisco (1988)
21. Pearl, J.: A constraint - propagation approach to probabilistic reasoning. In: Kanal, L.N., Lemmer, J.F. (eds.) Uncertainty in Artificial Intelligence. Machine Intelligence and Pattern Recognition, vol. 4, pp. 357–369. North-Holland (1986)
22. Pearl, J.: Fusion, propagation, and structuring in belief networks. Artif. Intell. **29**(3), 241–288 (1986)
23. Petiot, G.: Merging information using uncertain gates: an application to educational indicators. In: Medina, J., et al. (eds.) Information Processing and Management of Uncertainty in Knowledge-Based Systems. Theory and Foundations - 17th International Conference, IPMU (2018) Cádiz, Spain, June 11-15, 2018, Proceedings, Part I. Communications in Computer and Information Science, vol. 853, pp. 183–194. Springer (2018)
24. Petiot, G.: Compiling possibilistic networks to compute learning indicators. In: Proceedings of the 13th International Conference on Agents and Artificial Intelligence-Volume 2: ICAART, pp. 169–176. INSTICC, SciTePress (2021)
25. Raouia, A., Amor, N.B., Benferhat, S., Rolf, H.: Compiling possibilistic networks: alternative approaches to possibilistic inference. In: Proceedings of the Twenty-Sixth Conference on Uncertainty in Artificial Intelligence. pp. 40–47. UAI'10, AUAI Press, Arlington, Virginia, United States (2010)

26. Shabani, Z., Eshaghian, M.: Decision support system using for learning management systems personalization. Am. J. Syst. Softw. **2**(5), 131–138 (2014)
27. Shachter, R.: Intelligent probabilistic inference. In: Kanal, L.N., Lemmer, J.F. (eds.) Uncertainty in Artificial Intelligence, pp. 371–382. North-Holland (1986)
28. Shachter, R.: Evidence absorption and propagation through evidence reversals. Mach. Intell. Pattern Recogn. **10** (2013). https://doi.org/10.1016/B978-0-444-88738-2.50021-X
29. Shenoy, P.P., Shafer, G.: Axioms for probability and belief-function propagation. In: Shachter, R.D., Levitt, T.S., Kanal, L.N., Lemmer, J.F. (eds.) Uncertainty in Artificial Intelligence. Machine Intelligence and Pattern Recognition, vol. 9, pp. 169–198. North-Holland (1990). https://doi.org/10.1007/978-3-540-44792-4_20
30. Zadeh, L.A.: Fuzzy sets as a basis for a theory of possibility. Fuzzy Sets Syst. **1**, 3–28 (1978)
31. Zawacki-Richter, O., Marín, V.I., Bond, M., Gouverneur, F.: Systematic review of research on artificial intelligence applications in higher education - where are the educators? Int. J. Educ. Technol. High. Educ. **16**, 1–27 (2019)
32. Zhang, N.L., Poole, D.: A simple approach to Bayesian network computations. In: Proceedings of the Tenth Canadian Conference on Artificial Intelligence, pp. 171–178 (1994)

Assured Deep Multi-Agent Reinforcement Learning for Safe Robotic Systems

Joshua Riley[1]([✉]), Radu Calinescu[1], Colin Paterson[1], Daniel Kudenko[2], and Alec Banks[3]

[1] University of York, Heslington, York, U.K.
jpr538@york.ac.uk
[2] L3S Research Center, Leibniz Universität Hannover, Hannover, Germany
[3] Defence Science and Technology Laboratory, Salisbury, U.K.

Abstract. Using multi-agent reinforcement learning to find solutions to complex decision-making problems in shared environments has become standard practice in many scenarios. However, this is not the case in safety-critical scenarios, where the reinforcement learning process, which uses stochastic mechanisms, could lead to highly unsafe outcomes. We proposed a novel, safe multi-agent reinforcement learning approach named Assured Multi-Agent Reinforcement Learning (AMARL) to address this issue. Distinct from other safe multi-agent reinforcement learning approaches, AMARL utilises quantitative verification, a model checking technique that guarantees agent compliance of safety, performance, and non-functional requirements, both during and after the learning process. We have previously evaluated AMARL in patrolling domains with various multi-agent reinforcement learning algorithms for both homogeneous and heterogeneous systems. In this work we extend AMARL through the use of deep multi-agent reinforcement learning. This approach is particularly appropriate for systems in which the rewards are sparse and hence extends the applicability of AMARL. We evaluate our approach within a new search and collection domain which demonstrates promising results in safety standards and performance compared to algorithms not using AMARL.

Keywords: Reinforcement Learning · Multi-Agent Systems · Quantitative verification · Assurance · Multi-Agent Reinforcement Learning · Safety-critical scenarios · Safe Multi-Agent Reinforcement Learning · Assured Multi-Agent Reinforcement Learning · Deep Reinforcement Learning

1 Introduction

Multi-agent reinforcement learning (MARL) is a machine learning technique that allows multiple agents to work within shared environments to solve complex sequential decision-making problems either cooperatively or competitively [47]. Agents find solutions to these decision-making problems by autonomously interacting with the environment, which can be modelled within a Markov decision process (MDP) framework

Supported by the Defence Science and Technology Laboratory.

[10]. An environment containing only a single reinforcement learning agent will learn the optimal solution, otherwise known as a policy, when it has discovered which actions in all states of the MDP lead to the highest cumulative reward. However, environments containing multiple agents require an extension to the MDP framework known as a multi-agent Markov decision process (MA-MDP) [38]. This extension is necessary because each agent acts independently of the others and, as they interact with the environment, other agents will be affected [30].

MARL has proved a successful approach for many of the scenarios in which it has been utilised, including but not limited to services such as service management and markets [3,6], planetary exploration [17], patrolling and security [28], medical applications, and disaster recovery [25,26]. This potential has its foundations in the fact that many real-world scenarios can be naturally framed as multi-agent problems.

However, MARL systems' potential is significantly limited in safety-critical scenarios due to the inherent stochasticity of the learning mechanisms that underpin them [46]. The unpredictable nature of these agents during the learning process restricts their usage in mission-critical and safety-critical applications. Randomness in agents' action selection could lead to mission failure and harm to the environment, sensitive equipment, humans, and the agents themselves. These issues are exacerbated further with multiple agents dynamically learning within the environment, making the environment non-static [4]. Furthermore, agents' learning with undefined environmental limitations could produce unanticipated solutions and behaviours; despite these solutions potentially meeting all expected safety requirements, it will prove challenging to portray these agents as trustworthy [11].

Reinforcement learning is based on the premise that agents receive numerical rewards for undertaking actions that are beneficial to completing the objectives or penalties for undertaking those actions which are detrimental. For multi-agent systems, the agents may find themselves in conflict, and where multiple goals exist, the potential for conflict is increased yet further. This may lead to scenarios in which the priorities of a single agent lead to a degradation of overall system performance.

In safety-critical scenarios, various states of the system associated with actions or locations carry with them a level of risk. It may not be possible to eliminate risk completely, but we will often wish to constrain the level of risk that the system can sustain and still be viewed as safe. If we over constrain the system with respect to safety, then the performance of the system may be unacceptable. Under such conditions, we wish to maximise the rewards associated with achieving the goals of the system while providing guarantees that a level of risk will not be exceeded.

Traditional approaches to MARL can find compromises between these conflicting goals but cannot guarantee that this compromise will meet safety requirements.

Several suggestions have been proposed in both single-agent reinforcement learning and MARL to address these issues. These focus both on optimisation and exploration mechanisms within reinforcement learning [11]. Despite limitations, the most promising suggestion for the development of safe MARL, which can be guaranteed to meet strict safety and functional requirements, is the constrained criterion [11]. The constrained criterion makes specific states and actions prohibited from use, both during and after learning. The limitation to this approach is the overly simplified constraining method, which can unnecessarily remove actions that would lead to high performance or remove the system's ability to complete its goal entirely. Research that complements the constrained criterion is focused on safe reinforcement learning for a single agent, which makes use of the constrained criterion as a foundation of its approach. The assured reinforcement learning approach [29] is a multi-step approach that makes use of quantitative verification to produce formal guarantees that a single reinforcement learning agent will meet strict safety and functional requirements.

Our preliminary work [36,37] uses assured reinforcement learning as a basis and introduces a multi-stage plug-in styled approach for safe MARL that produces formal guarantees through the use of quantitative verification. This work was framed with a simple cooperative, homogeneous, two-agent system with the goal of patrolling a safety-critical scenario while avoiding unnecessary risk. Previous work also included differing MARL algorithms, increased system sizes, and heterogeneous systems.

In this extended work, we significantly extend our preliminary approach in several ways. First, we augment the approach to support the use of Deep MARL, which allows efficient learning in highly complex environments, in which non-Deep approaches would be unable to find appropriate solutions, as can be seen by its use in current literature [31]. Second, we demonstrate our approach working alongside intrinsically curious agents [39]. These agents are characterised by eager exploration into unknown states, facilitating faster learning in environments with sparse rewards. Lastly, we integrate and evaluate our approach with a more realistic simulation by utilising ML-Agents [20], a MARL testing adaption of the Unity games engine, which is currently receiving heightened attention from the RL research community because of its rendering abilities, simulated physics, and plug-in style.

2 Background

2.1 Markov Decision Process

An MDP is a formalism for representing a sequential decision-making problem that has aspects of stochastic behaviour [43]. The MDP is a model of the agents and the environment in which they are operating. It describes how the environment changes as the agents take different actions. Probabilities associated with actions allow for stochasticity within the model to be described.

An MDP is a tuple (S, A, P, R) where:

- S is a finite set of states representing the current environmental state including the agents.
- A is a finite set of actions representing the capabilities of the agents.
- $P : S \times A \times S$ is then a state transition function such that for any $s, s' \in S$ and $a \in A$, which is an allowed action in s, s'.
- $P(s, a, s')$ is the probability of transitioning to state s' when undertaking action a in state s.
- $R : S \times A \times S \rightarrow \mathbb{R}$ is a reward function such that $R(s, a, s') = r$ is the reward associated with taking an action a in state s which leads to s'.

As a Markov decision process is primarily formed from states and actions, state action pairing can be selected that will allow an agent to navigate an MDP with an optimal policy. One way in which to solve an MDP is with the Bellman Eq. 1, where state-action pairs (s, a) are used to distinguish the most effective actions in each state from the initial state of the MDP to the terminal state, using γ as a discount factor for the value of the future state.

$$V(s) = \max_a(R(s, a) + \gamma V(S'))$$ (1)

2.2 Multi-Agent Markov Decision Process

An MA-MDP, otherwise known as a Markov game, is a mathematical framework that captures multiple agents or processes within a system [30]. An MA-MDP's rewards explicitly change due to the choices of each agent, allowing rewards from an MA-MDP to be assigned to the agent that has made the said move. However, to solve an MA-MDP, the actions and objectives of all agents or processes must be considered.

| | | Player Two | |
		Conservative	Greedy
Player One	C...	5; 5	0; 10
	G...	10; 0	0; 0

Fig. 1. Two player reward maximisation game.

Considering the simplified two-player game in Fig. 1, players one and two both aim to maximise their returned reward at the end of the game. Each player has two possible actions. The first to act greedily, taking all of the rewards, leaving the other player with nothing. The second is to act conservatively, taking half of the available reward. If both players act greedily, they will receive no reward, but if they both act conservatively, they will both receive half of the reward. We can see from this simple example that each player's actions affect the other players in the game.

Suppose the players are able to observe all other player choices and outcomes. In that case, they are likely to opt for the conservative choice, as they are both guaranteed a reward, despite the possibility of achieving higher rewards with the greedy choice. In a Markov game, it is desirable to reach a Pareto-optimal or Nash equilibrium strategy, which is defined as finding a strategy in which no player can perform another action to receive a greater reward without decreasing the reward received by all other players [32].

2.3 Abstract Markov Decision Process

AMDPs are a high-level representation of an MDP, where states and actions are aggregated based on similarities. This is necessary for many practical scenarios since encoding all possible state combinations will lead to a state-space explosion and an MDP, which can not be solved using conventional computing. Consider, for example, an agent's speed which is real-valued. To capture all possible speeds would require an infinite number of states. More practically, we may, through an analysis of the system, define 3 three discrete levels {stop, slow, fast} with the reasoning that these are sufficient to capture the problem at hand. For this reason, AMDPs are commonly used in safety engineering [9]. This approach can drastically simplify the process. Actions too can be aggregated such that several actions can be abstracted to a single state, meaning the AMDP captures only the relevant information needed for high-level planning.

2.4 Single-Agent Reinforcement Learning

Reinforcement learning is an optimisation approach derived from behavioural psychology, involving positive and negative reinforcement [43]. An MDP may be solved using a reward function designed to signal the functional value of taking actions within a state. These numerical reward signals will be sent to the agent in the form of a positive or a negative number, depending on the functionality of the state action pairing. In this way, an agent learns how to solve an MDP based on previous experiences and the reward it obtained for undertaking actions in particular states. Learning the optimal policy requires the agent to interact with the environment repeatedly such that the state action pairings gradually improve. These repeated interactions are termed episodes.

The behavioural choices of the agent within the MDP should be governed in a way that will allow the agent to both explore the MDP and exploit the knowledge it has already acquired in order to learn efficiently. There are several ways in which these behavioural choices can be governed. A typical example of one of these choices is the ϵ-greedy approach. This approach involves the agent initially taking random actions (exploration) with a high frequency. Over time, making use of a degrading ϵ value, the rate at which exploratory actions are taken will decrease and instead, actions that maximise its current reward (exploitation) will be preferred [43,46].

Arguably the most well-known implementation of reinforcement learning, Q-learning [41], uses the ϵ-greedy technique to govern agents behavioural choices. Q-learning is an off-policy learning technique, meaning that it makes decisions not wholly dictated by its current policy. The update function of Q-learning, Eq. 2, shows how a state action pairing (s, a) is updated based on a decaying learning rate α. A discount factor γ determines how significant immediate and potential future rewards are to the learning agent.

$$\hat{Q}_{t+1}(s_t, a_t) = \hat{Q}_t(s_t, a_t) + \alpha \left(r_{t+1} + \gamma \max_{b \in A} \left\{ \hat{Q}_t(s_{t+1}, b) \right\} - \hat{Q}_t(s_t, a_t) \right) \quad (2)$$

The agent learning within the MDP will eventually converge to an optimal policy by storing the functional values of state-action pairs within a Q-matrix and updating and referencing these values. A policy is a collection of state action pairings throughout the entirety of the MDP, which the agent should take while in a certain state. Therefore, an optimal policy is found by collecting state action pairings that provide the maximum cumulative reward possible for the learning agent [43].

2.5 Multi-Agent Reinforcement Learning

MARL is a natural progression from single-agent reinforcement learning [4]. It uses similar methods but applies this to multiple agents learning within a shared environment, framed as an MA-MDP. MARL environments are significantly more complex than single-agent environments due to the fact that agents must learn within an environment that contains other agents. Due to this non-static environment, MA-MDPS must be utilised as multiple agents working in a shared environment break the Markovian principle due to the impact of the other agents on the environment [43]. Outside of this, agents may also have to learn how to work collaboratively to achieve goals or work against adversarial agents to achieve the best performance. There has been a myriad of methods proposed to overcome these difficulties.

Due to the complexity of these systems, it has become a standard to utilise deep neural networks to allow agents to learn efficiently within these shared environments [16].

2.6 Deep Reinforcement Learning

As the complexity of environments in which RL is being applied increases, the problem of creating appropriate state-space models of environments becomes increasingly difficult. This has led to the rise of Deep Reinforcement Learning, where artificial neural networks are combined with traditional RL techniques. Artificial neural networks [27] are inspired by the interconnection of neurons in the human brain and consist of a large number of simple computational units connected in a layered structure to provide a complex mapping of inputs to outputs. This complex map may then be used to represent an abstraction of the environment or the state-action space.

A common type of neural network is known as the Deep Q-Network (DQN) [8], which combines neural networks with the q-learning reinforcement learning algorithm. The DQN attempts to predict the Q-values of a state-action pair while using a softmax function to produce a probability distribution for action selection from the Q-values of the actions within a state to facilitate exploration during the learning process.

$$\text{Target}(s_t, a_t) = r_t + \gamma \cdot \max_a Q(s_{t+1}, a) \tag{3}$$

The equation which allows the DQN to make predictions based on the q-values of state action pairings can be seen in Eq. 3 and is very reminiscent of the Q-learning update function seen in Eq. 2.

Proximal Policy Optimization. Proximal policy optimisation (PPO), at the time of writing, is a relatively new but successful online policy gradient method that has been used in many scenarios [40]. Policy gradient methods, as seen in the policy gradient loss function in Eq. 4, uses an estimated relative value of the selected action $\hat{A}_t$, and compares this to the predicted value. If the value of $\hat{A}_t$ is greater than what was predicted, then the probabilities of certain actions being taken in the policy π_θ will increase, and if the value of $\hat{A}_t$ is lower than what was predicted, the probabilities are lowered. When iterated over learning steps, stronger policies emerge by increasing the possibilities of positive actions.

$$L^{PG}(\theta) = \hat{E}_t[\log\pi_\theta(a_t|s_t)\hat{A}_t] \tag{4}$$

PPO, unlike DQN, does not use a replay buffer to revisit the agent's experiences and instead learns directly from what the agent encounters. However, unchecked, this can lead to issues; policies can be invalidated due to experience parameters being updated too much with limited experience. This issue has prompted algorithms such as PPO to adopt a truncated approach to objective function updates, as seen in Eq. 5. Where θ is a policy parameter; $\hat{E}_t$ is the empirical expectation over time steps; r_t shows the ratio of probabilities under old and new policies, and ϵ is a hyper-parameter typically set at 0.1–0.2.

$$L^{CLIP}(\theta) = \hat{E}_t[\min(r_t(\theta)\hat{A}_t, \; \mathrm{clip}(r_t(\theta), 1 - \epsilon, 1 + \epsilon)\hat{A}_t)] \tag{5}$$

We can see that the PPO objective function makes use of a standard policy gradient objective $r_t(\theta)\hat{A}_t$ that facilitates actions with positive outcomes being chosen with higher probability, and also, uniquely, a truncated version of the policy gradient objective $clip(r_t(\theta), 1 - \epsilon, 1 + \epsilon)\hat{A}_t$. This truncated or *clipped* policy gradient objective function allows intelligently constrained gradient steps without significant overhead. The general idea behind this truncated function is to increase the probability of actions that promote positive outcomes, but not too much, in case it becomes detrimental. This idea, in essence, keeps new policies from deviating too far too quickly from the current policy.

It also makes sense that if a gradient step is taken that is detrimental, the step should be reversed. For this purpose, the two objective function terms are subjected to min, which will become effective if the function is negative. Thus, the algorithm will allow the probability of actions being taken to be decreased proportionally to the detrimental outcome.

Curiosity Driven Deep Reinforcement Learning. The foundations of reinforcement learning are built upon reward signals to guide agents towards correct and desirable behaviour [43]. However, in many real-world scenarios, rewards are not always available to an agent or are very sparse within the environment that the agent is navigating [34]. Furthermore, these sparse rewards can lead to very inefficient learning and a failure to find a policy that satisfies the goal. Curiosity-driven exploration is one technique proposed to overcome the problem of sparse rewards [34].

This technique makes use of both external rewards and what are termed "intrinsic curiosity rewards". These intrinsic curiosity rewards encourage the agent to explore areas of the environment that it has not previously explored, especially those areas that are deemed to be 'interesting'. One may consider this technique as follows: firstly, the agent makes predictions about the outcomes of possible actions; next, the agent attempts these actions and records the outcome; If the prediction is inaccurate, it is deemed to be an interesting area of the environment, and a higher curiosity reward is received. The more inaccurate the prediction, the more interesting this area is perceived to be.

Despite the benefits of curiosity-driven exploration, it is known to promote undesirable and unsafe behaviour to a greater degree than traditional RL methods given its method of exploration [39].

2.7 Quantitative Verification

Quantitative verification (QV) is a formal technique that allows for the analysis of probabilistic models. Automated probabilistic model checking has been applied to a wide range of real-world problems to produce guarantees for safety, reliability, performance, resource usage [22]. QV has been successfully applied to systems modelled as MDPs and, as such, is a natural fit with reinforcement learning.

Unlike simulation and testing, quantitative verification is exhaustive, using efficient algorithms and linear mathematics to analyse the entire graph of states and transitions. While this makes quantitative verification computationally expensive, it offers the strength of mathematical proof, and openly available probabilistic model checking tools have been developed, including PRISM [24] and STORM [7].

The verification of MDPs is accomplished by establishing labels for states within the model, these labels being atomic propositions for relevant properties. Labelling these states makes it possible to perform analysis on the feasibility of properties involving probability and temporal relationships between events.

Introducing these atomic propositions allows us to check if a desirable state can be reached within a certain probability without first entering states which are undesirable. These properties are expressed using probabilistic computational tree logic (PCTL), a form of probabilistic temporal logic [14]. For a set of atomic propositions AP, a state formula Φ and a path formula Ψ are defined in PCTL as:

$$
\Phi :: = true \mid a \mid \neg\Phi \mid \Phi_1 \wedge \Phi_2 \mid P_{\bowtie p}[\Psi],
$$
$$
\Psi :: = X\Phi \mid \Phi_1 U\Phi_2 \mid \Phi_1 U^{\leq l}\Phi_2
\tag{6}
$$

where $a \in$ AP, $\bowtie \in \{<, \leq, \geq, >\}$, $p \in [0,1]$ and $k \in \mathbb{N}$; and a PCTL reward state formula [23] is defined as:

$$
\Phi :: = R_{\bowtie r}[I^{=k}] \mid R_{\bowtie r}[C^{\leq k}] \mid R_{\bowtie r}[F\Phi] \mid R_{\bowtie r}[S],
\tag{7}
$$

where $r \in \mathbb{R}_{\geq 0}$. PCTL used within probabilistic model checkers such as PRISM uses the grammar above and allows complex properties to be expressed with relative ease. For example, to analyse the probability of reaching a finishing state within 20-time steps is expressed by $P = ?[F^{\leq 20} finished]$.

3 Domain Example

In order to evaluate our approach for Deep MARL, we created a three-dimensional navigation domain as shown in Fig. 2. The domain consists of 9 rooms labelled r_a to r_i each room then contains a flag that the agents must collect. Rooms are connected by hallways, h_i, in which security cameras are placed. The coloured areas of the hallway

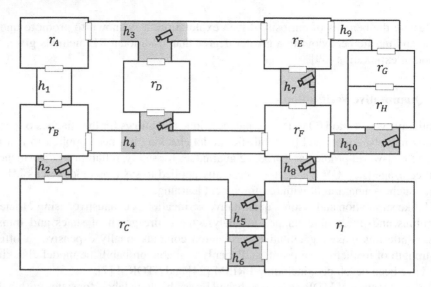

Fig. 2. Domain Example including rooms, hallways, and cameras.

Table 1. Probability of Agent Disruption Mechanism Failing.

Camera Location	Probability of Disruption Failure
h_2	0.05
h_3	0.1
h_4	0.1
h_5	0.05
h_6	0.1
h_7	0.05
h_8	0.05
h_{10}	0.15

show the coverage of these cameras. If an agent enters one of these coloured areas, then there is a probability that the mission fails.

While this domain is framed as an infiltration mission, some features are largely applicable to a wide range of scenarios, including search and rescue and maintenance tasks. For example, although we use cameras and detection, there could be areas where the loss of a robot is higher due to environmental features such as radiation, landslide risk.

In this domain, we are attempting to collect as many flags as possible with 3 robots while minimising the chances of detection by the security cameras since it is impossible for the agents to patrol all of the rooms without passing by a camera.

The agents must find a suitable balance between these conflicting goals.

Each of the agents is assumed to have a device that can disrupt the security cameras when they are in the surveillance zones, but the probability of avoiding detection is not certain and is dependent on the area of the environment in which the camera is located.

The probability of disruption device failing in each location is shown in Table 1.

The agents within this environment must learn how to navigate through rooms and corridors and effectively search within the environment space to collect as many objectives as possible. If we frame this problem that we have described in a real-world application, such as a search and rescue operation, our goal would be to find important objectives and safely return the expensive robotic hardware that we deploy. These two goals are, by their nature, conflicting. The more objectives an agent finds, the less likely it is that all agents will return safely. Viewing this problem in such as way, we set functional and safety constraints that we expect from the system within the environment, allowing us to formally state the acceptable functional and safety parameters for the problem domain, these being C_1 and C_2, respectively. These parameters were chosen to demonstrate the approach within this domain and the features that it holds.

- C_1 The probability of agents remaining undetected during the operation should not fall below 0.7.
- C_2 The agents should collect at least five objectives.

Furthermore, past these constraints, there are conflicting criteria that the system must attempt to optimise, these being O_1 and O_2.

- O_1 Maximise the probability of the system being undetected.
- O_2 Maximise the number of objectives collected.

4   Approach

In order to produce safe multi-agent reinforcement learning policies, we propose a four-stage plug-in styled approach called assured multi-agent reinforcement learning (AMARL), as shown in Fig. 3.

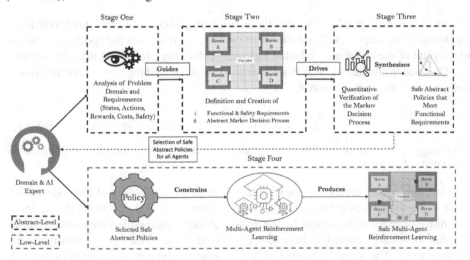

Fig. 3. Assured Multi-Agent Reinforcement Learning Approach.

Stage One involves a domain expert collecting and analysing that information about the environment and agent behaviours that may be deemed relevant to the problem at hand. Such information includes important states, agent actions, potential risk, performance and safety requirements. This information will be crucial in the construction of the AMDP and, as such,

1. All agent states within the environment S will include location states, failure states, success states, and transitions, the exact details of this are environment-dependent.
2. The behaviours of agents and capabilities of states will be mapped to actions A within stage two and are required to be identified.
3. Numerical reward structures can be used to capture system performance and safety qualities, such as the risk of agents being damaged R.
4. Mission objectives and constraints ω can be defined as probability, time steps, reachable states, and cumulative rewards.

An example of an abstraction choice is an environment with two rooms that can be accessed through two separate corridors. If the cost and payoff of using each corridor are the same, this can be abstracted into a single method of transitioning. At the same time, if there are differences between these corridors, such as requiring more energy to navigate through, both of these transition methods should be captured.

When discussing abstraction, it should be noted that systems that contain heterogeneity, meaning the possible behaviours of agents are not shared. This heterogeneity can also be captured within the AMDP at this stage.

Stage Two takes the information from stage one and uses the PRISM language to construct an AMDP model. An example of a statement in the PRISM language is presented below:

```
[action] guard -> prob_1 : update_1 + ... + prob_n : update_n;
```

An *action* is a label that describes the action being taken and allows synchronisation and reward-based updates. When the guard evaluates to true, then the update statements to the right of the arrow are evaluated and with probability prob_i then update_i occurs.

The code fragment below shows a general example describing two agents' transition options when they are in room A:

```
// In room A and making a movement choice
[visitA_B_1]  !done & r1=A & visitsA<N -> 1:(r1'=A)&(visitsA'=visitsA+1);
\\robot 1 visits room B
[visitA_D_2]  !done & r2=A & visitsB<N -> 1:(r2'=D)&(visitsD'=visitsD+1);
\\robot 2 visits room D
```

Here the *action* labels are given labels to aid in the readability of the code where *visit* is the act of moving from one room to another, and A_B_1 denotes that agent 1 will move from room A to room B. The *done* variable is used within the model to show whether the mission objectives have been completed. *done* is, therefore, a terminal state for the model. The variables named $r1$ and $r2$ contain the current location of agent 1 and 2 respectively. *visitA* and *visitsB* are used as a counter to see how many times room A or B respectively has been visited and N being the maximum amount of times a room should be visited. The variables, *done*, $r1$, $r2$, and *visits*, form the guard to constrain the model's transitions. Finally, $\rightarrow$ marks the separation between the guard and the update, with the notation to the right of → being the variables that are updated once the transition has fired.

The final part of the model to be defined is the reward functions. These allow us to assess the performance of the policy with respect to the functional and safety constraints. An example of a reward function is:

```
rewards "Objective_Collection_Rewards"
    [visitA_B_1]   true : 1;
    [visitA_D_1]   true : 3;
    [visitA_E_1]   true : 2;
end rewards
```

Here, the labels are used to associate a transition, previously defined, to a reward value. The *true* guard indicates that whenever this transaction occurs then the reward function adds the allocated numerical reward to the accumulated reward.

To further demonstrate how the PRISM language is applied to problems, we offer a diagram in Fig. 4, of an agent R_1 in a more complex MDP with two abstracted states, these being rooms r_A and r_B. The variables used in this model will be $R1$, which will hold the agent's location, and $G1$, which will be a Boolean variable to state whether the objective has already been collected previously. Here the robot has two transitions it can take within the model, move from r_A to r_B, and from r_B to r_A, the incentive to transition is to collect objective G_1. The PRISM model for this simple domain can be described using the code fragments in the image, including the transitions and reward observations.

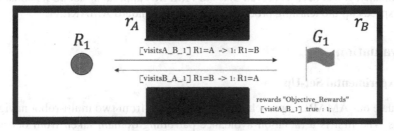

Fig. 4. Simple two state AMDP with related PRISM code.

Stage Three combines the abstracted model from stage two and the provide functional and safety requirements from stage one to conduct a quantitative verification of the model. The requirements to be verified are encoded as PCTL. Some examples of PCTL are expressed below:

1. $R\{\text{"goals"}\} \geq 3$ [F finished]
2. $R\{\text{"risk"}\} \leq 0.3$ [F finished]
3. $P \geq 0.99$ [!energyDepleted U finished]

The first property is a functional requirement that states that by the time the model reaches the state *finished*, the number of goals reached must be at least 3. The second states that the risk should be less than 0.2 when the episode is complete. The final property says that the probability of completing the task without running out of energy should be greater than 0.99.

With both the AMDP provided by stage two and the defined safety and functional requirements, QV can now be used over the defined model, governed by the requirements set. QV will potentially synthesise multiple policies for the model that meet all requirements, and a single policy may then be selected from this set. Due to the QV process, the produced policies are guaranteed to meet these requirements, which is where our formal assurances are produced. However, if the model has considerable inconsistencies with the actual domain space or the requirements are too constricting, it may be necessary to return to step one to reevaluate the structure and requirements of the domain. If the steps are followed correctly, this stage will produce safe policies for all agents modelled in the AMDP.

Stage Four is the final stage in our AMARL approach and involves the agents utilising a reinforcement learning technique/techniques within the non-abstracted environment. However, the behaviours within this environment are constrained using the safe abstract policies produced in stage three. The abstract policies constrain and partition the domain space, agent actions, and tasks. While under the constraint of these abstracted policies, the reinforcement learning agents can utilise the stochastic action selection that drives their exploratory actions, with assurances that their safety will be guaranteed to a certain level.

It is more than likely that agents will enter risky situations during their learning process, but as this cannot be repeated continuously due to the constraints, we can allow agents to run their learning process and also their fixed policies after learning with confidence. Lastly, while this process focused on producing safe MARL policies and not optimality, it has been observed that our AMARL approach, due to its constrained nature, speeds up the learning process compared to standard AMARL.

5   Evaluation

5.1   Experimental Set-Up

To evaluate our AMARL approach, we look at results from two multi-robot navigation domains. The first is a radiation avoidance patrolling domain taken from our earlier work [36], where agents must visit patrol points multiple times while conserving battery and minimising radiation exposure. The second is the multi-agent guarded flag domain described in Sect. 3, where agents must collect flags while minimising the risk of being captured by security cameras.

For each of these domains, we ran a minimum of two experiments. The first experiments did not utilise our AMARL approach and solely made us use traditional reinforcement learning techniques, acting as a baseline. The second experiments involve using our AMARL approach to constrain the state-space with the learning parameters for each domain are described in their relevant sections.

Domain-relevant functional and safety performance data is collected after each learning episode to evaluate the system's performance during learning. In addition, the converged policies from our multi-agent guarded flag collection domain are evaluated many times to ensure the validity of the conclusions drawn from this evaluation.

The radiation avoidance patrolling domain is implemented using a ROS simulator [35]. ROS is a robotics operating system capable of interfacing with a broad range of robotic systems. The second domain, being the multi-agent guarded flag collection, is simulated using the Unity games engine [20], an engine capable of powerful rendering, physics simulation, and easily integrated AI. An image from the unity engine domain can be seen in Fig. 5, showing the agents used. The quantitative verification process in our experiments is driven by the probabilistic model checking tool PRISM [24]. PRISM is a tool that allows us to express our safety and functional requirements through its reward extended PCTL properties, which has been utilised in the area of autonomous agent research previously [13,29].

Fig. 5. Multi-agent guarded flag collection domain showing an agent (left) and a room with a flag (right).

5.2 Radiation Avoidance Patrolling Domain

Our radiation avoidance patrolling domain, as seen in Fig. 6, contains five rooms, each of which must be visited a minimum of three times. Two robots share the responsibility of visiting the rooms, and moving between rooms has a corresponding battery cost. The batteries are assumed to be finite, and the robots attempt to maximise their overall remaining battery. This domain is inspired by autonomous agents working within nuclear power plants. As such, room four contains highly irradiated material, which the robots must inspect to meet mission objectives but limit their time within to reduce the risk of sustaining damage. There are multiple ways that agents can enter and exit this room, and this must be factored in due to the path lengths and corresponding travel time each option has. The longer the travel time, the more risk the agents will be subjected to when in the room. These risks can be seen displayed in Table 2.

The functional constraints that the system should meet can be seen below, in C1 and C2; however, in regards to battery, a secondary constraint can be derived, the need to preserve battery for after the mission is complete, we define this as the robotic system having 35% of its battery remaining. Finally, C3 describes the safety constraints regarding radiation exposure, defined as reducing and keeping the risk of damage to below 20% probability.

– C1: Visit each room a minimum of three times.
– C2: Complete all tasks without exhausting their batteries.
– C3: The amount of time spent in room 4 should be minimised.

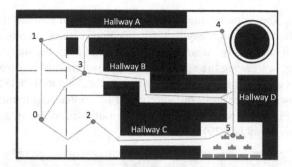

Fig. 6. Radiation Avoidance Patrolling Domain. From the Original Publication [36].

For the reinforcement learning process, we assign a reward for each patrol point that the agents visit, depending on how often it has been visited and how long it has been since its last visitation. We also assign a punishment triggered when an agent receives damage in the irradiated zone, ending the learning episode. We run Q-learning on our agents who act non-centralised, with a discount factor $\gamma = 0.7$ and a learning rate of $\alpha = 0.3$. Finally, we use an exploration rate of $\epsilon = 0.5$, which was found experimentally through interaction with the domain.

Table 2. Options for entering and leaving room 4 and the corresponding risk of damage.

Entrance	Exit	Exposure Time	Risk
Hallway A	Hallway A	30 (seconds)	0.03
Hallway A	Hallway D	34 (seconds)	0.04
Hallway D	Hallway D	46 (seconds)	0.07
Hallway D	Hallway A	34 (seconds)	0.04

Following our approach, we construct an AMDP with each room represented as a state and the transitions between rooms represented as actions with both agents represented within this AMDP. We then ran QV over this AMDP, and PRISM synthesised a policy that met the desired functional and safety requirements. We describe the safety and battery properties as rewards within the AMDP, which is standard practice when using PRISM [13,29], and our desired goal of visiting patrol points three times as a formal state in the AMDP. We then use this abstract policy to constrain our patrolling problem. Running the unconstrained and constrained MARL for 200 episodes on the domain allowed us to produce some preliminary results as shown in Fig. 7.

Figure 7 shows the cumulative risk of the system over learning episodes on the left and the individual battery consumption of robots within the system on the right over episodes. The dotted horizontal line on each graph is the relative functional and safety constraint defined for this domain, and the triangle shows a successful episode for the system. We sample across the learning episodes to determine how the system has functioned throughout the learning run and find that our AMARL approach allows the system to comply both consistently and reliably in terms of functionality and safety constraints. From early in the learning process out approach allowed the agents to meet

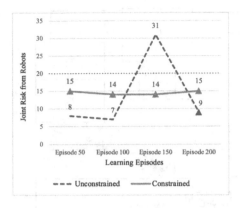 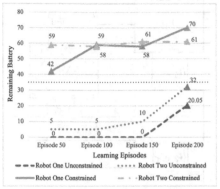

Fig. 7. Cumulative Risk and Battery Outcomes from Initial Patrolling Domain. From the Original Publication [36].

these constraints and meet all the functional objectives. This efficient learning is due to the constrained search space that requires less exploration. Traditional learning, however, takes much longer to find a functional policy, often falling greatly below the battery constraint and with unpredictable spikes in risk due to the unchecked stochasticity of reinforcement learning.

5.3 Multi-Agent Guarded Flag Collection

Our multi-agent guarded flag collection, described Sect. 3, was implemented with three agents using deep reinforcement learning, Proximal Policy Optimization and intrinsic curiosity.

The agents receive a reward of 1 for reaching a goal that can be found near the centre of every room, and being caught by a security camera resulted in the termination of the episode. Through experimentation, negative rewards between -0.1 to -1 were used for punishing the captured agents. The higher the punishment, the more the incentive to explore effectively was lowered.

In addition, the agent receives small rewards when finding novel experiences through the use of intrinsic curiosity. Due to intrinsic curiosity, the neural network makes use of two distinct reward signals, extrinsic, which is given by collecting flags or getting caught, and intrinsic, through intrinsic curiosity. The extrinsic reward signal has a strength of 1. While curiosity has a strength of 0.01, both have a discount factor of $\gamma = 0.99$. In order to incorporate intrinsic curiosity, we lower the learning rate to $\alpha = 0.003$. These parameters were found through experimental measures to produce the behaviour required.

A total of 1400 learning episodes were run for each experiment, with 6,000 steps per episode. A total of two types of learning methods are evaluated, the unconstrained PPO and intrinsic curiosity and our AMARL approach with PPO and intrinsic curiosity.

In regards to AMARL, we produce an AMDP that, similarly to our previous domain, captures the rooms as states and the transitions between actions with the corresponding

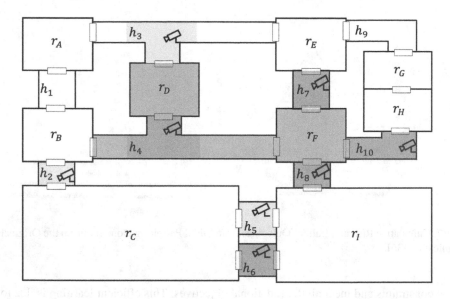

Fig. 8. Constraining Safe Abstract Policy with Inaccessible Areas in Grey.

risk they hold. Goals and risks are tracked using the reward structures within PRISM, and based on this description, PRISM was able to synthesis a safe abstract policy for us to constrain our learning. This abstract policy allowed the system to collect a maximum of 7 flags from the environment while disallowing actions that resulted in a cumulative risk greater than 0.3. A visualisation of this constraining abstract safe policy can be seen in Fig. 8, with grey spaces representing areas that are now inaccessible.

We present the results of our experiments within Figs. 9 and 10. These graphs show the cumulated risk and reward from collecting goals which the systems gained during the episodes in the learning runs. These graphs hold information on the unconstrained deep MARL as well as MARL constrained using our AMARL approach.

When looking at the rewards that the unconstrained MARL gathers during the learning process, it is clear that unconstrained MARL is working within a larger state-space given the disparity of the number of goals reached. Furthermore, the time it takes for the unconstrained MARL to learn to capture a significant number of goals also alludes to a greater search space available to the system. This disparity of the goals collected can also be attributed to intrinsic curiosity. While it allows the system to locate sparse rewards easier, it also encourages it to try new things to a much greater extent than traditional reinforcement learning, potentially pulling it away from known goals. AMARL, while still affected by intrinsic curiosity due to the ordered and constrained state-space, is more consistent in the goals it collects and learns to collect these at a faster pace. The ability of AMARL to bring greater consistency to traditional reinforcement learning and a technique known to bring greater stochasticity to behaviour is one of our approaches key contributions.

Unconstrained MARL suffers from unpredictability, leading to a lack of trust in the systems that make use of it; when looking at the risk results from this experiment, this

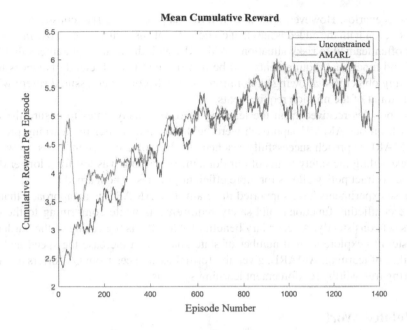

Fig. 9. Reward Received by the Systems.

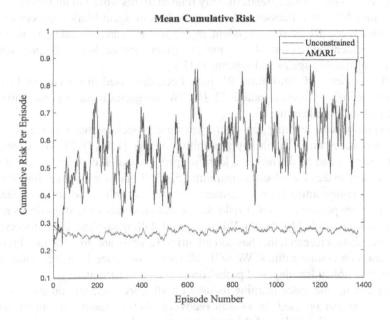

Fig. 10. Cumulative Risk Received by Systems.

unpredictability is clear to see. The system's risk levels fluctuate throughout the learning process, often violating the safety requirement showing that even reward signals that attempt to balance the conflicting functional and safety requirements are not trustworthy in these scenarios. However, with our AMARL approach, the risk constraint is never violated, even with the added issues that come with intrinsic curiosity, whose inquisitive nature often leads it to risky situations. AMARL, with the formal guarantees that both safety and functional requirements will be met through QV, efficiently balances these conflicting objectives, allowing exploration, goal collection, and assured safety within the constraint of the mission requirements.

The policies received from the learning were run many times to ensure the constraints from our AMARL approach were held during and after the learning process. Our AMARL approach successfully reached six flags on a consistent basis, as well as never exceeding the safety limits of our domain. If learning was left for a longer duration, the abstract policy allows for more efficient policies to be learned.

These experiments have supported the claim that AMARL is an approach that can balance conflicting functional and safety requirements while conforming to the constraints set consistently. A secondary benefit of AMARL is the easing of the burden on the system to explore a great number of state spaces and increase the speed and predictability of learning. AMARL, given the formal assurances from QV, offers a way of delivering trustworthy reinforcement learning systems.

6   Related Work

The Safe RL and safe MARL trends directly related to this work fall under the umbrella of constrained Markov Processes and constrained multi-agent Markov processes. Constrained based safe RL is very prevalent in the research area of safe RL as a whole and has been identified as one of the most promising approaches to the production of safety-critical suitable agents and systems [11].

Multiple variants of constrained RL have been discussed in the current literature, falling into degrees of safety standards [2, 15]. We categories these as conservative-safe learning and soft-safe learning.

Conservative-safe learning can define learning processes that remove the ability to enter into states that contain any possibility of risk [1, 15, 18, 21, 44]. Conversely, soft-safe learning can be defined as a learning process that allows agents to enter into risky states and makes use of soft constraints [5, 45]. Finally, we define threshold-safe learning as a compromise between conservative-safe learning and soft-safe learning, where agents are permitted to enter risky states, but only under the strict limits set by a permitted risk threshold [19, 29, 42]. With our work falling into this last category.

Some identified research that has had attention recently are grouped into broad categories based on commonalities. We will call these safe space learning, critic-teacher shielding, safe policy learning, and probabilistic based constraint.

As we call it, safe space learning focuses on all works that rely on some assumed safe space that can be used for system recovery [44]. Secondly, it can incorporate research where a region/policy of the environment that the agent will use to solve functional requirements while gradually increasing/changing this safe region [45].

Safe space learning, while this is a broad definition, generally groups research together that rely greatly on the assumption that certain areas of the environment will be safe to facilitate learning in a 'safe' way.

Our defined critic-teacher shielding research grouping consists of work that focuses on action monitoring and manipulation based on synthesised 'shields' that enforce safety properties [1, 19]. It also includes work that utilises safety critics, which are trained in environments before being implemented into future problems and allowing the critic to guide the agent away from risky behaviour [42].

Safe policy learning consists of work that utilises policies that are deemed to be safe to aid in the exploration process of the learning approach, such as interactively generating policies throughout a state-space to guide exploration [21]. While also including work that interacts with the agent's policy during runtime, allowing action selection to be altered based on the perceived safety of said action, such as work utilising Lyapunov functions [18].

Finally, we identify research that, in some way, introduces probabilistic model checking to provide, to varying degrees, formal guarantees to the safety of a system. This includes work that uses probabilistic model checking to allow a threshold approach to safety, including safe probabilistic shields, such as those which we described earlier [19], and work which provides formal guarantees to functional and safety objectives by applying an abstract safe policy over the state space to constrict agent learning [29].

Safe MARL can be seen to follow these trends with current research pushing these ideas into a MAS setting. Utilising constrained MDPs is a common approach [12], but as well as this, shielding [1] and actor-critic methods have been utilised [33]. Lastly, following on from research in safe RL, which utilises probabilistic model checking, you have our AMARL approach, which was the first approach to utilise probabilistic model checking to this end in MARL [36, 37].

7 Conclusion

We presented a four-stage, plug-in style approach that combines QV with MARL to produce formal assurances that functional, reliability and safety requirements will be met during and after the learning process and efficiently balanced these conflicting objectives. Using partial information of a domain, an AMDP is constructed, and functional and safety requirements can guide QV over said AMDP. Expressing these requirements using PCTL allows complex user requirements to be efficiently described within the QV tool. This process allows formally assured safe abstract policies to be synthesised that are used to constrain the low-level domain problem for safe MARL to be run within these constraints.

As a result, unlike traditional MARL, our AMARL approach can be used in a myriad of safety-critical and mission-sensitive scenarios with a significant level of trustworthiness, which is a great limitation to the practical use of MARL. Furthermore, through two experimental domains, we show that our approach is reliable and can be used with varied and current reinforcement learning techniques, such as deep reinforcement learning and intrinsic curiosity.

Future directions of this work include the ability for AMARL to be utilised in changing environments, allowing functional and safety requirements to be continued to be met despite unforeseen changes to risk levels and available transitions within an MDP.

Possible additions to this approach could be the incorporation of Petri-nets as a way to describe the processes of a system rather than constructing the MDP within the QV tool. Petri-nets are commonly used within multi-agent systems, so this would be a non-trivial addition in terms of the reachability of our approach. We also consider the difficulty of accurately representing a problem as an MDP and propose extending the approach to identify and correct inconsistencies in the AMDP and the low-level problem. Lastly, a more robust evaluation of our AMARL approach would be highly beneficial towards promoting the trustworthiness of AMARL.

References

1. Alshiekh, M., Bloem, R., Ehlers, R., Könighofer, B., Niekum, S., Topcu, U.: Safe reinforcement learning via shielding. In: Thirty-Second AAAI Conference on Artificial Intelligence (2018)
2. Brunke, L., et al.: Safe learning in robotics: from learning-based control to safe reinforcement learning. arXiv preprint arXiv:2108.06266 (2021)
3. Bui, V.H., Nguyen, T.T., Kim, H.M.: Distributed operation of wind farm for maximizing output power: a multi-agent deep reinforcement learning approach. IEEE Access 8, 173136–173146 (2020)
4. Buşoniu, L., Babuška, R., De Schutter, B.: Multi-agent reinforcement learning: an overview. In: Srinivasan, D., Jain, L.C. (eds.) Innovations in Multi-Agent Systems and Applications - 1. Studies in Computational Intelligence, vol. 310, pp. 183–221. Springer, Heidelberg (2010). https://doi.org/10.1007/978-3-642-14435-6_7
5. Cheng, R., Orosz, G., Murray, R.M., Burdick, J.W.: End-to-end safe reinforcement learning through barrier functions for safety-critical continuous control tasks. In: Proceedings of the AAAI Conference on Artificial Intelligence, vol. 33, pp. 3387–3395 (2019)
6. Danassis, P., Filos-Ratsikas, A., Faltings, B.: Achieving diverse objectives with AI-driven prices in deep reinforcement learning multi-agent markets. arXiv preprint arXiv:2106.06060 (2021)
7. Dehnert, C., Junges, S., Katoen, J.-P., Volk, M.: A storm is coming: a modern probabilistic model checker. In: Majumdar, R., Kunčak, V. (eds.) CAV 2017. LNCS, vol. 10427, pp. 592–600. Springer, Cham (2017). https://doi.org/10.1007/978-3-319-63390-9_31
8. Fan, J., Wang, Z., Xie, Y., Yang, Z.: A theoretical analysis of deep q-learning. In: Learning for Dynamics and Control, pp. 486–489. PMLR (2020)
9. Faria, J.M.: Machine learning safety: an overview. In: Proceedings of the 26th Safety-Critical Systems Symposium, York, UK, pp. 6–8 (2018)
10. Garcia, F., Rachelson, E.: Markov decision processes. Markov Decision Processes in Artificial Intelligence, pp. 1–38 (2013)
11. García, J., Fernández, F.: A comprehensive survey on safe reinforcement learning. J. Mach. Learn. Res. 16(1), 1437–1480 (2015)
12. Ge, Y., Zhu, F., Huang, W., Zhao, P., Liu, Q.: Multi-agent cooperation q-learning algorithm based on constrained Markov game. Comput. Sci. Inf. Syst. 17(2), 647–664 (2020)
13. Gerasimou, S., Calinescu, R., Shevtsov, S., Weyns, D.: UNDERSEA: an exemplar for engineering self-adaptive unmanned underwater vehicles. In: 2017 IEEE/ACM 12th International Symposium on Software Engineering for Adaptive and Self-Managing Systems (SEAMS), pp. 83–89. IEEE (2017)
14. Hansson, H., Jonsson, B.: A logic for reasoning about time and reliability. Formal Aspects Comput. 6(5), 512–535 (1994)

15. Hasanbeig, M., Abate, A., Kroening, D.: Cautious reinforcement learning with logical constraints. arXiv preprint arXiv:2002.12156 (2020)
16. Hernandez-Leal, P., Kartal, B., Taylor, M.E.: Is multiagent deep reinforcement learning the answer or the question? A brief survey. Learning **21**, 22 (2018)
17. Huang, Y., Wu, S., Mu, Z., Long, X., Chu, S., Zhao, G.: A multi-agent reinforcement learning method for swarm robots in space collaborative exploration. In: 2020 6th International Conference on Control, Automation and Robotics (ICCAR), pp. 139–144. IEEE (2020)
18. Huh, S., Yang, I.: Safe reinforcement learning for probabilistic reachability and safety specifications: a Lyapunov-based approach. arXiv preprint arXiv:2002.10126 (2020)
19. Jansen, N., Könighofer, B., Junges, S., Serban, A., Bloem, R.: Safe reinforcement learning using probabilistic shields (2020)
20. Juliani, A., et al.: Unity: a general platform for intelligent agents. arXiv preprint arXiv:1809.02627 (2018)
21. Junges, S., Jansen, N., Dehnert, C., Topcu, U., Katoen, J.-P.: Safety-constrained reinforcement learning for MDPs. In: Chechik, M., Raskin, J.-F. (eds.) TACAS 2016. LNCS, vol. 9636, pp. 130–146. Springer, Heidelberg (2016). https://doi.org/10.1007/978-3-662-49674-9_8
22. Kwiatkowska, M., Norman, G., Parker, D.: Probabilistic symbolic model checking with PRISM: a hybrid approach. In: Katoen, J.-P., Stevens, P. (eds.) TACAS 2002. LNCS, vol. 2280, pp. 52–66. Springer, Heidelberg (2002). https://doi.org/10.1007/3-540-46002-0_5
23. Kwiatkowska, M., Norman, G., Parker, D.: Stochastic model checking. In: Bernardo, M., Hillston, J. (eds.) SFM 2007. LNCS, vol. 4486, pp. 220–270. Springer, Heidelberg (2007). https://doi.org/10.1007/978-3-540-72522-0_6
24. Kwiatkowska, M., Norman, G., Parker, D.: PRISM 4.0: verification of probabilistic real-time systems. In: Gopalakrishnan, G., Qadeer, S. (eds.) CAV 2011. LNCS, vol. 6806, pp. 585–591. Springer, Heidelberg (2011). https://doi.org/10.1007/978-3-642-22110-1_47
25. Lee, H.R., Lee, T.: Multi-agent reinforcement learning algorithm to solve a partially-observable multi-agent problem in disaster response. Eur. J. Oper. Res. **291**(1), 296–308 (2021)
26. Liao, X., et al.: Iteratively-refined interactive 3D medical image segmentation with multi-agent reinforcement learning. In: Proceedings of the IEEE/CVF Conference on Computer Vision and Pattern Recognition, pp. 9394–9402 (2020)
27. Liu, W., Wang, Z., Liu, X., Zeng, N., Liu, Y., Alsaadi, F.E.: A survey of deep neural network architectures and their applications. Neurocomputing **234**, 11–26 (2017)
28. Luis, S.Y., Reina, D.G., Marín, S.L.T.: A multiagent deep reinforcement learning approach for path planning in autonomous surface vehicles: the Ypacaraí lake patrolling case. IEEE Access **9**, 17084–17099 (2021)
29. Mason, G.R., Calinescu, R.C., Kudenko, D., Banks, A.: Assured reinforcement learning with formally verified abstract policies. In: 9th International Conference on Agents and Artificial Intelligence (ICAART), York (2017)
30. Nowé, A., Vrancx, P., De Hauwere, Y.M.: Game theory and multi-agent reinforcement learning. In: Wiering, M., van Otterlo, M. (eds.) Reinforcement Learning. Adaptation, Learning, and Optimization, vol. 12, pp. 441–470. Springer, Berlin (2012). https://doi.org/10.1007/978-3-642-27645-3_14
31. OroojlooyJadid, A., Hajinezhad, D.: A review of cooperative multi-agent deep reinforcement learning. arXiv preprint arXiv:1908.03963 (2019)
32. Pardalos, P.M., Migdalas, A., Pitsoulis, L.: Pareto Optimality, Game Theory and Equilibria, vol. 17. Springer, Heidelberg (2008). https://doi.org/10.1007/978-0-387-77247-9
33. Parnika, P., Diddigi, R.B., Danda, S.K.R., Bhatnagar, S.: Attention actor-critic algorithm for multi-agent constrained co-operative reinforcement learning. arXiv preprint arXiv:2101.02349 (2021)

34. Pathak, D., Agrawal, P., Efros, A.A., Darrell, T.: Curiosity-driven exploration by self-supervised prediction. In: International Conference on Machine Learning, pp. 2778–2787. PMLR (2017)
35. Portugal, D., Iocchi, L., Farinelli, A.: A ROS-based framework for simulation and benchmarking of multi-robot patrolling algorithms. In: Koubaa, A. (ed.) Robot Operating System (ROS). SCI, vol. 778, pp. 3–28. Springer, Cham (2019). https://doi.org/10.1007/978-3-319-91590-6_1
36. Riley, J., Calinescu, R., Paterson, C., Kudenko, D., Banks, A.: Reinforcement learning with quantitative verification for assured multi-agent policies. In: 13th International Conference on Agents and Artificial Intelligence, York (2021)
37. Riley, J., Calinescu, R., Paterson, C., Kudenko, D., Banks, A.: Utilising assured multi-agent reinforcement learning within safety-critical scenarios. Procedia Comput. Sci. **192**, 1061–1070 (2021). Knowledge-Based and Intelligent Information & Engineering Systems: Proceedings of the 25th International Conference KES 2021
38. Rizk, Y., Awad, M., Tunstel, E.W.: Decision making in multiagent systems: a survey. IEEE Trans. Cogn. Dev. Syst. **10**(3), 514–529 (2018)
39. Rosser, C., Abed, K.: Curiosity-driven reinforced learning of undesired actions in autonomous intelligent agents. In: 2021 IEEE 19th World Symposium on Applied Machine Intelligence and Informatics (SAMI), pp. 000039–000042. IEEE (2021)
40. Schulman, J., Wolski, F., Dhariwal, P., Radford, A., Klimov, O.: Proximal policy optimization algorithms. arXiv preprint arXiv:1707.06347 (2017)
41. Spano, S., et al.: An efficient hardware implementation of reinforcement learning: the q-learning algorithm. IEEE Access **7**, 186340–186351 (2019)
42. Srinivasan, K., Eysenbach, B., Ha, S., Tan, J., Finn, C.: Learning to be safe: deep rl with a safety critic. arXiv preprint arXiv:2010.14603 (2020)
43. Sutton, R.S., Barto, A.G.: Reinforcement Learning: An Introduction. MIT Press, Cambridge (2018)
44. Thananjeyan, B., et al.: Recovery RL: safe reinforcement learning with learned recovery zones. IEEE Robot. Autom. Lett. **6**(3), 4915–4922 (2021)
45. Wachi, A., Sui, Y.: Safe reinforcement learning in constrained Markov decision processes. In: International Conference on Machine Learning, pp. 9797–9806. PMLR (2020)
46. Wiering, M.A., Van Otterlo, M.: Reinforcement learning. Adapt. Learn. Optim. **12**(3), 729 (2012)
47. Zhang, K., Yang, Z., Başar, T.: Multi-agent reinforcement learning: a selective overview of theories and algorithms. In: Vamvoudakis, K.G., Wan, Y., Lewis, F.L., Cansever, D. (eds.) Handbook of Reinforcement Learning and Control. SSDC, vol. 325, pp. 321–384. Springer, Cham (2021). https://doi.org/10.1007/978-3-030-60990-0_12

How to Segment Handwritten Historical Chronicles Using Fully Convolutional Networks?

Josef Baloun[1,2]([✉]) [iD], Pavel Král[1,2]([✉]) [iD], and Ladislav Lenc[1,2]([✉]) [iD]

[1] Department of Computer Science and Engineering, University of West Bohemia,
Univerzitní, Pilsen, Czech Republic
{balounj,pkral,llenc}@kiv.zcu.cz
[2] NTIS - New Technologies for the Information Society, University of West Bohemia,
Univerzitní, Pilsen, Czech Republic

Abstract. This paper deals with historical document image segmentation with focus on chronicles available in the Porta fontium portal. We build on our previously published database that has precise pixel-level annotations in PAGE format but also utilise other datasets for transfer learning in order to improve the results. We discuss a series of experiments that evaluate possibilities how to train a neural model for image, text and background segmentation. The outcome, in a form of segmentation method with relatively low computational costs and great results, is integrated into the Porta fontium portal to improve its possibilities of searching and publication of the documents.

Keywords: Page segmentation · Chronicle · Historical document · Text · Image · Background · Fully convolutional neural network · Pixel labeling · Artificial page

1 Introduction

Archival documents such as old periodicals and chronicles are a valuable source of information. Preserve it and make it available for researchers and for general public is thus of a great importance. Current standard is to scan the materials and publish it in digital form through various portals and databases. However, scanning is only the first step in the digitisation process. Modern technologies allow to further process the document images and can provide many ways of intelligent search, classification and visualisation which is a great benefit for people working with the documents.

Project Porta fontium[1] is an example of efforts to provide the researchers and other interested persons with an efficient search in archival materials. It covers the Czech-Bavarian border area which has a common history before the World War II. After the war, the regions on both sides of the border where separated. It is thus a logical step to re-connect it and provide the related documents at one place.

In our work we concentrate on the development of efficient methods how to index and search in the vast data collections. A very important part of the processing pipeline

---

[1] http://www.portafontium.cz/.

© Springer Nature Switzerland AG 2022
A. P. Rocha et al. (Eds.): ICAART 2021, LNAI 13251, pp. 181–196, 2022.
https://doi.org/10.1007/978-3-031-10161-8_9

is segmentation of the document images. Especially the issue of text localisation is crucial. Text segmentation has a long history dating back to the late 1970 s s when Optical Character Recognition (OCR) was addressed and it was necessary to extract single characters. "In order to let character recognition work, it is mandatory to apply layout analysis including page segmentation." [12] Today, most approaches tend to extract text lines instead of characters, but the importance of this step remains the same. There is also a need for extracting images that can be further processed and allow image search.

We focus on chronicles and their segmentation into text, image and background areas. These segments are crucial for further processing. For example OCR engines require a text input, but it could behave unpredictably when the input is an image or a graphic element. In such a case, the usability of the result could be harmed due to the produced noise. We can also provide image search or provide only pages that contain images.

To be able to train segmentation models that are usually based on deep learning neural architectures, we have to provide the model with a sufficient amount of training data. In our previous work [2], we have created a novel segmentation dataset that is designed for model training as well as for benchmarking purposes. We have utilised the dataset for initial experimentation with a Fully Convolutional Network (FCN) architecture and we have achieved promising results on real chronicle data. We have also presented an approach to automatically create artificial pages that can be used for data augmentation. In this paper, we go further and try to find efficient ways how to train a segmentation model with decent portion of data and evaluate several ways that can improve the model performance. Focusing mainly on the experiments and discussion, we provide more experiments on the input resolution, balancing the classes, post-processing the output and also examine the use of different training data including transfer learning and manual extension. Finally, we discuss the integration and usage on real data in the Porta fontium.

2   Related Work

This section first summarises recent methods for page segmentation and then it provides a short overview of available datasets.

2.1   Methods

There are many methods that were designed for the task of page segmentation which can be categorised into top-down and bottom-up categories. Historically, the segmentation problem was usually solved by conservative approaches based on simple image operations and on connected component analysis. Recent trend is to use neural networks for this task.

A page segmentation method using connected components and a bottom-up approach is presented in [5]. This method includes digitisation, rotation correction, segmentation and classification into text or graphics classes. Another method based on background thinning that is independent of page rotation is presented in [11]. These standard computer vision methods usually fail on handwritten document images, because it is difficult to binarise pages due to significantly low quality. It is also hard to extract characters since they are usually connected.

The above mentioned issues are successfully solved by approaches using Convolutional Neural Networks (CNN) that brought a significant improvement in many machine learning tasks including computer vision. An example of a CNN for historical document page segmentation is presented in [4]. Super-pixels (groups of pixels with similar characteristics) are identified in the image and they are classified using the network that takes 28×28 pixels as an input. The result of the classification is then assigned to the whole super-pixel.

Alternatively, every pixel can be classified separately using a sliding window. The problem of this approach is computational inefficiency because a large amount of computation is repeated as the window moves pixel by pixel. This problem is solved by Fully Convolutional Networks (FCNs) where one of the most efficient topology is U-Net [14]. This network was initially used for biomedical image segmentation but can be used in many other segmentation tasks including page segmentation.

Another architecture is presented by Wick & Puppe in [17]. This network is proposed for page segmentation of historical document images. In contrast to U-Net, it does not use skip-connections and uses transposed convolutional layer instead of upsampling layer followed by convolutional layer. The speed improvement is achieved mainly due to the small input size (260×390 pixels).

In order to achieve the best results in competitions, there were proposed also networks like the one presented by Xu et al. in [18]. This network uses the original resolution of images and provides many more details in the output.

There are many architectures that solve the segmentation problem very well. However, the main issue of this task consists in the availability of appropriate training data because the relevant data is the key point of approaches based on neural networks.

2.2 Datasets

There are several datasets for a wide range of tasks. Unfortunately, a significant number of datasets are inappropriate for our task, because the documents differ significantly.

ChronSeg. [2] dataset focuses on the segmentation of handwritten historical chronicles and it is available through website[2]. It contains training, validation, testing and experimental parts containing totally 58 (double-sided) pages with precise ground-truth for text, image and graphic regions in PAGE format. There are five different chronicles present in the dataset.

Diva-hisdb. [16] is a publicly available dataset with detailed ground-truth for text, comments and decorations. It consists of three manuscripts and 50 high-resolution pages for each manuscript. These manuscripts have similar layout features. The first two manuscripts come from the 11th century. They are written in Latin language using the Carolingian minuscule script. The third manuscript is from the 14th century and shows a chancery script in Italian and Latin. Unfortunately, the pages contain no images.

---

[2] https://corpora.kiv.zcu.cz/segmentation/.

IAM-HistDB. [7] contains handwritten historical manuscript images together with ground-truth for handwriting recognition systems. Currently, it includes three datasets: Saint Gall, Parzival and Washington.

Saint Gall database [6] contains 60 page images of a handwritten historical manuscript from 9th century. It is written in Latin language and Carolingian script.

Parzival database [8] is composed of 47 page images of handwritten historical manuscript from 13th century. The manuscript is written in Medieval German language and Gothic script.

Washington database [8] is created from the George Washington Papers. There are word and text line images with transcriptions. The provided ground-truth is not intended for page segmentation, but Saint Gall Database contains line locations that can be used for text segmentation.

Layout Analysis Dataset. [1] is precisely annotated for page layout analysis and contains suitable regions for our task. The dataset contains a huge amount of page images of different document types. There is a mixture of simple and complex page layouts with varying font sizes. The problem is that the documents are printed and consist mostly of modern magazines and technical journals so the page layout is totally different to our chronicles in most cases.

Competition Datasets at PRImA Website. There are also competition datasets at PRImA website[3]. These datasets has to be requested first and consist mainly of news-papers, books and typewritten notes. The number of annotated pages is usually around ten per dataset. Similarly as in the Layout Analysis Dataset, the text is printed and the page layout is different to our chronicle images.

3 FCN Architecture

We utilise a model that is based on U-Net [14], see Fig. 1 for the details . The architecture is designed to segment the entire input page at once. It uses padding in the convolutional layers, so there is no need for input image padding which could be problematic if the region with the padding colour is present in the image. Then this region could be understood by the network as a position at the borders and result in wrong predictions. There is usually a lot of noise at the borders of scanned document pages that should be suppressed. The padding in the convolutional layers allows that and also preserves dimensions so that the input resolution matches the output resolution.

Shared parameters in the convolutional layers allow variable input dimensions. In order to prevent skip-connection dimension inconsistency, the model input dimension has to be multiple of $2^4 = 16$ (given by four 2×2 max-pooling layers).

If there is a high-resolution input, the memory limitations appear. Then, there is again the need to trade-off between localisation accuracy and the use of context as discussed in [14]. The high resolution input can be processed in the sliding window manner using small context of the page or it can be down-sampled and processed with

---

[3] https://www.primaresearch.org/datasets.

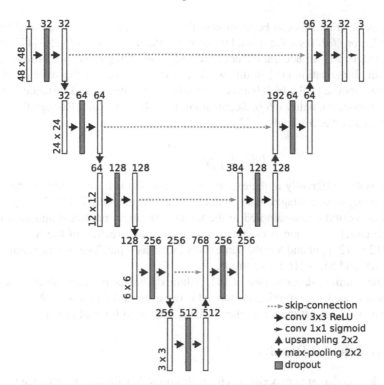

Fig. 1. FCN model architecture; values for 48 × 48 input: Boxes represent feature maps (dimensions are denoted on the left side, the number of channels is indicated above the box) [2].

less details, bigger context but worse localisation accuracy. To reduce computational costs, the input image size is limited to 512 × 512 pixels. This setup has been identified based on our preliminary experiments and it is also supported by the work of Wick and Puppe [17] where the authors used input of 260 × 390 pixels.

ReLU activation function is used in all but the output layer where sigmoid is utilized in order to produce three binary (segmentation) masks. The Binary Cross-Entropy loss function is used to allow the classification of the pixel into more classes since there could appear regions that correspond to more classes (e.g. image overlaid with text).

4 Experimental Setup

According to the ChronSeg paper [2], we utilise the same input images and GT masks for the experiments. The dataset contains training, validation, testing and experimental parts. Thus the experiments are evaluated on the validation part and the combined setup also on the test part of the dataset.

For evaluation, the classification metrics *accuracy*, *precision*, *recall* and *F1 score* are used, since the task is a pixel-labelling problem. Each pixel is binary classified for each channel so that True Positive (TP), True Negative (TN), False Positive (FP) or

False Negative (FN) sets can be identified. Further, the pixel modification of Intersection over Union (*IoU*) (see Eq. 1) and Foreground Pixel Accuracy (*FgPA*) [17] are used. FgPA is practically an accuracy calculated only over foreground pixels that are estimated using binarisation [15] in this work. For the *combined* setup we calculate also the Panoptic metric [10] which handles semantic segmentation and instance segmentation. The Panoptic Quality (*PQ*), Segmentation Quality (*SQ*) and Recognition Quality (*RQ*) are obtained accordingly to [3].

$$IoU = \frac{TP}{TP + FP + FN} \tag{1}$$

If not stated differently in the experiment, the model is trained only on the training part containing 6 page images that contain pictures. As depicted in Fig. 2, the grey level input image is first down-sampled to the target resolution, predicted and then resized back. The target resolution is obtained as the nearest correction of the resolution that fits the 512×512 input and has the same aspect ratio as input. The input resolutions can be 512×400 and 512×416 for example.

For the training, dropout rate of 0.2, Adam optimiser [9] and the early stopping technique are used. The training is stopped if the average IoU on the validation part is not improving. The best model (highest IoU) is then used for evaluation.

5   Experimental Results

We have designed a set of experiments for techniques that are used to enhance the recognition results if only small amount of data are available. Namely, we experiment with extending the training data, transfer learning and loss function weighting. The automatic creation of artificial pages from the existing ones is also presented as a data augmentation approach that deals with the problem of class imbalances and brings significant improvements. We also evaluate the influence of input resolution and a post-processing step. The results are reported in Table 1 and compared to the *baseline* setup which represents the model trained only on the 6 pages of chronicles that contains the image. Based on the experiments the *combined* setup of the model is made.

5.1   Input Resolution

The input resolution of the image is important since there are usually memory limitations and the compromise between computational costs, amount of details and avail-

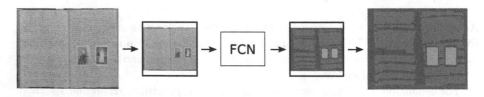

Fig. 2. Input image segmentation process: The input limit of 512×512 pixels is represented by squares before and after FCN box [2].

Table 1. Average results (in %) of the experiments on the validation part: *Baseline* is a referential setup with 512×512 input limit and the model is trained only on 6 pages that contain images. Baseline setup modifications are presented in next three blocks (different input size, loss function weighting, training data). Based on the experiments, the *combined* setup is reported in the next block. The last block contains modifications to the combined setup using post-processing, transfer learning and extended training data. All the modifications are closely described in Sects. 5 and 6.

	Accuracy	Precision	Recall	F1 score	IoU	FgPA
Baseline	95.3	91.8	92.6	92.0	85.5	98.5
128×128 input	86.6	79.9	82.7	80.7	68.0	93.4
256×256 input	93.9	89.9	91.8	90.7	83.1	98.4
1024×1024 input	95.5	94.1	91.6	92.6	86.5	98.8
Weighted sep. areas	95.3	94.6	90.7	92.3	85.9	99.0
Weighted classes	94.9	92.5	91.4	91.8	85.0	98.3
Augmentation	95.5	93.2	92.7	92.8	86.7	98.4
Artificial pages	96.1	94.0	94.3	94.0	88.9	99.2
Printed pages	95.5	94.2	92.1	93.0	87.1	98.8
Transfer learning	94.8	94.0	89.8	91.6	84.6	98.5
Combined	96.4	94.5	94.3	94.2	89.2	99.2
Post-process	95.9	93.4	94.6	93.9	88.6	99.0
Pre-trained	82.4	73.6	73.8	65.8	52.0	90.1
Fine-tuned	95.8	94.7	91.9	93.1	87.2	99.0
Extended	96.3	95.1	93.3	94.1	89.0	99.4

able context for the prediction has to be made. Hypothetically, the neighbourhood of the pixel can be more important than local pixel details. Therefore the model is trained with 128, 256, 512 and 1024 input size limit. For a human, the limits lower than 512 results in images that are hard to read. On the other hand, 1024 limit is comfortable for reading the text. The limit of 512 is somewhere between.

Fig. 3. Example predictions with different input limits (from left: input image, 128×128, 256×256, 512×512 and 1024×1024 input limits).

The results are reported in Table 1 and the example predictions are illustrated in Fig. 3. The 128 limit seems too low and results in a lot of noise and a significant drop in IoU. The 256 limit is applicable but noise is still present. The limits of 512 and 1024 are visually comparable. For the 1024 limit, there is an improvement in the presented metrics at the cost of higher computational demands. With different setup using artificial pages and augmentation, this difference is vanishing as can be seen in Table 2.

Table 2. Average results (in %) of different input limits with artificial pages and image augmentation setup [2].

	Accuracy	Precision	Recall	F1 score	IoU	FgPA
512×512	96.1	94.6	93.8	94.1	88.9	99.1
1024×1024	96.6	94.7	94.0	94.2	89.2	99.2

Alternatively, the network can be trained on smaller crops (e.g. 512×512) and then the predictions can be made for the whole page at once thanks to the shared parameters. So no composing of sub-results is necessary. Together with sliding window approach, this scenario is not appropriate for the architectures that use padding in the convolutional layers, because the padding provides a lot of information for predictions in border areas. In such a case, the model tends to amplify the noise at the borders of predicted samples as presented in Fig. 4. On the other hand, that information can be used for the noise suppression. For example, if there is mainly background class at the borders of the training samples, the model will more likely predict the border as background.

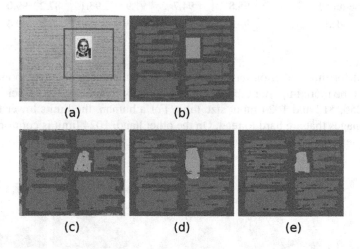

Fig. 4. Prediction examples: (a) input image, (b) ground-truth, (c) prediction of the model trained on crops (example training sample in green box of (a) and (b)), (d) *baseline* model prediction, (e) model prediction with weighted loss function for separating area [2].

5.2   Loss Function Weighting

Weighting of the loss function is used to improve the separation of the components as proposed in the U-Net paper [14]. The idea is that the component separating areas

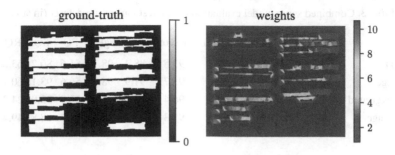

Fig. 5. Calculated weights for loss function weighting to improve the separation of the components [2].

are more important for training thus the loss function has more weight as illustrated in Fig. 5.

$$w(x) = w_0 \cdot \exp\left(-\frac{(d_1(x) + d_2(x))^2}{2\sigma^2}\right) \cdot (1 - \text{gt}(x)) + 1 \tag{2}$$

Weights are calculated for text and image channels according to Eq. 2, where x is the pixel position, $d_1(x)$ and $d_2(x)$ stands for the distance to two nearest components. The ground-truth value of the pixel is denoted as $\text{gt}(x)$. Parameter w_0 is set to 10 according to the U-Net paper and increased $\sigma = 10$ is used because of wider gaps between components.

The results of *weighted sep. areas* in Table 1 slightly improved. At the same time, the component separation is visually much better as illustrated in Fig. 4.

The weighting of the loss function can be used also for weighting classes to deal with class imbalances. For the given channel of the training sample, the weight of the binary class is edited based on its area. For example, the image class has usually bigger weight than no-image class. The weights should be also limited, otherwise the high values can cause problems during training. The best achieved results with *weighted classes* setup is presented in Table 1 and does not lead to an improvement. It increases the amount of noise in the output and the training can be problematic. Thus it is not very useful, since the training samples seem already good balanced.

5.3   Training Data Extension

Even though the *baseline* setup trained on 6 pages achieved promising results, better results can be expected when providing more training data. The image augmentation is a good approach for automatic extension of training data. The same transformations are applied on the input image and corresponding ground-truth as illustrated in Fig. 6. For the *augmentation* improvement in Table 1, the skew, slight rotations and grid based random distortions are used. As discussed previously, it is good to have the background class at the input borders to suppress noise. Since the grid based random distortion preserves borders, it is the most suitable.

The dataset contains also experimental part with annotated pages without images. These *no-image* pages are problematic for training because of class imbalances. On the

Table 3. Combined setup model evaluation on the test part of the dataset (in %).

	Accuracy	Precision	Recall	F1 score	IoU	FgPA	PQ	SQ	RQ
Text	96.3	95.8	92.1	93.8	88.4	98.7	51.6	80.2	63.8
Image	99.1	93.7	98.0	95.7	91.9	98.7	56.6	93.1	60.1
Background	96.1	96.5	96.4	96.4	93.1	99.0	22.9	93.0	24.3
Average	97.2	95.4	95.5	95.3	91.2	98.8	43.7	88.8	49.4

other hand, they contain specialities like different writing styles and decorations that are useful for training. To be able to use them, the images are added randomly into a no-image page as depicted in Fig. 7 with reasonable size and position restrictions. The image size ranges from 10×10 pixels up to 60 % of the page dimensions and the image can not touch the borders. These pages can be easily used for the training (see Fig. 8). Table 1 shows remarkable improvement for generated *artificial pages*.

Fig. 6. From left: (1) input image and its ground-truth, (2) augmented image, (3) image augmented only with random_distortion [2].

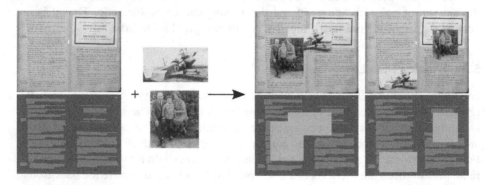

Fig. 7. Creation of artificial pages: Images are added randomly into document page [2].

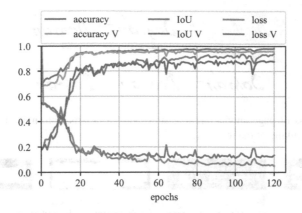

Fig. 8. Training process with using artificial pages for training does not indicate any problems caused by the generated samples (*V* denotes validation set.) [2].

Printed pages setup experiments with training the model on the training set extended by printed documents from the experimental part. According to Table 1, the features learned from the printed pages can be useful and improve the results especially if there is small amount of training samples. On the other hand, this approach leads to predictions with more noise and does not work well if combined together with other approaches.

5.4   Combined Setup

The best results (see Table 1) were achieved with the *combined* training setup that weights the loss function for separating area ($w_0 = 5$ and $\sigma = 10$), artificial pages creation, grid based random distortions for image augmentation and input is limited to 512×512 pixels.

The results on the testing part of the dataset are provided in Table 3 and one example prediction can be seen in Fig. 11.

5.5   Post-processing

The idea for this experiment is to post-process the prediction to imitate the page text annotation process that is illustrated in Fig. 9. To do that, the binarised image is masked with each separate component in the predicted text mask. This step imitates the noise removal and manual annotation. To shrink the region, the result is dilated with kernel k and the contour of the component is filled. After that, the erosion with the same kernel k is applied according to Fig. 10. The setting of kernel k is problematic since the annotation is done manually and for each page different shrinking setup can be used. Experimentally, the $k = (38, 45)$ is used. The small components for text and image channels are discarded and finally, the background is edited.

Although the comparison of Figs. 11 and 12 seems promising, the basic *post-process* does not improve the IoU results as could be seen in Table 1, since it tends to fill the

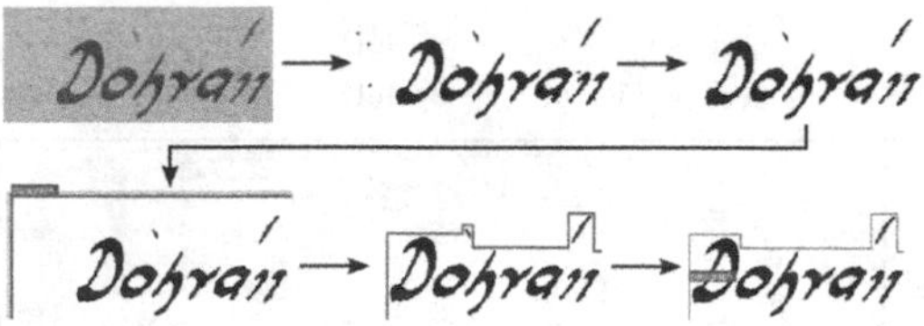

Fig. 9. The process of page annotation consists of image binarisation, noise removal, manual annotation and shrinking of the region. [2].

Fig. 10. Post-process example (from left: component from text mask prediction, masked binarised image, dilation, erosion).

Fig. 11. Combined setup model example prediction of the page from test set [2].

separating area in some predicted regions (see Fig. 10). On the other hand compared to the Table 3, the RQ improves significantly while SQ remains comparable resulting in better PQ as presented in Table 4.

5.6 Transfer Learning

Transfer learning model/setup in Table 1 is pre-trained on the printed documents from Layout Analysis Dataset and then fine-tuned as the *baseline* setup. The results are slightly worse and the model mispredicts the handwritten text as image more likely. On the other hand, it works better for the glued printed text blocks. This is probably due to the learned features for printed documents during pre-training. The fine-tuning is very fast and takes about 20 epochs compared to 160 epochs for the *baseline* setup. If the model is trained further for roughly the same number of epochs as *baseline*, the results are comparable.

Fig. 12. Post-processed combined setup model prediction example.

The combined setup is also used for the transfer learning and results are reported for *pre-trained* model and *fine-tuned* model separately. For the fine-tuned model, the characteristics are the same as in the previous case. The predictions of pre-trained model are not usable as could be seen in Fig. 13.

Fig. 13. From left: the input image, prediction of pre-trained model, prediction after fine-tuning (23 epochs).

6 Porta Fontium Integration and Method Tuning

The model allows automatic text, image and background segmentation of the chronicles with relatively low computational costs. These days, the result allows to filter the chronicles or pages that contain images as illustrated in Fig. 14. This can help the researchers studying the arts for example. It has also a great potential to further utilise the output for image search and handwritten text recognition to improve search options.

When testing the system on a large variety of different chronicles and thus previously unseen samples, the problems of mispredictions showed up. Using prediction masks, the two main problematic regions were identified. The first is image regions that were previously unseen in the training set. The second is text region with different

Table 4. Post-processed combined setup model evaluation on the test part of the dataset (in %).

	Accuracy	Precision	Recall	F1 score	IoU	FgPA	PQ	SQ	RQ
Text	95.9	93.7	93.0	93.3	87.4	98.8	59.4	79.2	75.1
Image	99.1	93.8	97.9	95.6	91.8	99.0	80.1	93.1	85.8
Background	95.5	95.5	96.1	95.8	92.0	99.0	52.8	91.9	56.9
Average	96.8	94.3	95.7	94.9	90.4	98.9	64.1	88.1	72.6

Fig. 14. Porta fontium extended functionality: The pages containing images are highlighted on the left side and can be browsed separately.

Table 5. Porta fontium model with extended data evaluation on the test part of the dataset (in %).

	Accuracy	Precision	Recall	F1 score	IoU	FgPA	PQ	SQ	RQ
Text	95.7	95.5	90.8	92.7	86.9	99.3	36.0	79.5	45.0
Image	99.2	96.0	98.0	96.9	94.1	99.3	63.1	94.0	66.2
Background	95.6	96.1	96.3	96.2	92.6	99.3	13.2	92.6	14.2
Average	96.8	95.9	95.0	95.3	91.2	99.3	37.5	88.7	41.8

writing style like decorative headings etc. The reason was determined as not enough training samples. There is a very limited set of images used for artificial pages during training. Also the decorative headings can be very diverse and not present among training samples.

To deal with this a huge amount of highly variable images from OpenImages [13] was used for artificial pages creation. The training set was also extended by newly annotated problematic pages containing decorative fonts, sketches etc. With *extended* data, a more general model is made while the results are still comparable to the specialised one as presented in Table 1. The results without post-processing presented in Table 5 are comparable to the combined setup results. The test part predictions are worse for the text but much better for the image class.

7 Conclusions and Future Work

This paper presents an approach to segment historical handwritten chronicles into text, image and background classes together with a series of experiments. These experiments are very useful for the final model integrated into Porta fontium to improve the search options.

Based on the experiments, we can say that high resolution is not crucial for the chronicle segmentation into text, image and background. FCN model can generalise well on the documents that are similar but it is hard to create one generalised FCN model that can segment pages of different types and characteristics (e.g. modern printed magazines and historical handwritten documents). In such a case, the model tends to output more noise than the specialised one. This makes the real usage difficult. In that case, the transfer learning can help in creation of specialised models allowing fast fine-tuning. As shown in the experiments, a small amount of the data can be sufficient and the results can be further improved with data augmentation approaches. Also extending the dataset for verified segmented samples and the iterative training could help significantly and reduce the costs of manual annotations.

We plan further studying the possibilities to normalise the different types of document images that could allow the usage of one generalised model. The idea is to pre-process the image to normalise the pixel representation since it is very different in terms of pixel values from which the predictions are made.

Acknowledgments. This work has been partly supported by Cross-border Cooperation Program Czech Republic - Free State of Bavaria ETS Objective 2014–2020 (project no. 211) and by Grant SGS-2022-016 Advanced methods of data processing and analysis.

References

1. Antonacopoulos, A., Bridson, D., Papadopoulos, C., Pletschacher, S.: A realistic dataset for performance evaluation of document layout analysis. In: 2009 10th International Conference on Document Analysis and Recognition, pp. 296–300 (2009). https://doi.org/10.1109/ICDAR.2009.271
2. Baloun., J., Král., P., Lenc., L.: Chronseg: Novel dataset for segmentation of handwritten historical chronicles. In: Proceedings of the 13th International Conference on Agents and Artificial Intelligence - Volume 2: ICAART, pp. 314–322. INSTICC, SciTePress (2021). https://doi.org/10.5220/0010317203140322
3. Chazalon, J., Carlinet, E.: Revisiting the coco panoptic metric to enable visual and qualitative analysis of historical map instance segmentation. In: Lladós, J., Lopresti, D., Uchida, S. (eds.) ICDAR 2021. LNCS, vol. 12824, pp. 367–382. Springer, Cham (2021). https://doi.org/10.1007/978-3-030-86337-1_25
4. Chen, K., Seuret, M., Hennebert, J., Ingold, R.: Convolutional neural networks for page segmentation of historical document images. In: 2017 14th IAPR International Conference on Document Analysis and Recognition (ICDAR), vol. 1, pp. 965–970. IEEE (2017)

5. Drivas, D., Amin, A.: Page segmentation and classification utilising a bottom-up approach. In: Proceedings of 3rd International Conference on Document Analysis and Recognition, vol. 2, pp. 610–614 (1995). https://doi.org/10.1109/ICDAR.1995.601970
6. Fischer, A., Frinken, V., Fornés, A., Bunke, H.: Transcription alignment of latin manuscripts using hidden markov models. In: Proceedings of the 2011 Workshop on Historical Document Imaging and Processing, pp. 29–36 (2011)
7. Fischer, A., Indermühle, E., Bunke, H., Viehhauser, G., Stolz, M.: Ground truth creation for handwriting recognition in historical documents. In: Proceedings of the 9th IAPR International Workshop on Document Analysis Systems, pp. 3–10 (2010)
8. Fischer, A., Keller, A., Frinken, V., Bunke, H.: Lexicon-free handwritten word spotting using character hmms. Pattern Recogn. Lett. **33**(7), 934–942 (2012)
9. Kingma, D.P., Ba, J.: Adam: a method for stochastic optimization. arXiv preprint arXiv:1412.6980 (2014)
10. Kirillov, A., He, K., Girshick, R., Rother, C., Dollár, P.: Panoptic segmentation. In: Proceedings of the IEEE/CVF Conference on Computer Vision and Pattern Recognition, pp. 9404–9413 (2019)
11. Kise, K., Yanagida, O., Takamatsu, S.: Page segmentation based on thinning of background. In: Proceedings of 13th International Conference on Pattern Recognition, vol. 3, pp. 788–792 (1996)
12. Kise, K.: Page segmentation techniques in document analysis. In: Doermann, D., Tombre, K. (eds.) Handbook of Document Image Processing and Recognition, pp. 135–175. Springer, London (2014). https://doi.org/10.1007/978-0-85729-859-1_5
13. Krasin, I., et al.: Openimages: a public dataset for large-scale multi-label and multi-class image classification. Dataset (2017). https://storage.googleapis.com/openimages/web/index.html
14. Ronneberger, O., Fischer, P., Brox, T.: U-Net: convolutional networks for biomedical image segmentation. In: Navab, N., Hornegger, J., Wells, W.M., Frangi, A.F. (eds.) MICCAI 2015. LNCS, vol. 9351, pp. 234–241. Springer, Cham (2015). https://doi.org/10.1007/978-3-319-24574-4_28
15. Sauvola, J., Pietikäinen, M.: Adaptive document image binarization. Pattern Recognition **33**(2), 225 – 236 (2000). https://doi.org/10.1016/S0031-3203(99)00055-2, http://www.sciencedirect.com/science/article/pii/S0031320399000552
16. Simistira, F., Seuret, M., Eichenberger, N., Garz, A., Liwicki, M., Ingold, R.: Diva-hisdb: a precisely annotated large dataset of challenging medieval manuscripts. In: 2016 15th International Conference on Frontiers in Handwriting Recognition (ICFHR), pp. 471–476. IEEE (2016)
17. Wick, C., Puppe, F.: Fully convolutional neural networks for page segmentation of historical document images. In: 2018 13th IAPR International Workshop on Document Analysis Systems (DAS), pp. 287–292 (2018). https://doi.org/10.1109/DAS.2018.39
18. Xu, Y., He, W., Yin, F., Liu, C.L.: Page segmentation for historical handwritten documents using fully convolutional networks. In: 2017 14th IAPR International Conference on Document Analysis and Recognition (ICDAR), vol. 1, pp. 541–546. IEEE (2017)

On the Relationship with Toulmin Method to Logic-Based Argumentation

Teeradaj Racharak$^{(\boxtimes)}$ and Satoshi Tojo

School of Information Science, Japan Advanced Institute of Science and Technology,
Ishikawa, Japan
{racharak,tojo}@jaist.ac.jp

Abstract. Toulmin presents a model of argumentation, in which claims can be justified in response to challenges. The model replaces the traditional concepts of 'claim' and 'premise' with new concepts of 'claim', 'data', 'warrant', 'qualifier', 'rebuttal', and 'backing'. Due to the significance of Toulmin's argumentation, this work investigates its relationship to our recently introduced logic-based argumentation [14]. We show that Toulmin's idea does not only give a visual interpretation of the logic-based argumentation, but also yields a human-understandable form. Finally, the paper wraps up the investigation's result and formalizes a novel 2-Tier argumentation framework, that combines the advantages of both Toulmin's model and the logic-based argumentation system.

Keywords: Toulmin model of argumentation · Formal argumentation · Deductive logic · Explainable artificial intelligence

1 Introduction

Argumentation is an important aspect of human intelligence. When humans are making decisions, they always search for pros and cons of arguments as well as their consequences to understand facing situations. This kind of argumentative reasoning can be formalized by utilizing a logical language for the premises and an appropriate consequence relation for showing that claims logically follow from the premises (*a.k.a. logic-based argumentation*) [14].

There are a number of proposals for logic-based formalization of argumentation (*cf.* [1, 3, 22] for the existing literature). These works allow the representation of arguments for claims, the representation of counterarguments against them, and the relationships between the arguments. Despite the diversity, an argument in logic-based argumentation is commonly defined as a pair of which the first item is a set of formulae that proves the second item (*i.e.* a logical formula). There been several investigations of and success with the use of proof techniques in logic. For instance, Prakken and Sartor [13] developed proof procedures to find acceptable arguments in Dung's semantics from a defeasible logic knowledge-base. As an example in propositional logic knowledge-base, Efstathiou and Hunter [5] proposed to generate arguments and counterarguments using the resolution principle and connected graph [10, 11].

Unfortunately, these existing approaches do not offer computational content of an argument in a form that is understandable by naive users. This is a vital aspect of

© Springer Nature Switzerland AG 2022
A. P. Rocha et al. (Eds.): ICAART 2021, LNAI 13251, pp. 197–207, 2022.
https://doi.org/10.1007/978-3-031-10161-8_10

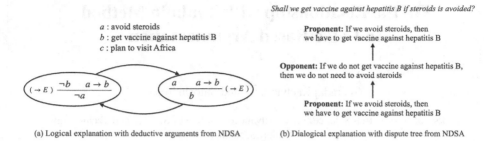

(a) Logical explanation with deductive arguments from NDSA   (b) Dialogical explanation with dispute tree from NDSA

Fig. 1. Logical (a) and dialogical (b) explanations from the NDSA framework.

developing explainable artificial intelligence (XAI) systems; reasoners should provide human-understandable explanations in order to facilitate the process of evolving the theory between explainers and explainees (*i.e.* a group of people who receive the explanations). To fill this gap, Racharak and Tojo [14] recently argued for the use of natural deduction (ND) [6], taken as a mean to identify an argument's structure from the proof, and demonstrated that the pattern represented by ND is close to what humans can perceive as an argument drawing a conclusion from any conjunction that it contains. This investigation results in the development of a novel logic-based framework called "natural deduction-based structured argumentation (NDSA)". Informally, NDSA allows to indicate explanations for any decisions made by deductive arguments computed in the framework and an argumentative dialogue that defends for its oppositions.

Figure 1 illustrates two types of explanation made by the recently introduced NDSA framework. Figure 1-(a) depicts an example of NDSA-based logical explanation with natural deduction. Since the hypotheses in natural deduction only appear on the top layers, this gives a benefit for yielding human-friendly arguments, compared with other deductive formalisms. For instance, a Hilbert-style axiomatization requires us to supply many axioms in the midst of a proof tree. As for the analytic tableau method, we need to show our goal to prove first on the top line, that is against our objective. Gentzen's sequent calculus [9] might be the most polished style of deduction; however, each sequent becomes a long and messy sequence of formulae and is thus difficult for proof's visualization. Furthermore, Fig. 1-(b) depicts an example of NDSA-based dialogical explanation with a dispute tree, allowing to visualize potential conflicts in reasoning.

It is worth mentioning that current studies on logic-based argumentation have mostly concerned on exploiting logic for modeling structured argumentation such as [1]; however, how it contributes to the development of explainable artificial intelligence (XAI) systems is not fully investigated yet. This paper is an extended study of [14], where the relationship between the proposed NDSA and the Toulmin's method is analyzed. Note that Toulmin's method is a classical approach in modern argumentation theories. Understanding its relationship to NDSA is valuable on offering human-interpretation in argumentative reasoning.

This work is organized as follows. Section 2 describes the background knowledge of the Toulmin's argumentation model and the NDSA framework recently introduced

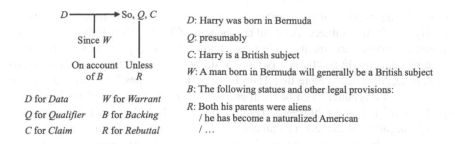

Fig. 2. Toulmin's layout of arguments with an example [15, pp. 104–5].

in [14]. Section 3 shows the manner in which the Toulmin's model provides an alternative interpretation of NDSA, yielding different viewpoints of explanation for adopted XAI systems in logic-based argumentation. Our related works and the conclusion are discussed in Sects. 4 and 5, respectively.

2   Preliminaries

2.1   Toulmin Model of Argumentation

This subsection reviews the basics of Toulmin's model of argumentation [15,16]. In his philosophical viewpoint, there exist other arguments than the formal ones, which offer more argument variants and different perspectives of interpretation.

Toulmin is perhaps most often read because of the simple representation of his argument diagram (cf. Fig. 2) [20]. While a formal logical argument often employs the dichotomy of premises and conclusions when formulating arguments, Toulmin's formalization breaks down each argument into six components: Data, Claim, Qualifier, Warrant, Backing, and Rebuttal. Figure 2 illustrates an intuition of each component with the Toulmin's classic example of arguing whether Harry, who may or may not, be a British subject.

When someone claims (C) that Harry is a British subject, apropos to Toulmin's view, it is natural to ask "what does this claim stand on?". An answer to this question can provide the data (D) on which the claim rests. For instance, "Harry was born in Bermuda". In addition, a further important question needs to be asked, *i.e.*, "why do you think that the datum gives support for your claim?". In other words, we need to use a warrant. In our example, it is "A man born in Bermuda will generally be a British subject". Warrants generally take the form of rule-like statements as illustrated in the example. A point to keep in mind here is that warrants are not necessary to be universal. As the example shows, the warrant is not that 'each' man born in Bermuda is a British subject, but merely that a man born in Bermuda will 'generally' be a British subject. As a result, the claim becomes that 'presumably' (Q) Harry is a British subject.

When the datum, qualified claim, and warrant are made explicitly, a further question has to be asked, *i.e.*, "why do you think that the warrant holds?". An answer to this question will supply the backing (B) for the warrant. In our example, Toulmin refers to the existence of statutes and other legal provisions (without specifying them) that can provide the backing of the warrant, *i.e.*, any person who is born in Bermuda will generally be a British subject. The final component of Toulmin's is Rebuttal (R) which indicates any counterarguments against the claim or any exception to it. In the example, the rebuttals might be "harry's parents could be aliens" or "he could have become a naturalized American". Note that Toulmin also distinguishes between a datum and the negation of a rebuttal; both of them are directly relevant to the claim in different ways. Here, the datum establishes a presumption of the British nationality, whereas by showing a negation of the rebuttal can confirm the presumption thereby created.

In sum, Toulmin distingiushes six kinds of elements in any arguments as follows. Firstly, claim is the starting assertion and must be justified when challenged. Secondly, datum provides the basis of the claim in response to the question: "what does the claim stand on?". Thirdly, warrant gives the connection between datum and claim. It is a general, hypothetical statement that authorizes the step of which an argument commits. Fourthly, qualifier indicates the strength of the step from datum to claim. Fifthly, backing shows why a warrant holds. Finally, rebuttal indicates circumstances in which the general authority of the warrant would have to be set aside, or exceptional circumstances which might be capable of defeating or rebutting the warranted conclusion.

2.2 NDSA: Natural Deduction for Structured Argumentation

Here, we suppose that a knowledge-base Δ is represented by classical propositional logic (PL); thereby proof theories in PL are investigated for construction of arguments and counterarguments from Δ. In [14], it is argued that reading a natural deduction (ND) proof from top to bottom yields a natural human-interpretable argument, initiating the formal development of the natural deduction for structured argumentation (NDSA) framework as follows.

Definition 1 ([14]). *Given a PL knowledge-base Δ, an argument for claim α supported by $\Phi \subseteq \Delta$ (denoted by $\langle \Phi, \alpha \rangle$) is a ND proof tree such that α is derivable (backwards) from α to Φ and $\neg\alpha$ is not derivable from Φ.*

Set Φ is called *supports* or assumptions; and also, α is called the *claim* of an argument. Note that the above definition imposes the consistency constraint to avoid the construction of illogical arguments (such as via *ex falso quodlibet*).

Example 1 Consider the Toulmin's classic example on Fig. 2, let a knowledge-base $\Delta_1 := \{(born\_in\_bermuda \land \neg arguably) \rightarrow british\_subject; born\_in\_bermuda ; aliens\_parent \rightarrow arguably; become\_american \rightarrow arguably\}$, where a semicolon (;) separates each logical formula in Δ_1 and $\neg$ denotes the classical negation. In the following, we show that $\{\neg arguably\} \cup \Delta_1 \vdash british\_subject$, where $\vdash$ indicates the derivation and $\{\neg arguably\}$ is an (uncancelled) hypothesis denoted by $[\cdot]$:

$$\frac{\dfrac{born\_in\_bermuda \quad [\neg arguably]}{born\_in\_bermuda \land \neg arguably} \quad (born\_in\_bermuda \land \neg arguably) \rightarrow british\_subject}{british\_subject}$$

Following Definition 1, we can say that $\langle \{\neg arguably\} \cup \Delta_1, british\_subject \rangle$ is an argument that supports the claim $british\_subject$.

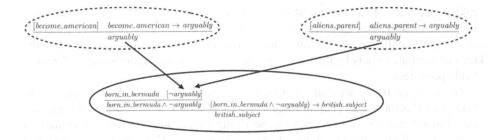

Fig. 3. An argumentation framework instantiated by the NDSA for Example 1.

Definition 2 ([14]). *Let $A := \langle \Phi, \alpha \rangle$ and $B := \langle \Psi, \beta \rangle$ be arguments. Then, we say that argument A attacks argument B iff $\exists \phi \in \Psi$ such that $\alpha \equiv \neg \phi$.*

From Example 1, it is worth observing that uncancelled hypotheses can be regarded as attacked points of an argument. For instance, in order to withdraw the claim $british\_subject$, one has to show that this claim is arguable (*cf.* Fig. 3), *i.e.*, by proving with the evidence that either the parents are aliens ($aliens\_parent$) or Harry has become an American ($become\_american$).

Definition 3 (NDSA [14]). *A NDSA framework is a triple $\langle \mathcal{L}, \Delta, \vdash_{ND} \rangle$, where $\mathcal{L}$ is a PL language, Δ is a knowledge-base modeled based upon language $\mathcal{L}$, and $\vdash_{ND}$ is a consequence relation represented by the natural deduction calculus.*

As investigated in [14], Definition 3 exploits the natural deduction because it enables to construct human-interpretable arguments in a sense that hypotheses appear on the top level of each argument and the claim appears on its leaf. Figure 3 illustrates an example of the argument and (potential) counterarguments in NDSA, initiating from the classic Toulmin's example in Sect. 2.1, in which the solid round indicates a valid logical argument, dashed rounds indicate potential counterarguments, and arrows indicate attack relations between arguments.

3 The Reception and Refinement of Toulmin's Model in Logic-Based Argumentation

Observe that the Toulmin's layout of arguments (Fig. 2) looks very resemblant to arguments instantiated from the NDSA framework (Fig. 3). In particular, each argument in an argumentation framework instantiated from NDSA corresponds to a Toulmin's argument and each of its attacking arguments corresponds to a rebuttal condition pointed out by the Toulmin's diagram.

In particular, there exists historical account of AI work taking up Toulmin's idea [20]. Specifically, Toulmin's idea, that logic should be regarded as a generalized form of jurisprudence, is taken up seriously in the 1990 s s in the field of artificial intelligence and law. Influenced by logic-based knowledge representation and Toulmin's method,

Prakken and Sartor [12] used an adapted first-order language as the basis of their formalism. In their system, arguments are built by applying Modus Ponens to rules, yielding an operationalization of Toulmin's idea. Prakken and Sartor also modelled specific kinds of rebuttal, namely by the attack of weakly negated assumptions and on the basis of rule priorities.

Hage [8] proposed another refinement of Toulmins's idea which is similar to Prakken and Sartor's work [12]. In Hage's approach, rules were formalized using predicates. For instance, the fact that the rule specifying thieves are punishable is formalized as 'Valid(rule(theft1, thief(x), punishable(x)))'. Here, 'theft1' corresponds to the name of a rule, 'thief(x)' the rule's antecedent, and 'punishable(x)' its consequent. A further refinement of Toulmin's view was given by Verheij *et al.* [21], which formalized two kinds of warrants, *i.e.*, legal rules and legal principles.

The key to the translation of Toulmin's model in the above works is to provide expressions in a concrete manner that a datum leads to a claim and a claim can be attacked from rebuttal. Furthermore, argument evaluation is defined in terms of winning strategies in dialogue games: an argument is called *justified* when it can be successfully defended against an opponent's counterarguments. The following subsections continue to analyze the reception and refinement of Toulmin's idea under the lens of logic-based argumentation.

3.1 Reasoning on NDSA and Admissible Sets

How does the NDSA framework relate to Toulmin's view? Obviously, similar to [8, 12, 21], NDSA has offered a precise explication on each part of Toulmin's view. This result is a direct consequence of using formal logic to formulate arguments, whereas Toulmin's only exists in the form of an informal philosophical expression. Moreover, it is shown in [14] that a formal elaboration of warrants and of rebuttals can be given in the form of the ND calculus and the notion of attack (Definition 2), yielding a systematic account of logical arguments' construction.

Indeed, a proposition is the claim of any Toulmin's argument if it can be logically derived using the ND proof calculus. Here, data of the claim is a set of hypotheses (but not uncancelled ones) used in the derivation, and warrants are the logical implication used by the rule ($\rightarrow E$) for the derivation. Consider the solid circle in Fig. 3, the claim is $british\_subject$, the datum is $born\_in\_bermuda$, and the warrant is the implication $(born\_in\_bermuda \land \neg arguably) \rightarrow british\_subject$.

As investigated by Toulmin, warrants can be either universally or presumably qualified. NDSA explicitly handles this two sorts of qualifiers at the granularity of the implication formulae, *i.e.*, if such formulae contain uncancelled hypotheses, those warrants are presumably and uncancelled ones can be attacked. Otherwise, they are universally qualified. Following this principle, the formula $(born\_in\_bermuda \land \neg arguably) \rightarrow british\_subject$ in Fig. 3 is classified as the presumption qualifier and $\neg arguably$ is opened to challenge. Note that, according to Definition 2, this challenge will be achieved if there exist arguments showing the contrary of such uncancelled hypotheses as its attacks. In Fig. 3, each arrow indicates an attack, where the head associates with an attacked argument, the tail associates with an attacking argument, and each uncancelled hypothesis denotes a challenged proposition (the rebuttal in the Toulmin's

Table 1. The relationship of Toulmin's and NDSA-based Arguments.

Toulmin's Element	NDSA's Element
Data	Hypotheses of natural deduction argument
Claim	Claim of natural deduction argument
Warrant	Implication rules used to derive the claim with the hypotheses
Qualifier	*Presumably* if there are uncancelled hypotheses, or *universally* otherwise
Backing	Maximal sub-proofs used to derive the warrants in natural deduction argument
Rebuttal	Other natural deduction arguments that derive the contrary of uncancelled hypotheses

idea). As the backings are simply reasons for the warrants in the Toulmin's, they are referred to the maximal sub-proof of each implication used to derive the claim in ND.

The above discussion explains how NDSA can provide explicitly a formal representation for the Toulmin's diagram. NDSA does not only provide a formal representation as it formalizes the Dung's abstract argumentation [4]. In fact, it also concerns a genuine extension of what Toulmin had in mind. The key idea is that an extension of an argumentation framework instantiated by NDSA can be thought of as a set of accepted arguments that defend all of the rebuttal. This set of arguments is called an *admissible* set in Dung's words. Note that Dung has studied three types of subsets of the set of admissible arguments for an argumentation framework: *stable*, *preferred*, and *grounded* extensions. Therefore, the recently introduced NDSA framework can significantly extend and provide the modelling of Toulmin's concept of rebuttal in a formal manner. Table 1 summarizes the relationship with Toulmin method to NDSA accordingly.

3.2 2-Tier AF: Two-Tier Argumentation Framework

Motivated by the relationship investigated previously, this subsection presents a further refinement of NDSA based on the Toulmin's structure, called a *2-tier argumentation framework* (2-Tier AF). Our main goal is to exploit the interpretability and readability of Toulmin's for lay people. Due to the obvious translation shown in Table 1, the 2-Tier AF is naturally defined as follows.

Definition 4. *Each Toulmin's diagram is an* argument *in the 2-Tier AF.*

Definition 4 obviously follows from the analysis that each derivation in NDSA corresponds to an argument based on the Toulmin's view. Next, we adopt the same understanding from our analysis to define an attack between arguments.

Definition 5. *Given a notion of* contrary *of claim in an argument, we say that an argument A* attacks *an argument B if the claim of argument A is the contrary of a datum of argument B and argument B is presumably.*

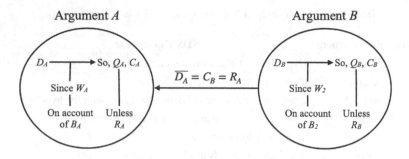

Fig. 4. An argumentation framework instantiated by a 2-Tier AF.

As in NDSA [14], the notion of attack between arguments in a 2-Tier AF depends only on attacking ('undercutting') uncancelled hypotheses. To complete the above definitions of argument and attack, we formally introduce the definition of 2-Tier argumentation framework as follows.

Definition 6 (2-Tier AF). *A 2-Tier argumentation framework is a septuple* $\langle \mathcal{D}, \mathcal{Q}, \mathcal{C}, \mathcal{W}, \mathcal{B}, \mathcal{R}, {}^{-} \rangle$ *in which*

- *Datum $D \in \mathcal{D}$, Qualifer $Q \in \mathcal{Q}$, Claim $C \in \mathcal{C}$, Warrant W, Backing $B \in \mathcal{B}$, and Rebuttal $R \in \mathcal{R}$ are elements of the Toulmin's diagram,*
- ${}^{-}$ *is a partial mapping from the set $\mathcal{D}$ of data into the set $\mathcal{C}$ of claims, where $\overline{D}$ is called the* contrary *of $D \in \mathcal{D}$.*

Note that ${}^{-}$ is defined as a partial mapping due to the fact that not every argument can be attacked. As in our analysis on NDSA, an argument is open for attack if it involves uncancelled hypotheses for deriving the claim. Figure 4 illustrates an example of an argumentation framework instantiated by a 2-Tier AF, where an attack is formalized by the contrary of datum D_A of argument A and the contrary is derivable on argument B, i.e., $\overline{D_A} = C_B = R_A$.

Obviously, the introduced 2-Tier AF is an instance of the Dung's abstract argumentation (AA), as in NDSA. Thus, all semantic notions for determining the 'acceptability' of arguments in AA are also applied to arguments in 2-Tier AF. This connection does not only provide benefits on the interpretability of logic-based arguments computed from the NDSA framework, but also gives potential for AI adoptions especially argument mining due to the available datasets [2].

4   Related Work

This section compares our investigation described in this paper with existing work on the relationship with the Toulmin's method for artificial intelligence.

Praken and Sartor [12] are perhaps the first researchers who are influenced by Toulmin's idea and applied it in the area of artificial intelligence and law. In their approach, an adapted first-order language was used as the basis of their formalism. The following illustrates a formal version of the rule that someone has legal capacity unless he can be shown to be a minor (taken from [12]):

$$r_1 : \sim x \text{ is a minor} \Rightarrow x \text{ has legal capacity}$$

Here, r_1 is the name of the rule, which can be used to refer to it. In addition, 'x is a minor' and 'x has legal capacity' are unary predicates. The tilde represents so-called *weak negation*, indicating that the rule's antecedent is fulfilled when it cannot be shown that x is a minor. It is not difficult to perceive that this mechanism corresponds to the presumably qualifier in the Toulmin's sense. If ordinary negation is used (*i.e.* $\neg x$ is a minor), the fulfillment of the antecedent would require to show that x is not a minor.

Hage's approach [8] is similar to the work of Prakken and Sartor. In [8], rules were first-and-foremost to be thought of as things with properties. Thus, each rule was formalized as a predicate. For instance, the same example would be expressed as 'Valid(rule(r_1, $\sim$minor(x), legal_capacity(x)))' in Hage's. In addition, Hage distinguished the validity of a rule from its applicability, in which the rule validity corresponded to the Toulmin's warrant.

A formal reconstruction of Toulmin's diagram is studied by Verheij [19]. In his study, the abstract argumentation logic DefLog [17] was employed to formulate each element of Toulmin's model except the notion of qualifier. Apropos to the analysis, Verheij has realized that the treatment of Toulmin's rebuttal is ambiguous as it associates with multiple kinds of attack, namely defeating (or rebutting) the warranted conclusion and undercutting in the sense of Pollock's argumentation. A side effect of his reconstruction was that arguments modelled according to Toulmin's diagram could be formally evaluated. A similar reconstruction of Walton's argumentation schemes was also studied by Verheij in [18].

Our result of this research is similar to Verheij's works [18,19] where a formal reconstruction of Toulmin's scheme is analyzed and explicitly explained. Indeed, our result differs from Verheij's in two perspectives. Firstly, our work analyzes the connection of Toulmin's idea to logic-based argumentation especially the recent NDSA framework. Unlike [18,19] which is specifically based on DefLog, NDSA can be utilized by any deductive logic with an appropriate consequence relation, providing with greater potential to be adopted. Secondly, we present an obvious translation between arguments instantiated by NDSA and Toulmin's arguments. Consider on the availability Toulmin-based annotation for argument mining [2,7], this contribution can enable researchers from both Knowledge Representation and Reasoning and Natural Language Processing to connect together and make further progress towards the automated argument reasoning.

5   Conclusion and Future Direction

This work extends the proposal in our previous paper [14]. Indeed, the reception and refinement of Toulmin's ideas in AI is investigated and analyzed under the lens of the NDSA framework. We show that when an argumentation framework is instantiated by NDSA, there exists an obvious translation from each instantiated argument to an argument in Toulmin's view and the attack between arguments is indicated through the contrary of each argument's claim.

More importantly, we demonstrate that the proposed 2-Tier argumentation framework (2-Tier AF) is an instance of the renowned Dung's abstract argumentation. Therefore, arguments modelled according to Toulmin's diagram can be formally evaluated through the mathematics of Dung. For instance, assuming that datum and warrant hold, but not a rebuttal, then the claim follows; when also a rebuttal is assumed, the claim does not follow. In addition, a rebuttal of a rebuttal can be shown to reinstate a claim. These illustrated circumstances can be formally evaluated through the notion of admissibility in Dung's sense, while retaining the original flavor of Toulmin's method.

Considering the available datasets [2, 7] annotated in Toulmin's method, we plan to develop machine learning models to automatically indicate each element of Toulmin's argument from text. Indeed, we are under the development of these systems and aim at integrating with our proposal in [14] towards an implementation of automated argument reasoning in future.

References

1. Besnard, P., Hunter, A.: A review of argumentation based on deductive arguments. In: Handbook of Formal Argumentation, pp. 437–484 (2018)
2. Cabrio, E., Villata, S.: Five years of argument mining: a data-driven analysis. In: IJCAI, vol. 18, pp. 5427–5433 (2018)
3. Chesñevar, C.I., Maguitman, A.G., Loui, R.P.: Logical models of argument. ACM Comput. Surv. (CSUR) 32(4), 337–383 (2000)
4. Dung, P.M.: On the acceptability of arguments and its fundamental role in nonmonotonic reasoning, logic programming and n-person games. Artif. Intell. 77(2), 321–358 (1995)
5. Efstathiou, V., Hunter, A.: Algorithms for generating arguments and counterarguments in propositional logic. Int. J. Approximate Reason. 52(6), 672–704 (2011)
6. Gentzen, G.: Untersuchungen über das logische schließen i. Mathematische zeitschrift 39(1), 176–210 (1935)
7. Habernal, I., Gurevych, I.: Argumentation mining in user-generated web discourse. Comput. Linguist. 43(1), 125–179 (2017)
8. Hage, J.: A theory of legal reasoning and a logic to match. Artif. Intell. Law 4(3), 199–273 (1996). https://doi.org/10.1007/BF00118493
9. Kleene, S.C., De Bruijn, N., de Groot, J., Zaanen, A.C.: Introduction to Metamathematics, vol. 483. van Nostrand New York (1952)
10. Kowalski, R.: A proof procedure using connection graphs. J. ACM (JACM) 22(4), 572–595 (1975)
11. Kowalski, R.: Logic for problem solving, vol. 7. Ediciones Díaz de Santos (1979)
12. Prakken, H., Sartor, G.: A dialectical model of assessing conflicting arguments in legal reasoning. In: Logical Models of Legal Argumentation, pp. 175–211. Springer (1996). https://doi.org/10.1007/978-94-011-5668-4_6
13. Prakken, H., Sartor, G.: Argument-based extended logic programming with defeasible priorities. J. Appl. Non-Class. Logics 7(1–2), 25–75 (1997)
14. Racharak, T., Tojo, S.: On explanation of propositional logic-based argumentation system. In: Rocha, A.P., Steels, L., van den Herik, H.J. (eds.) Proceedings of the 13th International Conference on Agents and Artificial Intelligence, ICAART 2021, vol. 2, Online Streaming, 4–6 February 2021, pp. 323–332. SCITEPRESS (2021)

15. Toulmin, S.E.: The Uses of Argument. Cambridge University Press, Cambridge (1958)
16. Toulmin, S.E.: The Uses of Argument. Updated Edition. Cambridge University Press, Cambridge (2003)
17. Verheij, B.: DefLog: on the logical interpretation of prima facie justified assumptions. J. Log. Comput. **13**(3), 319–346 (2003)
18. Verheij, B.: Dialectical argumentation with argumentation schemes: an approach to legal logic. Artif. Intell. Law **11**(2), 167–195 (2003). https://doi.org/10.1023/B:ARTI.0000046008.49443.36
19. Verheij, B.: Evaluating arguments based on toulmin's scheme. Argumentation **19**(3), 347–371 (2005). https://doi.org/10.1007/s10503-005-4421-z
20. Verheij, B.: The toulmin argument model in artificial intelligence. In: Argumentation in Artificial Intelligence, pp. 219–238. Springer (2009). https://doi.org/10.1007/978-0-387-98197-0_11
21. Verheij, B., Hage, J.C., Van Den Herik, H.J.: An integrated view on rules and principles. Artif. Intell. Law **6**(1), 3–26 (1998). https://doi.org/10.1023/A:1008247812801
22. Vreeswijk, G., Prakken, H.: Logical systems for defeasible argumentation. In: Handbook of Philosophical Logic vol. 4, pp. 219–318 (2001). https://doi.org/10.1007/978-94-017-0456-4_3

Informer: An Efficient Transformer Architecture Using Convolutional Layers

Cristian Estupiñán-Ojeda[(✉)], Cayetano Guerra-Artal[(✉)],
and Mario Hernández-Tejera[(✉)]

University of Las Palmas de Gran Canaria, 35017 Las Palmas de Gran Canaria, Spain
cristian.estupinan101@alu.ulpgc.es,
{cayetano.guerra,mario.hernandez}@ulpgc.es

Abstract. The use of Transformer based architectures has been extended in recent years, reaching the level of State of the Art (*SOTA*) in numerous tasks in the field of Natural Language Processing (*NLP*). However, despite the advantages of this architecture, it has some negative factors, such as the high number of parameters it uses. That is why the use of this type of architecture can become expensive for research teams with limited resources. New variants have emerged with the purpose of improving the efficiency of the Transformer architecture, addressing different aspects of it. In this paper we will focus on the development of a new architecture that seeks to reduce the memory consumption of the Transformer, meanwhile is able to achieve a SOTA result in two different datasets [14] for the Neural Machine Translation (*NMT*) task.

Keywords: Deep learning · Transformer · Neural Machine Translation · Convolutional layers

1 Introduction

The field of Natural Language Processing has gained special relevance in recent years. This is due to the rise of new techniques to deal with the different NLP tasks. With the advent of the Transformer networks [22] for the NMT task, it has been proven that their use in other NLP tasks results in superior performance, ranking as SOTA in many of them. We have the case of the Large-BERT network [7], which focuses on the language modeling task. Its development resulted in the GPT-3 model [3], which has become a SOTA in its field (*with over 175 billion number of parameters*). As well as the G-Shard network [12], which deals the NMT task with approximately 600 billion parameters.

One of the main drawbacks of this type of architecture is its high cost. By increasing the number of parameters, its performance increases without affecting the convergence of the model. For this reason, training this type of network becomes very expensive for research teams with limited resources. To address this issue, new architectures are emerging and seeking to improve the efficiency of these models, from reducing the complexity of the models, such as the Linformer [24], to modifying the learnable patterns [10], (see Table 1).

© Springer Nature Switzerland AG 2022
A. P. Rocha et al. (Eds.): ICAART 2021, LNAI 13251, pp. 208–217, 2022.
https://doi.org/10.1007/978-3-031-10161-8_11

In this work we will focus on Informer [15], in which a novel concept of Information Organization is presented by replacing one of the layers that make up the Transformer architecture, specifically the feed-forward layer by a set of convolutional layers. With this, not only the reduction in computational consumption is achieved, but also an improvement in performance is reached. Experimental results show a higher performance with respect to other models based on Transformer [22,24] in an English-Vietnamese dataset of NMT [14]. In this work, experiments were carried out on a second German-English dataset [14], thus allowing a validation on the results obtained in two different datasets, obtaining also another SOTA level in this second dataset.

2 Previous Work

We will focus on the most relevant Transformer based architectures, such as the Linformer [24] in which a modification of the Transformer architecture is presented (see Fig. 1). Authors demonstrate that the context of the mapping matrix P is Low Rank, therefore the complexity of the model can be reduced from $\mathcal{O}(n^2)$ complexity to $\mathcal{O}(n)$ complexity by introducing linear projections in the Key and Value matrices, (see Fig. 2 and Fig. 3). This idea has the advantage of being applicable to almost any type of Transformer based architecture, which is why it has become the basis of this work. Its only drawback is that it cannot be used in the decoder stage, because in that case, flexibility would be lost during the network inference process.

The datasets used in this paper are IWSLT15 English-Vietnamese and the IWSLT15 German-English [14], both datasets need moderate resources and are widely used. The current SOTAs are [15,23] respectively.

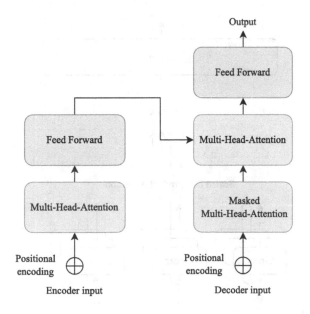

Fig. 1. Extracted from [15]. Overall Transformer architecture [22].

Table 1. Extracted from [21]. "Efficient Transformer Models presented in chronological order. Class abbreviations include: FP = Fixed Patterns or Combinations of Fixed Patterns, M = Memory, LP = Learnable Pattern, LR = Low Rank, KR = Kernel and RC = Recurrence. Furthermore, n generally refers to the sequence length and b is the local window (or block) size. We use subscript g on n to denote global memory length and n_c to denote convolutionally compressed sequence lengths".

Model/Paper	Complexity	Decode	class
Memory Compressed[†] [13]	$\mathcal{O}(n_c^2)$	yes	FP+M
Image Transformer[†] [16]	$\mathcal{O}(n \cdot m)$	yes	FP
Set Transformer[†] [11]	$\mathcal{O}(nk)$	no	M
Transformer-XL[†] [6]	$\mathcal{O}(n^2)$	yes	RC
Sparse Transformer [4]	$\mathcal{O}(n\sqrt{n})$	yes	FP
Reformer[†] [10]	$\mathcal{O}(n \log n)$	yes	LP
Routing Transformer [18]	$\mathcal{O}(n \log n)$	yes	LP
Axial Transformer [8]	$\mathcal{O}(n\sqrt{n})$	yes	FP
Compressive Transformer[†] [17]	$\mathcal{O}(n^2)$	yes	RC
Sinkhorn Transformer[†] [20]	$\mathcal{O}(b^2)$	yes	LP
Longformer [2]	$\mathcal{O}(n(k+m))$	yes	FP+M
ETC [1]	$\mathcal{O}(n_g^2 + nn_g)$	no	FP+M
Synthesizer [19]	$\mathcal{O}(n^2)$	yes	LR+LP
Performer [5]	$\mathcal{O}(n)$	yes	KR
Linformer [24]	$\mathcal{O}(n)$	no	LR
Linear Transformers[†] [9]	$\mathcal{O}(n)$	yes	KR
Big Bird [25]	$\mathcal{O}(n)$	no	FP+M

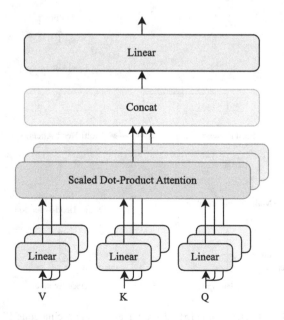

Fig. 2. Extracted from [15]. Transformer Multi-Head-Attention mechanism [22].

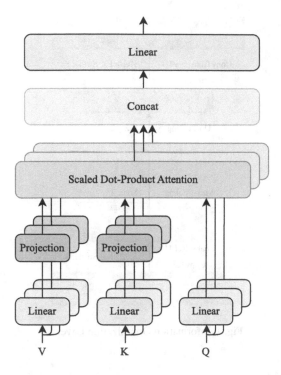

Fig. 3. Extracted from [15]. Linformer Multi-Head-Attention mechanism [24].

3 Information Organization Layer

The feed-forward layer of the Transformer networks is in charge of applying the transformations on the data coming from the self-attention layer. This layer is located in both the encoder and decoder stacks. It has a larger number of parameters with respect to the other layers present in the Transformer. Therefore, there is a high consumption of resources by the use of this layer. In Informer [15], the novel Information Organization layer is presented. This is composed of convolutional layers that replace the feed-forward layers of the encoder stack. The use of these convolutional layers reduces the feature representation space while maintaining at least the same performance, achieving a reduction in the used resources.

The Information Organization layer consists of a first convolutional layer that is responsible for reducing the feature space of the model from a size of 512 to 64 (multi-head size of the self-attention stage). This is done by modifying the kernel and stride sizes, having a number of channels equal to the maximum sequence size of the dataset used. This is followed by a max-pooling layer, in charge of halving this feature size to 32. Finally, it ends with the unpooling and transposed convolutional layers that perform the reverse process, returning the feature space to the size of 512 (see Fig. 4). This layer is applied during the encoder stage, this is because it is necessary to fix the sequence size in order to use it. To maintain flexibility during the inference process, it has been chosen not to apply it on the decoder stack.

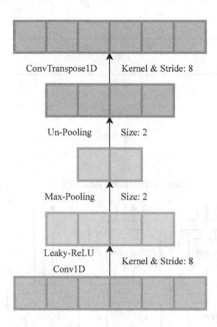

Fig. 4. Information Organization Layer.

4   Experiments

Experiments have been performed with two different NMT datasets [14]. The first, IWSLT15 English-Vietnamese dataset, has approximately 133K training sentences, while the IWSLT15 German-English dataset has approximately 194K sentences.

4.1   Training Details

A comparison among different Transformer models has been developed to test the effectiveness of the Information Organization layer. We have compared our model with the canonical Transformer proposed in [22], as well as the Linformer model [24], which is used as a basis for this architecture. The hyper-parameters used are the same for all the models tested, so that we can perform a fair comparison, these are the ones used in [22]. For the models using the Linformer implementation, convolutional projections have been applied along with max-pooling layers to reduce the sequence size to an effective size of 4. We fixed a total of 100 epochs for all models, and a batch size of 64. Finally, for the English-Vietnamese and German-English datasets, we have applied byte-pair encoding sizes of 4192 and 8192 respectively and the maximum sequence size established is 200.

We have eliminated very long sentences (*size larger than 200 tokens*) in the training sets. 52 in the English-Vietnamese set and 47 in the German-English set. No sentences have been removed from the test sets for a fair comparison with other models.

4.2   Results Analysis

If we analyze the performance obtained using the Information Organization layer, we see that it clearly outperforms the Transformer and Linformer models with convolutional projections (see Table 2). Approximately 4 points of BLEU-1 over on the English-Vietnamese and 5 points on the German-English dataset with only 100 training epochs. We obtain a new SOTA result for the latter. Also, it is observed in the validation curves that the performance is consistently superior throughout the training, distancing from the rest of the models (see Fig. 5 and Fig. 6). Likewise, this result is replicated in the perplexity curves (see Fig. 7 and Fig. 8).

Table 2. BLEU-1 results for IWSLT15 English-Vietnamese and IWSLT15 German-English datasets.

Model	EN-VI Val	EN-VI Test	DE-EN Val	DE-EN Test
Transformer	29.50	29.35	28.33	31.52
Conv. Linformer	29.43	30.39	28.59	31.55
Inf. Organization	33.32	33.34	33.37	36.69

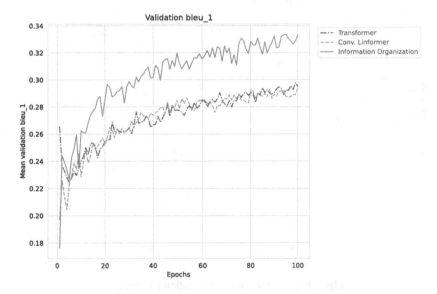

Fig. 5. English-Vietnamese validation BLEU-1.

With respect to memory consumption, in both datasets the use of Convolutional Linformer and Information Organization techniques produces a saving in memory allocated by the tensors. Around 2 gigabytes in both datasets, which corresponds to an approximate 14% improvement with respect to the total consumption of the Transformer model (see Fig. 9).

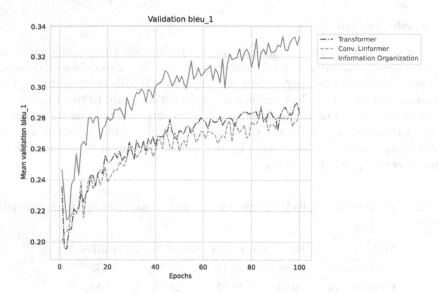

Fig. 6. German-English validation BLEU-1.

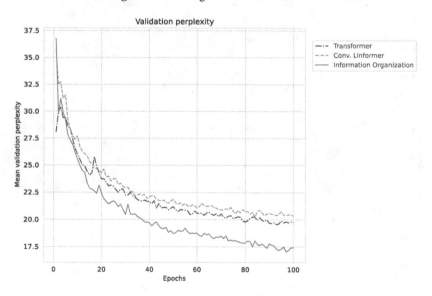

Fig. 7. English-Vietnamese validation perplexity.

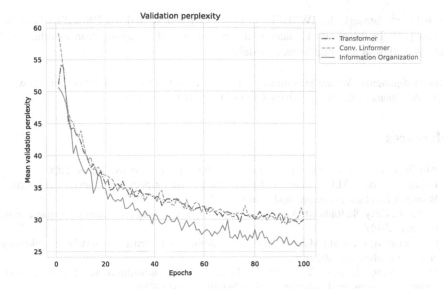

Fig. 8. German-English validation perplexity.

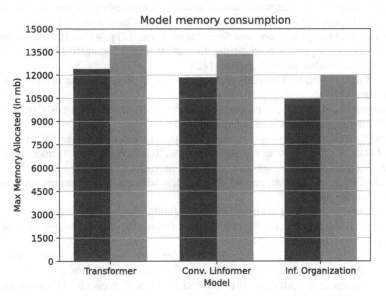

Fig. 9. Memory consumption comparison.

5 Conclusions

The use of the Information Organization layer improves the efficiency of Transformer based models. With this layer, memory consumption can be reduced by about 14% and superior performance results are achieved. We have tested its application on two different datasets, the IWSLT15 English-Vietnamese and the IWSLT15 German-English [14]. In future work, there is the possibility of its application in other NLP tasks, as well as other Transformer models.

Acknowledgements. We are grateful to the University of Las Palmas de Gran Canaria, which has partially financed this work with the ULPGC COVID 19-09 project.

References

1. Ainslie, J., et al.: ETC: encoding long and structured inputs in transformers (2020)
2. Beltagy, I., Peters, M.E., Cohan, A.: Longformer: The long-document transformer (2020)
3. Brown, T.B., et al.: Language models are few-shot learners (2020)
4. Child, R., Gray, S., Radford, A., Sutskever, I.: Generating long sequences with sparse transformers (2019)
5. Choromanski, K., et al.: Masked language modeling for proteins via linearly scalable long-context transformers (2020)
6. Dai, Z., Yang, Z., Yang, Y., Carbonell, J., Le, Q.V., Salakhutdinov, R.: Transformer-XL: attentive language models beyond a fixed-length context (2019)
7. Devlin, J., Chang, M.W., Lee, K., Toutanova, K.: BERT: pre-training of deep bidirectional transformers for language understanding. In: Proceedings of the 2019 Conference of the North American Chapter of the Association for Computational Linguistics: Human Language Technologies, (Long and Short Papers), vol. 1, pp. 4171–4186. Association for Computational Linguistics, Minneapolis, June 2019. https://doi.org/10.18653/v1/N19-1423, https://www.aclweb.org/anthology/N19-1423
8. Ho, J., Kalchbrenner, N., Weissenborn, D., Salimans, T.: Axial attention in multidimensional transformers (2019)
9. Katharopoulos, A., Vyas, A., Pappas, N., Fleuret, F.: Transformers are RNNs: fast autoregressive transformers with linear attention (2020)
10. Kitaev, N., Kaiser, Ł., Levskaya, A.: Reformer: the efficient transformer (2020)
11. Lee, J., Lee, Y., Kim, J., Kosiorek, A.R., Choi, S., Teh, Y.W.: Set transformer: a framework for attention-based permutation-invariant neural networks (2019)
12. Lepikhin, D., et al.: GShard: scaling giant models with conditional computation and automatic sharding (2020)
13. Liu, P.J., et al.: Generating wikipedia by summarizing long sequences (2018)
14. Luong, M.T., Manning, C.D.: Stanford neural machine translation systems for spoken language domains. In: Stanford (2015)
15. Ojeda, C., Artal, C., Tejera, F.: Informer, an information organization transformer architecture. In: Proceedings of the 13th International Conference on Agents and Artificial Intelligence - Volume 2: ICAART, pp. 381–389. INSTICC, SciTePress (2021). https://doi.org/10.5220/0010372703810389
16. Parmar, N., et al.: Image transformer (2018)
17. Rae, J.W., Potapenko, A., Jayakumar, S.M., Hillier, C., Lillicrap, T.P.: Compressive transformers for long-range sequence modelling. In: International Conference on Learning Representations (2020). https://openreview.net/forum?id=SylKikSYDH
18. Roy, A., Saffar, M., Vaswani, A., Grangier, D.: Efficient content-based sparse attention with routing transformers (2020)
19. Tay, Y., Bahri, D., Metzler, D., Juan, D.C., Zhao, Z., Zheng, C.: Synthesizer: rethinking self-attention in transformer models (2020)
20. Tay, Y., Bahri, D., Yang, L., Metzler, D., Juan, D.C.: Sparse sinkhorn attention (2020)

21. Tay, Y., Dehghani, M., Bahri, D., Metzler, D.: Efficient transformers: a survey (2020)
22. Vaswani, A., et al.: Attention is all you need. ArXiv (2017)
23. Wang, D., Gong, C., Liu, Q.: Improving neural language modeling via adversarial training (2019)
24. Wang, S., Li, B.Z., Khabsa, M., Fang, H., Ma, H.: Linformer: self-attention with linear complexity (2020)
25. Zaheer, M., et al.: Big bird: transformers for longer sequences (2020)

Improving the Generalization of Deep Learning Classification Models in Medical Imaging Using Transfer Learning and Generative Adversarial Networks

Sagar Kora Venu$^{(\boxtimes)}$ (iD)

Harrisburg University of Science and Technology, Harrisburg, PA 17101, USA
SKora@my.HarrisburgU.edu
https://www.harrisburgu.edu/

Abstract. Data sets for medical images are generally imbalanced and limited in sample size because of high data collection costs, time-consuming annotations, and patient privacy concerns. The training of deep neural network classification models on these data sets to improve the generalization ability does not produce the desired results for classifying the medical condition accurately and often over-fit the data on the majority of class samples. To address the issue, we propose a framework for improving the classification performance metrics of deep neural network classification models using transfer learning: pre-trained models, such as Xception, InceptionResNet, DenseNet along with the Generative Adversarial Network (GAN) - based data augmentation. Then, we trained the network by combining traditional data augmentation techniques, such as randomly flipping the image left to right and GAN-based data augmentation, and then fine-tuned the hyper-parameters of the transfer learning models, such as the learning rate, batch size, and the number of epochs. With these configurations, the Xception model outperformed all other pre-trained models achieving a test accuracy of 98.7%, the precision of 99%, recall of 99.3%, f1-score of 99.1%, receiver operating characteristic (ROC) - area under the curve (AUC) of 98.2%.

Keywords: Generative adversarial networks · Transfer learning · Medical imaging · Deep learning classification · Chest X-ray's

1 Introduction

In general, medical image datasets, such as Chest X-ray images, are usually imbalanced and come with limited samples due to the high costs of obtaining the data and time-consuming annotations. Training a deep neural network model on such datasets to accurately classify the medical condition does not yield the desired results. Every so often over-fits the majority class samples' data. Usually, transfer learning and data augmentation are performed on the training data to improve the deep learning model's classification performance to address the issue.

First, for classification tasks with limited datasets, transfer learning is adopted. It improves learning in a new domain by transferring knowledge from a related domain, reducing the neural network's training time and generalization error. It is a common

© Springer Nature Switzerland AG 2022
A. P. Rocha et al. (Eds.): ICAART 2021, LNAI 13251, pp. 218–235, 2022.
https://doi.org/10.1007/978-3-031-10161-8_12

practice in the field of computer vision to use transfer learning for limited datasets via pre-trained models. The pre-trained models are those trained on large benchmark datasets, where the models have already learned to extract a wide variety of features, which can be used as a starting point to learn on a new task in a related domain. To enhance the models' performance, it is not uncommon to overlook the fine-tuning of the hyper-parameters of transfer learning models.

Second, to balance the datasets, there are a few traditional methods. Random over-sampling, which produces copies of minority class samples, and Synthetic Minority Over-sampling Technique (SMOTE) [11], which generates synthetic data from dataset samples from nearest k-nearest neighbors. These methods of augmentation are not guaranteed to be advantageous and are only well suited to low-dimensional data. Deep generative models such as Generative Adversarial Networks (GANs) are known to augment high-dimensional image data effectively.

To address the issues of class imbalance and limited sample sizes for classification tasks, we propose a framework for improving the classification performance metrics of deep neural network classification models using transfer learning: pre-trained models, such as Xception, InceptionResNet, DenseNet, and along with the GAN - based data augmentation. We show the proposed framework in the Fig. 1. In one of our previous studies, we explored the GANs in creating artificial instances of chest X-ray images [24]. In another study, we investigated transfer learning to classify pneumonia from chest X-ray images [23]. In this study, we evaluated the combination of GAN - based data augmentation and transfer learning approaches.

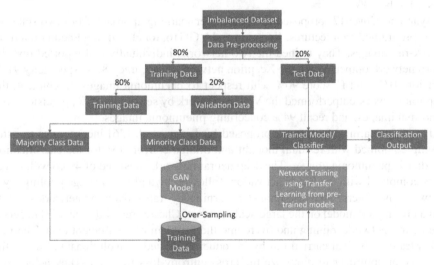

Fig. 1. Proposed framework.

The rest of the paper is structured as follows: In Sect. 2, we briefly present the related work from the literature. We introduce the materials and methods used in the study in Sect. 3. In Sects. 4 and 5, we present the results of the proposed framework and discuss our findings. Finally, in Sect. 6, we conclude our study by providing directions to future work.

2   Related Work

The lack of availability of large, labeled datasets is one of the significant problems with deep learning in medical imaging. As mentioned in Sect. 1, Medical images are not only annotated expensively but also time-consuming. By producing synthetic samples with real images' appearance, Generative Adversarial Networks (GANs) provide a novel way to create additional information from a dataset. In this section, we briefly review the literature on the use of transfer learning and GANs in the analysis of medical image data.

2.1   Transfer Learning in Medical Imaging

Rajpurkar et al. [36] developed an algorithm CheXNet, a 121-layer Dense convolutional neural network (DenseNet) that detects Pneumonia from chest X-ray images at a level exceeding the practicing radiologists. They trained their network on the ChestX-ray14 dataset released by Wang et al. [43] and assessed the performance with four practicing radiologists on the f1 score metric. CheXNet achieved an f1 score of 0.435, higher than the radiologist's average of 0.387. They later extended the CheXNet model to detect all 14 diseases in the ChestX-ray14 dataset and achieved state-of-the-art results on all 14 diseases. Similarly, Antin et al. [6] utilized transfer learning approach from a pre-trained model, DenseNet121 to classify Pneumonia from chest X-ray image dataset [43]. The only reported metric on the test data is the area under the curve (AUC), which they reported to be 60%.

Ayan and Ünver [7] proposed to use transfer learning approach from two state-of-the-art pre-trained architectures, Xception and VGG16, for classifying Pneumonia from chest X-ray images. They trained the two networks individually and reported that the Vgg16 network outperformed the Xception network by accuracy 87%, specificity 91%, precision 91%, and f1 score 90% with respect to pneumonia images. In contrast, the Xception network outperformed the Vgg16 network by sensitivity 85%, precision 86% for normal images, and recall 94% concerning pneumonia images.

The deep learning framework proposed by Liang et al. [26] incorporates transfer learning combined with residual thought and dilated convolution for the classification of pediatric pneumonia images. The deep neural network consisted of 49 convolutional layers combined with the ReLU activation, followed by a global average pooling layer and two dense layers. They used transfer learning by transferring the network weights from a pre-trained model on the large-scale dataset: ChestX-ray14 dataset [43] to accelerate neural network training and overcome the problem of insufficient data. The network's training is then carried out by introducing dilated convolutions and using the Adam as an optimizer to minimize the cross-entropy loss function. They achieved a test recall of 96.7%, and an f1 score of 92.7% in classifying Pneumonia from the chest X-ray image dataset [22].

Chouhan et al. [13] proposed a deep learning framework combined with the use of transfer learning to classify Pneumonia from chest X-ray images by adopting an ensemble-based approach to pre-trained architectures, such as AlexNet, InceptionV3, DenseNet121, ResNet18, and GoogLeNet. They trained the AlexNet for 200 epochs with an initial learning rate of 0.001 and then retrained with a learning rate of 0.00001.

To prevent overfitting and improving generalization, they trained the DenseNet121 and InceptionV3 for 100 epochs and the GoogLeNet for 50 epochs. The network training is performed using Adam as an optimizer to minimize the cross-entropy loss function. Unfortunately, the authors did not provide details on the metrics/methods used to choose the learning rate and the number of epochs used to train the network. The final prediction was based on majority voting by combining the results of pre-trained neural networks in the Pneumonia classification. Their proposed ensemble model achieved an accuracy of 96.4% with a recall of 99.62% on unseen data from the Guangzhou Women and Children's Medical Center dataset [22].

Similarly, Hashmi et al. [18] proposed a weighted classifier that optimally combined the weighted predictions from the state-of-the-art deep learning models ResNet18, Xception, InceptionV3, DenseNet121, and MobileNetV3 for Pneumonia classification from chest X-ray images. They achieved a test accuracy of 98.43%, and an AUC score of 99.76% on the unseen data from the Guangzhou Women and Children's Medical Center pneumonia dataset [22]. In another study, Rahman et al. [34] used transfer learning from pre-trained networks such as AlexNet, ResNet18, DenseNet201, and SqueezeNet for classifying Pneumonia from chest X-ray images. The authors did not mention any details on the hyper-parameters used for the study. They showed that DenseNet201 outperformed the other three pre-trained networks, achieving a 98% accuracy on Pneumonia classification from the chest X-ray image dataset [22].

2.2 Generative Adversarial Networks in Medical Imaging

Bowles et al. [9] demonstrated GAN's feasibility to create synthetic data for two brain segmentation tasks. They used Progressive Growing of GANs [21], which improved the training stability at large image sizes to generate synthetic data. They reported that when synthetic data created using GAN's combined with the training data improved the Dice Similarity Coefficient anywhere from one and five percentage points. Similarly, Beers et al. [8] also used Progressive Growing of GANs for generating realistic medical images in two different domains. First, they could generate realistic fundus photographs exhibiting vascular pathology associated with retinopathy of prematurity (ROP). Second, they were able to generate synthetic multi-modal magnetic resonance images of glioma. In another research, Korkinof et al. [25] explored the use of progressively trained generative adversarial networks (GANs) for generating highly realistic, high-resolution synthetic Full Field Digital Mammograms (FFDM). They reported achieving the highest resolution of 1280×1024 pixels.

In another study, Sandfort et al. [38] evaluated the CycleGAN [46] for data augmentation in CT segmentation tasks by first transforming the contrast CT images to non-contrast CT images and then generated synthetic non-contrast CT images [32,39,45]. They trained the network by comparing the segmentation performance of a U-Net [15] trained on the original dataset compared to a U-Net trained on the combined dataset of original data and synthetic non-contrast images demonstrated substantial improvement in the segmenting performance of the CT images, with the Dice score increasing from 0.09 to 0.66.

In another research, Welander et al. [44], evaluated two unsupervised GAN models, such as CycleGAN [46] and UNIT [27] for image-to-image translation of T1- and

T2- weighted MR images, by comparing generated synthetic MR images to ground truth images. They also evaluated two supervised models; a modification of Cycle-GAN (CycleGAN_s) and a pure generator model (Generator_s), and reported that all the GAN models would synthesize visually realistic MR images [17,42]. Iqbal and Ali [20] proposed another Generative Adversarial Network for Medical Imaging, MI-GAN, for synthesizing Retinal images. They used the STARE [5], and DRIVE [3] datasets for evaluating the MI-GAN model and reported that they achieved a Dice coefficient of 0.837 on the STARE dataset and a Dice coefficient of 0.832 on the DRIVE dataset.

Dar et al. [16] demonstrated an end-to-end image synthesis approach for MRI that successfully estimated the image in the target contrast given the image in the source contrast, by utilizing conditional generative adversarial networks, cGANs [29], with pixel-wise and cycle-consistency loss functions. They trained the conditional GAN on three datasets, such as MIDAS dataset [10], the IXI dataset [4], and the BRATS dataset [1]. In order to generate realistic lung nodule samples, Chuquicusma et al. [14] proposed the use of unsupervised learning through the Deep Convolutional Generative Adversarial Networks (DCGANs). Likewise, Salehinejad et al. [37] showed an improvement in chest pathology classification performance by augmenting the original imbalanced data set with DCGAN. Similarly, in another study, the DCGAN was investigated by Madani et al. [28] to generate chest X-ray images for the augmentation of the original data and trained a convolutional neural network to classify cardiovascular abnormalities, showing a higher classification accuracy.

In another study, Qin et al. [33] investigated data sampling methods such as undersampling the majority class, in which the majority class in the training dataset was randomly dropped to achieve a 1:1 ratio between classes, and over-sampling/augmentation of the minority class, such as affine transformations and GAN-based data augmentation, to learn from the imbalanced and limited chest X-ray dataset. They reported achieving improved classification metrics with an accuracy of 89.9%, recall of 89.7%, the precision of 93.8%, F1score of 91.7%, and an AUC of 95.4% in detecting pneumonia with GAN-based data augmentation when trained with a deep convolutional neural network.

The combination of fine-tuning the hyper-parameters of transfer learning models and GAN-based data augmentation has received very little attention in the literature. This study addresses improving the classification performance metrics of an imbalanced and limited dataset by fine-tuning the hyper-parameters of the transfer learning models and utilizing GAN-based data augmentation.

3   Materials and Methods

3.1   Dataset Description and Pre-processing

We used a chest X-ray image dataset published by [22] and chest X-ray images generated using GANs by [24] for all the experiments conducted in this study. The dataset by Kermany et al. comprises 5,856 chest X-ray images in total, of which 1583 images labeled as Normal and 4273 images labeled as Pneumonia. The chest X-ray images in the dataset are in varying sizes, i.e., all the chest X-ray images' dimensions are not the same. However, the deep neural network architectures utilized in this study as part of transfer learning expect all the images to be in a common dimension. For example,

Xception architecture expects the dimensions of the image (width × height × no. of Channels) to be 299 × 299 × 3, and width and height should be no smaller than 71. The dimension of the input image will also vary by the type of deep neural network architecture. For example, the DenseNet201 architecture expects the input image shape to be (224 × 224 × 3), with width and height no smaller than 32, and InceptionResNet-V2 expects the input image shape to be (299 × 299 × 3), with width and height no smaller than 75. To have common dimensions accepted by all the architectures used in this study, we initially resized all the chest X-ray images to have the shape of (224×224×3). Once the images are resized to 224 × 224 × 3, we created TFRecords of the images to train on Tensor Processing Units (TPUs) and one-hot encoded the labels. The dataset was then shuffled and split into training and test sets, of which 4,684 images in the training set (Normal Images: 1,266 and Pneumonia images: 3,418), and 1,172 images in the test set (Normal images: 317, and Pneumonia images: 855). We further split the training dataset to have 80% as training data (3,748 images in total, of which 1013 are Normal images and 2735 are Pneumonia images) and 20% as validation data (936 images in total, of which 253 are Normal images and 683 are Pneumonia images). We show a Normal image and Pneumonia image sample in Fig. 2.

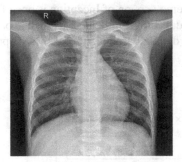 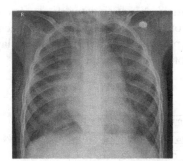

(a) Normal Image.   (b) Pneumonia Image.

Fig. 2. Sample of Normal and Pneumonia Images.

To balance the training dataset, we have combined the Normal chest X-ray images generated with GANs [24] to the original training dataset to have an equal proportion of Normal and Pneumonia Images. The images generated with GANs are resized to 224×224×3 to match the dimensions of the training data and we created TFRecords of the GAN generated images. We show a sample of Normal chest X-ray image generated using GANs in Fig. 3.

Each pre-trained model expects a specific kind of input pre-processing, and they all have the methods to pre-process the inputs before passing them to the model. For example, the Xception and InceptionResNetV2 networks expects to have the input pixel values scaled between −1 and 1, the DenseNet network expects to have the input pixel values scaled between 0 and 1.

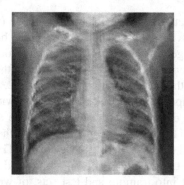

Fig. 3. Normal Chest X-ray image generated using GAN.

3.2 Transfer Learning Models

In the following sub-sections, we will discuss in detail the pre-trained models used in this study, such as Xception, DenseNet, and InceptionResNetV2.

Xception. Xception network, also known as extreme version of Inception is one of the state-of-the-art neural network architectures introduced by Chollet [12], which is based on depth-wise separable convolution layers. The detailed architecture of the Xception network is shown in the Fig. 4.

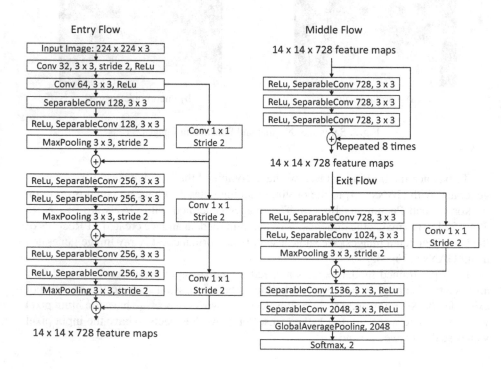

Fig. 4. Xception Architecture.

The entire architecture consists of three flows, namely, the Entry flow, the Middle flow, and the Exit flow. The entry flow consists of four blocks, with traditional convolutional layers in the first block and depth-wise separable convolutional layers in the remaining three blocks. There is only one block of depth-wise separable convolution layers in the middle flow, repeated eight times. The exit flow has two blocks: the first block has the depth-wise separable convolutional layers, and the second block consists of depth-wise separable convolutional layers followed by a GlobalAveragePooling layer and a dense layer with softmax activation to output the probability of the input image being Normal or Pneumonia.

The Entry flow takes the pre-processed image of size $224 \times 224 \times 3$ as an input, followed by two traditional convolutions. to output the representation of size $14 \times 14 \times 728$. The Middle flow takes the representation of size $14 \times 14 \times 728$ as input to output the representation of size $14 \times 14 \times 728$. The Exit flow takes the representation of size $14 \times 14 \times 728$ as input to output the probability of image as Normal or Pneumonia.

DenseNet. Huang et al. [19] introduced Densely Connected Convolutional Networks (DenseNet), which won the best paper award at the CVPR 2017 conference [2]. The DenseNet architecture is shown in Fig. 5, which connects each layer of the network in a feed-forward manner to every other layer. In other words, all previous layers' feature maps are used as inputs into each layer, and its own feature maps are used as inputs into all subsequent layers [19]. With L layers, the DenseNet network has $L(L+1)/2$ direct connections compared to L connections of a traditional convolutional network, thereby significantly reducing the network's overall learnable parameters.

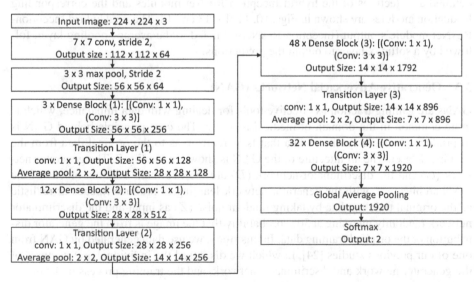

Fig. 5. DenseNet201 Architecture.

As shown in Fig. 5, the DenseNet network takes an image of size $224 \times 224 \times 3$ as input. The image then goes through an initial convolutional layer with a kernel size of 7×7 and a stride of 2 to output a representation of size $112 \times 112 \times 64$, followed by a MaxPooling operation with a kernel size of 3×3 and a stride of 2, halving the representation size to $56 \times 56 \times 64$. The $56 \times 56 \times 64$ representation is subjected to a series of dense blocks and transition layers. Each dense block consists of a 1×1 convolution, followed by a 3×3 convolution, and each transition block consists of a 1×1 convolution followed by a 2×2 average pooling operation. The final dense block's output is a representation of size $7 \times 7 \times 1920$, which is passed on to the global average pooling layer with a softmax activation to output the probability of the image as Normal or Pneumonia.

InceptionResNet. Szegedy et al. [41] introduced the InceptionResNet architecture based on the Inception Architectures family by replacing the Inception modules with the Inception-ResNet hybrid modules. The network training is significantly accelerated due to the presence of residual connections in the network. The InceptionResNet network architecture is shown in Fig. 6a. The InceptionResNet network takes an image of size $224 \times 224 \times 3$ as input, followed by a Stem module where the input image undergoes a series of convolutions as shown in Fig. 6b. The output of final convolution in the stem module is followed by a Max-Pooling layer to output a representation of size $25 \times 25 \times 192$. The output from the stem module is passed on to the Inception - A block as shown in Fig. 9 to output a representation of size $25 \times 25 \times 320$. The output from the Inception - A block is subjected to a series of hybrid Inception-ResNet modules and Reduction modules, such as Inception-ResNet-A followed by a Reduction-A module, Inception-ResNet-B followed by a Reduction-B module, and Inception-ResNet-C. The detailed architectures of the hybrid Inception-ResNet modules and the corresponding Reduction modules are shown in Figs. 10, 11, 12, 13 and 14. The final hybrid Inception-ResNet module's output (Inception-ResNet-C) is fed to the average pooling layer, followed by a softmax layer to output the predictions.

3.3 Generative Adversarial Networks (GAN)

GANs are gaining traction as effective tools for dealing with data imbalance, which is quite common in the domain of medical imaging. The core principle behind GAN is to produce plausible synthetic data that is as realistic as to the original data from the training dataset. The architecture of the GAN is shown in the Fig. 7. The generator network (G) and the discriminator network (D) are the two main building blocks of the GAN architecture, with the generator network learning to produce images as realistic as the original training data by taking random noise (Z) as input and the discriminator network randomly guessing at 50% probability that the image is from the generator distribution or the original training data. In this study, we use data generated by GAN from one of our previous studies [24], in which we discussed the individual architectures of the generator network and discriminator network, and the training process in detail.

4   Results

As per the proposed framework, we over-sampled the minority class samples using GAN's and trained the deep neural network by fine-tuning the hyper-parameters of

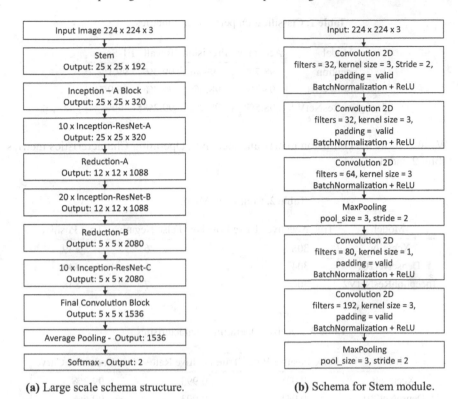

Input Image 224 x 224 x 3
Stem Output: 25 x 25 x 192
Inception – A Block Output: 25 x 25 x 320
10 x Inception-ResNet-A Output: 25 x 25 x 320
Reduction-A Output: 12 x 12 x 1088
20 x Inception-ResNet-B Output: 12 x 12 x 1088
Reduction-B Output: 5 x 5 x 2080
10 x Inception-ResNet-C Output: 5 x 5 x 2080
Final Convolution Block Output: 5 x 5 x 1536
Average Pooling - Output: 1536
Softmax - Output: 2

Input: 224 x 224 x 3
Convolution 2D filters = 32, kernel size = 3, Stride = 2, padding = valid BatchNormalization + ReLU
Convolution 2D filters = 32, kernel size = 3, padding = valid BatchNormalization + ReLU
Convolution 2D filters = 64, kernel size = 3 BatchNormalization + ReLU
MaxPooling pool_size = 3, stride = 2
Convolution 2D filters = 80, kernel size = 1, padding = valid BatchNormalization + ReLU
Convolution 2D filters = 192, kernel size = 3, padding = valid BatchNormalization + ReLU
MaxPooling pool_size = 3, stride = 2

(a) Large scale schema structure.   **(b)** Schema for Stem module.

Fig. 6. InceptionResNet Architecture and Stem Module.

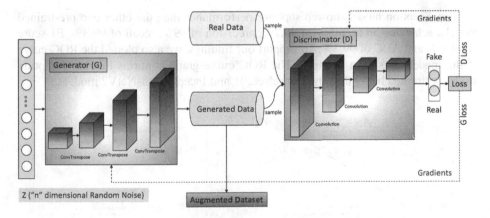

Fig. 7. GAN Architecture.

the transfer learning models, such as the learning rate, batch size and the number of epochs to train the model. We trained the network using three pre-trained models, such as Xception, DenseNet201, and InceptionResNetV2 individually. We show the classification metrics, such as accuracy, precision, recall, and F1-score in Table 1.

Table 1. Classification performance metrics.

Model	Accuracy	Precision	Recall	F1-Score
Xception	98.7%	99%	99.3%	99.1%
DenseNet201	98.4%	98.5%	99.3%	98.9%
InceptionResNetV2	98.5%	98.7%	99.2%	99%

We also show the confusion matrix and Receiver Operating Characteristics metrics in Tables 2 and 3.

Table 2. Confusion Matrix.

Model	True Negative	False Positive	False Negative	True Positive
Xception	308	9	6	849
DenseNet201	304	13	6	849
InceptionResNetV2	306	11	7	848

Table 3. Receiver Operating Characteristics.

Model	False Positive Rate	True Positive Rate	Area Under the Curve
Xception	0.028	0.993	99.3%
DenseNet201	0.041	0.993	99.6%
InceptionResNetV2	0.035	0.992	99.5%

The Xception model showed superior performance than the other two pre-trained models, achieving an accuracy of 98.7%, precision of 99%, recall of 99.3%, F1-score of 99.1%, and AUC of 99.3%. To support our findings, we also plotted the ROC curve of the models as shown in Fig. 8. The ROC curve graph confirms that the Xception model performed better than the DenseNet201 and InceptionResNetV2 models.

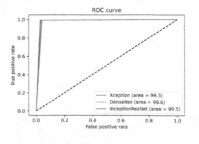

(a) ROC Curve.

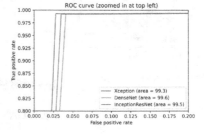

(b) ROC Curve - Zoomed in at top left.

Fig. 8. Receiver Operating Characteristics Curve.

4.1 Comparison of Results with Other Recent Similar Works

We compare the results of this study with other recent similar works in this section - see Table 4. The proposed model results, i.e., over-sampling of the minority class samples using GAN's and training the neural network by fine-tuning the transfer learning models' hyper-parameters, outperformed all the previous studies in the majority of the classification metrics. As discussed in the Sect. 4, the Xception architecture achieved the best classification metrics with an accuracy of 98.7%, precision of 99%, recall of 99.3%, F1-score of 99.1% and ROC-AUC of 99.3%.

Table 4. Comparison of results with other recent similar works.

	Accuracy	Precision	Recall	F1 Score	AUC
Kermany et al. [22]	92.80	87.20	93.20	90.10	96.80
Nahid et al. [31]	97.92	98.38	97.47	97.97	-
Stephen et al. [40]	93.73	-	-	-	-
Qin et al. [33]	89.90	93.80	89.70	91.70	95.40
Chouhan et al. [13]	96.39	93.28	**99.62**	96.35	99.34
Rajaraman et al. [35]	96.20	97.00	99.50	-	99.00
Hashmi et al. [18]	98.43	98.26	99.00	98.63	**99.76**
Mittal et al. [30]	96.36	-	-	-	-
Rahman et al. [34]	98.00	97.00	99.00	98.10	98.00
Kora Venu [23]	98.46	98.38	99.53	98.96	99.60
Kora Venu et al. [24]	95.50	96.20	97.70	97.00	93.60
Current work	**98.70**	**99.00**	99.30	**99.10**	99.30

5 Discussion

Medical image datasets generally come by limited samples and are often imbalanced on majority class samples. Transfer learning from pre-trained models, i.e., the models trained on a large-scale benchmark datasets like Imagenet, is commonly used for classification tasks when encountered with small datasets, which is more common in the medical imaging domain. Often over-sampling of minority class samples or under-sampling of majority class samples, or augmentation of minority class samples using traditional data augmentation techniques, such as position or color augmentation, is carried out to balance the dataset before training the model to This makes sure that the trained model's classification performance is not biased against the majority class samples. In this study, we proposed a framework where we over-sampled the minority class samples using Generative Adversarial Networks and then fine-tuned the hyper-parameters of transfer learning models to improve the classification performance of the trained model. Using Generative Adversarial Networks for data augmentation has two significant advantages, i.e., 1. Diversity - GAN's can generate more varied images than the sampling or traditional data augmentation techniques, and 2. Fidelity - GAN's improve the quality of generated images. Before training the models on TPU's, the models were fine-tuned and compiled. The results show that the combination of GAN-based data augmentation and fine-tuning of the transfer learning models' hyper-parameters demonstrates a significant improvement in classification metrics.

6 Conclusions and Future Work

The lack of availability of large, labeled datasets is one of the significant problems with deep learning classification tasks in the domain of medical imaging. We demonstrated the ability to generate synthetic samples of chest X-ray images using Generative Adversarial Networks in one of our previous studies [24], and we demonstrated that fine-tuning the hyper-parameters of the transfer learning models improves classification performance metrics in another study [23]. These studies gave confidence and motivation in conducting the present research by combining the GAN-based data augmentation for over-sampling the minority class samples to balance the dataset and fine-tuning the hyper-parameters of the transfer learning models. We later trained the deep neural network classification models on three pre-trained state-of-the-art transfer learning models, such as Xception, DenseNet201, and InceptionResNetV2. The Xception model outperformed the other two models achieving the test accuracy of 98.7%, the precision of 99%, recall of 99.3%, f1-score of 99.1%, receiver operating characteristic (ROC) - area under the curve (AUC) of 98.2%. Future work may include the investigation of other GAN methods for generating synthetic data, such as Wasserstein GAN with a gradient penalty, and the investigation of the generalization of the proposed framework to improve the classification performance metrics of other common medical conditions.

Appendix

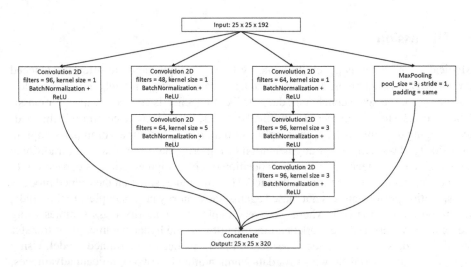

Fig. 9. Inception - A Block.

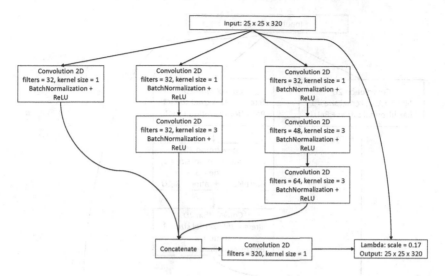

Fig. 10. InceptionResNet - A Block.

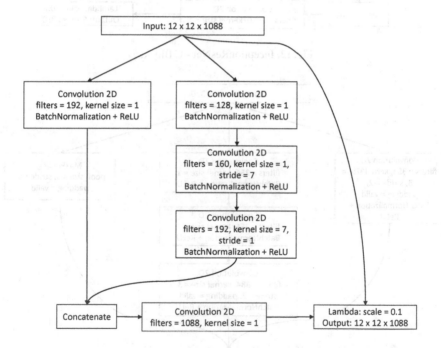

Fig. 11. InceptionResNet - B Block.

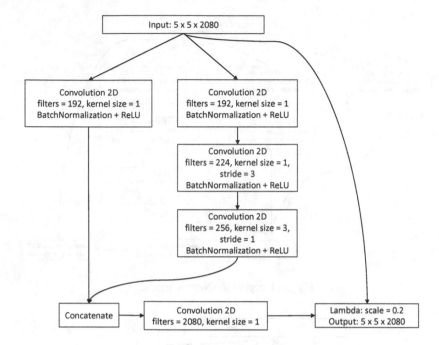

Fig. 12. InceptionResNet - C Block.

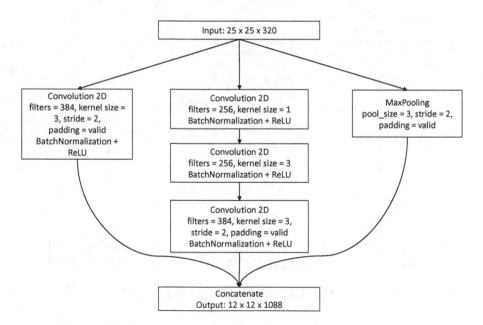

Fig. 13. Reduction - A Block.

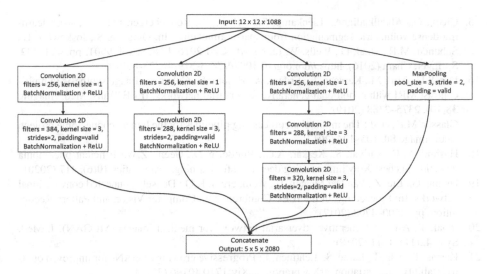

Fig. 14. Reduction - B Block.

References

1. Brats 2015 - MICCAI Brats 2017. https://sites.google.com/site/braintumorsegmentation/home/brats2015. Accessed 27 Jan 2021
2. CVPR 2017. https://cvpr2017.thecvf.com/program/main_conference#cvpr2017_awards. Accessed 31 Oct 2020
3. Introduction - drive - grand challenge. https://drive.grand-challenge.org/DRIVE/. Accessed 27 Jan 2021
4. IXI dataset - brain development. https://brain-development.org/ixi-dataset/. Accessed 27 Jan 2021
5. The stare project. https://cecas.clemson.edu/~ahoover/stare/. Accessed 27 Jan 2021
6. Antin, B., Kravitz, J., Martayan, E.: Detecting pneumonia in chest X-rays with supervised learning. Semanticscholar.org (2017)
7. Ayan, E., Ünver, H.M.: Diagnosis of pneumonia from chest X-ray images using deep learning. In: 2019 Scientific Meeting on Electrical-Electronics & Biomedical Engineering and Computer Science (EBBT), pp. 1–5. IEEE (2019)
8. Beers, A., et al.: High-resolution medical image synthesis using progressively grown generative adversarial networks. arXiv preprint arXiv:1805.03144 (2018)
9. Bowles, C., et al.: Gan augmentation: augmenting training data using generative adversarial networks. arXiv preprint arXiv:1810.10863 (2018)
10. Bullitt, E., et al.: Vessel tortuosity and brain tumor malignancy: a blinded study1. Acad. Radiol. **12**(10), 1232–1240 (2005)
11. Chawla, N.V., Bowyer, K.W., Hall, L.O., Kegelmeyer, W.P.: Smote: synthetic minority oversampling technique. J. Artif. Intell. Res. **16**, 321–357 (2002)
12. Chollet, F.: Xception: deep learning with depthwise separable convolutions. In: Proceedings of the IEEE Conference on Computer Vision and Pattern Recognition, pp. 1251–1258 (2017)
13. Chouhan, V., et al.: A novel transfer learning based approach for pneumonia detection in chest X-ray images. Appl. Sci. **10**(2), 559 (2020)
14. Chuquicusma, M.J.M., Hussein, S., Burt, J., Bagci, U.: How to fool radiologists with generative adversarial networks? A visual turing test for lung cancer diagnosis (2018)

15. Çiçek, Ö., Abdulkadir, A., Lienkamp, S.S., Brox, T., Ronneberger, O.: 3D U-Net: learning dense volumetric segmentation from sparse annotation. In: Ourselin, S., Joskowicz, L., Sabuncu, M.R., Unal, G., Wells, W. (eds.) MICCAI 2016. LNCS, vol. 9901, pp. 424–432. Springer, Cham (2016). https://doi.org/10.1007/978-3-319-46723-8_49

16. Dar, S.U., Yurt, M., Karacan, L., Erdem, A., Erdem, E., Çukur, T.: Image synthesis in multi-contrast MRI with conditional generative adversarial networks. IEEE Trans. Med. Imaging 38(10), 2375–2388 (2019)

17. Glasser, M.F., et al.: The minimal preprocessing pipelines for the human connectome project. Neuroimage 80, 105–124 (2013)

18. Hashmi, M.F., Katiyar, S., Keskar, A.G., Bokde, N.D., Geem, Z.W.: Efficient pneumonia detection in chest Xray images using deep transfer learning. Diagnostics 10(6), 417 (2020)

19. Huang, G., Liu, Z., Van Der Maaten, L., Weinberger, K.Q.: Densely connected convolutional networks. In: Proceedings of the IEEE Conference on Computer Vision and Pattern Recognition, pp. 4700–4708 (2017)

20. Iqbal, T., Ali, H.: Generative adversarial network for medical images (MI-GAN). J. Med. Syst. 42(11), 1–11 (2018)

21. Karras, T., Aila, T., Laine, S., Lehtinen, J.: Progressive growing of GANs for improved quality, stability, and variation. arXiv preprint arXiv:1710.10196 (2017)

22. Kermany, D.S., et al.: Identifying medical diagnoses and treatable diseases by image-based deep learning. Cell 172(5), 1122–1131 (2018)

23. Kora Venu, S.: An ensemble-based approach by fine-tuning the deep transfer learning models to classify pneumonia from chest X-ray images. In: Proceedings of the 13th International Conference on Agents and Artificial Intelligence - Volume 2: ICAART, pp. 390–401. INSTICC, SciTePress (2021). https://doi.org/10.5220/0010377403900401

24. Kora Venu, S., Ravula, S.: Evaluation of deep convolutional generative adversarial networks for data augmentation of chest X-ray images. Future Internet 13(1) (2021). https://doi.org/10.3390/fi13010008. https://www.mdpi.com/1999-5903/13/1/8

25. Korkinof, D., Rijken, T., O'Neill, M., Yearsley, J., Harvey, H., Glocker, B.: High-resolution mammogram synthesis using progressive generative adversarial networks. arXiv preprint arXiv:1807.03401 (2018)

26. Liang, G., Zheng, L.: A transfer learning method with deep residual network for pediatric pneumonia diagnosis. Comput. Methods Programs Biomed. 187, 104964 (2020)

27. Liu, M.Y., Breuel, T., Kautz, J.: Unsupervised image-to-image translation networks. arXiv preprint arXiv:1703.00848 (2017)

28. Madani, A., Moradi, M., Karargyris, A., Syeda-Mahmood, T.: Chest X-ray generation and data augmentation for cardiovascular abnormality classification. In: Angelini, E.D., Landman, B.A. (eds.) Medical Imaging 2018: Image Processing, vol. 10574, pp. 415–420. International Society for Optics and Photonics, SPIE (2018). https://doi.org/10.1117/12.2293971

29. Mirza, M., Osindero, S.: Conditional generative adversarial nets. arXiv preprint arXiv:1411.1784 (2014)

30. Mittal, A., et al.: Detecting pneumonia using convolutions and dynamic capsule routing for chest X-ray images. Sensors 20(4), 1068 (2020)

31. Nahid, A.A., et al.: A novel method to identify pneumonia through analyzing chest radiographs employing a multichannel convolutional neural network. Sensors 20(12), 3482 (2020)

32. Pickhardt, P.J., et al.: Population-based opportunistic osteoporosis screening: validation of a fully automated CT tool for assessing longitudinal BMD changes. Br. J. Radiol. 92(1094), 20180726 (2019)

33. Qin, X., Bui, F.M., Nguyen, H.H.: Learning from an imbalanced and limited dataset and an application to medical imaging. In: 2019 IEEE Pacific Rim Conference on Communications, Computers and Signal Processing (PACRIM), pp. 1–6. IEEE (2019)

34. Rahman, T., et al.: Transfer learning with deep convolutional neural network (CNN) for pneumonia detection using chest X-ray. Appl. Sci. **10**(9), 3233 (2020)
35. Rajaraman, S., Candemir, S., Kim, I., Thoma, G., Antani, S.: Visualization and interpretation of convolutional neural network predictions in detecting pneumonia in pediatric chest radiographs. Appl. Sci. **8**(10), 1715 (2018)
36. Rajpurkar, P., et al.: CheXNet: radiologist-level pneumonia detection on chest X-rays with deep learning. arXiv preprint arXiv:1711.05225 (2017)
37. Salehinejad, H., Valaee, S., Dowdell, T., Colak, E., Barfett, J.: Generalization of deep neural networks for chest pathology classification in X-rays using generative adversarial networks. CoRR abs/1712.01636 (2017). http://arxiv.org/abs/1712.01636
38. Sandfort, V., Yan, K., Pickhardt, P.J., Summers, R.M.: Data augmentation using generative adversarial networks (CycleGAN) to improve generalizability in CT segmentation tasks. Sci. Rep. **9**(1), 1–9 (2019)
39. Simpson, A.L., et al.: A large annotated medical image dataset for the development and evaluation of segmentation algorithms. arXiv preprint arXiv:1902.09063 (2019)
40. Stephen, O., Sain, M., Maduh, U.J., Jeong, D.U.: An efficient deep learning approach to pneumonia classification in healthcare. J. Healthcare Eng. **2019** (2019)
41. Szegedy, C., Ioffe, S., Vanhoucke, V., Alemi, A.: Inception-v4, inception-ResNet and the impact of residual connections on learning. arXiv preprint arXiv:1602.07261 (2016)
42. Van Essen, D.C., et al.: The WU-Minn human connectome project: an overview. Neuroimage **80**, 62–79 (2013)
43. Wang, X., Peng, Y., Lu, L., Lu, Z., Bagheri, M., Summers, R.M.: ChestX-ray8: hospital-scale chest X-ray database and benchmarks on weakly-supervised classification and localization of common thorax diseases. In: Proceedings of the IEEE Conference on Computer Vision and Pattern Recognition, pp. 2097–2106 (2017)
44. Welander, P., Karlsson, S., Eklund, A.: Generative adversarial networks for image-to-image translation on multi-contrast MR images-a comparison of CycleGAN and unit. arXiv preprint arXiv:1806.07777 (2018)
45. Yan, K., Wang, X., Lu, L., Summers, R.M.: DeepLesion: automated mining of large-scale lesion annotations and universal lesion detection with deep learning. J. Med. Imaging **5**(3), 036501 (2018)
46. Zhu, J.Y., Park, T., Isola, P., Efros, A.A.: Unpaired image-to-image translation using cycle-consistent adversarial networks. In: Proceedings of the IEEE International Conference on Computer Vision, pp. 2223–2232 (2017)

An Interpretable Word Sense Classifier
for Human Explainable Chatbot

Rohan Kumar Yadav$^{(\boxtimes)}$, Lei Jiao, Ole-Christoffer Granmo, and Morten Goodwin

Centre for Artificial Intelligence Research, University of Agder, Grimstad, Norway
{rohan.k.yadav,lei.jiao,ole.granmo,morten.goodwin}@uia.no

Abstract. Explainable Artificial Intelligence (AI) based chatbot is one of the most ambitious and unsolved sectors of conversational AI. Recently, there has been a boom in the neural network architecture such as BERT and GPTs that understand the sense of such words/phrases in the sentence. However, such models fail to explain the logical reasoning behind the language understanding thereby making the base of chatbot unreliable. In this paper, we design and extend the previous TM based Word Sense Disambiguation task on complete 20 words as well as design a fully explainable word sense classifier using the Tsetlin Machine (TM) that supports the chatbot to understand the concept of the word/phrases. Our experiments show that the proposed model performs on par with the state-of-the-art accuracy on the publicly available CoarseWSD-balanced dataset. In addition, we explore in-depth how each interpretable clause of TM carries context information that can be easily explained by a human for designing a trustful chatbot.

Keywords: Explainable AI · Tsetlin machine · Word sense disambiguation · Chatbot

1 Introduction

Virtual assistants and task-oriented chatbots integrated within software programs provide a variety of options for automating activities and assisting with the usage of complicated features. Despite the promise of these chatbots, many users are annoyed by them and may quit them after a series of failed conversations [31]. For example *Clippy* [19] was first included in the Microsoft Office suite in 1996 [2] to help users with a variety of word processing tasks, only to be withdrawn four years later due to poor customer response.

At the fundamental algorithmic level, recent advances in machine learning (ML) and Natural Language Processing (NLP) have greatly improved chatbot capabilities. However, complexities of natural language understanding [8,23] and limited training sets, poor conversational understanding [1], and unexplained response are still major roadblocks to fully achieving the potential of human-chatbot interaction. For instance, a key example is a chatbot unable to explain to the user about the intent of its response either correct or incorrect. Recently most of the complex models correctly understand the sense of words thereby making chatbots more accurate. On the other hand, such

© Springer Nature Switzerland AG 2022
A. P. Rocha et al. (Eds.): ICAART 2021, LNAI 13251, pp. 236–249, 2022.
https://doi.org/10.1007/978-3-031-10161-8_13

an accurate model does not offer an explainable model for the human to understand the concept underneath the prediction. Similarly, a simple interpretable language model provides explainable justification of the prediction but fails to perform well and only relies on labelled data. This may lead to conversational dead-ends or breakdowns.

A breakdown generally takes place in the case when chatbot fails to recognize the user intent in a query [18]. In a simple sense, chatbot appears to be a blackbox to the user making it tough to figure out why something does not work, what actions are truly viable, and how to get back on track. This lack of transparency has an influence on users' opinions of the system's utility and trustworthiness [10,22,32]. Hence, in this work, we design an interpretable model for word sense disambiguation (WSD) that classifies the various sense of the word for a better understanding of language.

WSD is the process of determining the meaning of homographs that are identically spelled, whose sense or meaning are determined by the context words in a phrase or paragraph. WSD is one of the most important NLP tasks, and it often fails to be integrated into NLP applications because it still revolves around the ideal solution of sense classification and indication [24]. Many supervised approaches attempt to solve the WSD problem by training a model on sense annotated data [16]. However, most of them fail to produce interpretable models with acceptable performance. Those models, which perform better in terms of accuracy and language understanding, are far from human-understandable. Since word senses are the base for understanding any language, it is a foremost important task to have a trustable model that can support a transparent user-friendly chatbot interface.

With the recent proliferation of chatbots, the limitations of the state-of-the-art WSD have become increasingly apparent. In the real scenario, chatbots are notoriously poor in distinguishing the meaning of words with multiple senses present in a user query. Take the word "book" in the sentence "I want to book a ticket for the upcoming movie", as an example. Indeed, a sophisticated chatbot that has a complex NLP model at the backend can identify "book" as "reservation" rather than "reading material". However, it does not explain why it has responded correctly (or incorrectly). Such unexplained model raises several questions, like: "How can we trust the model?" or "How did the model make the decision?". Answering these questions will increase the trustworthiness of a chatbot. For instance, choosing word senses incorrectly might have unfavorable implications, such as leading a chatbot astray or incorrectly classifying a CV.

Although certain rule-based approaches, such as decision trees, are relatively simple to interpret, others are beyond the scope of thorough interpretation [30], such as Deep Neural Networks (DNNs). Despite the high accuracy of DNNs, their "blackbox" nature limits their impact on real-life application [26]. DNN's weights and biases are in the form of fine-tuned continuous values, making it difficult to discern the context words that influence classification decisions. Hence, several simple approaches like the Naive Bayes classifier, logistic regression, decision trees, random forest, and support vector machine are still extensively employed because of their simple interpretation. However, they only provide reasonable accuracy when the amount of data available is minimal.

In this paper, we design an interpretable word sense disambiguation on a full CoarseWSD balanced dataset that can be used as the sense classifier for chatbot interface to understanding natural language. By proposing a unique model for language patterns, we hope to strike a feasible compromise between accuracy and interpretability. TM is a pattern recognition method that composes patterns in propositional logic comprehended by humans. We show how our algorithm learns relevant patterns from context words and investigate which context words influence each word sense's classification. We extend the previous work of TM on WSD (4 words) [34] to complete 20 words extending the previous task by 16 words. We also introduced the global interpretation along with local interpretation for explainability on chatbot domain.

2   Related Work

The field of WSD research is gaining traction in the NLP community, and it has recently made significant progress [3,35]. In an essence, there are two types of WSD methods: knowledge-based and supervised WSD. Knowledge-based approaches rely on the semantic structure of lexical knowledge bases to determine the meaning of ambiguous words [21]. BabelNet's semantic structure, for example, has been used to assess word similarity [9]. The advantage of such models is that they do not require annotated or unannotated data and instead rely primarily on synset relationships. Traditional techniques to supervise WSD typically rely on extracting features from the context words that surround the target word [37].

The success of deep learning has significantly fueled WSD research. In addition to typical supervised WSD, embedding is becoming more common for capturing word senses [20]. Majid et al. also improve the state-of-the-art supervised WSD by assigning vector coefficients to generate more exact context representations and then using PCA dimensionality reduction to find a superior feature transformation [27]. For the lexical sample task of the Senseval dataset, Salomonsson introduces a supervised classifier based on bidirectional LSTM [14]. Other machine learning algorithms have handled contextually aware word embedding extensively across various areas. The work on neural network embedding is perhaps the most important [15,25]. When it comes to interpretability, our study differs significantly from past efforts because existing approaches provide complicated vectorized embeddings that are rarely human interpretable. This is one of the most vital bottlenecks of NLP models into real-life applications.

Recently, NLP models have been dominated by the DNN model based on attention [29]. Even though the attention mechanism brings some sort of interpretation of the prediction, it still does not provide a faithful explanation of the model. It interprets the prediction based on the weightage of each input on the output. But this is merely a numerical value rather than a transparent and explainable model. In a user-end explainable chatbot, the model should be able to explain the logic behind the learning as well as the reasoning for a particular prediction.

All of these contributions demonstrate that supervised neural models can attain the state-of-the-art accuracy without taking into account external language-specific information. However, due to their black-box nature [7], such neural network models are criticized for being difficult to interpret. In this study, we use the newly developed Tsetlin machine (TM) to introduce interpretability that supports the backend of the chatbot for WSD. The TM paradigm is inherently interpretable by producing rules in propositional logic [11,13,36]. TMs have demonstrated promising results in various classification tasks involving image data [12], NLP tasks [4,5,28,33], and board games

[11]. Although the TM works with binary data, current research reveals that a threshold-based representation of continuous input allows the TM to function well in situations when binary data is not available, such as disease outbreak forecasting [2].

3 Proposed Tsetlin Machine Based Word Sense Disambiguation

3.1 Tsetlin Machine

A new game-theoretic approach that organizes a decentralized team of Tsetlin Automata (TA) is at the core of the TM. Based on disjunctive normal form (DNF), the strategy directs the TAs to learn the arbitrarily complex propositional formula. Notwithstanding its ability to learn complex nonlinear patterns, TM is interpretable in the sense that it decomposes problems into self-contained sub-patterns that may be interpreted separately. Each sub-pattern is represented by a conjunctive clause, which is a series of literals, each of which represents an input bit or its negation. As a result, sub-pattern representation and evaluation are both Boolean. In comparison to other approaches, this makes the TM computationally efficient and hardware friendly.

Let $X = [x_1, x_2, ..., x_n]$ be the feature vector (input) for the TM, which is thus a simple bag of words constructed from the text corpus. The feature vector is then fed to a TM classifier, whose overall architecture is shown in Fig. 1. Multiclass TM consists of multiple TM and each TM has several TA teams which is expanded in Fig. 1(b). X is the input to the TM. For this task, each sense is seen as a class, and the context of the word to be disambiguated is the feature vector (the bag of words). If there are q classes and m sub-patterns per class or per sense, the senses can be classified using $q \times m$ conjunctive clauses, $C_i^j, 1 \leq j \leq q, 1 \leq i \leq m$:

$$C_i^j = \left(\bigwedge_{k \in I_i^j} x_k\right) \wedge \left(\bigwedge_{k \in \bar{I}_i^j} \neg x_k\right), \tag{1}$$

where I_i^j and $\bar{I}_i^j$ are non-overlapping subsets of the input variables. A specific subset is in charge of determining whether propositional variables are included in the clause and whether or not they are negated. In greater detail, the input variable indices in I_j^i relate to the literals that are included as is, and the indices of input variables in $\bar{I}_j^i$ correspond to the negated ones.

Clauses with odd indexes are given positive polarity $(+)$ and those with even indexes are given negative polarity $(-)$ to distinguish the class pattern from other patterns (1-vs-all). Positive polarity clauses vote in favor of the target class, while negative index clauses vote against it. Finally, according to Eq. (2), a summation operator aggregates the votes by subtracting the number of negative votes from the number of positive votes.

$$f^j(X) = \Sigma_{i=1}^m (-1)^{m-1} C_i^j(X). \tag{2}$$

In a multi-class TM, the final decision is made by an argmax operator to classify the input based on the highest sum of votes, as shown in Eq. (3):

$$y = \text{argmax}_j \left(f^j(X)\right). \tag{3}$$

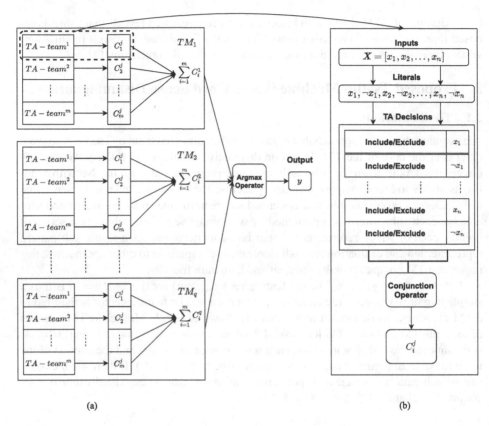

(a)   (b)

Fig. 1. The architecture of (a) multiclass Tsetlin Machine, (b) a TA-team forms the clause C_i^j, $1 \leq j \leq q, 1 \leq i \leq m$ [34].

3.2 Training of the Proposed WSD Model

The TM's training is described in depth in [11]. Here, we only look at how data is used to extract word senses. Consider the following training example: $(\boldsymbol{X}, \hat{y})$. The input to the TM is represented by the input vector $\boldsymbol{X}$ - a bag of words. The sense of the target word is the target $\hat{y}$. TM learning is overseen by several teams of TAs. A clause is assigned one TA per literal, as shown in Fig. 1(b). A deterministic automaton, known as a TA, learns the best action from a set of options presented by the environment. As shown in Fig. 2, each TA in the TM has $2N$ states and chooses between two actions: Action 1 and Action 2. The TA's current state determines its course of action. Each TA in TM has the option of excluding (Action 1) or including (Action 2) its allocated literal. The structure of the clause is dictated by the TA team's decisions, and the clause can therefore provide an output for the given input $\boldsymbol{X}$. Thereafter, the state of each TA is updated based on its current state, the output of the clause C_i^j for the training input $\boldsymbol{X}$, and the target $\hat{y}$.

We offer an example to demonstrate the training process, showing how a clause is constructed by excluding and including words. As shown in Fig. 3, we consider the

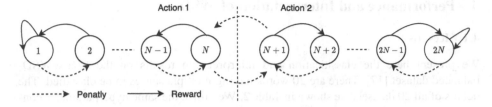

Fig. 2. Representation of two actions of TA.

bag of words for "Text Corpus 2": (apple, like, orange, and more), converted to binary form "Input 2". There are eight TAs with ($N = 100$) states per action that co-produce a single clause, as seen in Fig. 4. With "more", "like", "orange", and "apple", the four TAs (TA' to the left in Fig. 4) vote for the intended sense, but the four TAs (TA' to the right in Fig. 4) vote against it. The rewarded terms are moved away from the central states while the penalized ones are moved closer to the center state. In Fig. 4, from the TAs to the left, we obtain a clause $C_1 =$ "apple" ∧ "like". For the time being, the status of "orange" is excluded. However, after seeing more evidence from "Input 2", the TA of "orange" is penalized for its current action, forcing it to switch from exclude to include in the end. As a result, after more updates, the word "orange" will be included to the clause, resulting in $C_1 =$ "apple" ∧ "like" ∧ "orange", which improves the precision of the sub-pattern and hence the classification.

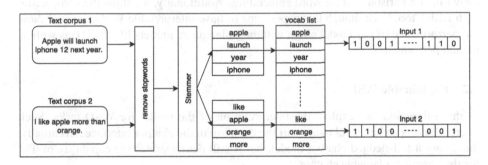

Fig. 3. Preprocessing of text corpus for input to TM.

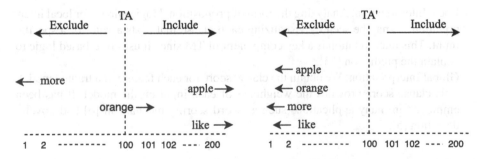

Fig. 4. Eight TA with 100 states per action that learn whether to exclude or include a specific word (or its negation) in a clause [34].

4 Performance and Interpretation of WSD

4.1 Results

We present here the classification and interpretation results on the CoarseWSD-balanced dataset [17]. There are 20 words having multiple senses to be classified. The details of all 20 datasets are shown in Table 2. We utilize the same hyperparameter configuration for all of the target phrases to train the TM for this task. Each word has been trained separately using different TMs. However, for real application, all of the TM are ensembled together and based on the target word whose sense has to be classified. Since it deals with only 20 words present in the CoarseWSD-balanced dataset, it represents a demo model for interpretable WSD Classifier for Human Explainable Chatbot. The performance for each word sense classification is shown in Table 2. As we can see that, we have obtained three models to compare with our proposed TM-based WSD in full CoarseWSD-balanced dataset [17]. The three models employ static embedding obtained from two sources, CommonCrawl and Base, and are trained using 1 layer neural network called FTX-B and FTX-C. In addition, we also consider BERT base with 1 layer neural network model called BRT-B. In order to have the performance comparison of these trained models with humans, we use the human performance from [17].

From Table 2, we can see that the proposed TM easily outperforms FTX-B by a significant margin in all the 20 words. In the case of FTX-C, TM still outperforms most of the available word senses. This is because of the enriched information in Common-Crawl in comparison to Base word embedding. Additionally, we show the comparison with BERT too. Even though this paper aims to have interpretable WSD, we still show the performance of our model along with huge language models like BERT as well as human performance.

4.2 Explainable WSD

In this subsection, we explore the interpretation of the model for WSD tasks. Such interpretation can be useful to support the decision in the chatbot interface. Eventually, this is not a full-fledged chatbot model, but it still demonstrates the capability of TM for the human explainable chatbot.

We will explore two types of interpretation using TM to design explainable WSD:

– Local Interpretation: Analyzing the form of propositional logic allows for local interpretation. It may be seen by visualizing each clause that casts a vote for a specific input. This interpretation is a key component of TM since it uses rule-based logic to explain the prediction [33].
– Global Interpretation: We obtain the clause score for each feature of a trained model. This clause score provides the weightage of each input on the model. It has been employed in many applications such as word scoring mechanism [6] and novelty detection [5].

Local Interpretation in WSD. Here, we detail the local interpretation of WSD by observing the propositional logic of each clause [11, 33]. We'll use a basic example

Table 1. Senses associated with each word that is to be classified.

Dataset	Sense1	Sense2	Sense3	Sense4	Sense5
Apple	apple inc	apple	NA	NA	NA
JAVA	computer	location	NA	NA	NA
Spring	hydrology	season	device	NA	NA
Crane	machine	bird	NA	NA	NA
Arm	architecture	arm	NA	NA	NA
Bank	bank	bank (geography)	NA	NA	NA
Bass	bass	guitar	NA	NA	NA
Bow	ship	arrow	music	NA	NA
Chair	chairman	chair	NA	NA	NA
Club	club	night club	weapon	NA	NA
Deck	ship	building	NA	NA	NA
Digit	numerical	anatomy	NA	NA	NA
Hood	comics	vehicle	headgear	NA	NA
Mole	animal	espionage	unit	sauce	espionage
Pitcher	pitcher	container	NA	NA	NA
Pound	mass	currency	NA	NA	NA
Seal	pinniped	musician	emblem	mechanical	NA
Square	square	company	town square	square number	NA
Trunk	botany	automobile	anatomy	NA	NA
Yard	yard	sailing	NA	NA	NA

with the noun "apple" as the target word for explanation purposes. For the sake of simplicity, we will explore two meanings of the word "apple", namely, Company (s_1) and Fruit (s_2). The text corpus for s_1 is about the apple as a company, whereas the text corpus for s_2 is about the apple as a fruit. To extract the clauses that vote for sense s_1, the input text is passed to the model and the clauses that vote for the presence of sense s_1 are observed as shown in Fig. 4. The token indices are used to represent the literals created by TM. The appropriate word tokens have been used in their place for clarity. As seen in Fig. 5, the green box signifies the literal's non-negated form, whereas the red box denotes the literal's negated ones. For example, the sub-pattern created by clause C_3 is $C_3 = \text{apple} \wedge \neg\text{orange} \wedge \neg\text{more}$. These clauses consist of included literals in conjunctive normal form (CNF), which contains several included randomly placed literals in each clause during training.

Table 2. Results on the full CoarseWSD balanced dataset: FastText-Base (FTX-B), FastText-CommonCrawl (FTX-C), 1 Neural Network BERT-Base (BRT-B) and Tsetlin Machine (TM).

Datasets	Micro-F1				Macro-F1				Humans
	FTX-B	FTX-C	BRT-B	TM	FTX-B	FTX-C	BRT-B	TM	
Apple	96.3	97.8	99.0	97.58	96.6	97.7	99.0	97.45	100
JAVA	98.7	99.5	99.6	99.38	68.4	84.3	99.8	99.35	100
Spring	86.9	92.5	97.4	90.78	78.8	96.4	97.2	90.76	100
Crane	87.9	94.9	94.2	93.63	88.0	94.8	94.1	93.62	98
Arm	92.1	97.0	99.4	97.93	93.1	97.2	99.6	96.93	100
Bank	79.5	87.7	99.8	97.36	78.5	89.2	97.8	93.32	98
Bass	84.8	86.0	81.1	87.77	87.0	87.8	79.6	78.20	90
Bow	80.5	92.1	96.3	92.52	81.0	91.7	97.0	91.89	98
Chair	75.3	85.4	96.2	90.15	75.00	84.2	94.7	89.73	98
Club	62.4	74.8	81.2	76.8	64.6	79.9	84.3	74.4	86
Deck	65.6	84.8	87.9	94.90	68.4	85.2	86.9	70.89	96
Digit	76.2	92.9	100.0	97.56	84.8	95.5	100.0	96.57	100
Hood	73.2	87.8	98.8	88.89	82.7	87.6	97.7	82.63	98
Mole	76.2	91.7	97.1	91.5	83.5	93.0	97.6	90.2	98
Pitcher	86.6	93.3	99.8	91.31	78.3	91.6	99.9	90.2	100
Pound	53.6	62.9	86.6	89.58	67.4	90.0	100.0	79.56	100
Seal	65.6	87.8	96.7	85.60	63.7	81.1	97.5	80.20	100
Square	63.3	82.1	88.4	80.5	69.1	69.1	89.1	75.62	96
Trunk	71.4	81.8	92.2	90.40	69.6	81.6	95.8	88.42	100
Yard	73.6	88.8	73.6	95.77	72.7	93.4	84.5	89.88	100

The literals in clauses that output 1 or vote for the presence of the class s_1 for I_{test} are collected first, as shown in Eq. (4):

$$L_t = \bigcup_{\substack{k,j, \\ \forall C_j=1}} \{x_k^j, \neg x_k^j\}, \qquad (4)$$

where x_k^j is the kth literal, i.e., x_k that appears in clause j and $\neg x_k^j$ is the negation of the literal. The next process is to look for literals (words) that appear frequently in L_t and correlate to the relevant words. Then a new function is defined, $\beta(h, H)$, which returns the number of the elements h in the set H. Thereafter, a set of the numbers can be formulated for all literals x_k and their negations $\neg x_k$ in L_t, $k \in \{1, 2, \ldots, n\}$, as shown in Eq. (5):

$$S_t = \left\{ \bigcup_{k=1:n} \beta(x_k, L_t), \bigcup_{k=1:n} \beta(\neg x_k, L_t) \right\}. \qquad (5)$$

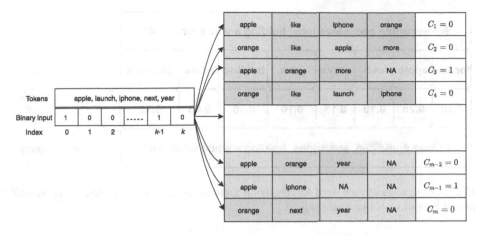

Fig. 5. Structure of clauses formed by the combination of sub-patterns. Green color indicates the literals that are included as original, red color indicates the literals that are included as the negated form and the blue color boxes indicates that there are no literals because not all the clauses has same number of literals [34]. (Color figure online)

Input text	Important words	Non-important words
	$\neg tree$	$\neg pilot$
	$\neg fruit$	$\neg variant$
	$\neg cherries$	$\neg evolution$
former apple ceo, steve jobs, holding a white iphone 4"	$\neg orchard$	$\neg earliest$
	$\neg garden$	$\neg anderson$
	$\neg pear$	$\neg palate$
	$\neg plant$	$\neg lifecycle$

Fig. 6. Important and non-important words for a given input context.

These elements are then ranked in descending order in set S_t, with the top η percent of the rank being considered as the important literals whereas the last η percent are considered as non-important literals.

To demonstrate interpretability, consider the following sample to extract the literals responsible for the classification of an input sentence: **"former apple ceo, steve jobs, holding a white iphone 4"**. After passing this information through the model, TM predicts the correct sense, and we look at the clauses that output 1. Each clause's literals are added together, and the number of appearances for each literal is computed. Since the bag-of-words representation is sparse, TM easily learns the negated literals more than the non-negated literals which give the model the logical reasoning based on nega-

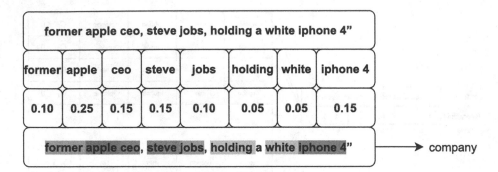

Fig. 7. Clause score of each word for classifying apple as company. Color represents the weightage of each word. (Color figure online)

tion. The local interpretation for the above-mentioned input context for being apple as a company is shown in Fig. 6. By using the most repeated literals in the clause, we can see that the explanation of TM for classifying apple as a company is that the context around the target word does not contain tree, fruit, cherries, orchard, garden, pear, and plant. Such interpretation also makes sense to human beings as we understand that if apple is not related to those important literals, then it most probably represents the company.

Global Interpretation. Once the model is trained, we can obtain the score for each feature from Eq. (2). The most important aspect of this interpretation is that it does not rely on negated logical reasoning, rather on the weightage of each feature on the model that satisfies the propositional logic. The global interpretation based on the clause score of each feature is shown in Fig. 7. As we can see, the words "apple" has the highest weightage being a target word. The context words such as "Steve", "ceo", and "iphone4" have the highest clause score followed by "jobs" and "former".

4.3 Application of Interpretation in Chatbot

Nowadays, the chatbot has become an integral part of many service-oriented organizations. Such increasing demand for chatbots also needs to be loyal and trustworthy for humans to rely on in daily tasks. Due to the massive development of pre-trained language models, the performance that supports chatbot to understand user's queries has gone drastically upwards. However, the explainable part of it still lacks a solid background because of the blackbox nature of the neural network. Hence, we here propose a simple application of TM for WSD based sense classifier chatbot. This model aims to design a sense classifier for a chatbot that explains its prediction to the user thereby building the first step towards a fully-fledged chatbot. Here we integrate both the local and global interpretation of TM to demonstrate its application in the chatbot domain as shown in Fig. 8. We can use both logical negation reasoning and clause score to explain the prediction to humans. This application can be a stepping stone in the field of human explainable chatbots.

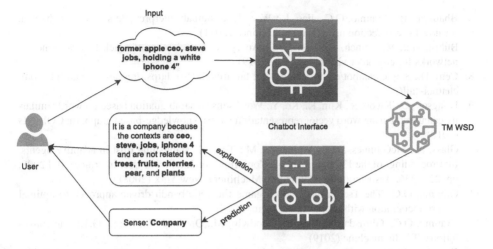

Fig. 8. Clause score of each word for classifying apple as company.

5   Conclusion

In this paper, we extended the 4-word CoarseWSD WSD task using Tsetlin Machine (TM) into full 20 words CoarseWSD-balanced WSD task. We employed the full dataset to train the TM on WSD and demonstrated the performance of the model. The proposed TM-based WSD achieves the state-of-the-art performance in most of the datasets, outperforming the basic setup of the neural network except BERT. In addition, we explore the local and global interpretation of TM. We showed that combining both local interpretability that gives logical reasoning with negation and global interpretability that gives weightage of each word using clause score boost the explanation of the model. Such high-level interpretation has a huge impact on real-life conversational AI such as chatbots. We also have proposed an application of TM on a chatbot that explains the prediction of sense as human understands the concept.

References

1. Why chatbots fail: Limitations of chatbots. https://medium.com/voice-tec
2. Abeyrathna, K.D., Granmo, O.C., Zhang, X., Jiao, L., Goodwin, M.: The regression Tsetlin machine: a novel approach to interpretable nonlinear regression. Philos. Trans. R. Soc. A: Math. Phys. Eng. Sci. **378** (2019)
3. Agirre, E., Edmonds, P.: Word Sense Disambiguation: Algorithms and Applications. Text, Speech and Language Technology, Springer, Heidelberg (2006). https://doi.org/10.1007/978-1-4020-4809-8
4. Berge, G.T., Granmo, O., Tveit, T.O., Goodwin, M., Jiao, L., Matheussen, B.V.: Using the Tsetlin machine to learn human-interpretable rules for high-accuracy text categorization with medical applications. IEEE Access **7**, 115134–115146 (2019). https://doi.org/10.1109/ACCESS.2019.2935416
5. Bhattarai, B., Granmo, O.C., Jiao, L.: Measuring the novelty of natural language text using the conjunctive clauses of a Tsetlin machine text classifier. arXiv abs/2011.08755 (2020)

6. Bhattarai, B., Granmo, O.C., Jiao, L.: Word-level human interpretable scoring mechanism for novel text detection using Tsetlin machines (2021)
7. Buhrmester, V., Münch, D., Arens, M.: Analysis of explainers of black box deep neural networks for computer vision: a survey (2019)
8. Cem, D.: 8 epic chatbot/conversational bot failures (2020). https://research.aimultiple.com/chatbot-fail/
9. Dongsuk, O., Kwon, S., Kim, K., Ko, Y.: Word sense disambiguation based on word similarity calculation using word vector representation from a knowledge-based graph. In: COLING (2018)
10. Glass, A., McGuinness, D.L., Wolverton, M.: Toward establishing trust in adaptive agents. In: Proceedings of the 13th International Conference on Intelligent User Interfaces, IUI 2008, pp. 227–236. Association for Computing Machinery, New York (2008)
11. Granmo, O.C.: The Tsetlin machine - a game theoretic bandit driven approach to optimal pattern recognition with propositional logic (2018)
12. Granmo, O.C., Glimsdal, S., Jiao, L., Goodwin, M., Omlin, C.W., Berge, G.T.: The convolutional Tsetlin machine (2019)
13. Jiao, L., Zhang, X., Granmo, O.C., Abeyrathna, K.D.: On the convergence of Tsetlin machines for the XOR operator. arXiv preprint arXiv:2101.02547 (2021)
14. Kågebäck, M., Salomonsson, H.: Word sense disambiguation using a bidirectional LSTM. In: CogALex@COLING (2016)
15. Khattak, F.K., Jeblee, S., Pou-Prom, C., Abdalla, M., Meaney, C., Rudzicz, F.: A survey of word embeddings for clinical text. J. Biomed. Inform.: X **4**, 100057 (2019)
16. Liao, K., Ye, D., Xi, Y.: Research on enterprise text knowledge classification based on knowledge schema. In: 2010 2nd IEEE International Conference on Information Management and Engineering, pp. 452–456 (2010). https://doi.org/10.1109/ICIME.2010.5477609
17. Loureiro, D., Rezaee, K., Pilehvar, M.T., Camacho-Collados, J.: Analysis and evaluation of language models for word sense disambiguation. Comput. Linguist. **47**, 387–443 (2021)
18. Luger, E., Sellen, A.: "Like having a really bad PA": the gulf between user expectation and experience of conversational agents. In: Proceedings of the 2016 CHI Conference on Human Factors in Computing Systems, CHI 2016, pp. 5286–5297. Association for Computing Machinery, New York (2016)
19. Meyer, R.: Even early focus groups hated clippy, June. https://www.theatlantic.com/
20. Mikolov, T., Sutskever, I., Chen, K., Corrado, G.S., Dean, J.: Distributed representations of words and phrases and their compositionality. arXiv abs/1310.4546 (2013)
21. Navigli, R., Velardi, P.: Structural semantic interconnection: a knowledge-based approach to word sense disambiguation. In: SENSEVAL@ACL (2004)
22. Porcheron, M., Fischer, J.E., Reeves, S., Sharples, S.: Voice interfaces in everyday life. In: Proceedings of the 2018 CHI Conference on Human Factors in Computing Systems, CHI 2018, pp. 1–12. Association for Computing Machinery, New York (2018)
23. Radlinski, F., Craswell, N.: A theoretical framework for conversational search. In: Proceedings of the 2017 Conference on Conference Human Information Interaction and Retrieval, CHIIR 2017, pp. 117–126. Association for Computing Machinery, New York (2017)
24. Raganato, A., Camacho-Collados, J., Navigli, R.: Word sense disambiguation: a unified evaluation framework and empirical comparison. In: Proceedings of the 15th Conference of the European Chapter of the Association for Computational Linguistics, Valencia, Spain: Volume 1, Long Papers, pp. 99–110 (2017)
25. Rezaeinia, S.M., Rahmani, R., Ghodsi, A., Veisi, H.: Sentiment analysis based on improved pre-trained word embeddings. Expert Syst. Appl. **117**, 139–147 (2019)
26. Rudin, C.: Stop explaining black box machine learning models for high stakes decisions and use interpretable models instead (2018)

27. Sadi, M.F., Ansari, E., Afsharchi, M.: Supervised word sense disambiguation using new features based on word embeddings. J. Intell. Fuzzy Syst. **37**, 1467–1476 (2019)
28. Saha, R., Granmo, O.-C., Goodwin, M.: Mining interpretable rules for sentiment and semantic relation analysis using Tsetlin machines. In: Bramer, M., Ellis, R. (eds.) SGAI 2020. LNCS (LNAI), vol. 12498, pp. 67–78. Springer, Cham (2020). https://doi.org/10.1007/978-3-030-63799-6_5
29. Vaswani, A., et al.: Attention is all you need. In: Advances in Neural Information Processing Systems, pp. 5998–6008 (2017)
30. Wang, Y., et al.: Clinical information extraction applications: a literature review. J. Biomed. Inform. **77**, 34–49 (2018). https://doi.org/10.1016/j.jbi.2017.11.011. http://www.sciencedirect.com/science/article/pii/S1532046417302563
31. Xiao, J., Stasko, J., Catrambone, R.: An empirical study of the effect of agent competence on user performance and perception. In: Proceedings of the Third International Joint Conference on Autonomous Agents and Multiagent Systems, AAMAS 2004, vol. 1, pp. 178–185. IEEE Computer Society, USA (2004)
32. Xu, W.: Toward human-centered AI: a perspective from human-computer interaction. Interactions **26**(4), 42–46 (2019)
33. Yadav, R.K., Jiao, L., Granmo, O.C., Goodwin, M.: Human-level interpretable learning for aspect-based sentiment analysis. In: The Thirty-Fifth AAAI Conference on Artificial Intelligence (AAAI 2021). AAAI (2021)
34. Yadav, R.K., Jiao, L., Granmo, O., Goodwin, M.: Interpretability in word sense disambiguation using Tsetlin machine. In: Proceedings of the 13th International Conference on Agents and Artificial Intelligence, Volume 2: ICAART, pp. 402–409. INSTICC, SciTePress (2021)
35. Yuan, D., Richardson, J., Doherty, R., Evans, C., Altendorf, E.: Semi-supervised word sense disambiguation with neural models. In: COLING (2016)
36. Zhang, X., Jiao, L., Granmo, O.C., Goodwin, M.: On the convergence of Tsetlin machines for the IDENTITY- and NOT operators. IEEE Trans. Pattern Anal. Mach. Intell. (2021, accepted)
37. Zhong, Z., Ng, H.T.: It makes sense: a wide-coverage word sense disambiguation system for free text. In: ACL (2010)

A Tsetlin Machine Framework for Universal Outlier and Novelty Detection

Bimal Bhattarai[✉], Ole-Christoffer Granmo, and Lei Jiao

Department of Information and Communication Technology, University of Agder,
Grimstad, Norway
{bimal.bhattarai,ole.granmo,lei.jiao}@uia.no

Abstract. Outlier and novelty detection are two of the most active study areas where a huge amount of research effort has been made over the past decades. Although there are several well-known outlier and novelty detection methods, it is difficult to find one that can effectively and simultaneously deal with both tasks across different data types. When studied in detail, outliers and novelties exhibit different characteristics. In this paper, we introduce a universal Tsetlin Machine (TM) framework for novelty and outlier detection. The framework consists of a TM generator and a machine learning classifier. To this end, we enhance the vanilla TM with a generator to produce a novelty score. The generator consists of the conjunctive clauses of the TM, which are used to form a representative pattern of a given input. We demonstrate that the clauses provide a succinct interpretable description of the trained input and that our scoring mechanism enables us to discern outlier and novel input. Empirically, we evaluate our TM framework on nine outlier datasets, five novelty tasks, and a one-class classification setup. In all experiments, we were able to either outperform or closely match state-of-the-art methods, with the added benefit of an interpretable propositional logic-based representation.

Keywords: Outlier detection · Novelty detection · Tsetlin Machine · One-class classification · Interpretable

1 Introduction

Outlier detection, alternatively referred to as anomaly detection, is the process of classifying unusual instances, events, or observations that do not conform to an expected pattern or other data points in a dataset. Generally, outliers exhibit unique characteristics and deviate significantly from normal data points. The fundamental premise behind the machine learning classifier is a generalization- to form a decision boundary that differentiates the new instances into classes. As a result, many machine learning methods have been widely used to identify anomalous data points. The common approach to deal with outliers is one-class classification, where the classifier creates decision boundaries to learn normal classes. And any deviation of data points from the normality is considered an outlier [4]. Because of these characteristics, outlier detection often plays a critical role in variety of application domains, including object detection [6,40],

© Springer Nature Switzerland AG 2022
A. P. Rocha et al. (Eds.): ICAART 2021, LNAI 13251, pp. 250–268, 2022.
https://doi.org/10.1007/978-3-031-10161-8_14

credit card fraud detection [23], network intrusion detection [58], sensor networks [57], medical information [47], and text analysis [7]. Apart from its widespread application, outlier detection poses a few challenges. To begin, there is a dearth of labeled data as outliers are rare. Second, it is difficult to propose universal mathematical formulations to define outliers that suit all datasets. Finally, the performance of outliers detection suffers from a large volume of complex data from a variety of application domains.

Novelty detection, on the other hand, is a process of recognizing that the test data is somehow different than the training data. The majority of supervised classifiers assume closed-world assumptions [46]. That is, the classes present in test data must have appeared during training. However, in open-world assumptions, [8], the new class might appear during the test time. The issue with neural network-based supervised classifiers that employ the standard softmax layer is that they erroneously force novel input into one of the previously seen classes by normalizing the class output scores to obtain a distribution that adds to 1.0. Instead, a robust classifier should be capable of flagging input as a novel and rejects labeling it with presently known classes. Therefore, the classifier should not be limited to assign a given example to previously trained classes; it should also be capable of detecting novel classes.

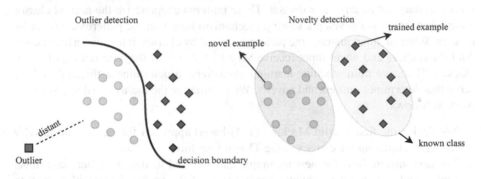

Fig. 1. Visualization of outlier detection and novelty detection [12].

Outliers and novelty are often used interchangeably. However, there are a few tiny distinctions depending on our observation and comprehension. In general, outliers emphasize statistical rarity and deviation than normal data instances. In some cases, outliers are the data points that make it more difficult for a model to converge. In contrast, novel data points from unknown classes that have never occurred in training samples. In such situation, the classifier should not assign the data point to one of the training classes. But it should flag them as novel input or reject. Figure 1 highlights the challenge of novelty detection. In a nutshell, the blue data points to the right in Fig. 1 represent training data, whereas the yellow data points to the right indicate novel data points. We will refer to the known data points as *positive examples* and the novel data points as *negative examples*. As illustrated in the figure, we see that the problem of novelty detection is inextricably linked to the problem of outlier detection [16]. However, as exemplified to the left in Fig. 1, the latter problem entails highlighting data points that belong to previously known class, yet deviating from the normal data points, e.g., due to measurement errors or anomalies (red point).

Given a set of example data points $X = (x_i, y_i)$, $x_i \in \mathcal{R}^s$, where $i = (1, 2, 3, \ldots, N)$ indexes the positive examples, s is the dimensionality of the data point x_i, and y_i is the label of x_i, assigning it a class. For any data point x_i, also known as a feature vector, a classifier function $\hat{y} = \mathcal{F}(x; X)$ is used to assign the data point a predicted class $\hat{y}$, after the function has been fitted to the training data X. Our objective is to identify a division boundary that can be used to distinguish outliers and novel input from typical input. To describe the boundary, we create a novelty scoring function $z(x; X)$, which is also fitted on X, and computes a novelty score. In other words, the classifier should return the appropriate class label while simultaneously discarding outliers and novel examples.

Paper Contribution. In this paper, we introduce a novel framework that makes use of rule-based logic for outlier and novel data classification. Although we proposed an early notion of text-based novelty detection in [12], this work presents an extended study encompassing outlier detection, novel architecture, and robust evaluation setups. To this end, we include state-of-the-art datasets and algorithms for both outlier and novelty detection. The novelty detection in text is further evaluated using a one-class classification configuration. Our framework enables us to use conjunctive clauses to represent frequent patterns in a dataset. These patterns characterize the normal classes comprehensively. We develop a scoring mechanism based on the patterns captured by clauses. When an input matches the pattern captured by clauses, it receives a high score. And the outliers and novel input receive very low scores as they are not captured by clauses. Then, we train machine learning classifiers to determine a threshold of the score that determines outliers and novelty. We summarize the main contributions of our work as follows:

- We devise the first Tsetlin Machine (TM)-based approach for outlier and novelty detection, utilizing the clauses of the TM architecture.
- We demonstrate how the new technique can be used to detect outliers and novel topics, and compare the technique against state-of-the-art baselines, with respect to a collection of classification datasets previously used for the evaluation.

The remainder of the paper is organized as follows. In Sect. 2, we discuss related works. Section 3 describes the proposed framework. We report experimental results and discussion in Sect. 4 before concluding our work in Sect. 5.

2 Related Work

Many existing research on outlier detection falls under the following categories: distribution-based, distance-based, clustering, and density-based [30]. It is discussed in [54] distance-based methods for defining outlier scores based on their nearest neighbors. Similarly, [15] performed an experimental evaluation of 12 methods based on nearest neighbors using ELKI software [3]. The non-parametric models [17] achieve good results but require a huge amount of data. To address this, another frequently used method, proximity-based model [14,41,45] assumes the outliers are located far from their nearest neighbors without requiring any training of the entire dataset. However, the effectiveness is significantly reduced because of the high dimensionality and volume of data.

In contrast to the distance-based method, the density-based method identifies less dense points locally as outliers. The local outlier factor (LOF) [14] is a well-known density-based algorithm that has inspired numerous studies on outliers detection. However, the increasing complexity of the algorithm is not suitable for dealing with a sparse dataset. Therefore, Principle Component Analysis (PCA) was employed in [49] to propose bounded LOF (BLOF). The connectivity-based outlier factor (COF) [50] addresses the shortcomings of LOF assuming that the outlier pattern is only low density in a spherical region defined by euclidean distances. Another approach of density-based approaches such as DBSCAN can detect outliers by considering them as small points in sparse space [21]. Several cluster-based methods have been proposed for determining the tightness of the clusters [31] but they are highly dependent on threshold parameters [19]. The cluster-based local outlier factor (CBLOF) [31] also attempts to distinguish small and large clusters by a quantitative measure.

In recent years, algorithms such as the One-Class Support Vector Machine (OC-SVM) [20] have been proposed that are not dependent on data distribution. It locates a hyperplane to distinguish normal data from outliers by projecting the data in high-dimensional space. Similarly, a one-class classification algorithm [32] exploits the probability density of the real data to separate outliers. Recent methods utilizing Generative Adversarial networks (GAN) [26] have achieved state-of-the-art performance by leveraging mini-max game theory to capture a representation of real data. The emerging research includes a deep convolutional generative adversarial network (AnoGAN) [55], and a generator with an encoder-decoder-encoder sub-networks (GANomaly) [5].

Novelty detection in the text is a relatively emerging research area. Several studies have been conducted on supervised multiclass classification in closed-world settings [9]. The common approach is the distance-based method [30] in which normal and novel data are clustered separately in a distance. OCSVM [20] and [51] are two additional approaches based on on one-class classifiers. Because of the lack of negative training samples, single-class classifiers struggle to maximize the class margin. A new method named center-based similarity space (CBS) [22] was proposed to use binary classifiers for transforming each document to a central similarity vector. The probabilistic method used in [33] threshold the entropy of the estimated class probability distribution. However, it requires prior knowledge to choose the entropy. An active learning model to classify novel data points while training is proposed in [43].

Many recent research on novel text classification uses GANs. In [25], GAN is used to generate a blend of normal and novel data. The generator is trained using feature matching loss, while the discriminator handles classification and novelty detection. Similarly, [8] proposed an approach called OpenMAX to estimate the probability of an input belonging to a novel class. Recent state-of-the-art GAN-based outlier detection called Single-Objective Generative Adversarial Active Learning (SO-GAAL) and Multi-Objective Generative Adversarial Active Learning (MO-GAAL) was proposed in [39]. The training of the generator is interrupted just before convergence in order to generate outliers that are utilized to train the discriminator for outlier detection. However, the method necessitates substantial problem-specific hyperparameter tuning. Another more recent unsupervised learning method COPOD [37] uses copulas for modeling multivariate data distribution. The method is computationally efficient and is insensitive to the dimension of the features. However, the method is ineffective when dealing with complex features and nonlinear relations.

3 Tsetlin Machine Framework

In this section, we propose a TM framework for outlier and novelty detection. The framework is composed of TM generator and classifier architecture. The generator produces the scores utilizing the clauses from TM. And the classifier is coupled with the generator to use the score for outlier and novelty classification.

3.1 TM Architecture for Generator

The TM, proposed in [27], is a recent approach to pattern classification, regression, and novelty detection [2,12,13,28]. It captures the frequent patterns of the learning problem using conjunctive clauses in propositional logic. Each clause is composed of a conjunction of literals, where a literal is a propositional/Boolean variable or its negation. Recent research indicates that the TM performs competitively with state-of-the-art deep learning networks in text classification [10,11,44,52,53] along with parallel and asynchronous architecture [1] for faster learning across diverse tasks. Additionally, theoretical studies have revealed robust convergence properties [34,56]. In what follows, we propose a new scheme that extends the TM with the capability to recognize outliers and novel patterns.

Figure 2 describes the building blocks of a TM. As seen, a vanilla TM takes a vector $X = (x_1, \ldots, x_o)$ of binary features as input (Fig. 3). We binarize text by using binary features that capture the presence/absence of terms in a vocabulary, akin to a bag of words, as done in [10]. However, as opposed to a vanilla TM, our scheme does not output the predicted class. Instead, it calculates a novelty score per class.

Together with their negated counterparts, $\bar{x}_k = \neg x_k = 1 - x_k$, the features form a literal set, $L = \{x_1, \ldots, x_o, \bar{x}_1, \ldots, \bar{x}_o\}$. A TM pattern is formulated as a conjunctive clause C_j^+ or C_j^-, where $j = (1, \ldots, m/2)$ denotes an index of a clause, and the superscript describes the polarity of a clause. In more detail, the total number of clauses, m, is divided into two parts, where half of the clauses are assigned a positive polarity and the other half are assigned a negative polarity. Any clause, regardless of the polarity, is formed by ANDing a subset of the literal set. For example, the jth clause with positive polarity, $C_j^+(X)$, can be expressed as:

$$C_j^+(X) = \bigwedge_{l_k \in L_j^+} l_k = \prod_{l_k \in L_j^+} l_k. \tag{1}$$

where $L_j^+ \subseteq L$ is the set of literals that are involved in the expression of $C_j^+(X)$ after training. For instance, given clause $C_1^+(X) = x_1 x_2$, it consists of the literals $L_1^+ = \{x_1, x_2\}$ and outputs 1 if $x_1 = x_2 = 1$. The output of a conjunctive clause is determined by evaluating it on the input literals. When a clause outputs 1, this means that it has recognized a pattern in the input. Conversely, the clause outputs 0 when no

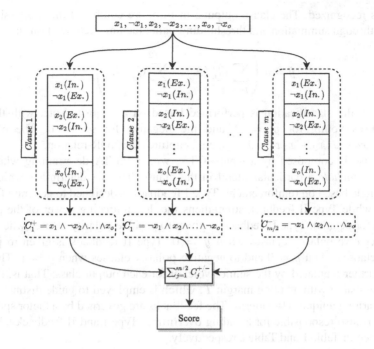

Fig. 2. Optimization of clauses in TM for generating score [12].

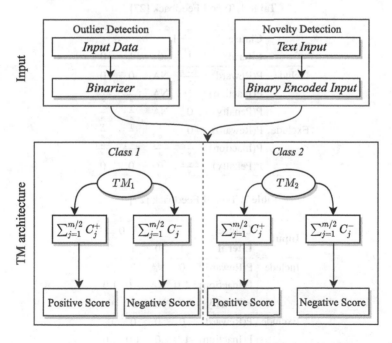

Fig. 3. Multiclass Tsetlin Machine (MTM) generator framework to produce the score for each class.

pattern is recognized. The clause outputs, in turn, are combined into a classification decision through summation and thresholding using the unit step function u:

$$\hat{y} = u \left(\sum_{j=1}^{m/2} C_j^+(X) - \sum_{j=1}^{m/2} C_j^-(X) \right). \tag{2}$$

That is, the classification is performed based on a majority vote, with the positive clauses voting for $y = 1$ and the negative for $y = 0$. The classifier $\hat{y} = u\left(x_1\bar{x}_2 + \bar{x}_1 x_2 - x_1 x_2 - \bar{x}_1\bar{x}_2\right)$, e.g., captures the XOR-relation.

A clause is composed by a team of TA, with each TA determining whether to *Exclude* or *Include* a particular literal in the clause. The TA determines which literals to include based on reinforcement: Type I feedback is designed to generate frequent patterns, while Type II feedback strengthens the discriminating power of the patterns (see [27] for details). Type I feedback is given to positive polarity clauses when $y = 1$ and to negative polarity clauses when $y = 0$. Type II feedback is given to positive polarity clauses when $y = 0$ and to negative polarity clauses when $y = 1$. The feedback is further regulated by the sum of votes v for each output class. That is, the total vote is compared with a voting margin T, which is employed to guide distinct clauses toward learning unique sub-patterns. The feedbacks are governed by a factor specificity s, which is also responsible for avoiding overfitting. Type I and II feedback tables are summarized in Table 1 and Table 2 respectively.

Table 1. Type I Feedback [27].

Input	Clause	1		0	
	Literal	1	0	1	0
Include	P(Reward)	$\frac{s-1}{s}$	NA	0	0
	P(Inaction)	$\frac{1}{s}$	NA	$\frac{s-1}{s}$	$\frac{s-1}{s}$
	P(Penalty)	0	NA	$\frac{1}{s}$	$\frac{1}{s}$
Exclude	P(Reward)	0	$\frac{1}{s}$	$\frac{1}{s}$	$\frac{1}{s}$
	P(Inaction)	$\frac{1}{s}$	$\frac{s-1}{s}$	$\frac{s-1}{s}$	$\frac{s-1}{s}$
	P(Penalty)	$\frac{s-1}{s}$	0	0	0

Table 2. Type II Feedback [27].

Input	Clause	1		0	
	Literal	1	0	1	0
Include	P(Reward)	0	NA	0	0
	P(Inaction)	1.0	NA	1.0	1.0
	P(Penalty)	0	NA	0	0
Exclude	P(Reward)	0	0	0	0
	P(Inaction)	1.0	0	1.0	1.0
	P(Penalty)	0	1.0	0	0

3.2   Classifier

We propose to use the score generated by the TM generator for outlier and novelty detection. This is because the score indicates how closely an input instance fits into either of the classes. The TM generator architecture produces four different outputs, two per class as shown in Fig. 3. In the case of an outlier or novel input, the scores produced from the generator are extremely low. Similarly, for normal input, the scores are typically high and we should be able to differentiate it into one of the training classes. The architecture of the classifier is depicted in Fig. 4. The TM generator is trained with only normal classes. For any given input instance the TM generator produces a score that is equal to the number of classes present while training. For example, in our scenario, we have two trained classes, and hence we have scores for each class. The scores from the generator are scaled and passed to simple machine learning classifiers, such as k-nearest neighbor (KNN), support vector machine (SVM), and logistic regression (LR). The output from the classifier is a binary i.e., 0 or 1, which indicates either the input instance is normal or outlier/novel. Another way to decide whether an input is an outlier or novel is by setting a threshold T. Then an input instance can be compared with T to determine if an instance is normal or not. The value of T specifies the minimum number of clauses that must fit the pattern of the input instance in order to qualify as an outlier or novelty. The classification function $\mathcal{F}(X)$ for a single class can accordingly be given as:

$$
\mathcal{F}(X) = \begin{cases} 1, \textbf{ if } \sum_{j=1}^{m/2} C_j^+(X) > T, \\ 1, \textbf{ if } \sum_{j=1}^{m/2} C_j^-(X) < -T, \\ 0, \textbf{ otherwise.} \end{cases}
$$

4   Experiments and Results

This section presents an experimental evaluation of the proposed TM framework for outlier and novelty detection. We conducted our experiment on the server - NVIDIA DGX-2 with dual Intel Xeon Platinum 8168, 2.7 GhZ, 16 × NVIDIA Tesla V100 and Ubuntu 18.04 LTS x64. We conduct distinct experiments for outlier detection and novelty detection because we are dealing with novelty detection using text data. We break both of the experiments in the following sub-section:

4.1   Outlier Detection

Datasets. We used 9 publicly available outlier detection benchmark datasets from the ODDS datasets [15]. In our experiment, we used 60% of the data for the training set and the remaining 40% as the validation set. The detailed statistics of the datasets are provided in Table 3.

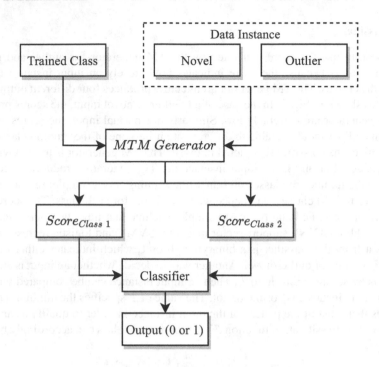

Fig. 4. Outlier/Novelty detection architecture.

Evaluation Measures. Accuracy is a well-established metric for comparing the performance of outlier detection. However, the accuracy ignores the false outliers and false inliers. As a result, in our work we use the Receiver Operating Characteristics (ROC) curve and corresponding AUC, which are insensitive to the number of outliers n, to measure the detection accuracy. The curve is calculated by plotting all potential choices of the true positive rate (the portion of outliers ranked among the top n) against the false positive rate (the portion of inliers ranked among the top n). The ROC AUC value, which ranges between 0 and 1, can be regarded as the average of the recall at n. A random outlier ranking would result in a ROC AUC value close to 0.5 i.e., a curve close to diagonal. In general, the greater the ROC AUC value, the better is the algorithm. [29] established that the ROC AUC value corresponds to the probability of a pair $(ou,\ in)$, where ou is some true outlier and in is some true inlier. The ROC AUC can then be denoted as:

$$ROC\ AUC = \begin{cases} 1, & \text{if } score(ou) > score(in), \\ 0, & \text{if } score(ou) < score(in), \\ 1/2, & \text{if } score(ou) \ = \ score(in). \end{cases}$$

Therefore, the ROC AUC has a direct probabilistic interpretation. Another measure we have used in our work is precision at n (which we denote as $P@n$). It is defined as the fraction of correct results in top n ranks [18]. For a dataset consisting of outliers O and inliers I, $P@n$ can be represented as:

$$P@n = \frac{|\ ou \in O \mid rank(ou) \leq n\ |}{n} \tag{3}$$

Here, we assume that the outlier ranking is unique.

Table 3. Description of the Datasets.

Dataset	Number		Dim.
	Normal	Outlier	
Cardio	1655	176	21
Breastw	444	239	9
Lympho	142	6	18
Ionosphere	225	126	33
Mammography	10923	260	6
Optdigits	5066	150	64
Pima	500	268	8
Speech	3625	61	400
Annthyroid	6595	534	21

Baseline Methods. We compare TM framework with 8 state-of-the-art outlier detection algorithms. The common outlier detection framework [58] is used to implement these algorithms. Table 4 summarize the baseline algorithms employed in our work.

Table 4. Baseline algorithms for outlier detection.

Method	Category	JIT Enabled	Multi-core
LOF [14]	Proximity	No	Yes
kNN [42]	Proximity	No	Yes
CBLOF [31]	Proximity	Yes	No
OCSVM [48]	Linear Model	No	No
ABOD [36]	Proximity	Yes	No
Isolation Forest [38]	Ensembling	No	Yes
HBOS [24]	Proximity	Yes	No
SO-GAAL [39]	Neural Net	No	No
MO-GAAL [39]	Neural Net	No	No
COPOD [37]	Copula	No	Yes

Emperical Evaluation. We compare the performance of the proposed model by comparing ROC AUC with other state-of-the-art outlier detection algorithms using 9 baseline datasets. To begin, we train TM with hyperparamter setting of 1000 clauses, a threshold T of 50, and specificity s of 5.0. Then, feed the score produced from TM generator as a feature to the machine learning classifier. To make our work computationally efficient, we employ simple classifiers such as Logistic Regression (LR) and Support Vector Machine (SVM).

The experimental outcomes are shown in Table 5 and Table 6. Table 5 illustrates the ROC AUC values of all algorithms, whereas the Table 6 illustrates the $P@n$ ranking.

For each dataset, the best result is highlighted in bold. The TM framework achieves the highest ROC AUC value on three out of eight datasets. In the remaining, the performance of TM is extremely competitive. Therefore, our method outperforms all other methods in average ROC AUC value. Similarly, our method achieves the highest $P@n$ value on four out of eight datasets. Additionally, it outperforms all other algorithms in terms of average precision value. The LOF performed poorly and yielded the least ROC AUC and precision values among the baseline algorithms. From observation, we find that our method achieves superior results as the dimension of the dataset increases. And, given that the majority of real-world datasets include a large number of dimensions, we expect that our method would be extremely efficient in such a case. It can also be noticed that while other algorithms produce inconsistent results for all datasets i.e., good for some datasets and bad for others, our proposed method provides very stable and efficient results across datasets. Our method uses clauses to capture the frequent pattern or the inliers. And the patterns formed by the clauses are used to accumulate votes for any input instance. When inliers are fed into the trained TM framework, the scores increase since the input matches majority of the patterns in the clauses. And for outliers, the score is typically low as there are little to no patterns in the clauses. As a result, our method can produce very distinctive scores for inliers and outliers resulting in improved performance.

Table 5. ROC-AUC scores of algorithm performance (average of 10 independent experiments, highest score highlighted in bold).

Data	ABOD	CBLOF	HBOS	IForest	KNN	LOF	OCSVM	COPOD	TM
Cardio	0.56	0.92	0.83	0.92	0.72	0.57	**0.93**	0.89	0.86
Breastw	0.39	0.96	0.98	0.98	0.97	0.47	0.96	**0.99**	0.94
Lympho	0.91	0.96	0.99	0.99	0.97	0.97	0.97	0.99	**1**
Ionosphere	**0.92**	0.89	0.56	0.84	0.92	0.87	0.84	0.83	0.82
Mammography	0.54	0.82	0.83	0.86	0.84	0.72	0.87	**0.89**	0.85
Optdigits	0.46	0.75	0.87	0.72	0.37	0.45	0.49	0.73	**0.75**
Pima	0.67	0.65	0.70	0.67	**0.70**	0.62	0.62	0.66	0.68
Speech	0.62	0.45	0.45	0.44	0.45	0.47	0.44	0.48	**0.66**
Annthyroid	**0.72**	0.62	0.56	0.64	0.69	0.69	0.60	0.69	0.70
AVG	0.64	0.68	0.77	0.78	0.73	0.64	0.76	0.79	**0.80**

Table 6. Average precision of detector performance (average of 10 independent experiments, highest score highlighted in bold).

Data	ABOD	CBLOF	HBOS	IForest	KNN	LOF	OCSVM	COPOD	TM
Cardio	0.23	**0.58**	0.44	0.50	0.33	0.15	0.50	0.57	0.48
Breastw	0.29	0.91	0.95	0.97	0.92	0.32	0.93	**0.98**	0.89
Lympho	0.51	0.80	0.92	0.95	0.82	0.82	0.81	0.89	**1**
Ionosphere	0.91	0.87	0.36	0.78	**0.92**	0.82	0.82	0.71	0.82
Mammography	0.023	0.13	0.12	0.23	0.16	0.11	0.18	**0.42**	0.2
Optdigits	0.027	0.062	**0.195**	0.055	0.022	0.028	0.027	0.053	0.15
Pima	0.51	0.47	0.56	0.50	0.51	0.42	0.46	0.54	**0.69**
Speech	0.039	0.021	0.027	0.017	0.021	0.024	0.021	0.019	**0.12**
Annthyroid	0.18	0.15	0.24	0.18	0.16	0.20	0.12	0.18	**0.25**
AVG	0.30	0.44	0.42	0.46	0.43	0.32	0.43	0.48	**0.51**

4.2 Novelty Detection in Text

The novelty detection is carried out on text data. In the experiment, we make one class novel by removing it out from the training process. While testing, the classifier should be able to reject the instances from novel class.

Datasets. We used the following datasets for evaluation.

- 20-newsgroup dataset: The dataset has total of 18,828 documents divided into 20 classes. In our experiment, we consider the two classes *"comp.graphics"* and *"talk.politics.guns"* as known classes and the class *"rec.sport.baseball"* is considered novel. We take 1000 samples from both known and novel classes for novelty classification.
- CMU Movie Summary corpus: The dataset contains a collection of 42,306 movie plot summaries extracted from Wikipedia and metadata extracted from Freebase. In our experiment, we consider the two movie categories *"action"* and *"horror"* as known classes and *"fantasy"* as novel.
- Spooky Author Identification dataset: The dataset contains 3,000 public domain books from the following horror fiction authors: *Edgar Allan Poe (EAP), HP Lovecraft (HPL),* and *Mary Shelley (MS)*. We train on written texts from *EAP* and *HPL* while treating texts from *MS* as novel.
- Web of Science dataset [35]: This dataset contains 5,736 published papers sorted into eleven categories organized under three main categories. We use two of the main categories as known classes, while the third as a novel class.
- BBC sports dataset: This dataset contains 737 documents from the BBC Sport website, divided into five sports article categories and collected between 2004 to 2005. In our work, we use *"cricket"* and *"football"* as the known classes and *"rugby"* as novel.

A Case Study. To cast light on the interpretability of our scheme, we here use substrings from the 20 Newsgroup dataset, demonstrating novelty detection on a few simple cases. First, we form an indexed vocabulary set V, including all literals from the dataset. The input text is binarized based upon the index of the literals in V. For example, if a word in the text substring has been assigned index 5 in V, the 5th position of the input vector is set to 1. If a word is absent from the substring, its corresponding feature is set to 0. Let us consider substrings from the two known classes and the novel class from the 20 Newsgroup dataset.

- **Class:** comp.graphics (known)
  Text: Presentations are solicited on all aspects of Navy-related scientific visualization and virtual reality.
  Literals: *"Presentations"*, *"solicited"*, *"aspects"*, *"Navy"*, *"related"*, *"scientific"*, *"visualization"*, *"virtual"*, *"reality"*.
- **Class:** talk.politics.guns (known)
  Text: Last year the US suffered almost 10,000 wrongful or accidental deaths by handguns alone. In the same year, the UK suffered 35 such deaths.
  Literals: *"Last"*, *"year"*, *"US"*, *"suffered"*, *"wrongful"*, *"accidental"*, *"deaths"*, *"handguns"*, *"UK"*, *"suffered"*.

- **Class:** rec.sport.baseball (Novel)
  Text: The top 4 are the only true contenders in my mind. One of these 4 will definitely win the division unless it snows in Maryland.
  Literals: *"top"*, *"only"*, *"true"*, *"contenders"*, *"mind"*, *"win"*, *"division"*, *"unless"*, *"snows"*, *"Maryland"*.

After training, the two known classes form conjunctive clauses that capture literal patterns reflecting the textual content. For the above example, we get the following clauses:

- C_1^+ = *"Presentations"* ∧ *"aspects"* ∧ *"Navy"* ∧ *"scientific"* ∧ *"virtual"* ∧ *"reality"* ∧ *"year"* ∧ *"US"* ∧ *"mind"* ∧ *"division"*
- C_1^- = ¬(*"suffered"* ∧ *"accidental"* ∧ *"unless"* ∧ *"snows"*)
- C_2^+ = *"last"* ∧ *"year"* ∧ *"US"* ∧ *"wrongful"* ∧ *"deaths"* ∧ *"accidental"* ∧ *"handguns"* ∧ *"Navy"* ∧ *"snows"* ∧ *"Maryland"* ∧ *"divisions"*
- C_2^- = ¬(*"presentations"* ∧ *"solicited"* ∧ *"virtual"* ∧ *"top"* ∧ *"win"*)

Table 7. Novelty score example when known text sentence is passed to the model.

Class	C_1^+	C_1^-	C_2^+	C_2^-
Known	+6	-3	+3	-5
Novel	+2	-1	+1	-2

Table 8. Accuracy (%) of different machine learning classifiers to detect novel class in various dataset.

Dataset	DT	KNN	SVM	LR	NB	MLP
20 Newsgroup	72.5	82	78.0	72.75	69.0	**82.50**
Spooky action author	53.42	57.89	63.15	52.63	58.68	**63.15**
CMU movie	61.05	64.73	62.10	55.00	58.94	**68.68**
BBC sports	84.21	85.96	75.43	70.17	73.68	**89.47**
Web of Science	64.70	67.97	69.93	67.10	62.09	**70.37**

Table 9. ROC-AUC scores of algorithm performance (average of 10 independent experiments, highest score highlighted in bold).

Algorithms	20 Newsgroup	Spooky action author	CMU movie	BBC sports	WOS
ABOD	0.701	0.617	0.54	0.528	0.565
CBLOF	0.703	0.651	0.54	0.549	0.545
HBOS	0.715	0.64	0.51	0.641	0.56
Isolation Forest	0.70	0.632	0.529	0.543	0.567
Average KNN	0.712	0.65	0.542	0.60	0.539
LOF	0.690	0.638	0.528	0.60	0.60
One-class SVM	0.695	**0.654**	0.539	0.534	0.55
SO-GAAL	0.638	0.57	0.557	0.501	0.49
MO-GAAL	0.546	0.516	0.571	0.558	0.503
COPOD	0.721	0.634	0.533	0.65	0.56
TM framework	**0.84**	0.64	**0.62**	**0.87**	**0.78**

Table 10. Average precision of detector performance (average of 10 independent experiments, highest score highlighted in bold).

Algorithms	20 Newsgroup	Spooky action author	CMU movie	BBC sports	WOS
ABOD	0.637	0.578	0.485	0.589	0.54
CBLOF	0.635	0.619	0.483	0.608	0.53
HBOS	0.644	0.603	0.473	0.642	0.54
Isolation Forest	0.646	0.608	0.48	0.611	0.544
Average KNN	0.648	**0.623**	0.485	0.653	0.53
LOF	0.635	0.605	0.48	0.65	0.57
One-class SVM	0.633	**0.623**	0.48	0.592	0.537
SO-GAAL	0.643	0.553	0.558	0.541	0.50
MO-GAAL	0.503	0.518	0.589	0.501	0.548
COPOD	0.652	0.605	0.50	0.653	0.54
TM framework	**0.77**	0.62	**0.59**	**0.82**	**0.73**

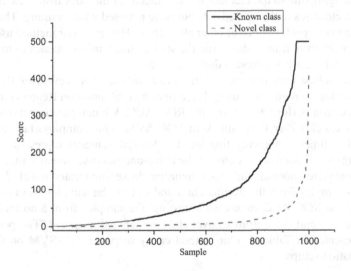

Fig. 5. Visualization of novelty score for known and novel classes [12].

Emperical Evaluation. We conducted two experiments: Novelty score generation and novelty classification. In the first experiment, we run TM for 100 epochs with hyper-parameter setting of 5000 clauses, a threshold T of 25, and a specificity s of 15.0. The score is produced using trained TM generator, where clauses votes are accumulated for the input pattern. In the second experiment, the classifiers are used on the score for novelty classification.

Table 8 shows the accuracy result from various classifiers. As seen, multilayer perceptron (MLP) (hidden layer sizes *100,30* and *ReLU* activation with stochastic gradient descent) is superior for all of the datasets. In our experiments, the 20 Newsgroups and BBC sports datasets yielded better results than the three other data sets, arguably because of the sharp distinctiveness of examples in the known and novel classes. This distinctiveness is shown in Fig. 5, where we plot and arrange the score of 1000 instances from both known and novel classes in ascending order. We observe that majority of the instances from the known class have a higher score than those belonging to the novel class. In all brevity, we believe that the clauses of a TM capture frequent patterns in the training data, and thus novel samples will emerge when they do not fit sufficiently with a large number of clauses. Thus, the number of triggered clauses can be used to calculate the novelty score. Additionally, the clauses generated by trained TM models should only to a small degree trigger on novel classes, resulting in distinctively low scores.

Table 9 and Table 10 presents the performance comparison of TM framework with other baseline algorithms. To ensure a fair comparison, the text input is preprocessed for the baseline algorithms using count vectorizer, term frequency-inverse document frequency (TF-IDF), and Principle component analysis (PCA). Additionally, for these approaches, we utilized the maximum possible outlier fraction (i.e., 0.5). Table 9 shows the ROC AUC scores for novelty detection. Our proposed method outperforms all other algorithms on four out of five datasets. Similarly, Table 10 shows the precision of detector values. Our method significantly outperforms all other methods. The novelty detection is challenging due to the fact that the validation set includes instances that exhibit similar characteristics to the trained data but were not used while training. This can be a reason for the poor performance of other algorithms. However, our method uses clauses to form a pattern from trained data. And the scoring mechanism enables us to eliminate the instances which are not present during training.

To ensure robust performance and that the results are not skewed by the data, we perform one-class classification using leave-one-out evaluation on Reuters dataset[1] and quantify detection performance using the ROC AUC. We compare our method with a strong one-class classifier, the cosine kernel OC-SVM, which employs fastText embedding with 300 dimension aggregating into fixed-length sentence representations using max-pooling over hidden activations. In the leave-one-out assessment setup, one of the classes is considered normal while the remaining classes are treated novel. We train the models on examples from the normal class and test on the samples from novel class. To compute the ROC AUC values while testing, the samples from a normal class are labeled as $y = 0$ and those from a novel class are labeled as $y = 1$. The performance result is presented in Table 11. Our method easily surpasses OC-SVM on five out of seven evaluation setups.

Table 11. ROC AUC (%) of one-class classification with leave-one-out evaluation on Reuters.

Normal class	OC-SVM	TM
earn	74.9	**86.27**
acq	80.2	**82.36**
crude	84.7	**85.5**
trade	**92.1**	91.15
money-fx	**73.8**	66
interest	82.8	**88.7**
ship	85.0	**94.4**

---

[1] http://www.daviddlewis.com/resources/testcollections/reuters21578/.

5 Conclusions

This paper proposes a universal interpretable TM framework to perform outlier and novelty detection on multiple datasets. We present a score-based TM framework that is capable of detecting both outlier and novel instances. We introduce the TM generator- a modified vanilla TM architecture, to produce a score based on the pattern learned by the clauses. Then, a machine learning classifier is adopted for classification using the scores obtained from the TM generator. We conducted comprehensive tests to evaluate the effectiveness of the TM framework using outlier and novelty datasets. Our findings demonstrate that our method is both effective and superior in both experimental setups.

In future work, we intend to explore outlier and novelty detection on high-dimension and large datasets. Additionally, a detailed experimental analysis of a text data can be added for novelty detection.

References

1. Abeyrathna, K.D., et al.: Massively parallel and asynchronous Tsetlin Machine architecture supporting almost constant-time scaling. In: The Thirty-Eighth International Conference on Machine Learning (ICML 2021) (2021)
2. Abeyrathna, K.D., Granmo, O.C., Zhang, X., Jiao, L., Goodwin, M.: The regression tsetlin machine: a novel approach to interpretable nonlinear regression. Phil. Trans. R. Soc. A **378**(2164), 20190165 (2019)
3. Achtert, E., Kriegel, H.-P., Zimek, A.: ELKI: a software system for evaluation of subspace clustering algorithms. In: Ludäscher, B., Mamoulis, N. (eds.) SSDBM 2008. LNCS, vol. 5069, pp. 580–585. Springer, Heidelberg (2008). https://doi.org/10.1007/978-3-540-69497-7_41
4. Aggarwal, C.C.: An introduction to outlier analysis. In: Outlier Analysis, pp. 1–34. Springer, Cham (2017). https://doi.org/10.1007/978-3-319-47578-3_1
5. Akcay, S., Atapour-Abarghouei, A., Breckon, T.P.: GANomaly: semi-supervised anomaly detection via adversarial training. In: Jawahar, C.V., Li, H., Mori, G., Schindler, K. (eds.) ACCV 2018. LNCS, vol. 11363, pp. 622–637. Springer, Cham (2019). https://doi.org/10.1007/978-3-030-20893-6_39
6. Banerjee, P., Yawalkar, P., Ranu, S.: Mantra: a scalable approach to mining temporally anomalous sub-trajectories. In: Proceedings of the 22nd ACM SIGKDD International Conference on Knowledge Discovery and Data Mining, pp. 1415–1424 (2016)
7. Basu, S., Bilenko, M., Mooney, R.J.: A probabilistic framework for semi-supervised clustering. In: Proceedings of the Tenth ACM SIGKDD International Conference on Knowledge Discovery and Data Mining, pp. 59–68 (2004)
8. Bendale, A., Boult, T.E.: Towards open set deep networks. In: The IEEE Conference on Computer Vision and Pattern Recognition (CVPR) (2016)
9. Bendale, A., Boult, T.E.: Towards open set deep networks. In: Proceedings of the IEEE Conference on Computer Vision and Pattern Recognition, pp. 1563–1572 (2016)
10. Berge, G.T., Granmo, O.C., Tveit, T.O., Goodwin, M., Jiao, L., Matheussen, B.V.: Using the tsetlin machine to learn human-interpretable rules for high-accuracy text categorization with medical applications. IEEE Access **7**, 115134–115146 (2019)
11. Bhattarai, B., Granmo, O.C., Jiao, L.: Explainable tsetlin machine framework for fake news detection with credibility score assessment. arXiv preprint arXiv:2105.09114 (2021)

12. Bhattarai, B., Granmo, O.C., Jiao, L.: Measuring the novelty of natural language text using the conjunctive clauses of a tsetlin machine text classifier. In: Proceedings of the 13th International Conference on Agents and Artificial Intelligence - Volume 2: ICAART, pp. 410–417 (2021)
13. Bhattarai, B., Granmo, O.C., Jiao, L.: Word-level human interpretable scoring mechanism for novel text detection using Tsetlin Machines (2021). https://doi.org/10.1007/s10489-022-03281-1. arXiv preprint arXiv:2105.04708
14. Breunig, M.M., Kriegel, H.P., Ng, R.T., Sander, J.: Lof: identifying density-based local outliers. In: Proceedings of the 2000 ACM SIGMOD International Conference on Management of Data, pp. 93–104 (2000)
15. Campos, G.O., et al.: On the evaluation of unsupervised outlier detection: measures, datasets, and an empirical study. Data Min. Knowl. Disc. 30(4), 891–927 (2016). https://doi.org/10.1007/s10618-015-0444-8
16. Chandola, V., Banerjee, A., Kumar, V.: Anomaly detection: a survey. ACM Comput. Surv. (CSUR) 41(3), 1–58 (2009)
17. Cohen, G., Sax, H., Geissbuhler, A., et al.: Novelty detection using one-class parzen density estimator. An application to surveillance of nosocomial infections. In: Mie, pp. 21–26 (2008)
18. Craswell, N.: Precision at n. In: Encyclopedia of Database Systems (2009). https://doi.org/10.1007/978-0-387-39940-9_484
19. Duan, L., Xu, L., Liu, Y., Lee, J.: Cluster-based outlier detection. Ann. Oper. Res. 168(1), 151–168 (2009). https://doi.org/10.1007/s10479-008-0371-9
20. Erfani, S.M., Rajasegarar, S., Karunasekera, S., Leckie, C.: High-dimensional and large-scale anomaly detection using a linear one-class svm with deep learning. Pattern Recogn. 58, 121–134 (2016)
21. Ester, M., Kriegel, H.P., Sander, J., Xu, X., et al.: A density-based algorithm for discovering clusters in large spatial databases with noise. In: kdd, vol. 96, pp. 226–231 (1996)
22. Fei, G., Liu, B.: Social media text classification under negative covariate shift. In: Proceedings of the 2015 Conference on Empirical Methods in Natural Language Processing, pp. 2347–2356 (2015)
23. Fiore, U., De Santis, A., Perla, F., Zanetti, P., Palmieri, F.: Using generative adversarial networks for improving classification effectiveness in credit card fraud detection. Inf. Sci. 479, 448–455 (2019)
24. Goldstein, M., Dengel, A.: Histogram-based outlier score (hbos): a fast unsupervised anomaly detection algorithm. KI-2012: Poster and Demo Track, pp. 59–63 (2012)
25. Goodfellow, I., et al.: Generative adversarial nets. Advances in neural information processing systems, 27 (2014)
26. Goodfellow, I., et al.: Generative adversarial networks. Commun. ACM 63(11), 139–144 (2020)
27. Granmo, O.C.: The Tsetlin machine - a game theoretic bandit driven approach to optimal pattern recognition with propositional logic. ArXiv abs/1804.01508 (2018)
28. Granmo, O.C., Glimsdal, S., Jiao, L., Goodwin, M., Omlin, C.W., Berge, G.T.: The convolutional tsetlin machine. arXiv preprint arXiv:1905.09688 (2019)
29. Hanley, J.A., McNeil, B.J.: The meaning and use of the area under a receiver operating characteristic (ROC) curve. Radiology 143(1), 29–36 (1982)
30. Hautamaki, V., Karkkainen, I., Franti, P.: Outlier detection using k-nearest neighbour graph. In: Proceedings of the 17th International Conference on Pattern Recognition, 2004. ICPR 2004, vol. 3, pp. 430–433. IEEE (2004)
31. He, Z., Xu, X., Deng, S.: Discovering cluster-based local outliers. Pattern Recogn. Lett. 24(9–10), 1641–1650 (2003)

32. Hempstalk, K., Frank, E., Witten, I.H.: One-class classification by combining density and class probability estimation. In: Daelemans, W., Goethals, B., Morik, K. (eds.) ECML PKDD 2008. LNCS (LNAI), vol. 5211, pp. 505–519. Springer, Heidelberg (2008). https://doi.org/10.1007/978-3-540-87479-9_51

33. Hendrycks, D., Gimpel, K.: A baseline for detecting misclassified and out-of-distribution examples in neural networks. arXiv preprint arXiv:1610.02136 (2016)

34. Jiao, L., Zhang, X., Granmo, O.C., Abeyrathna, K.D.: On the convergence of tsetlin machines for the XOR operator. arXiv preprint arXiv:2101.02547 (2021)

35. Kowsari, K., Brown, D., Heidarysafa, M., Meimandi, K., Gerber, M., Barnes, L.: Hdltex: hierarchical deep learning for text classification. In: 2017 16th IEEE International Conference on Machine Learning and Applications (ICMLA), pp. 364–371 (2017)

36. Kriegel, H.P., Schubert, M., Zimek, A.: Angle-based outlier detection in high-dimensional data. In: Proceedings of the 14th ACM SIGKDD International Conference on Knowledge Discovery and Data Mining, pp. 444–452 (2008)

37. Li, Z., Zhao, Y., Botta, N., Ionescu, C., Hu, X.: Copod: copula-based outlier detection. In: 2020 IEEE International Conference on Data Mining (ICDM), pp. 1118–1123. IEEE (2020)

38. Liu, F.T., Ting, K.M., Zhou, Z.H.: Isolation forest. In: 2008 Eighth IEEE International Conference on Data Mining, pp. 413–422. IEEE (2008)

39. Liu, Y., et al.: Generative adversarial active learning for unsupervised outlier detection. IEEE Trans. Knowl. Data Eng. 32(8), 1517–1528 (2019)

40. Mao, J., Wang, T., Jin, C., Zhou, A.: Feature grouping-based outlier detection upon streaming trajectories. IEEE Trans. Knowl. Data Eng. 29(12), 2696–2709 (2017)

41. Radovanović, M., Nanopoulos, A., Ivanović, M.: Reverse nearest neighbors in unsupervised distance-based outlier detection. IEEE Trans. Knowl. Data Eng. 27(5), 1369–1382 (2014)

42. Ramaswamy, S., Rastogi, R., Shim, K.: Efficient algorithms for mining outliers from large data sets. In: Proceedings of the 2000 ACM SIGMOD International Conference on Management of Data, pp. 427–438 (2000)

43. Rebuffi, S.A., Kolesnikov, A., Sperl, G., Lampert, C.H.: icarl: incremental classifier and representation learning. In: Proceedings of the IEEE Conference on Computer Vision and Pattern Recognition, pp. 2001–2010 (2017)

44. Saha, R., Granmo, O.-C., Goodwin, M.: Mining interpretable rules for sentiment and semantic relation analysis using tsetlin machines. In: Bramer, M., Ellis, R. (eds.) SGAI 2020. LNCS (LNAI), vol. 12498, pp. 67–78. Springer, Cham (2020). https://doi.org/10.1007/978-3-030-63799-6_5

45. Salehi, M., Leckie, C., Bezdek, J.C., Vaithianathan, T., Zhang, X.: Fast memory efficient local outlier detection in data streams. IEEE Trans. Knowl. Data Eng. 28(12), 3246–3260 (2016)

46. Scheirer, W.J., de Rezende Rocha, A., Sapkota, A., Boult, T.E.: Toward open set recognition. IEEE Trans. Pattern Anal. Mach. Intell. 35(7), 1757–1772 (2012)

47. Schlegl, T., Seeböck, P., Waldstein, S.M., Schmidt-Erfurth, U., Langs, G.: Unsupervised anomaly detection with generative adversarial networks to guide marker discovery. In: Niethammer, M., Styner, M., Aylward, S., Zhu, H., Oguz, I., Yap, P.-T., Shen, D. (eds.) IPMI 2017. LNCS, vol. 10265, pp. 146–157. Springer, Cham (2017). https://doi.org/10.1007/978-3-319-59050-9_12

48. Schölkopf, B., Platt, J.C., Shawe-Taylor, J., Smola, A.J., Williamson, R.C.: Estimating the support of a high-dimensional distribution. Neural Comput. 13(7), 1443–1471 (2001)

49. Tang, J., Ngan, H.Y.: Traffic outlier detection by density-based bounded local outlier factors. Inf. Technol. Ind. 4(1) (2016)

50. Tang, J., Chen, Z., Fu, A.W., Cheung, D.W.: Enhancing effectiveness of outlier detections for low density patterns. In: Chen, M.-S., Yu, P.S., Liu, B. (eds.) PAKDD 2002. LNCS (LNAI),

vol. 2336, pp. 535–548. Springer, Heidelberg (2002). https://doi.org/10.1007/3-540-47887-6_53

51. Tax, D.M., Duin, R.P.: Support vector data description. Mach. Learn. **54**(1), 45–66 (2004)

52. Yadav, R.K., Jiao, L., Granmo, O.C., Goodwin, M.: Distributed word representation in Tsetlin Machine. arXiv preprint arXiv:2104.06901 (2021)

53. Yadav, R.K., Jiao, L., Granmo, O.C., Goodwin, M.: Human-level interpretable learning for aspect-based sentiment analysis. In: The Thirty-Fifth AAAI Conference on Artificial Intelligence (AAAI-21) (2021)

54. Zhang, J.: Advancements of outlier detection: a survey. ICST Trans. Scalable Inf. Syst. **13**(1), 1–26 (2013)

55. Zhang, L., et al.: Probabilistic-mismatch anomaly detection: do one's medications match with the diagnoses. In: 2016 IEEE 16th International Conference on Data Mining (ICDM), pp. 659–668. IEEE (2016)

56. Zhang, X., Jiao, L., Granmo, O.C., Goodwin, M.: On the convergence of tsetlin machines for the identity-and not operators. In: IEEE Transactions on Pattern Analysis and Machine Intelligence (2021)

57. Zhang, Y., Meratnia, N., Havinga, P.: Outlier detection techniques for wireless sensor networks: a survey. IEEE Commun. Surv. Tutorials **12**(2), 159–170 (2010)

58. Zhao, Y., Nasrullah, Z., Li, Z.: Pyod: a python toolbox for scalable outlier detection. J. Mach. Learn. Res. **20**, 1–7 (2019)

Adding Supply/Demand Imbalance-Sensitivity to Simple Automated Trader-Agents

Dave Cliff$^{(\boxtimes)}$ ⓘ, Zhen Zhang ⓘ, and Nathan Taylor ⓘ

Department of Computer Science, University of Bristol, Bristol BS8 1UB, UK
csdtc@bristol.ac.uk, zhangzhen@enactusunnc.org

Abstract. In most major financial markets nowadays very many of the participants are "robot traders", autonomous adaptive software agents empowered to
buy and sell quantities of tradeable assets, such as stocks and shares, currencies, and commodities; in the past two decades such robots have largely replaced
human traders at the point of execution. This paper addresses the question of how
to make minimally simple robot traders sensitive to any imbalance between supply and demand that may occur in the market in the course of a trading session.
Such imbalances typically are transient, and their occurrence is unpredictable, but
when they do arise any human traders would automatically shift the prices that
they quote, to reflect their expectations (grounded in basic microeconomics) that
a momentary excess supply is an indication that prices are about to fall, while
an excess demand is an indication that prices are about to rise. This can result in
prices moving against a trader that is attempting to buy or sell a large quantity
of some asset. In this paper we describe our work on exploring the use of *multi-
level order-flow imbalance* (MLOFI) as a usefully robust instantaneous measure of
supply/demand imbalance, and we show how MLOFI can be used to give simple
robot traders an *opinion* about where prices are heading in the immediate future,
which mean that our imbalance-sensitive trading robots can serve as a platform
for experimental study of issues arising in Nobel laureate Robert Shiller's recent
work on *Narrative Economics*.

Keywords: Market impact · Adaptive trader agents · Financial markets ·
Multi-agent systems

1 Introduction

In recent years Nobel prize-winner Robert Shiller has introduced [32] and popularised
[33] the notion of *narrative economics* in which economic phenomena that defy explanation by conventional approaches can be better understood by reference to the *narratives* (i.e. the stories, the commentaries) told and believed by economic agents within
the system of interest. As an example, in [33] Shiller argues that the stratospheric rise
in price of cryptocurrencies like Bitcoin (which, by conventional economic analyses,
should arguably be valueless) can be explained as a consequence of the stories that people tell each other, and themselves believe, about the future prospects of the currency as
an investment. In the simplest case, a positive feedback loop of self-fulfilling prophecies

© Springer Nature Switzerland AG 2022
A. P. Rocha et al. (Eds.): ICAART 2021, LNAI 13251, pp. 269–293, 2022.
https://doi.org/10.1007/978-3-031-10161-8_15

can occur where everyone involved in the market convinces themselves that the price is set to rise, and so they seek to purchase more of the asset, and their enthusiasm draws in more buyers, and the consequent excess of demand over supply results in the price going up; this price increase then further confirms the beliefs of the market participants and draws additional in new buyers, and so the loop cycles around with the price rising on each iteration. Such economic "manias"' have long been documented (see e.g. [24]), but Shiller's analysis goes into greater depth, drawing analogies between the spread of narratives through the population of agents involved in some market, and the spread of infected individuals in a population of organisms experiencing an epidemic (or indeed a pandemic); and Shiller calls for new empirical research to track the spread of narratives (e.g. in online news and social media posts), and the changing nature of the narratives themselves (i.e., how the stories people tell each other change over time, creating new variants, in much the same was a mutations in a pathogen also create new variants).

In their 2021 prize-winning ICAART paper, Lomas & Cliff [25], showed how agent-based models (ABMs) could be used to study narrative economics, as an alternative to the empirical approach laid out by Shiller. Lomas & Cliff noted that a narrative, a story, is merely the external expression of an *opinion*, and there is a long-standing research theme in the social science simulation research literature that aims to understand how individuals in a population might influence others to change their opinion, or might themselves alter their own opinion as a result of interaction with other individuals: this field, known as *opinion dynamics* (OD) has seen the development of several notable models over the past 25 years, and Lomas & Cliff showed how these OD models could be integrated into agent-based models of contemporary automated financial markets in which traders buy and sell some asset by posting orders to an automated central exchange (such as a real-world stock-exchange, or a cryptocurrency trading website). The key innovation in Lomas & Cliff's work was that each trader-agent in their automated markets would determine the price that it was willing to buy or sell at by taking account of its opinion, and its opinion could be affected by 'social' interactions with other traders in the market, via one of the established OD models. Although there is a long tradition of agent-based models of financial markets (see e.g. [5,11,23,39]), Lomas & Cliff were the first to integrate opinions into such market models.

And, although the OD literature is extensive, almost all of it explores models in which the opinions being held and altered by each agent are abstract and have no external reference that could establish whether a specific opinion is actually correct or not (e.g. the opinions could be about politics, or religion – topics on which people hold deeply-felt personal opinions, each believing their own opinion to be true, but for which there is no single objectively correct opinion); because of the abstract nature of the agents' opinions, many simulation experiments in OD research start by randomly assigning initial opinions to each agent, using draws from a distribution over the entire range of possible opinions. In much of the most widely referenced OD work, such as the Bounded Confidence (BC) model [22], the Relative Agreement (RA) model [16,27], and the Relative Disagreement (RD) model [28], each agent in the ABM holds a single opinion that is represented as a real-valued number in the range $[-1, +1]$.

Lomas & Cliff's work is different from much of the existing OD literature because the trader-agents' opinions about the future price of an asset cannot sensibly be initialised by random assignments over the space of all possible prices. Furthermore, in Lomas & Cliff's work, an agent's opinion about whether the price of an asset will fall or rise in the immediate future can subsequently be established as either true or false, because either the price later really did go up, or it really did not. That is, the agents in Lomas & Cliff's model hold opinions about something that they can later shown to be wrong about: this also is unusual within the OD literature.

In this paper, we explore methods by which trader-agents in an automated market can reliable be given a means of forming an opinion about near-term movements in the price of an asset traded on the market. Technically, because the price is the only distinguishing variable about units of an asset, it is a *commodity*, but the model market used here is a close approximation of what happens in any major real-world financial market (in which, for example, individual share certificates are also, technically, commodity goods – because if I am selling one share of Apple Inc at $148, while you are selling one AAPL at $150, an interested buyer would distinguish between your share and my share purely on the basis of price).

Unsurprisingly, opinions about near-term movements in the price of an asset traded on an exchange are very important in real-world financial markets, which have seen an explosive prevalence of automated trading systems being installed and replacing human traders over the past 20 years. Financial markets populated by human traders often exhibit so-called *market impact*, where the prices quoted by traders shift in the direction of anticipated change, as a reaction to the arrival of a large (i.e., "block") buy or sell order for a particular asset: that is, mere knowledge of the presence of the block order is enough to trigger a change in the traders' quote-prices, before any transaction has actually taken place, because the traders know that a block buy order is likely to push the price of the asset up, and a block sell order is likely to push the price down, and so they adjust their quote-prices accordingly, in anticipation of the shift in price that they foresee coming as a consequence of the block-trade completing. This is bad news for the trader trying to buy or sell a block order: the moment she reveals her intention to buy a block, the market-price goes up; the moment she reveals her intention to sell, the price goes down. From the perspective of a block-trader, the market price *moves against her*, whether she is buying or selling, and this happens not because of the *price* she is quoting, but because of the *quantity* that she is attempting to transact.

Block-traders' collective desire to avoid market impact has long driven the introduction of automated trading techniques such as "VWAP engines" (which break block orders into a sequence of smaller sub-orders that are released into the market over a set period of time, with the intention of achieving a specific volume-weighted average price, hence VWAP), and has also driven the design of major new electronic exchanges such as London Stock Exchange's (LSE's) *Turquoise Plato* trading venue [26], in which block-traders are allowed to obscure the size of their blocks in a so-called *dark pool* market, with LSE's automated matching engine identifying one or more willing counterparties and only making full details of the block-trade known to all market participants after it has completed: see [30] for further discussion.

Many of the world's major financial markets now have very high levels of automated trading: in such markets most of the participants, the traders, are "robots" rather than humans: i.e., software systems for automated trading, empowered with the same legal sense of agency as a human trader, and hence "software agents" in the most literal sense of that phrase. Given that these software agents typically replace more than one human trader, and given that those human traders were widely regarded to have required a high degree of intelligence (and remuneration) to work well in a financial market, it is clear that the issue of designing well-performing robot traders presents challenges for research in agents *and* artificial intelligence, and hence is a research topic that is central to the themes of the ICAART conference.

This paper addresses the question of best how to give robot traders an appropriate anticipatory sensitivity to large orders, such that markets populated entirely by robot traders also show market-impact effects. This is desirable because the impact-sensitive robot traders will get a better price for their transactions when block orders do arrive, and also because simulated markets populated by impact-sensitive automated traders can be studied to explore the pros and cons of various impact-mitigation or avoidance techniques. We show here that well-known and long-established trader-agent strategies can be extended by giving them appropriately robust sensitivity to the imbalance between buy and sell orders issued by traders on the exchange, orders that are aggregated on the market's limit order-book (LOB), the data-structure at the heart of most electronic exchanges.

To the best of our knowledge, the first paper to report on the use of an imbalance metric to give ABM automated traders impact-sensitivity was the 2019 publication by Church & Cliff [6], in which they demonstrated how a minimal nonadaptive trader-agent called *Shaver* (which, following the convention of practice in this field, is routinely referred to in abbreviated form via a psuedo-ticker-symbol: "SHVR") could be extended to show impact effects by addition of an imbalance metric, and Church & Cliff gave the name *ISHV* to their Imbalance-SHVR trader-agent [6]. SHVR is a trader-agent strategy built-in to the popular open-source financial exchange simulator called BSE [2], which Church & Cliff used as the platform for their research. Although Church & Cliff deserve some credit for the proof-of-concept that ISHV provides, we argue here that the imbalance-metric they employed is too fragile for practical purposes because very minor changes in the supply and demand can cause their metric to swing wildly between the extremes of its range. One of the major contributions of our paper here (which is revised and extended from [44][1] is the demonstration that a much better, more robust, metric known as *multi-level order-flow imbalance* (MLOFI) can be used instead of the comparatively very fragile metric proposed by Church & Cliff. Another major contribution of this paper is our demonstration of the addition of MLOFI-based impact-sensitivity to the very well-known and widely cited public-domain adaptive trader-agent strategies ZIP [8] and AA [40,41]. Although our primary aim was to add impact sensitivity to these two machine-learning-based trader-agent strategies, we also demonstrate in this paper that ISHV can be altered/extended to use MLOFI, and our improvement of Church & Cliff's work in that regard is an additional contribution of this paper.

The extended versions of the AA, ZIP, and ISHV trader-agent strategies that we introduce here are named ZZIAA, ZZIZIP, and ZZISHV respectively. In this paper,

---

[1] The primary extensions of the present paper, relative to its progenitor [44], are that Sect. 1 has been rewritten, all results in Figs. 5, 6 and 7 have been freshly re-generated, and all of Sect. 3.2 is newly added.

after our criticism of Church & Cliff's methods, we describe a more mathematically sophisticated approach to measuring imbalance, which is more robust, and which we incorporate into our agent extensions. We then present results from testing our extended trader-agents on BSE, the same platform that was used in Church & Cliff's work. Full details of the work reported here are available in [46], and all the relevant source-code has been made freely available on *GitHub* [45].

Section 2 of this paper presents an overview of relevant background material: this is repeated verbatim from [44] and readers already familiar with automated trading systems, contemporary electronic financial exchanges, and the mathematics of order-flow imbalance, can safely skip ahead straight to Sect. 3. In Sect. 3 we describe the steps taken to add MLOFI-based impact-sensitivity to ZIP, AA, ISHV, and PRZI; and illustrative results from ABMs populated by those extended trading algorithms are presented.

2 Prior Work

2.1 Automated Traders

Since the mid-1990s researchers in universities and in the research labs of major corporations such as IBM and Hewlett-Packard have published details of various strategies for autonomous trader-agents, often incorporating AI and/or machine learning (ML) methods so that the automated trader can adapt its behaviors to prevailing market conditions. Notable trading strategies in this body of literature include: Kaplan's "Sniper" strategy [31]; Gode & Sunder's ZIC [20]; the ZIP strategy developed at Hewlett-Packard [8]; the GD strategy reported by Gjerstad & Dickhaut [19] the MGD and GDX strategies developed by IBM researchers [37,38]; Gjerstad's HBL [18]; Duffy & Unver's NZI [17]; Vytelingum's AA [40,41]; the Roth-Erev approach (see e.g. [29]); Arifovic & Ledyard's IEL [1]; and the recently-introduced PRZI [7], described further in Sect. 3.2. However, for reasons discussed at length in a recent review of key papers in the field [34] this sequence of publications concentrated on the issue of developing trading strategies for orders where the quantities were all in the same order of magnitude (and often, where the quantity was fixed at one, a single unit per order). That is, *none* of the key papers listed here deal with trading strategies for outsize block orders, and none of them directly explore the issue of how an automated trader can best deal with, or avoid, market impact.

Trader-agent strategies such as Sniper, ZIC, ZIP, GD and MGD were all developed to operate in electronic markets that were based on old-school open-outcry trading pits, as were common on major financial exchanges until face-to-face human-to-human bargaining was replaced by negotiation of trades via electronic communication media; but more recent work has concentrated on developing trading agents that issue bids and asks (i.e. quotations for orders to buy or to sell) to a centralised electronic exchange (such as a major stock-market like NYSE or NASDAQ or LSE) where the exchange's *matching engine* then either matches the trader's quote with a willing counterparty (in which case a transaction is recorded between the two counterparties, the buyer and the seller) or the quote is added to a data-structure called the *Limit Order Book* (LOB) that is maintained by the exchange and published to all traders whenever it changes. The LOB aggregates and anonymises all outstanding orders: it has two sides or halves: the bid-side and the ask-side. Each side of the book shows a summary of all outstanding orders, arranged from best to worst: this means that the bid-side is arranged in descending price-order, and the ask side is arranged in ascending price-order, such that at the "top of the book" on the two sides the best bid and ask are visible. For all orders currently sat on the LOB, if there are multiple orders at the same price then the quantities of those orders are aggregated together, and often multiple orders at the same price will be later matched with a counterparty in a sequence given by the orders' arrival times, in a first-in-first-out fashion. The public LOB shows only, for each side of the book, the prices at which orders have been lodged with the exchange, and the total quantity available at each of those prices: if no orders are resting at the exchange for a particular price, then that price is usually omitted from the LOB rather than being shown with a corresponding quantity of zero. Illustrations of LOBs appear later in this paper.

The difference between the price of the best bid on the LOB at time t and the price of the best ask at t is known as the *spread*. The mid-point of the spread (i.e. the arithmetic mean of the best bid and the best ask) is known as the *mid-price* which is denoted here by P_{mid}. The mid-price is very commonly used as a single-valued statistic to summarise the current state of the market, and as an estimate of what the next transaction price would be. However, the midprice pays no attention to the quantities that are bid and offered. If the current best bid is for a quantity of one at a price of $10 and the current best ask is for a quantity of 200 at a price of $20 then the mid-price is $15 but that fails to capture that there is a much larger quantity being offered than being bid: basic microeconomics, the theory of supply and demand, would tell even the most casual observer that with such heavy selling pressure then actual transaction prices are likely to trend down – in which case the mid-price of $15 is likely to be an overestimate of the next transaction price. Similarly, if the bid and ask prices remain the same but the *imbalance* between supply and demand is instead reversed, then the fact that there is a revealed desire for 200 units to be purchased but only one unit on sale at the current best ask would surely be a reasonable indication that transaction prices are likely to be pushed up by buying pressure, in which case the mid-price of $15 will turn out to be an underestimate. This lack of quantity-sensitivity in the mid-price calculation leads many market practitioners to instead monitor the *micro-price*, denoted here by P_{micro}, which is a quantity-weighted average of the best bid and best ask prices, and which does move in the direction indicated by imbalances between supply and demand at the top of the LOB: see, e.g., [4].

To the best of our knowledge the first impact-sensitive ABM trader-agent was *ISHV* [6]. ISHV is based on the *SHVR* trader built into the popular *BSE* public-domain financial-market simulator [2,9]. A SHVR trader simply posts the buy/sell order with its price set one penny higher/lower than the current best bid/ask. This single instruction gives it a parasitic nature, in the sense that it can mimic the price-convergence behaviour of other strategies being used by other traders in the market.

Instead of shaving the best bid or offer by one penny, Church & Cliff's ISHV trader instead chooses to shave by an amount Δ_s which varies with Δ_m defined in Eq. 1:

$$\Delta_m = P_{\text{micro}} - P_{\text{mid}} \tag{1}$$

The difference of the micro-price and the mid-price can identify the degree of supply/demand imbalance to a useful extent. If $\Delta_m \approx 0$, there is no obvious imbalance in the market. If $\Delta_m < 0$, then the quantities of the best bid and the best offer on the LOB indicate that supply exceeds demand and the subsequent transactions prices are likely to decrease; whereas $\Delta_m > 0$ indicates that demand outweighs supply and subsequent transaction prices will have an upward tendency.

Church & Cliff give pseudocode for ISHV in [6] and source-code for a Python implementation is freely available at [2]. ISHV implements a function that maps from Δ_m to Δ_s to determine how much it will shave off its price. For an ISHV buyer, if $\Delta_m < 0$, SHVR 'predicts' the price will shift in its favour and shaves its price as little as possible (the exchange's minimum tick-size Δ_p – often one penny or one cent – is chosen as the value for Δ_s): we might say that in this situation SHVR is *relaxed* However, if $\Delta_m > 0$, ISHV 'predicts' that later prices will be worse and so it attempts to shave a large amount off, using $\Delta_s = C\Delta_p + M\Delta_m\Delta_p$, where C and M are two constants that determine the SHVR's response to the imbalance (they are the y-intersect and gradient for a linear response function; nonlinear response functions could be used instead): in such a situation we might say that SHRV is *urgent*. The algorithm for an ISHV seller is the same *mutatis mutandis*. Church & Cliff showed that ISHV can identify and respond appropriately to the presence of a block order signal at the top of the LOB.

2.2 Critique of Church & Cliff

Church & Cliff were careful to flag their ISHV trader as only a proof-of-concept (PoC): ISHV was developed to enable the study of coupled lit/dark trading polls such as LSE *Turquoise Plato* system in commercial operation in London, as mentioned in the Introduction to this paper. Without impact-sensitive trader-agents, it is not possible to build agent-based models of contemporary real-world trading venues such as LSE Turquoise Plato. Having experimented further with Church & Cliff's PoC system, we came to realise that there are severe limitations in ISHV: these limitations stem from the fact that Eq. 1, which is at the heart of ISHV, uses values *only found at the top of the LOB*: Eq. 1 involves only the price and quantity of the best bid and the best ask. As we will demonstrate in the next section, this makes the method introduced by Church & Cliff so fragile that it is unlikely to be usable in anything but the simplest of simulation studies; as we show in the next section, for real-world markets it is necessary to look deeper into the LOB, to delve below the top of the LOB.

For brevity, we will limit ourselves here to presenting a qualitative illustrative example which demonstrates how wildly fragile the Church & Cliff method is. For a longer and more detailed discussion, see Chap. 3 of [46].

Consider a situation in which the top of the LOB has a best bid price of $10 and a best ask price of $20, as before, and where the quantity at the best bid is 200 and at the best ask is 1. As we explained in the previous section, this huge imbalance between supply and demand at the top of the book indicate that the excess demand is likely to push transaction prices up in the immediate future. Church & Cliff's ISHV does the right thing in this situation.

Now consider what happens if the next order to arrive at the exchange is a bid for $11 at a quantity of 1. Because this fresh bid is at a higher price than the current best bid, it is inserted at the top of the bid-side of the LOB. The previous best-bid, for 200 at

$10, gets shuffled down to the second layer of the LOB. At that point, the best bid and the best ask each show a quantity of one, and so ISHV acts as if there is no imbalance in the market, despite the fact when viewing *the whole LOB* it is clear that the quantity bid is now 201 (i.e. 1 at \$11 and 200 at \$10) while the ask quantity is still only 1: if anything, the imbalance has *increased* but ISHV reacts as if it had *disappeared* because ISHV looks only at the top of the LOB.

There is more that could be said, but this should be enough to convince the reader that any impact-sensitive trader-agent algorithm that looks only at the data at the top of the LOB is surely going to get it wrong very often, because it is ignoring the supply and demand information, the quantities and the prices, which lie deeper in the LOB. What we introduce in the rest of this paper addresses this problem.

2.3 Measuring Imbalance

A reliable metric is needed to capture the quantity imbalance between the supply side and the demand side, at multiple levels in the LOB (i.e., not just the top) and which can quantitatively indicate how much the imbalance will affect the market. We first discuss the Order-Flow Imbalance (OFI) metric introduced by [10] and then describe the extension of this into a reliable Multi-Level OFI (MLOFI) metric recently reported by [43]. After that, we show how MLOFI can be used to give robust impact-sensitivity to ISHV [6], AA [40,41], and ZIP [8]. AA and ZIP are of particular interest because in previous papers published at IJCAI and at ICAART it was demonstrated that these two strategies can each reliably outperform human traders [12–15].

Order Flow Imbalance (OFI). Cont *et al.* argued that previous studies modelling impact are extremely complex, and that instead a single factor, the order flow imbalance (OFI), can adequately explain the impact ($R^2 = 67\%$ in their research) [10]. They indicated that OFI has a positive linear relation with mid-price changes, and that the market depth D is inversely proportional to the scope of the relationship. OFI means the net order flow at the bid-side and the ask-side, and the market depth, D, represents the size at each bid/ask quote price.

To calculate the OFI they focused on the "Level 1 order book", i.e. the best bid and ask at the top of the LOB. Between any two events ($event_n$ and $event_{n-1}$), only one change happens in the LOB (check the condition from top to bottom, and from left to right; in other words, we should compare the change of price first and if the price does not change, then compare the change of quantity). Using $D \uparrow$ and $D \downarrow$ to respectively denote an increase and a reduction in demand; and $S \uparrow$ and $S \downarrow$ to denote an increase/decrease in supply, Cont et al. had:

$$p_n^b > p_{n-1}^b \vee q_n^b > q_{n-1}^b \implies D \uparrow$$
$$p_n^b < p_{n-1}^b \vee q_n^b < q_{n-1}^b \implies D \downarrow$$
$$p_n^a < p_{n-1}^a \vee q_n^a > q_{n-1}^a \implies S \uparrow$$
$$p_n^a > p_{n-1}^a \vee q_n^a < q_{n-1}^a \implies S \downarrow$$

where p^b is the best bid price; q^b the size of the best bid price; p^a the best ask price; and q^a the size of the best ask price. The variable e_n is defined to measure this tick change between two events, ($event_n$ and $event_{n-1}$), shown in Eq. 2, where I can be regarded as a Boolean variable.

$$e_n = I_{\{p_n^b > p_{n-1}^b\}} q_n^b - I_{\{p_n^b \le p_{n-1}^b\}} q_{n-1}^b$$
$$-I_{\{p_n^a < p_{n-1}^a\}} q_n^a + I_{\{p_n^a \ge p_{n-1}^a\}} q_{n-1}^a \tag{2}$$

The rules for I are as follows, and only one of them will happen between any two consecutive events:

1. if p^b increases, $e_n = q_n^b$
2. if p^b decreases, $e_n = -q_{n-1}^b$
3. if p^a increases, $e_n = q_{n-1}^a$
4. if p^a decreases, $e_n = -q_n^a$
5. if p^b remains same and $q_n^b \ne q_{n-1}^b$, $e_n = q_n^b - q_{n-1}^b$
6. if p^a remains same and $q_n^a \ne q_{n-1}^a$, $e_n = q_{n-1}^a - q_n^a$

If $N(t_k)$ is the number of events during $[0, t_k]$, then OFI_k refers to the cumulative effect of e_n that has occurred over the time interval $[t_k - 1, t_k]$, as shown in Eq. 3.

$$OFI_k = \sum_{n=N(t_{k-1})+1}^{N(t_k)} e_n \tag{3}$$

After this, a linear regression equation can be built, per Eq. 4, where $\Delta P_k = (P_k - P_{k-1})/\delta$ and δ is the tick size (1 cent in Cont et al.'s experiments), β is the price impact coefficient, and ε_k is the noise term mainly caused by contributions from lower levels of the LOB:

$$\Delta P_k = \beta OFI_k + \varepsilon_k \tag{4}$$

Moreover, Cont et al. stated that the market depth, D, is an important contributing factor to the fluctuations, and is inversely proportional to mid-price changes. They defined the average market depth, AD_k, in the "Level 1 order book" as shown in Eq. 5; and β can be measured by AD_k, shown in Eq. 6, where λ and c are constants and v_k is a noise term.

$$AD_k = \frac{1}{2(N(T_k) - N(T_k) - 1)} \sum_{N(T_{k-1})+1}^{N(T_k)} (q_n^B + q_n^A) \tag{5}$$

$$\beta_k = \frac{c}{AD_k^\lambda} + v_k \tag{6}$$

Given Eqs. 4 and 6, the relationship between ΔP and OFI and AD is constructed as seen in Eq. 7, according to which, Cont et al. ran the linear regression by using the 21-trading-day data from 50 randomly chosen US stocks, and the average $R^2 = 67\%$. They demonstrated that OFI is positive in relation to the change of mid-price. If $OFI > 0$, meaning a net inflow on the bid side or a net outflow on the ask side, the mid-price has a significantly increasing momentum, and the higher OFI is, the more the mid-price will increase. Conversely, if $OFI < 0$, meaning a net outflow on the bid side or a net inflow on the ask side, the mid-price has a significantly decreasing momentum, and the lower OFI is, the more the mid-price will decrease.

$$\Delta P_k = \frac{c}{AD_k^\lambda} OFI_k + \epsilon_k \tag{7}$$

OFI is clearly a useful metric, but it operates only on values found at the top of the LOB, i.e. the best bid and ask. In that sense, it is as sensitive to changes at the top of the book as is the Church & Cliff Δ_m metric. Next we describe how OFI can be extended to be sensitive to values at multiple levels in the LOB, which gives us Multi-Level OFI, or MLOFI.

Multi-level Order Flow Imbalance. Fortunately, [43] demonstrated how to measure multi-level order flow imbalance (MLOFI). A quantity vector, v, is used to record the OFI at each discrete level in the LOB: see Eq. 8, where m denotes the depth of price level in the LOB. The level-m bid-price refers to the m-highest prices among bids in the LOB, and the level-m ask-price refers to the LOB's m-lowest priced asks.

$$v = \begin{pmatrix} MLOFI_1 \\ MLOFI_2 \\ ML\ddot{O}FI_m \end{pmatrix} \tag{8}$$

The time when an n_{th} event occurs is denoted by τ_n; $p_b^m(\tau_n)$ signifies the level-m bid-price; $p_a^m(\tau_n)$ denotes the level-m ask-price; $q_b^m(\tau_n)$ refers to the total quantity at the level-m bid-price, and $q_a^m(\tau_n)$ refers to the total quantity at the level-m ask-price.

Similar to the OFI defined in Sect. 2.3, the level-m OFI between two consecutive events occurring at times τ_s and τ_n ($s = n - 1$) can be calculated as follows:

$$\Delta W^m(\tau_n) = \begin{cases} q_b^m(\tau_n), & \text{if } p_b^m(\tau_n) > p_b^m(\tau_s) \\ q_b^m(\tau_n) - q_b^m(\tau_s), & \text{if } p_b^m(\tau_n) = p_b^m(\tau_s) \\ -q_b^m(\tau_m), & \text{if } p_b^m(\tau_n) < p_b^m(\tau_s) \end{cases} \tag{9}$$

and

$$\Delta V^m(\tau_n) = \begin{cases} -q_a^m(\tau_m), & \text{if } p_a^m(\tau_n) > p_a^m(\tau_s) \\ q_a^m(\tau_n) - q_a^m(\tau_s), & \text{if } p_a^m(\tau_n) = p_a^m(\tau_s) \\ q_a^m(\tau_n), & \text{if } p_a^m(\tau_n) < p_a^m(\tau_s) \end{cases} \tag{10}$$

where $\Delta W^m(\tau_n)$ measures the order flow imbalance of the bid side in the level-m and $\Delta V^m(\tau_n)$ measures the order flow imbalance of the ask side in the level-m.

From Eqs. 9 and 10, we can get the MLOFI in the level-m over the time interval $[t_k - 1, t_k]$:

$$MLOFI_k^m = \sum_{\{n | t_{k-1} < \tau_n < t_k\}} e^m(\tau_n) \tag{11}$$

where

$$e^m(\tau_n) = \Delta W^m(\tau_n) - \Delta V^m(\tau_n) \tag{12}$$

We now give four illustrative examples of the MLOFI mechanism in action: for ease of explanation, we'll only consider the 3-level OFI, and we'll assume that there is only evert one event that occurs during the time interval $[t_{k-1}, t_k]$.

Case 1: New Order at Level-1 of the LOB. Figure 1 shows the situation of the LOB at time t_{k-1}, and then the updated LOB at time t_k after a new buy order has arrived.

Limit Order Book time = t_{k-1}					Limit Order Book time = t_k			
Bid Q	Bid P	Ask P	Ask Q		Bid Q	Bid P	Ask P	Ask Q
7	90	95	3		**5**	**93**	95	3
2	87	98	5		**7**	**90**	98	5
10	82	100	1		**2**	**87**	100	1

Fig. 1. Left: the initial LOB at time t_{k-1}; Right: the updated LOB at time t_k after a new buy order has been added: details of the LOB changed as a result are highlighted in bold font. In the column headings, P stands for Price and Q stands for Quantity.

- Level-1: since $p_b^1(t_k) > p_b^1(t_{k-1})$ (i.e. 93 > 90), $MLOFI_k^1 = q_b^1(t_k) = 5$;
- Level-2: since $p_b^2(t_k) > p_b^2(t_{k-1})$ (i.e. 90 > 87), $MLOFI_k^2 = q_b^2(t_k) = 7$;
- Level-3: since $p_b^3(t_k) > p_b^3(t_{k-1})$ (i.e. 87 > 82), $MLOFI_k^3 = q_b^3(t_k) = 2$;

So, the quantity vector v_k is:

$$v_k = \begin{pmatrix} 5 \\ 7 \\ 2 \end{pmatrix} \tag{13}$$

All three numbers in v_k are positive, which indicates the upward trend of the price.

Case 2: Partial Fulfillment or Cancellation. A new sell limit order crosses the spread, or a buy limit order at the best-bid position cancels. Figure 2 shows the resultant LOB.

Limit Order Book time = t_{k-1}					Limit Order Book time = t_k			
Bid Q	Bid P	Ask P	Ask Q		Bid Q	Bid P	Ask P	Ask Q
7	90	95	3		**2**	90	95	3
2	87	98	5		2	87	98	5
10	82	100	1		10	82	100	1

Fig. 2. Left: the initial LOB at time t_{k-1}; Right: the updated LOB at time t_k after the quantity available at the best bid price is altered, either as a result of one or more sellers hitting that bid price with a total quantity of five, or five items are deleted from the LOB as a result of one or more order cancellations. Format as for Fig. 1.

Level-1: as $p_b^1(t_k) = p_b^1(t_{k-1})$ (i.e. 90 = 90), $MLOFI_k^1 = q_b^1(t_k) - q_b^1(t_{k-1})$ $= 2 - 5 = -3$;
Level-2: as $p_b^2(t_k) = p_b^2(t_{k-1})$ (i.e. 87 = 87), $MLOFI_k^2 = q_b^2(t_k) - q_b^2(t_{k-1})$ $2 - 2 = 0$;
Level-3: as $p_b^3(t_k) = p_b^3(t_{k-1})$ (i.e. 82 = 82), $MLOFI_k^2 = q_b^3(t_k) - q_b^3(t_{k-1}) = 0$;

So the quantity vector v_k is:

$$v_k = \begin{pmatrix} -3 \\ 0 \\ 0 \end{pmatrix} \tag{14}$$

where -3 at Level 1 indicates a potential downward trend for the price, because the total demand on the bid side decreases.

Case 3: Full Fulfillment or Cancellation. This is similar to Case 2, but (as illustrated in Fig. 3) assumes that all orders at Level 1 in the ask book (A_1) are transacted by an incoming buy order, or that the orders making up A_1 are cancelled. In this case, we need to consider the change on the ask side.

Limit Order Book time = t_{k-1}			
Bid Q	Bid P	Ask P	Ask Q
7	90	95	3
2	87	98	5
10	82	100	1

Limit Order Book time = t_k			
Bid Q	Bid P	Ask P	Ask Q
7	90	98	5
2	87	100	1
10	82	**105**	**7**

Fig. 3. Left: the initial LOB at time t_{k-1}; Right: the updated LOB at time t_k after the quantity available at the best ask price is entirely consumed, either as a result of one or more buyers lifting that ask price with a total quantity of three, or three items being deleted from the ask side of the LOB as a result of one or more order cancellations. The whole ask side of the LOB shifts up, revealing previously hidden sell orders at a price of 105. Format as for Fig. 1.

Here we have:

$A_1: p_a^1(t_k) > p_a^1(t_{k-1}) \implies \Delta V^1(t_k) = -q_a^1(t_{k-1}) = -3; MLOFI_k^1 = -\Delta V^1(t_k) = 3;$

$A_2: p_a^2(t_k) > p_a^2(t_{k-1}) \implies \Delta V^1(t_k) = -q_a^2(t_{k-1}) = -5; MLOFI_k^2 = -\Delta V^1(t_k) = 5;$

$A_3: p_a^3(t_k) > p_a^3(t_{k-1}) \implies \Delta V^1(t_k) = -q_b^2(t_{k-1}) = -1; MLOFI_k^3 = -\Delta V^1(t_k) = 1;$

So the quantity vector v_k shown in Eq. 15 demonstrates that if the supply reduces or a buy has sufficient interest to transact, the price tends to go up (Fig. 4).

$$v_k = \begin{pmatrix} 3 \\ 5 \\ 1 \end{pmatrix} \tag{15}$$

Limit Order Book time = t_{k-1}			
Bid Q	Bid P	Ask P	Ask Q
7	90	95	3
2	87	98	5
10	82	100	1

Limit Order Book time = t_k			
Bid Q	Bid P	Ask P	Ask Q
7	90	95	3
100	89	98	5
2	87	100	1

Fig. 4. Left: the initial LOB at time t_{k-1}; Right: the updated LOB at time t_k after a block bid order arrives, at a price that is below the current best. Format as for Fig. 1.

Case 4: New Order at Level-m of the LOB. Assuming now that a new large-sized order comes to the level-2 ask, if we only consider order flow imbalance in the top level of the LOB, we cannot detect this new block order. This is the reason why we choose to use MLOFI.

As there is no change in the level-1 bid, $MLOFI_k^1 = 0$. Because a new order comes to the second-level bid, $p_b^2(t_k) > p_b^2(t_{k-1})$ (i.e. $89 > 87$) and $MLOFI_k^2 = q_b^2(t_k) = 100$. Based on the same rule, $MLOFI_k^3 = q_b^3(t_k) = 2$. So, the quantity vector v_k is:

$$v_k = \begin{pmatrix} 0 \\ 100 \\ 2 \end{pmatrix} \qquad (16)$$

If we only care about first-level order flow imbalance, we get $OFI = 0$. However, if we consider second and third levels, we get $MLOFI_k^2 = 100$ and $MLOFI_k^3 = 2$, which indicate a huge surplus on the demand side. If a trader can obtain this information and take action accordingly, it may result in larger profits or smaller losses.

3   Adding MLOFI-Impact to Robot Traders

In our work thus far, we have explored adding MLOFI-based impact-sensitivity to Vytelingum's [40] AA trading strategy, creating an extended AA that we refer to as ZZIAA. The impact-sensitivity source-code that we developed for ZZIAA was then added to Cliff's [8] ZIP strategy, giving ZZIZIP, and to the ISHV strategy introduced by Church & Cliff [6], giving ZZISHV: how we did this, and the results we got, are described in Sect. 3.1, which is adapted from [44] and was in turn abridged from [46]. Then Sect. 3.2 describes our work on adding MLOFI-based impact sensitivity to the recently-developed PRZI strategy [7], which is adapted and abridged from [36] but was not described at all in [44].

3.1   Simple Robot Traders with Impact: AA, ZIP, and ISHV

Implementation. In this section we describe how ZZIAA is created, by the addition of MLOFI-style imbalance-sensitivity to the original AA trader strategy. Our intention for ZZIAA was to develop an "impact-sensitivity" module of code that is not deeply embedded into the original AA [40] so that, if successful, this relatively independent module could also easily be applied to other trading algorithms. For this reason we chose the Widrow-Hoff delta rule to update the quote of the ZZIAA towards an impact-sensitive quote, as shown in Eq. 17. The $p_{AA}(t+1)$ is derived from the long-term and short-term factors using the information at time t (see [40]), and $\tau(t)$ is the target price computed with consideration of MLOFI:

$$p_{IAA}(t+1) = p_{AA}(t+1) + \Delta(t) \qquad (17)$$

where

$$\Delta(t) = \beta(\tau(t) - p_{AA}(t+1)) \qquad (18)$$

and

$$\tau(t) = p_{benchmark}(t) + o_{offset}(t) \qquad (19)$$

The core of the IAA derivation is how to find $\tau(t)$, which consists of two parts, the benchmark price $p_{benchmark}(t)$ and $o_{offset}(t)$. The $p_{benchmark}(t)$ depends on whether the mid-price exists. As Eq. 20 shows, if the mid-pice is available, we can set $p_{\text{benchmark}}(t)$ as the mid-price, but if it is not, we set $p_{\text{benchmark}}(t)$ as $p_{AA}(t + 1)$, which can be obtained at time t.

$$p_{\text{benchmark}}(t) = \begin{cases} p_{\text{mid}}(t), & \text{if } \exists p_{\text{mid}} \\ p_{AA}(t+1), & \text{if } \nexists p_{\text{mid}} \end{cases} \quad (20)$$

The $o_{\text{offset}}(t)$ is derived from the MLOFI and the average depth. Assume that we consider M numbers of levels MLOFI in the LOB, shown in Eq. 21, and that each MLOFI captures the last N events shown in Eq. 22.

$$a(t) = \begin{pmatrix} \text{MLOFI}_1(t) \\ \text{MLOFI}_2(t) \\ \dots \\ \dots \\ \text{MLOFI}_M(t) \end{pmatrix} \quad (21)$$

where

$$\text{MLOFI}_M(t) = \sum_{n=1}^{N} e_n^m \quad (22)$$

We can define the average market depth for m levels in a similar way:

$$d(t) = \begin{pmatrix} \text{AD}_1(t) \\ \text{AD}_2(t) \\ \dots \\ \text{AD}_M(t) \end{pmatrix} \quad (23)$$

where:

$$\text{AD}_M(t) = \frac{1}{N} \sum_{n=1}^{N} \frac{q_{M_n}^a + q_{M_n}^b}{2} \quad (24)$$

Knowing the quantity vector $a(t)$, we need a mechanism to switch this vector to a scalar. Similar to Eq. 7, we define the offset as Eq. 25.

$$v_{\text{offset}} = \sum_{i=0}^{i=m-1} \alpha^i \frac{c * \text{MLOFI}_{(i+1)}(t)}{\text{AD}_{(i+1)}(t)} \quad (25)$$

where α is the decay factor (initialized as 0.8) and c is a constant (we use $c = 5$). Note: if $AD_m(t) = 0$, the item $\alpha^{m-1} \frac{c*\text{MLOFI}_m(t)}{\text{AD}_m(t)}$ will not be counted.

To summarise, our work extends AA by the novel introduction of prior contributions to the econometrics of LOB imbalance from Cont et al. and of Xu et al. in the following ways:

- Cont et al. and Xu et al. run linear regressions to build their model and use statistical methods to test the significance of factors. The constants such as c come from modelling real-world data. However our version does not run a linear regression and the constants such as c and α are determined based on previous studies [10,43]. We can check the model's performance by exploring different values of constants.
- In the prior work, $MLOFI_M(t)$ and $AD_M(t)$ are influenced by the events within a specified time interval. In contrast, in our work, $MLOFI_M(t)$ and $AD_M(t)$ are calculated based on the last N events that occurred in the LOB, regardless of length of the time interval between successive events.

Results. Because our MOLFI-based "impact sensitive" module added to AA was deliberately developed in a non-intrusive way, it can easily be replicated into any other algorithm. In this section we first show results from ZZIAA and then we follow those with results from adding the MLOFI module to ISHV (giving ZZISHV), and to ZIP (giving ZZIZIP). Because of space limitations, the performance comparisons shown here focus on situations where the imbalance would cause a problem for the non-imbalance sensitive versions of the trader agents – and we demonstrate that our extended trader agents are indeed superior. Extensive sets of further results are presented in [46], which demonstrate that the extended trader-agents perform the same as the unextended versions in situations where there is no imbalance to be concerned about in the LOB.

For each A:B comparison we ran 100 trials in BSE [2], the same open-source simulator of a financial exchange that was used by Church & Cliff. Each trial involved creating a market where there were N traders of type A (e.g., ZIP) and N traders of type B (e.g., ZZIZIP) who were allocated the role of buyers, and similarly N of type A and N of type B who were allocated the role of sellers. Thus one market trial involved a total of $4N$ trader-agents: for the results presented here we used $N = 10$. As is entirely commonplace in all such experimental work, buyers were issued with assignments of cash, and sellers with assignments of items to sell, and each trader was given a private *limit price*: the price below which a seller could not sell and above which a buyer could not buy. The distribution of limit prices in the market determines that market's supply and demand curves, and the intersection of those two curves indicates the *competitive equilibrium price* that transaction prices are expected to converge to.

Although very many of the previous trader-agent papers that we have cited here have monitored the *efficiency* of the traders' activity in the market, we instead monitored *profitability* (which only differs from efficiency by some constant coefficient). Each individual market trial would allow the traders to interact via the LOB-based exchange in BSE for a fixed period of time, and at the end of the session the average profit of the Type A traders would be recorded, along with the average profit of the Type B traders. In the results presented here we conducted 100 independent and identically distributed market trials for each A:B comparison, giving us 100 pairs of profitability figures. To summarise those results we plot as box-and-whisker charts the distribution of profitability values for traders of Type A, the distribution of profitability values for traders of Type B, and the distribution of profitability-difference values (i.e., for each of the 100 trials, for trial t compute the difference between the profitability of Type A traders and the profitability of Type B traders in trial i). We used the Wilcoxon-Mann-Whitney U Test to determine whether the differences we observed were significant.

ZZIAA. Figure 5 summarises the comparison data generated between AA and ZZIAA. In the U test, when comparing the ZZIAA with AA, $p = 0.007$ which meant that the profit difference between ZZIAA and AA was statistically significant.

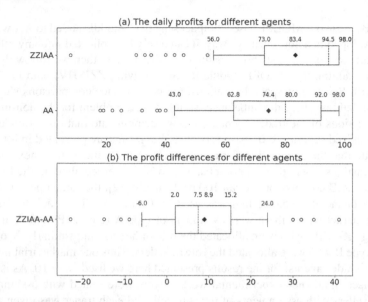

Fig. 5. Profit distributions from original AA tested against ZZIAA: upper figure shows profit data for ZZIAA and AA; lower figure shows the difference in profits calculated across paired data for the two types of agent.

Comparison of ZZISHV and ISHV. We can see from Fig. 6 that the profit generated by ZZISHV was much greater than ISHV. However, this only means that ZZISHV is better than ISHV under this particular market condition, and this might not be the case under other market conditions. In the test, the outperformance of ZZISHV can easily be explained: as a seller, when ISHV met favourable imbalances, it worked like SHVR and posted a price one penny lower than the current best ask; in contrast, under the same condition, ZZISHV chose to set price Δ_p higher than the current best ask and seek for transaction opportunities some time later. For example, assume that the current best ask is 70 and ISHV will post an order with the price equal to 69. Assume that ZZISHV gets the offset value equal to 20 from the "impact-sensitive" module, and the quoted price will be 90.

The aim of both ISHV and ZZISHV is the same: to be sensitive to imbalances in the market. The former uses a function that maps from Δ_m to Δ_s to achieve this objective and Δ_m is generated based on the mid- and micro-prices in the market. In contrast, the latter uses MLOFI to achieve the goal. The biggest difference between ISHV and ZZISHV is that ISHV can only be sensitive to imbalances at the top of the LOB and the MLOFI mechanism helps ZZISHV to be sensitive to m-level imbalances on the LOB and thus detect them earlier than ISHV in some cases. The drawback comes in determination of appropriate parameter values for both ISHV and ZZISHV, where trial-and-error is the best current option. In the map function of ISHV ($\Delta_s = C\Delta_p \pm M\Delta_m\Delta_p$ if the imbalance is significant), the parameters C and M were somewhat arbitrarily set in [6] to C = 2 and M = 1. For ZZISHV, when quantifying MLOFI, we use Eq. 25, and the key parameter c and decay factor α are artificially determined. We

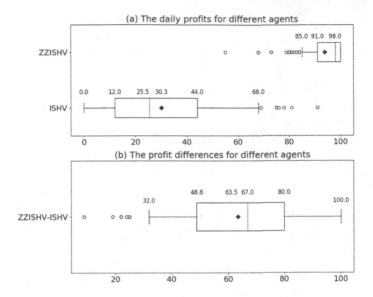

Fig. 6. Performance of ZZISHV and ISHV when facing large-sized orders from the bid side. Format as for Fig. 5.

set $m = 5$ (consistent with the result from [10]) and $\alpha = 0.8$. The optimal values of these parameters are not known; poor choices of these constants may cause agents to perform badly.

Comparison of ZZIZIP and ZIP. ZZIZIP is ZIP with the addition of the MLOFI module. In the example we present here, sellers will face an excess imbalance from the demand side. The box plots in Fig. 7 illustrate the results: ZZIZIP has less variance than ZIP and their median profitability was slightly higher than that of ZIP; in the second figure, we can see that although there were some outliers on both the top and bottom, and the bottom whisker was located below zero, the whole box was distributed beyond zero. Employing the U Test, we got $p = 0.002$ and can therefore conclude that the profit generated by ZZIZIP was statistically significantly greater than ZIP. Despite this, it is worth noting that the average difference in profitability is less than half of the difference between AA and IAA, given that other conditions remain unchanged. So, our next question is: what causes the smaller difference in profits between ZZIZIP and ZIP?

To answer this, we need to examine how ZIP works. ZIP uses the Widrow-Hoff Delta rule to update its next quote-price towards its current target price. The current target price is based on the last quote price in the market. Due to this, the last quote price affects the bidding behaviour of ZIP considerably. In this test, on the ask side, the 10 ZIP sellers were not impact-sensitive and the 10 ZZIZIP sellers were. But, although the ZIP traders were not themselves impact-sensitive, they were affected by the quote prices coming from the ZZIZIP active in the same market, and so the ZIPs' quote prices approached the ZZIZIPs' to some extent. In other words, this adaptive mechanisms

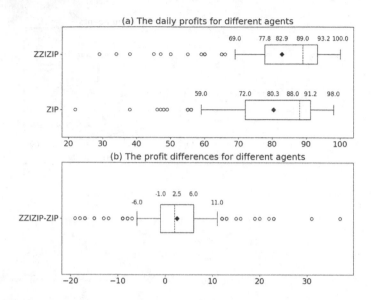

Fig. 7. Performance of ZIP and ZZIZIP when facing large-sized orders from the bid side. Format as for Fig. 5.

within the non-impact-sensitive ZIP gave it a degree of impact-sensitivity, because it was influenced by the activities of the impact-sensitive traders in the market. In the test, if we treat ZZIZIP and ZIP as a group, the average profit generated is 84.82 (95% CI: [82.16, 87.48]). If we replace 10 ZZIZIPs with 10 ZIPs (total 20 ZIP sellers), the average profit of ZIP is 79.21 (95% CI: [77.11, 81.31]). With the presence of ZZIZIP, all sellers tend to make more profit.

3.2 MLOFI Opinionated PRZI Traders for Narrative Economics

Having established in the previous section that MLOFI works well for giving autonomous trader-agents a robust sensitivity to supply/demand imbalance, we turn now to use of MLOFI in an agent-based model of a financial market in which the agents' trading activities are driven at least in part by their opinion of future events in the market, and in which agents interact with one another via two channels: posting buy/sell orders at the central financial exchange, which either result in an immediate transaction or are added to the LOB; and 'social' interactions in which agents active in the market engage in some number of pairwise interactions with one or more other agents which can result in the opinions of the interacting agents being altered via some opinion dynamics (OD) model. That is, this is where we bring things back to the narrative economics of Nobel laureate Robert Shiller [32,33], and the agent-based modelling work of Lomas & Cliff [25], all of which was discussed in the Introduction section of this paper.

In a paper released in early 2021, Cliff [7] introduced a new minimal-intelligence automated trading algorithm named *Parameterized-Response Zero Intelligence*, or

PRZI. PRZI's response is parameterized in the sense that its behavior at any one time is governed by the current value of its strategy parameter, denoted by $s \in [-1, +1] \in \mathbb{R}$. In common with many of the trading strategies reviewed in Sect. 2, a PRZI trader stochastically generates the prices for its bid or offer orders as iid draws from some random distribution. For example, Gode & Sunder's [20] ZIC strategy uses a uniform distribution bounded on one side by trader i's limit price λ_i (the price that i may not pay above when buying, or sell below when selling) and bounded on the other side by a system constant. The space of possible trading strategies that PRZI can exhibit does include ZIC, as the case when $s = 0$; but as s is moved further from zero, towards $s = \pm 1$, the shape of the PRZI trader's distribution function smoothly deforms to be skewed to the left or the right, giving rise to stochastically-generated quote-prices that are reasonable models of the trader either becoming more *urgent* in the pricing of its quotes (i.e., more likely to generate a quote-price that is attractive to potential counter-parties, so more likely to lead to a transaction, but at the cost of making less profit on the transaction when it does happen) or more *relaxed* in the pricing of its quotes (i.e., more likely to generate profit, but less attractive to the counterparty side and hence likely to result in a longer wait before a willing counterparty is found). At the absolute extremes of $s = -1$ and $s = +1$, the most urgent PRZI trading strategy is identical to the GVWY strategy introduced in [2,9] which simply generates quote price of λ_i with probability 1, maximising the chances of a transaction but offering the strong likelihood of making no profit at all; while the least urgent PRZI strategy is identical to the SHVR strategy introduced in [2,9] which simply adds one penny to the price of the best bid, or shaves one penny of the price of the best ask.

Just as Lomas & Cliff added opinions-dynamics to the pre-established ZIC [20] and NZI [17] strategies to give new *opinionated* extensions referred to as OZIC and ONZI, we add opinions to PRZI to give OPRZI. If an OPRZI trader i at time t has opinion-value $o_i(t) \in [-1, +1] \in \mathbb{R}$ then what is required is to map this onto i's strategy at time t denoted by $s_i(t)$, i.e. $s_i(t) = F(o_i(t))$ s.t. $s_i(t) \in [-1, +1] \in \mathbb{R}$. However, a moment's thought reveals that in our ABM a trader's opinion can be affected by more than one factor: specifically there is the *local* influence of the trader's social interactions with other traders (i.e., the opinion dynamics aspect, the narrative economics factor); and then there is the *global* factor that all traders in the market can see the exchange's LOB, and any imbalance on the LOB (as measured by MLOFI) will also affect a trader's opinion of where prices are heading in the near-term.

Let the market be populated by a total of N_P trader-agents each running OPRZI, and let $o_i(t)_l \in [-1, +1] \in \mathbb{R}$ denote trader i's *local* opinion, which is maintained via an opinion dynamics model such as BC [22], RA [16,27], or RD [28]; and let $o_i(t)_g \in [-1, +1] \in \mathbb{R}$ denote the *global* opinion, which i derives from data published to all by the market's central exchange – in principle, different traders could have ways of computing $o_i(t)_g$, but in the initial studies reported here we give the same method to all traders, and they all use $o_i(t)_g = \sigma(MLOFI(t))$ where $\sigma(.)$ is a sigmoidal function with asymptotes at ± 1 s.t. $o_i(t)_g \in [-1, 1]$.

For completeness we need also to define the global opinion factor $o_i(t)_g$ in the situations where one or both sides of the LOB are empty, in which case MLOFI is undefined. In a real market there are two plausible commentaries on a situation in which one or both sides of the LOB are empty: one would involve words to the effect of "...*well, the market's only just opened, and there's clearly not enough information in the LOB, not enough market activity yet, to form a judgement, so we'll stick with global opinion of zero, i.e. we'll sit on the fence for the time being*"; while the other could be along the lines of "...*there's a major supply/demand imbalance because one side of the LOB is empty while the other side is not, and so there must be very heavy excess demand or supply and so the global opinion should go fully to +1 or −1 depending on which side is empty*". In a real market, which of those two narratives you'd settle upon would depend on wider context, such as how long the market has been open and what the total order volume is on the nonempty side of the LOB: if the market has only just opened, and there are just the first few orders populating the LOB, then $o_i(t)_g = 0$ is a reasonable assumption (the alternative, assuming +1 or −1, might introduce some fairly large opinion-swings at the start of the market) but if you're mid-way through a trading session and the LOB has previously been well populated with orders on both sides of the book but you then find one side of the LOB emptying, that could be a sign that there has been a major reduction in supply/demand, and then assuming $o_i(t)_g = \pm1$ would make much more sense. In the interests of minimality, in the work reported here $o_i(t)_g = 0$ has been used if either/both sides of the LOB are empty, because that's less likely to introduce wild swings; exploring alternative approaches remains a topic for further work.

The local and global sources of opinion are combined as a simple linear weighted combination:

$$o_i(t) = \omega_i(t)o_i(t)_l + (1 - \omega_i(t))o_i(t)_g \qquad (26)$$

where $\omega_i(t) \in [0, 1] \in \mathbb{R}$ is trader i's opinion-weighting: if $\omega_i = 0$, the trader ignores local opinion and pays attention only to global opinion; if $\omega_i = 1$ then it ignores global information and is influenced only by the opinions of other traders that i interacts with. Such a simple linear combination of global and local opinions has also recently been shown in [21] to be useful in an agent-based model of opinion dynamics among a population of bettors gambling on the outcome of horse-racing events.

We first established a set of baseline results from a market in which nothing happens, and in which all traders hold moderate (near-zero) opinions: these results were then used for comparison in analysis of results from subsequent experiments where controlled interventions were made, and results observed. All our results from markets populated by OPRZI traders are visualized and analyzed in [36]. In this paper, we limit ourselves to presenting one set of key illustrative results, in which the market is first allowed to run for a period of time to stabilise to a steady state, and then at a predetermined time denoted t_I, we inject extreme opinions into some number N_I of the traders in the market, and observe the subsequent spread of extreme opinions in the market, and the effect those extreme opinions have on the dynamics of transaction prices on the exchange.

The manner in which extreme opinions are injected into the market requires some care when (as with the RA [16,27] and RD [28] opinion-dynamics models) the extent to which one agent's opinion can be affected by another can be dependent on how close those two agents' opinions are before they interact: intuitively, this captures the everyday observation that someone who (for example) holds right-of-centre political view is more likely to be influenced to a slightly further right-wing view by interactions with a fellow right-winger, than they are to be convinced to move toward the left by interacting with an individual who holds extreme left-wing views; once the difference in opinions between two agents is too great, they lose the ability to influence one another. As is explained at length in [36], this required that the injection of extremist into the market is done with some sophistication: the agents selected to be made to hold extreme views are set on a trajectory where their opinion is made slightly more extreme on each timestep, so that they can influence some number of moderates to start moving to a more extreme opinion (who will then in turn influence other moderates, and so on). This is in contrast to making the injection of extremists as a sudden step-change in the selected agents' opinions, which would immediately render them all as absolute extremists but would leave them without any influence over the remaining moderates.

Figure 8 shows a scatter-plot of transaction prices in a single ABM experiment where the market is populated by OPRZI traders, all of whom hold initially moderate opinions, and where at $T_I = 300$ some number of extremists are injected, whose opinions steadily ramp up to be ever more positive, eventually stopping at the system limit

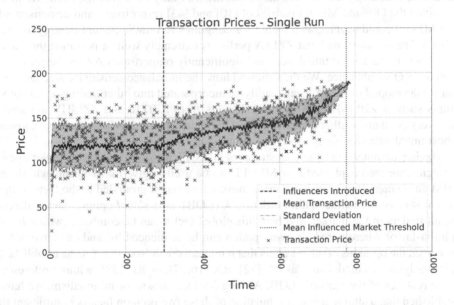

Fig. 8. Transaction-price time-series: data-points marked by crosses come from a single experiment in which at time $T_I = 300$ (indicated by the vertical dashed line) a number of the OPRZI trader-agents are injected into the market, to become progressively more extreme, holding ever more positive opinions, which influence other moderate or neutral traders to also become more positive. As more traders' opinions are increasingly positive, indicating that a price rise is imminent, the OPRZI buyers bid more urgently and the OPRZI sellers offer at relaxed prices, and so the distribution of transaction prices rises in the period after T_I.b The vertical dotted line at time of approx. 780 marks the point at which all traders have become extremists, at which point the session is halted. The solid dark line shows the mean transaction price, and the gray-shaded envelope indicates plus and minus one standard deviation, for 200 i.i.d. repetitions of this experiment.

of $o_i(t) = +1.0$. As time progresses, their influence raises the opinion of previously moderate or neutral traders to also become more positive. As more traders' opinions are increasingly positive, indicating that a price rise is imminent, the OPRZI buyers bid more urgently and the OPRZI sellers offer at relaxed prices, and so the distribution of transaction prices rises in the period after T_I. The experiment is terminated when all traders hold extreme-positive views with opinion-values greater than some pre-set threshold (e.g. $o_i(t) \geq 0.95; \forall i$).

4   Discussion and Conclusion

We know of no agent-based model (ABM) prior to Church & Cliff's [6] in which trader-agents are given a sensitivity to quantity imbalances between the bid and ask sides of the LOB. Such imbalances are often (but not always) caused by the arrival of one or more block orders on one side of the LOB. In this paper we have provided a constructive critique of Church & Cliff's method, pointing out the extreme fragility of imbalance-sensitivity metrics like theirs that monitor only the top of the LOB. We then explained the OFI and MLOFI metrics of [10] and [43] respectively, and demonstrated how MLOFI could be integrated within Vytelingum's AA trading-agent strategy to give ZZIAA. We demonstrated that ZZIAA performs extremely well: it performs the same as AA when there is no imbalance, and significantly outperforms AA in the presence of major LOB imbalance. We then showed how the imbalance-sensitivity mechanisms that we developed for ZZIAA can readily be incorporated into other trading-agent algorithms such as ZIP [8] and SHVR [9]. Results from ZZIZIP and ZZISHV are similarly very good and further demonstrate that the mechanisms developed here have given robust imbalance-sensitivity to a range of trader-agent strategies.

Having demonstrated the robustness of MLOFI in long-established trader-agent strategies, we then explained how MLOFI can be used to give trader-agents within an ABM an *opinion* about near-term price movements that is grounded in the facts of the current state of the market's limit order book (LOB), as a *global* opinion-factor affecting all traders in the market, and how this global factor can be combined with a *local* opinion-factor where a trader's own opinion can be influenced by, and can have influence over, the opinions of other traders that it interacts with 'socially' (via an established opinion-dynamics model such as BC [22], RA [16,27], or RD [28]) without reference to the realities of the market's LOB. Aiming for Occam's-razor minimalism, we have established that a simple linear combination of these two opinion factors is sufficient to give an ABM that seems well set to serve as a platform for examining various aspects in Shiller's thinking on narrative economics.

In future work we intend to explore the addition of MLOFI-based impact-sensitivity to contemporary adaptive trader-agents based on deep learning neural networks [3,42], and we are currently exploring mechanisms that will allow opinionated traders to *introspect*, such that when their opinions about future events turn out to be wrong, they change the way that they form subsequent opinions. Complete details of the work described here are given in [36,46] and all of our relevant source-code for the ABMs described here has been made freely available as open-source code on GitHub [35,45], enabling other researchers to examine, replicate, and extend our work.

References

1. Arifovic, J., Ledyard, J.: Individual evolutionary learning with many agents. Knowl. Eng. Rev. **27**(2), 239–254 (2012)
2. BSE: Bristol Stock Exchange open-source financial exchange simulator (2012). gitHub repository. https://github.com/davecliff/BristolStockExchange
3. le Calvez, A., Cliff, D.: Deep learning can replicate adaptive traders in a limit-order-book financial market. In: Proceedings of the IEEE Symposium Series on Computational Intelligence (SSCI-2018), pp. 1876–1883 (2018)
4. Cartea, A., Jaimungal, S., Penalva, J.: Algorithmic and High-Frequency Trading. Cambridge University Press, Cambridge (2015)
5. Chen, S.H.: Agent-Based Computational Economics: How the Idea Originated and Where it is Going. Routledge (2018)
6. Church, G., Cliff, D.: A simulator for studying automated block trading on a coupled darks/lit financial exchange with reputation tracking. In: Proceedings of the European Modelling and Simulation Symposium (2019)
7. Cliff, D.: Parameterized-response zero-intelligence traders. SSRN: 3823317 (2021)
8. Cliff, D.: Minimal-intelligence agents for bargaining behaviors in market-based environments. Hewlett-Packard Labs Technical Report HPL-97-91 (1997)
9. Cliff, D.: An open-source limit-order-book exchange for teaching and research. In: Proceedings of the IEEE Symposium Series on Computational Intelligence (SSCI-2018), pp. 1853–1860 (2018)
10. Cont, R., Kukanov, A., Stoikov, S.: The price impact of order book events. J. Fin. Economet. **12**(1), 47–88 (2014)
11. Darley, V., Outkin, A.: A NASDAQ Market Simulation: Insights on a Major Market from the Science of Complex Adaptive Systems. World Scientific, Singapore (2007)
12. Das, R., Hanson, J., Tesauro, G., Khephart, J.: Agent-human interactions in the continuous double auction. In: Proceedings IJCAI-2001, pp. 1169–1176 (2001)
13. De Luca, M., Cliff, D.: Agent-human interactions in the continuous double auction, redux. In: Proceedings ICAART-2011 (2011)
14. De Luca, M., Cliff, D.: Human-agent auction interactions: adaptive-aggressive agents dominate. In: Proceedings IJCAI-2011 (2011)
15. De Luca, M., Szostek, C., Cartlidge, J., Cliff, D.: Studies of interactions between human traders and algorithmic trading systems. Driver Review 13, UK Government Office for Science, Foresight Project on the Future of Computer Trading in Financial Markets (2011)
16. Deffuant, G., Neau, D., Amblard, F.: How can extremism prevail? A study based on the relative agreement interaction model. J. Artif. Soc. Soc. Simul. **5**(4), 1 (2002). http://jasss.soc.surrey.ac.uk/5/4/1.html
17. Duffy, J., Ünver, M.U.: Asset price bubbles and crashes with near-zero-intelligence traders. Econ. Theor. **27**, 537–563 (2006)
18. Gjerstad, S.: The impact of pace in double auction bargaining. Working paper, Department of Economics, University of Arizona (2003)
19. Gjerstad, S., Dickhaut, J.: Price formation in continuous double auctions. Game. Econ. Behav. **22**(1), 1–29 (1997)
20. Gode, D.K., Sunder, S.: Allocative efficiency of markets with zero-intelligence traders. J. Polit. Econ. **101**(1), 119–137 (1993)
21. Guzelyte, R., Cliff, D.: Narrative economics of the racetrack: an agent-based model of opinion dynamics in in-play betting on a sports betting exchange. In: Rocha, A.P., Steels, L., van den Herik, J. (eds.) Proceedings of the 14th International Conference on Agents and Artificial Intelligence (ICAART2022), vol. 1, pp. 225–236. SciTePress (2022)

22. Hegselmann, G., Krause, U.: Opinion dynamics and bounded confidence: models, analysis and simulation. J. Artif. Soc. Soc. Simul. **5**(3), 2 (2002). http://jasss.soc.surrey.ac.uk/5/3/2.html

23. Hommes, C., LeBaron, B. (eds.): Computational Economics: Heterogeneous Agent Modeling. North-Holland (2018)

24. Kindleberger, C.: Manias, Panics, and Crashes: A History of Financial Crises. Palgrave Macmillan, 7 edn. (2017)

25. Lomas, K., Cliff, D.: Exploring narrative economics: an agent-based modeling platform that integrates automated traders with opinion dynamics. In: Rocha, A.P., Steels, L., van den Herik, J. (eds.) Proceedings of the 13th International Conference on Agents and Artificial Intelligence (ICAART2021), vol. 1, pp. 137–148. SciTePress (2021)

26. London Stock Exchange Group: Turquoise trading service. Description Version 3.35.5 (2019)

27. Meadows, M., Cliff, D.: Reexamining the Relative agreement model of opinion dynamics. J. Artif. Soc. Soc. Simul. **15**(4), 4 (2012). http://dx.doi.org/10.18564/jasss.2083

28. Meadows, M., Cliff, D.: The Relative disagreement model of opinion dynamics: where do extremists come from? In: 7th International Workshop on Self-Organizing Systems (IWSOS), pp. 66–77 (2013). https://doi.org/10.1007/978-3-642-54140-7_6

29. Pentapalli, M.: A comparative study of Roth-Erev and modified Roth-Erev reinforcement learning algorithms for uniform-price double auctions. Ph.D. thesis, Iowa State University (2008)

30. Petrescu, M., Wedow, M.: Dark pools in European equity markets: emergence, competition and implications. ECB Occasional Paper 193 (2017)

31. Rust, J., Palmer, R., Miller, J.H.: Behaviour of trading automata in a computerized double auction market. In: The Double Auction Market: Theories and Evidence, pp. 155–198. Addison Wesley (1992)

32. Shiller, R.: Narrative economics. Technical report 2069, Cowles Foundation, Yale University, January 2017

33. Shiller, R.: Narrative Economics: How Stories Go Viral & Drive Major Economic Events. Princeton University Press, Princeton (2019)

34. Snashall, D., Cliff, D.: Adaptive-aggressive traders don't dominate. In: van den Herik, J., Rocha, A.P., Steels, L. (eds.) ICAART 2019. LNCS (LNAI), vol. 11978, pp. 246–269. Springer, Cham (2019). https://doi.org/10.1007/978-3-030-37494-5_13

35. Taylor, N.: BSE. https://github.com/nwtay/BSE

36. Taylor, N.: Explorations in agent-based models of narrative economics. Master's thesis, Department of Computer Science, University of Bristol (2021)

37. Tesauro, G., Das, R.: High-performance bidding agents for the continuous double auction. In: Proceedings of 3rd ACM Conference on E-Commerce, pp. 206–209 (2001)

38. Tesauro, G., Bredin, J.L.: Strategic sequential bidding in auctions using dynamic programming. In: Proceedings of First International Joint Conference on Autonomous Agents and Multiagent Systems: part 2, pp. 591–598 (2002)

39. Tesfatsion, L., Judd, K. (eds.): Handbook of Computational Economics, Vol. 2: Agent-Based Computational Economics. North-Holland (2006)

40. Vytelingum, K., Cliff, D., Jennings, N.: Strategic bidding in continuous double auctions. Artif. Intell. **172**(14), 1700–1729 (2008)

41. Vytelingum, P.: The structure and behaviour of the continuous double auction. Ph.D. thesis, University of Southampton (2006)

42. Wray, A., Meades, M., Cliff, D.: Automated creation of a high-performing algorithmic trader via deep learning on level-2 limit order book data. In: Proceedings of the IEEE Symposium Series on Computational Intelligence (SSCI-2020) (2020)

43. Xu, K., Gould, M., Howison, S.: Multi-level order-flow imbalance in a limit order book. SSRN 3479741 (2019)
44. Zhang, Z., Cliff, D.: Market impact in trader-agents: adding multi-level order-flow imbalance-sensitivity to automated trading systems. In: Rocha, A.P., Steels, L., van den Herik, J. (eds.) Proceedings of the 13th International Conference on Agents and Artificial Intelligence (ICAART2021), vol. 2, pp. 426–436 (2021)
45. Zhang, Z.: (2020). https://github.com/davecliff/BristolStockExchange/tree/master/Zhen Zhang
46. Zhang, Z.: An impact-sensitive adaptive algorithm for trading on financial exchanges. Master's thesis, University of Bristol Department of Computer Science (2020)

Advances in Measuring Inflation Within Virtual Economies Using Deep Reinforcement Learning

Conor Stephens[✉] and Chris Exton[✉]

University of Limerick, Limerick, Ireland
13123947@studentmail.ul.ie, chris.exton@ul.ie

Abstract. This paper assesses an improved framework for evaluating the performance of economies within online multiplayer games. Games in this medium traditionally require a great deal of testing and analysis to assess the outcomes and affects of player interactions. This process is normally imperfect and time consuming, leading a lot of games developers and publishers to maintain a lot of risk during the development and launch of multi-million dollar projects.

The framework and example project presented within this paper uses deep reinforcement learning to simulate economic interactions between learning agents. This is possible by having agents learn from player demonstrations to interact with game systems such as *Battling, Collecting Resources* and *Crafting Weapons* which allows them to co-ordinate and cooperate to achieve long-term goals in the game. This paper shows recent breakthroughs in relation to training these agents to the variety of metrics learning agents can generate to help games designers test and polish multiplayer experience, which have proved hard to quantify and measure without extensive play testing.

This paper is an extension paper to our publication in ICAART 2021 [21], within this paper includes the following additions:
- Further discussion on the economic properties of Eve Online
- An evaluation of how player demonstrations can accelerate the training time for both agent's policies
- A measured example of how this tool can balance multiplayer game economies through parameter tuning.

Keywords: Artificial intelligence · Games design · Reinforcement learning · Game economies

1 Introduction

Multiplayer video games can contain virtual economies which support the games design and systems, providing both the means and the motive to player actions and goals. Throughout the last two decades, multiplayer game economies have suffered from economic forces working against both the players and the games designers and publishers, these flaws have arisen from unwanted inflation to incorrect player priorities. This project and framework can evaluate most economy designs found within Massively Multiplayer Online games (MMO) the base metric this paper looks at is inflation.

Supported by Lero: The Irish Software Research Centre.

A. P. Rocha et al. (Eds.): ICAART 2021, LNAI 13251, pp. 294–314, 2022.
https://doi.org/10.1007/978-3-031-10161-8_16

Inflation can become an epidemic within a game's virtual world and form a massive internal problem when compared to real-world economies. The creation of resources that can be exchanged for in-game currency is tied to player mechanics; an example would be when a player receives an additional resource upon completion of a quest.

Systems or mechanics that result in the creation of economic value are effectively printing money. This process results in the devaluing of the currency in the game, if it is hard capped or connected to a rising rate of production such as in the game *Eve Online*. Gameplay causing an unstoppable inflow of resources has caused rampant inflation within MMO games [1]. An early example was in *Asherons Call:* the in-game currency became so inflated that shards were used instead of money. Similarly, the developers of *Gaia Online* would donate $250 to charity if the players discarded 15 trillion Gold (Gold was the in-game currency used for transactions) [12]. A traditional solution would be for game designers to create a counterweight such as a sink to prevent problems within the game's internal balance. *Sinkholes* are key tools for game's designers when designing economies within virtual economies allowing some resources to be removed from the economy. Sinkholes are mechanics that take currency out of the games system, sometimes referred to as "Drains" within machination diagrams [2]. Typical sinkholes found within online games are Auction Fees and Consumable Items which are only available from NPC's (Non-Playable Characters). Players however will endeavour to avoid these taxes and attempt to amass vast amounts of currency and items as quickly as possible.

MMO titles which have featured virtual economies have frequently experienced periods of hyper-inflation due to player behaviour. *Ultima Online*, an incredibly successful early MMO released in 1997 was an early example of the issues players could present to game designers. *Ultima Online's* creator Richard Garriott explained in an interview how players destroyed the virtual ecology within seconds by over-hunting and depleting the world of animals within the simulated eco-system [14]. Within *Ultima Online* the spawning of new carnivorous animals was connected to the availability of herbivorous animals. The two types of animals were balanced so players would attack herbivorous animals such as wolves and bears as they had resources connected to game progress. When the game went live problems started to surface; resources were being depleted at an alarming rate and destroying the game's ecosystem due to players over hunting herbivores for fun. To solve this problem future games did not restrict the rate that enemies would spawn, MMO games such as *World of Warcraft* and *Star Wars: The Old Republic* uses sinkholes to manage the imbalance set within their economies.

1.1 Proposed System

The framework that we propose assesses inflation within an in-game economy by measuring the price of resources within the game over time. In this framework the economy is simulated by using reinforcement learning agents playing as both the supplier and consumer within a simplified game economy both aiming to gain more wealth through the game systems. This research aims to show the power of reinforcement learning for both *Game Balance* [5] ensuring the game is challenging and fair for different types of players whilst also assessing the game's economy for potential inflation allowing key stakeholders to better understand how changes within the virtual economy can influence player interactions such as trade without releasing the game or extensive user testing. This paper is built upon two clear objectives:

1. Measure the upper limits of inflation within a multiplayer game economy;
2. Provide a tool for simulating different changes to a game's economy for analysis.

2   Related Works

This work is compromised by ideas and methodologies from a wide variety of fields, but it is most focused on areas within the study of games, from games design and automated design, all the way to higher level sub-disciplines for games designers such as game balance and game theory. This work incorporates ideas structures and concepts from artificial intelligence such as deep reinforcement learning and Monte Carlo simulations and parameter tuning and optimisation. A brief overview of the most relevant disciplines can be found within this section.

2.1   Parameter Tuning

A discipline and challenge found within both Games Design and Artificial Intelligence; within AI parameters are the values for the weights and biases found inside each neuron of a neural network. Optimisation methods such as Stochastic Gradient Descent provide improved values for a neural networks parameters when optimised towards a certain goal, goals within Artificial Intelligence could be anything between supervised learning on cancer scans to reinforcement learning improving an agent's policy. Parameter Tuning in games development is normally grouped with games design. Within the structure of any games design all mechanics and systems that use comparisons to evaluate game state are given real data to evaluate, an example of this is the different numbers such as damage, durability and accuracy attached to a weapon. These specific values are parameters of the game and are key to evaluating transitive mechanics throughout the balancing process, these values are tweak to create the expected aesthetics and dynamics of the games design.

2.2   Game Balance

Game Designers rely on a variety of practices to ensure fair and fun experiences for players by analysing mechanics and systems. In order for designers to create these experiences, the designer assesses the fairness, challenge, meaningful choices, and randomness of the different events and challenges within the game. Several terms have emerged over the years to define and explain aesthetics within common genres, one such term is 'Game Feel' [22] a practice of making the mechanics, i.e. "moving parts" of a game more impactful by adding effects such as:

- Screenshake;
- Particle effects;
- Post processing.

An oversimplification of game balance can be defined as "do the players feel the game is fair" [3]. To successfully balance a game, a variety of considerations and tolerances depending on the game, genre and audience must be considered.

Cost Curve Analysis. Game Balance was traditionally achieved using analytical methods such as cost-curve analysis, spreadsheet and Excel macros. Tools and techniques to evaluate the validity of game parameters evolved over the years. A new addition to the game's designers tool belt are machination diagrams, a more visual and interactive framework to test the internal game balance [2]. Each of these methods follows a reductive process that allows the designers to see the impact when values are changed within the games' internal systems. A more traditional tool when balancing transitive systems Cost-curve analysis as an example associates every mechanics, systems and items within the game with a benefit and a cost [6] value, this type of analysis shows the designer if any individual component deviates too much from the mean. Designers place the the the cost increases of an item in line with the benefit of a game, mechanic or resource, each item within the world have been refereed to as the *Jedi Curve* within *Magic The Gathering* [8]. The cost-benefit relationship between each item forms the shape of the curve. During the balancing process, a designer can use it to see where a specific game component fits within the system. Small imbalances are allowed, as choosing the most efficient or effective item creates an interesting decision for the player. However, game mechanics that are obviously too high on the cost curve are traditionally identified for a redesign or a small nerf (making a mechanic a worse option to improve the variety of possible options). This approach works well with traditional arcade games and role playing games. However, this approach is less effective in multiplayer games due to less defined relationships and chaos that can attributed to multiplayer environments.

2.3 Automated Game Testing

Game testing has traditionally relied on human play testers or scripted play testing requiring prior knowledge of the game and systems, especially during early development of the game. Play testing is an integral component of user testing games to ensure a fun and engaging experience for players, designed to review design decisions within interactive media such as games and to measure the aesthetic experience of the game compared to the designer's intentions [9]. Huge strides have been taken to automate this process using learning agents trained with a variety of supervised and reinforcement learning approaches [4]. Reinforcement learning (RL) models have allowed learning agents to achieve human-like performance in a wide variety of, a wide variety of developers and researchers have been experimenting with machine learning to test their games. An example of this in practice is *King's* automated play testing of their Match-3 "Crush Saga" games where they trained agents to mimic human behaviour and using these agents within simulations, designers can test new level designs [10]. This testing has a lot of different use cases and contexts depending on the department spearheading the initiative. Quality assurance departments may consider employing trained bots/learning agents to test the game levels, mechanics and players to detect bugs. Examples include: missing collisions within the level geometry; finding holes in the narrative events that can hard/soft lock players from progressing; *modl.ai* is an excellent example of a company which offers this service to games developers and publishers.

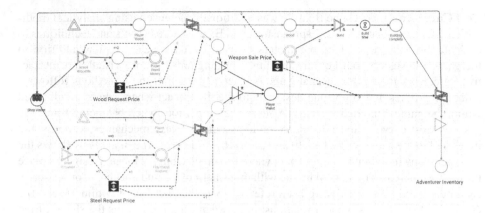

Fig. 1. Crafting Machinations Diagram [21].

3 History of Economies in Games

MMOs feature some of the most impressive economic interactions between agents found in video games. Lots of research has been done to explore virtual economies [7]. This research identified some necessary mechanics that are required to allow fluctuations in value for virtual currencies. These mechanics, which include the creation of the currency using in-game mechanics, can be formulated as: 'Be directly connected to real-world currency'. An early example of this link between physical and game currency can be found in *Entropia Universe*, a free-to-play MMO released in 2003 where 1 USD is tied to 100 PED (Project Entropia Dollars) on a fixed exchange rate [16]. There are ethical concerns for this mechanic regarding how the currency is stored and how it can be used for gambling as a key game mechanic.

Online multiplayer game economies include an extensive range of possible systems, the base of a virtual economy consists of currencies, resources and rulesets for how these resources should be exchanged between both player and nonplayer entitities. When designers talk about balancing game economies, they generally mean balancing mechanics that feature conversion between two resources. In game economies, game designers define how players obtain the currency and by how much of each currency key resources cost in the game. This paper discusses game economies that are significantly affected by supply and demand between multiple players. To facilitate this specific in-game mechanics, a first requirement would be allowing players to sell items within the world and the second would be having different requirements for different types of players incentivising trading and cooperation.

MMO's markets experience periods of stagnations and fluctuations similar to modern stock markets, this is very different from traditional single-player games where the prices of items in shops are a key balance consideration. A good example of this was explored earlier in *Eve Online* where each seller has a different set price for the resource they are selling. The cost and availability of resources and processed items within the world are key when considering both player progression and the difficulty of achieving particular quests and challenges. Within single player games, the prices of items can be set to allow sufficient challenge without giving the player an un-surmountable hurdle to cross, multiplayer games can feature supply and demand, which can affect the players ability to progress within the game world. Other techniques found in 'free to play' games are illiquidity; (players have to convert one currency into another before they can make certain purchases).

Due to the infinite nature of enemies found within MMO games, alongside the persistence of player inventories throughout multiple years of updates and promotions can cause issues to arrise either inadvertently or by error (exploits and bugs). Key items which were once rare may quickly become common place, eroding the value of them to players, this erosion is not only to player inventories but to developers margins due to players being motivated by scarce and hard to find content. Many games create prestige and scarcity by allowing players to own physical space (for example, land and property) in *Second Life* or spaceships and space-stations (as it is done in *Eve Online*). This economy is different from the game play-based economy where the property is a finite resource that can be traded endlessly. It also has different types of values based on location and amenities, e.g. citadels near trading posts are worth more due to footfall similarly to real estate in real-world cities.

Large Massive Multiplayer Online (MMO) games such as *RuneScape* and *World of Warcraft* (WoW) have tackled the issue of hyperinflation over the years with various levels of success. MMO's have experimented with integrating real-world financial policies to curb inflation. These solutions include creating a reserve currency to put a minimum value in the in-game currency. It is also worth implementing illiquidity in the transnational mechanics within the game's auctions and trading systems. These design considerations are slow to develop and it is difficult to measure the effects accurately before the game's release.

3.1 Eve Online

RuneScape operates trade squares to players allowing them to exchange their goods. Runescape servers operate up to 2000 players at a time. *Eve Online* is hosted centrally among all players. To achieve this functionality, the marketplace system of Eve Online was structured similarly to the NASDAQ [24]. The NASDAQ handles all trades digitally, allowing the exchange to efficiently and transparently display thousands of companies to millions of investors. Eve Online has an in-game currency called ISK with a conversion rate of 6 USD to 1 Billion ISK which players can convert both ways.

Eve Online has probably the most consequential and intricate economic system of any MMO game, one of the most relevant considerations and designs considerations within *Eve Online's* is the sales tax [23]. Eve Online's sales tax, these taxes are applied to millions of transactions every day. After the transaction a proportion of the sale is given to the Secure Commerce Commission which was around 2% which is one of the economic sinks baked into the game's design. This tax was changed to 5% in June 2019. This change encouraged players to facilitate their own trade in Citadels eventually reducing the price down for in-game trade to 1%.

4   Testing Economies

Artificial Intelligence techniques have provided some means for testing and evaluating economic policy and fiscal design. *Salesforce* showed how using a learning environment; different tax policies can be tested and assessed on specific economies [25]. The AI economist is capable of using reward signals from the learning environment such as the positive affirmation of earning money and the punishment of being taxed to create incentives for the agents to relax and enjoy their day and to work within their society and contribute. This work highlights the great potential in finding optimal tax rates and policies to generate the most income for the government without creating disincentives for the agents working when they could be resting.

Games developers have traditionally used modelling techniques to test economies within games [2]. Machinations is a graph-based programming language created by *Joris Dormans* with a syntax that supports the flow of resources between players. A modern equivalent is the excellent Machinations.io web app that modernises the previous machinations toolset. Machinations allow game's designers to model the creation, flow and destruction of resources within the economy. It also allows resources to be exchanged and converted within a visual interactable simulation.

5   Parameter Tuning

Parameter Tuning when being discussed as a component of a game's design "Involves making low-level changes to game mechanics settings such as character movement parameters, power-up effect, or control sensitivity." [27] Within a multiplayer games such as the example project this environment simulates, these parameters include the individual parameters of each monster including:

- Weapon Damage
- Health Points
- Accuracy
- Speed
- Transitive Type

Individually changing each component of each monster and each weapon is an incredibly tiring process; a way of assessing the accuracy and validity of so many parameters is to test the wider game and optimise towards that using methods such as gradient descent or parameter optimisation. To achieve this we have assessed the affect of changing the difficulty of collecting resources to the rate of inflation within the game world. This measures whether making the world less plentiful with resources can prevent unwanted scenarios for players and developers.

6   Methods

This research aims to measure inflation within a game economy. This is achieved by using a game economy as a learning environment for reinforcement learning agents and tracking transactions between them after collecting resources from the world around them. Industry standard tools are used for the game engine and sample code to make this work more accessible for game development professionals. The process to achieve this can be broken into 3 steps:

1. Implement a simple MMO economy using Unity game engine;
2. Train learning agents to play the game allowing them to create, sell and win resources from the game world;
3. Assess the game economy by deploying the trained learning agents within the game world and record the price of transactions.

This framework assesses sample virtual economies within a simulated MMO game using learning agents to simulate the needs and desires of different players. The sample economy is a circular economy between two different types of agents, **Adventurer Agents** and **Crafting Agents**. Crafting Agents post resource requests that Adventurer Agents can choose to collect for the reward similar to a guild system within a modern MMO. Both sets of agents within this learning environment are dependent on cooperation and bartering between each other to progress in the game. The two agents have separate reward signals; Crafting Agents are rewarded based on the success of their business practice. If an Craftsman Agent sells an item for a profit, it receives a reward. This reward signal is the percentage profit of the sale that was made. The reward signal that fuels the Adventurer Agents would be more similar to a career progression. The Adventurer Agent has two reward signals, the first is financial if an agent makes money it receives a reward. The second reward signal is when the adventurer agent buys an item that improves its stats and a passive one that the increase in the agents stats is a reward signal. The implementation for the agent's policy was possible using ml-agents an open-source plugin for Unity [15] that allows for the development of reinforcement learning agents within Unity.

6.1 Economy Design

Traditional MMO economies are facilitated by the supply and demand provided by the game's players. The demand within the in-game economy is achieved by having players needing different types of weapons and resources to achieve their short term objectives within the game. Examples include how Warriors and Mages in *World of Warcraft* would desire different equipment, allowing both to sell unwanted or useless equipment to each other. This example project features a similarly designed structure. Consisting of two layers, the first is between different types of Adventurer agents which there are three types of adventurer's: *Swordsman, Brawler and Archer* agents. Different types of adventurers can use different types of weapons such as Bows and Swords. The second layer is between Craftsmen agents and Adventurer agents, Craftsmen agents are business focused while Adventurer agents are battle focused. Craftsman agents spend money to receive resources to make equipment which they sell for a profit. Adventurer agents in an opposite approach use the equipment to collect resources that they sell to craftsman agents. Both agents have to cooperate to prosper within this economy, allowing a wide variety of interactions and influences. The supply is achieved by having mechanics within the game that creates and changes different resources; these include loot drops from battles, and crafting resources into more valuable weapons that will sell at a higher price to buyers.

The game's internal economy was tested as a machination diagram, as shown in Fig. 1. The economy is based on Craftsman and Adventurer agents agreeing on the price of resources and items to facilitate trade. This agreement within the system can be seen in the two types of *Registers* within the machination diagram. The first register type is for the Craftsman agent that allows them to set the price of the request. Moreover, it is an interactive pool that Adventurer agents can use to agree on the price. This interaction locks negotiations for both parties. The second type of register within this diagram is the price for the crafted weapon. This register allows the craftsman to change the price of the weapon even when they have no stock of the weapon. When an Adventurer agent interacts with the Trade node, this exchanges the item in the shop with the Adventurer agent's money. The values chosen for the different outcomes were based on play testing the economy design with different parameters to ensure neither the Adventurer nor the Craftsman runs out of money, which could bring the simulation and economy to a standstill. This was possible using Monte Carlo techniques to simulate players using the Machinations.io [18]. The economy as shown in Fig. 1 was simulated over 1000 time-steps within the environment over 20 iterations for each configuration of the items specific statistics. An example of the balancing process can be seen in Fig. 9 which shows the steady upwards direction of the economy and the constant progression and purchasing throughout the simulation. A Monte Carlo search for games design is a popular strategy for exploring the search space of strategies and game states [26,28].

Table 1. Enemy Loot Drops [21].

Area	Name	Health	Damage	Wood	Metal	Gem	Scale
Forest	Owl	10	2	1			
Forest	Buffalo	10	5	2	1		
Mountain	Bear	15	5	2	2		
Mountain	Gorilla	20	5	2	2	1	
Sea	Narwhale	15	6	1	1	2	
Sea	Crocodile	22	4		2	2	
Volcano	Snake	20	5			2	1
Volcano	Dragon	25	6		2	1	2

6.2 Adventure Agents

Each Adventurer agent can access three unique game systems where they can interact with other agents, a flow diagram of the different systems can be found in Fig. 3.

Request System. The request system is similar to a guild in *World Of Warcraft*; Adventurers can see all active resources that Crafting agents requested and the reward when the request is complete. Adventurer agents can choose up to five individual requests to fulfil.

Battle System. Agents are able to travel within the virtual world. There are four different environments *Forest, Mountain, Sea and Volcano* each with varying types of enemies to encounter. When the agent enters an area, a random battle occurs which is designed similarly to Pokemon battles; the authors used *Brackey's* turn-based combat framework for the implementation of this system. Players can choose to *Attack, Heal or Flee* during combat. If either the players' or enemies' health points drop to zero the game is over. If the player was victorious, a loot drop occurs with items and probabilities based on the enemy that the agent defeated. Specific loot values for different enemy types can be found in Table 1. The main challenge of the battle system is to manage the player's health points between battles and battling enemies that have sufficient chance to drop resources needed for each agent's accepted requests.

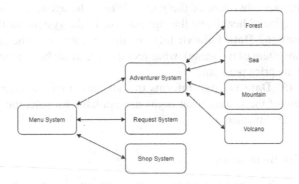

Fig. 2. Adventurer System.

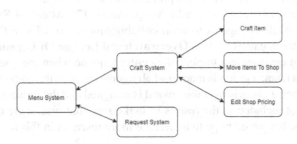

Fig. 3. Shop System.

Shop System. The shop system allows Adventurer Agents have access to the weapons that Craftsman agents have submitted to their shops. Adventurer Agents can purchase items from them. Each weapon is placed within the Adventurer's inventory and a weapon is equipped if it is the strongest weapon in the agents inventory. Better equipment allows the Adventurers to encounter stronger enemies and receive more loot. If the agent's health drops to zero, it loses the battle and suffers a loss of 5 units of gold from the Adventurer agents wallet.

Sensors. The adventurer agent has six unique sensors to inform each agent of its current state and the visible state of the systems around them, agent sensors normalize scalar data and use one hot encoding for categorical data

- **Base Sensor (7 Data Points):** Informs the agent to its money, health, current-active-system & adventurer-type.
- **Inventory Sensor (8 Data Points):** Informs the agent to its current weapon, current-damage & number of weapons.
- **Current Request Sensor (18 Data Points):** Informs agent to the requests they have accepted, the number of crafting materials that is required and the number of crafting materials they have obtained.
- **Adventurer Sensor (18 Data Points):** Informs the adventurer (if the adventurer is in the adventure subsystem of the game) Where the agent is, what the agent is fighting, both fighters' health and the current state of the system for that agent.
- **Request Sensor (62 Data Points):** Informs the adventurer (if the adventurer is in the request subsystem of the game), what requests are available, the number of items required, and the price per item.
- **Shop Sensor (55 Data Points):** Informs the adventurer (if the adventurer is in the shop subsystem of the game), what items are available for sale, the prices, and the shop the items are attached to.

6.3   Co-operative Behaviours

A new addition to the simulated economy is co-operative battles between multiple players and AI instances, this more closely mirrors the types of battles found within MMO games. Agents are rewarded and punished as a group in this instance using MA-POCA (MultiAgent POsthumous Credit Assignment) [17] instead of SAC to train the actors. MA-POCA allows agents to train collaboratively. To achieve this system, we use a queue similar to games such as **Overwatch** and **League Of Legends**. Adventurer Agents choose an environment to play, they enter a queue when the queue has enough players to make a team, a group is made and all agents move to the battle where they can fight together, when a game is over the reward is assigned and the group is de-registered. This system is not included in the results to make sure that results are consistent with previous samples, but we do hope to undertake more research in this area in the future.

6.4   Crafting Agents

Each Crafting agent has two different abilities. (A flow graph can be found in Fig. 3).

Request System. The ability to input requests for materials which include *Wood, Metal, Gems and Dragon Scales*. Craftsman Agents can change both the number of the resources they require and the price they are willing to pay for it. This system is similar to a guild request found in many traditional MMO's. From this marketplace, Adventurer agents will take requests which they can fulfil through battling and exploration.

Crafting System. The crafting system allows each agent can craft a variety of weapons using the resources they have received. The third and final ability of the Crafting agent is how the agents interact with their shopfront. Agents can put items in their shopfronts to replenish stock. They also have the ability to increase and decrease the price of each item. There are five unique weapons that a Craftsman could create with different crafting requirements; this can be seen in Table 3.

Craftsman agents have a passive inflow of money into their wallets, This source within the *Machinations* diagram, this design consideration prevents stagnation within the system when agents may have no money, this prevents a lack or requests being made which would remove incentive and reward from the Adventurer Agents.

Table 2. Weapon Stats & Crafting Requirements [21].

Item Name	Damage	Durability	Wood Req.	Metal Req.	Gem Req.	Scale Req.
Beginner	7	5	2	2		
Intermediate	9	6	3	3		
Advanced	10	7	2	2	1	
Epic	12	7	2	2	2	
Master	13	8	3	3	3	
Ultimate	15	10	3	3	3	2

Sensor

- **Base Sensor (9 Data Points):** Shows the agent its current money, the system it is currently using, and the number of resources they have of each type.
- **Config Sensor (24 Data Points):** Captures the crafting requirements for different weapons to inform the agent when making decisions in different game systems.
- **Request Sensor (33 Data Points):** Shows the agent, the requests they have made (number of items, and price) and the current average price for that kind of request.
- **Crafting Sensor (56 Data Points):** Shows the current resources the agent has and the requirements of different weapons.

6.5 Training

Each agent is trained using Soft Actor-Critic (SAC) policies using multi-agent reinforcement learning; this is possible by using Unity's excellent ML-Agents package [15]. ML-Agents allows developers and designers to train learning agents within Unity game environments. The knowledge is achieved by using *Self Play* within the environment [20]. Self Play improves the learning process by having multiple agents within the environment use previous versions of the agent's policy. Self Play stabilises the agents learning by allowing a positively trending reward within the learning environment. This was implemented within the learning environment by having half of the Adventurer and Craftsman agents infer their decisions from previous versions of the policy.

Behavioural Cloning/Imitation Learning. "Behavioural Cloning is a method by which human subcognitive skills can be captured and reproduced in a computer program" [19]. There are a variety of different types of learning algorithms that try to mimic human behaviour and make a policy for a learning agent based on a player's interaction with the learning system, policys that are built using this paradigm can be separated into Imitation Learning and Behavioural Cloning. Imitation learning uses pairs and observations and actions from a demonstration to learn a policy, meanwhile Behavioural Cloning trains an agent's policy to exactly mimic the actions shown in a set of demonstrations. Unity ml-agent's has the capacity for both we evaluated the difficulty of training both Adventurer and Craftsman Agent's policies using a combination of *Behavioural Cloning, GAIL and Curiosity Learning*. 3 Demonstrations of approximately 2 min were recorded for both agents and used to evaluate different training algorithms for the agent's policy.

GAIL of (Generative Adversarial Imitation Learning) [13] uses adversarial neural networks to reward the agent for behaving similarly to the demonstrations. Within the adversarial structure the discriminator network is trained to distinguish between the *Action-State* pairs of the expert demonstration and the reinforcement learning agent. Meanwhile the agent's policy network which acts as the **Generator network** for the data used by the **Discriminator** is trained to learn a policy that produces similar action-state pairs to the demonstration, and is rewarded when its pairs pass as demonstrations to the Discriminator Network.

The accelerated training of the agents is as follows:

- **Behavioural Cloning:** used first in pre-training
- **GAIL:** used with extrinsic reward within the learning environment
- **RL (SAC):** used to complete learning and generalisation within the learning environment

Curriculum Learning. Before deciding to supplement the learning with GAIL, experiments were made to use curriculum learning to accelerate the learning process within the simulation. The curriculum reward signals would reward behaviour that would guide the agents towards achieving their objectives and can be found in Fig. 3. Curriculum learning allows the agent to learn a simpler problem. In this learning environment we created mini objectives for both kinds of learning agents.

Training Results. Results for the training can be found in Fig. 4 this shows the steps within the learning environment it took the respected policy to achieve an average cumulative reward of 1 within the learning environment. We took this value as a good baseline for training performance for each policy; this is shown in the graph having either behavioural cloning or GAIL making the biggest difference when training the agent to perform - the results show significant improvement over the original policy. This graph hides the computational time pre-training took, however it was negligible with the small sample set of demonstrations that were used.

6.6 Economy Sinks

Both the adventurer, crafting and virtual environments for the game were designed to sustain a healthy supply-demand curve to regulate the prices between the different weapons and resources. However, the base environment has a traditional feature

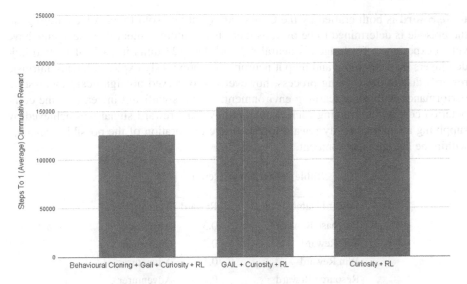

Fig. 4. Steps To 1 (Average) Cumulative Reward.

of online game economies that have been the cause of previous instances of hyperinflation. Such hyperinflation is caused by the infinite monsters within the adventuring system, potentially allowing the cost of resources to plummet for the Crafting Agents. The game is designed to prevent hyperinflation by having excess rewards removed from the in-game economy. This is achieved by having each Adventurer agent discard items if they do not have a current request for that item. This mechanic is a similar mechanic to how *Monster Hunter's* request system works by having unique issues for the early application, preventing the player collecting all potentially early game items within their first journey into the wild area.

6.7 Training

The reward signal for both Adventurer and Craftsman agents was to incentivize the agents to coordinate with each other. This was achieved by rewarding the *Craftsman Agents* for selling items, with the reward signal being the percentage profit made during a sale. The learning agent is rewarded when it earns money. This is achieved when an agent completes a resource request. The Adventurer agent is penalised with a penalty of -0.1 to punish the agent for its failure. Adventurer agents have a similar reward signal; every time they earn money, they receive a proportional reward signal ranging between 0-0.8 based on the value of money they have gained. Adventurers earn money when they complete a resource request. Both agents' policies are updated using *Soft-Actor Critic* a learning algorithm for reinforcement learning [11]. Soft Actor-Critic allows higher levels of entropy within the system, enabling further exploration of the stochastic action distribution.

Each episode during training is started by resetting every agent's inventory and wallet, giving them the starting value of 100 gold units and no weapons. When the **Ulti-**

mate Sword is both crafted by the Craftsman agent and sold to an Adventurer agent, the episode is determined to be over, as there is no future content that the agents have yet to experience. Each agent's neural network has 128 units in each of its two hidden layers between input and output neurons. We previously explored having intrinsic rewards during the training process, however, we observed no significant increase in performance within the learning environment; with a significant increase in the computation cost whilst training each agent's policy. This reward signal was achieved by supplying a small curiosity reward to encourage exploration of the possible scenarios within the learning environment.

Table 3. Curriculum Rewards [21].

Reward Name	Reward	Agent
Purchase Reward	0.3	Adventure
Sell Reward	0.2	Craftsman
Win Reward	0.1	Adventurer
Resource Reward	0.1	Adventurer
Resource Complete Reward	0.2	Adventurer
Craft Reward	0.4	Craftsman

6.8 Parameter Tuning

Crafting Requirements. Using the trained agents within the simulation, we can change the required resources needed for crafting items as shown in the graph bellow 5. Scarcity of weapons is controlled by randomly increasing the required resources

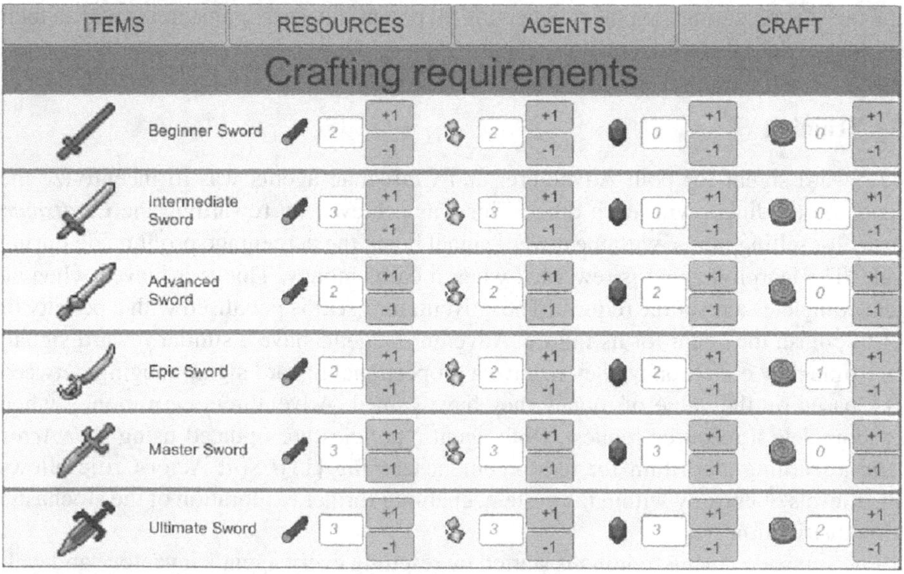

Fig. 5. Resource Tuning.

of each item randomly by 1 resource at a time. This requires Craftsman agents to input more resources, it requires Adventurer agents to take on more battles.

6.9 Data Collection

After successful training of both the Craftsman and Adventurer agents' policies, the trained models were then used within the learning environment to generate and collect data. Data was collected by recording the sale prices of weapons within the simulation. This was recorded as Comma Separated Value (CSV) data alongside the time within the simulation that the exchange occurred.

To record the parameters for crafting each Crafting Map, (a list of required resources and how many resource is needed for each weapon) is output at the beginning of the simulation with a key to map between game events and the configuration parameters.

7 Inflation Results

The beginning results of this paper are a continuation of the results from the initial paper [21]. As show by the sale price of *Beginner* and *Advanced swords* shown in Fig. 6 and Fig. 7. The trend lines in both diagrams show a clear upwards trajectory within the virtual economy, the shape of the graph lines provides a more interesting picture showing a more in-depth look at the particulars of this game's economy. As shown in the graphs, between the 5th and 10th hour of simulation, the price increases for both weapons. This could be seen as a higher level of demand for the item from the Adventurer agents. This is quickly followed by a decrease in price representing a small dip within the game's economy, potentially relieving the burden on the Adventurer agents within the economy and having the burden of more competitive prices affecting the Shop agents reward signal.

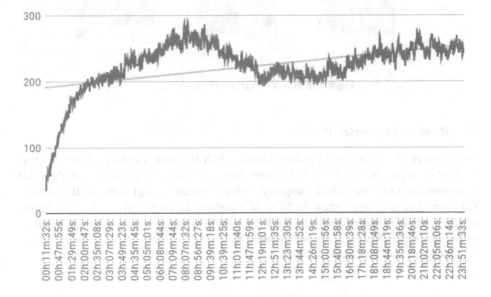

Fig. 6. Sale value of Beginner Swords [21].

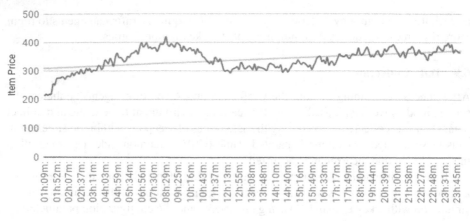

Fig. 7. Sale value of Advanced Swords [21].

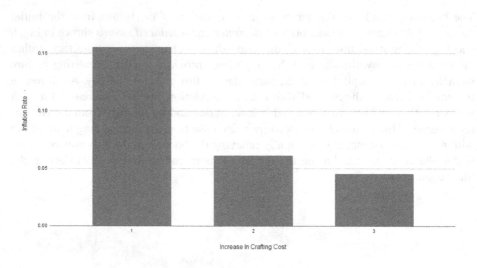

Fig. 8. Inflation Vs Crafting Difficulty [21].

7.1   Results - Parameter Tuning

As shown in Fig. 8 the rate of inflation over a 24 h simulation reduces if we increase
the crafting cost. We infer this is because items become less plentiful and the price
of resource requests decreases compared to the standard configuration of the system.
This would be similar to when the GDP of a country is smaller the cost of goods and
services are also smaller due to the higher availability of labor. Considering the effect
on the economy, we would also recommend tweaking the durability of items to change
how long they can stay in the system.

8   Discussion and Future Work

Virtual Economies within online games have grown in popularity as a design component in both single player free-to-play game and massive multiplayer AAA games published on consoles and PC's. Testing and evaluating multiplayer games is becoming harder to achieve due to the compounding factors of the bigger game world, (4 km by 4 km maps) are and multiplayer mechanics (multiple high profile games such as *Fall Guys* and *Fortnight* having 100 player online multiplayer). The authors recommend automated agents for testing the different systems in multiplayer video-games. Better testing ensures the stakeholder's confidence more robust allowing accurate evaluation of the systems before releasing them to the public a vital precaution to ensure consistent profitability of the game throughout its life cycle. Testing virtual economies has the potential of allowing companies to protect their assets whilst earning higher and more consistent revenue during the products life cycle. Other techniques to test game economies such as machinations and analysis of player data allows developers to assess the health of the game's economy. However, these approaches are possible only during prototyping and may not encapsulate the entire possibility space of the game's mechanics. This framework offers a middle ground that allows key stakeholders of the game to test the same economic systems found within the game. Moreover, it allows player motivation to be modelled in the form of the reward signal found within our learning environment.

Future work within this research should explore the effectiveness of this approach in different types of economies with other starting parameters. Comparing different economies would make it possible to evaluate the effect of inflation within economies containing positive or negative feedback loops. *Monopoly* with a very high level of positive feedback within the game has a history of exploding inflation and competition as a core premise. Comparing this economy to a more serious game with a negative feedback loop such as *This War of Mine* could highlight the exact difference in flow between these two very different experiences.

The authors propose using this framework in a more extensive online game with multiple mechanics for gaining money and resources. This could potentially allow game designers to assess the impact of different play styles and systems on the games internal economy. This research could be extended by training another neural network whose responsibility is to view transactions between agents in order to predict inflation within the economy during the simulation. This neural network could be used within the game to prevent fraud or hyperinflation in a way similar to how credit card companies prevent fraud in their systems.

Appendix

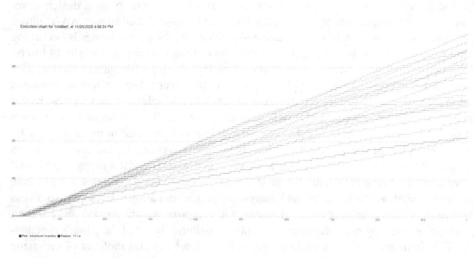

Fig. 9. Monte Carlo testing of Economy Design [21].

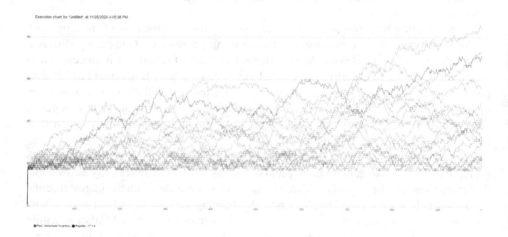

Fig. 10. Monte Carlo Item Purchase Frequency [21].

References

1. Achterbosch, L., Pierce, R., Simmons, G.: Massively multiplayer online role-playing games: the past, present, and future. Comput. Entertain. **5**(4), 1–33 (2008). https://doi.org/10.1145/1324198.1324207
2. Adams, E., Dormans, J.: Game Mechanics: Advanced Game Design, 1st edn. New Riders Publishing, USA (2012)
3. Becker, A., Görlich, D.: Game balancing - a semantical analysis (2019)

4. Bergdahl, J., Gordillo, C., Tollmar, K., Gisslén, L.: Augmenting automated game testing with deep reinforcement learning. CoRR abs/2103.15819 (2021). https://arxiv.org/abs/2103.15819

5. Beyer, M., et al.: An integrated process for game balancing (2016). https://doi.org/10.1109/CIG.2016.7860425

6. Carpenter, A.: Applying risk analysis to play-balance rpgs (2003)

7. Castronova, E.: On virtual economies. Game Studies 3 (2002)

8. Credits, E.: Perfect imbalance - why unbalanced design creates balanced play (2012). https://www.youtube.com/watch?v=e31OSVZF77w. In comment section. Accessed 26 Oct 2021

9. Fullerton, T.: Game Design Workshop. A Playcentric Approach to Creating Innovative Games, pp. 248–276 (2008). https://doi.org/10.1201/b22309

10. Gudmundsson, S., et al.: Human-like playtesting with deep learning, pp. 1–8 (2018). https://doi.org/10.1109/CIG.2018.8490442

11. Haarnoja, T., Zhou, A., Abbeel, P., Levine, S.: Soft actor-critic: off-policy maximum entropy deep reinforcement learning with a stochastic actor. In: Proceedings of Machine Learning Research, vol. 80, pp. 1861–1870. PMLR, Stockholmsmässan, Stockholm (2018). http://proceedings.mlr.press/v80/haarnoja18b.html

12. Haufe, V.: Hyperinflation in gaia online — know your meme. https://knowyourmeme.com/memes/events/hyperinflation-in-gaia-online (2014). Accessed 08 May 2020

13. Ho, J., Ermon, S.: Generative adversarial imitation learning. CoRR abs/1606.03476 (2016). http://arxiv.org/abs/1606.03476

14. Hutchinson, L.: War stories: lord British created an ecology for Ultima Online but no one saw it (2018). https://arstechnica.com/gaming/2018/12/an-afternoon-with-lord-british-creating-ultima-onlines-unknown-virtual-ecology

15. Juliani, A., et al.: Unity: a general platform for intelligent agents. CoRR abs/1809.02627 (2018). http://arxiv.org/abs/1809.02627

16. Kieger, S.: An exploration of entrepreneurship in massively multiplayer online role-playing games: second life and entropia universe. J. Virtual Worlds Res. 2 (2010). https://doi.org/10.4101/jvwr.v2i4.643

17. Lowe, R., Wu, Y., Tamar, A., Harb, J., Abbeel, P., Mordatch, I.: Multi-agent actor-critic for mixed cooperative-competitive environments. CoRR abs/1706.02275 (2017). http://arxiv.org/abs/1706.02275

18. Raychaudhuri, S.: Introduction to Monte Carlo simulation. In: 2008 Winter Simulation Conference, pp. 91–100 (2008). https://doi.org/10.1109/WSC.2008.4736059

19. Sammut, C.: Behavioral cloning. In: Sammut, C., Webb, G.I. (eds) Encyclopedia of Machine Learning. Springer, Boston (2011). https://doi.org/10.1007/978-0-387-30164-8_69

20. Silver, D., et al.: Mastering chess and shogi by self-play with a general reinforcement learning algorithm. CoRR abs/1712.01815 (2017). http://arxiv.org/abs/1712.01815

21. Stephens, C., Exton, C.: Measuring inflation within virtual economies using deep reinforcement learning. In: Proceedings of the 13th International Conference on Agents and Artificial Intelligence, vol. 2, pp. 444–453. ICAART. INSTICC, SciTePress (2021). https://doi.org/10.5220/0010392804440453

22. Swink, S.: Game Feel: A Game Designer's Guide to Virtual Sensation. Morgan Kaufmann Game Design Books, Taylor & Francis (2009). https://books.google.ie/books?id=i9GfunWcB-oC

23. Works, H.M.: What eve online's tax havens teach us about new york's future. https://www.youtube.com/watch?v=2t25bsqlTM8 (2021). In comment section. Accessed 25 Oct 2021

24. Works, H.M.: Why eve onlines market system might be too efficient for its own good. https://www.youtube.com/watch?v=ijhAILUNz_s (2021). In comment section. Accessed 25 Oct 2021

25. Zheng, S., et al.: The AI economist: Improving equality and productivity with AI-driven tax policies (2020)
26. Zook, A., Riedl, M.O.: Learning how design choices impact gameplay behavior. IEEE Trans. Games **11**(1), 25–35 (2019). https://doi.org/10.1109/TG.2018.2812763
27. Zook, A., Fruchter, E., Riedl, M.: Automatic playtesting for game parameter tuning via active learning (2019)
28. Zook, A., Harrison, B., Riedl, M.O.: Monte-Carlo tree search for simulation-based strategy analysis (2019)

Practical City Scale Stochastic Path Planning with Pre-computation

Kamilia Ahmadi[✉] and Vicki H. Allan

Utah State University, Logan, Utah 84341, USA
kamelia.ahmadi@gmail.com, vicki.allan@usu.edu

Abstract. This work prescribes a practical city scale path planning in the presence of traffic delays. Edge weights are not fixed and are stochastically defined based on the mean and variance of travel time on them. One main objective is to minimize the running time of the overall procedure at query time, and hence the response time to the shortest-path queries are crucial. Agents are car drivers who are moving from one point to another point at different times of the day/night. Agents pursue two types of goal. The first group desires the path with the highest probability of reaching their destination before their desired arrival time. They look for the most secure route. The second group are the agents who are open to take a riskier decision if it helps them in having the shortest en-route time. Pre-computation and approximation has been used in order to scale the path planning process and make it practical in city scale route planning. The city graph is partitioned to smaller groups of nodes using community detection and clustering methods, and each partition is represented by its exemplar. In query time, source and destination pairs are connected to their respective exemplars and the path between those exemplars is found. Paths are stored in distance oracles for different time slots of day/week in order to expedite the query time. Distance oracles are updated weekly in order to capture the recent changes in traffic. The proposed framework handles queries in real time while the approximate paths are 3 to 5% longer than exact paths.

Keywords: Stochastic path planning · Congestion-aware modeling · Community detection methods · Distance oracles · Approximation

1 Introduction

When the volume of traffic is greater than the capacity of the streets congestion is likely to happen. In the era of accelerated urbanization around the world, practical path planning approaches considering the level of congestion are more critical than ever before [1,4,18]. In modeling city scale traffic, congestion changes throughout the day which results in having uncertain travel time on the road segments [14,27]. One of the main approaches is stochastic path planning framework which city is modelled as a graph and the graph's edge weights are the mean and variance of the travel time on each edge during the given time interval. Travel time is defined as a random variable as its value depends on the

© Springer Nature Switzerland AG 2022
A. P. Rocha et al. (Eds.): ICAART 2021, LNAI 13251, pp. 315–339, 2022.
https://doi.org/10.1007/978-3-031-10161-8_17

time of the day and day of the week. Travel time variability is one of the most useful indicators to measure the performance and reliability of a transportation systems [7].

In this work we adopted stochastic path planning framework and modelled agents as car drivers which pursue different goals. Two types of agents have been modelled for a given origin, destination pair: a) the agents that look for a path that maximizes the probability of reaching the destination within a given deadline and b) the agents who look for the shortest en-route time while the probability of making the deadline is at least a given threshold. A path planner satisfies the agents' goals by minimizing the path costs over the travel time random variable toward the agents' goals. Edge weights are defined as mean and variances of travel time for each time slot. While the mean shows the average traffic on the edge, variance reflects how far the values are spread out from their average value with respect to all of the changes and uncertainties in network congestion. The data for extracting edge weights is the historical traffic logged data of the preceding 12 months.

This paper focuses on a scalable algorithm for stochastic path planning under congestion. The main objective of this work is to minimize the query time in order to handle the large number of requests in the real world domain. The approach uses a stochastic path planning framework and improves the query time utilizing pruning, graph partitioning, pre-processing and approximation techniques. A key part is to find region-based partitions in the city graph and represent each region with an exemplar. Instead of planning a path from a source node to the destination node, we connect each node to the closest exemplar considering the direction to the destination and find a path between exemplars. This enables responding to path finding queries in real time with an approximate path instead of an exact path. In the pre-processing phase, all of the paths from every pair of exemplars for every time slot of each day of the week is stored by the distance oracles. An approximate distance oracle is a data structure that efficiently answers path planning queries in graphs. Therefore, in the query time, a source and destination are connected to their corresponding exemplar, and the path from two exemplars is retrieved. Distance oracles are updated every week with respect to the data of the preceding 12 months in order to reflect the recent traffic pattern changes such as seasonality, events, and weather conditions on the congestion of each edge.

2   Previous Work

Stochastic path planning in scale is challenging in real time due to the high volume of queries and dynamic nature of traffic. Fan et al. [10] determine the optimal route by selecting the best next direction at each junction using stochastic dynamic programming problem. Their approach uses a standard successive approximation algorithm. The problem is their algorithm has no finite bound on the maximum number of iterations to converge on cyclic road networks.

Nie and Wu [20] proposed a framework which calculates the optimal a-priori path in query time using a multi-criteria label-correcting algorithm by generating all non-dominated paths based on the first-order stochastic dominance condition (FSD). The proposed algorithm provides an approximate solution in pseudo-polynomial time in the best case, but since the number of FSD non-dominated paths grows exponentially with network size; the run time of the solution is exponential in the worst-case.

Nikolova et al. [22] presented a framework for reliable stochastic combinatorial optimization that includes mean-risk minimization and probability tail model. Their algorithm is independent of the feasible set structure and uses solutions for the underlying linear (deterministic) problems as oracles for solving the corresponding stochastic models. They showed the problem can be solved in $n^{log(n)}$ time if we assume distribution of the travel time random variable is Gaussian. The solution utilizes pre-computation in path planning but still the time complexity of their provided solution are $n^{log(n)}$ which is not practical in real world domain.

Samaranayake et al. [29] presented a label-setting approach to speed up the computation of stochastic path finding based on zero-delay convolution, and localization techniques for determining an optimal order of policy computation. Their proposed approach is still too slow to be implemented in scalable navigation systems.

Gutman, et al. [15] used pruning as a technique to speed up the stochastic planning process. In their model, a node is expanded if its reach value is larger than some threshold. A node with higher reach is a node that appears the most in the shortest paths between pairs of nodes. Reach values are obtained in a pre-processing step. Arc-flag acceleration method [6] also uses pruning to tackle the stochastic path planning at scale. They divide the graph into a set of regions and a Boolean vector representing roads. For each region, the corresponding road value is true if the edge is used by at least one path ending in the corresponding region. Then, any edge without the Boolean corresponding to the region is pruned. One of the major limitations of both mentioned methods is it takes a long time to respond to changes in the network due to the vast amount of computation, even in pre-processing phase.

Contraction hierarchies [14] and arc-flags [6] use bidirectional search in pre-processing. However, speedup techniques that rely on bidirectional search are not applicable to the stochastic path planning problem, because the final and intermediate solutions are a function of the remaining time budget and remaining time budget is not deterministic. When performing a bidirectional search, the reverse search needs to stochastically estimate the time budget at each step, hence there are cases where bi-directional search might not converge.

PACE [33] is a path centric stochastic path planning which estimates the cost of paths instead of edges. Their path finding builds upon the 'path + another edge' pattern to find paths for each source, destination pairs. They store the paths between possible pairs from trajectory data and retrieve in query time. Their approach has the following shortcomings for use in the real world domain: a) estimating the costs of paths highly depends on trajectory data which may suffer from sparsity [17], b) best path is picked after finding candidate paths and estimating the joint cost distribution of the paths which is not real time, and c) their only model finds high probability path.

Lim et al. [27] showed how to solve the scalable stochastic path finding in $\Theta(nlog_n)$ time where n is number of nodes in the network. They assume edge weights in the city graph are independent and distribution of travel time is Gaussian. Their approach is quasi-polynomial with a rate of growth between polynomial and exponential and use a data structure that occupies space roughly proportional to the size of the network for storing distance oracles.

Ahmadi et al. [4] proposed a framework that can answer large scale stochastic path planning queries in real time using graph clustering, pruning, pre-computation, and approximation with two agent goals of highest probability path and shortest en-route time. They used historical traffic data and consider the changes of traffic at different time slots of a day in each day of the week. They reduce the city graph to partitions and pre-compute paths for representative of partitions. Pre-computed paths are updated every week in order to reflect the recent changes. Current work extends the work and enriches the framework in the following ways:

- Expanding graph partitioning methods by adding *meanshift* clustering and *Walktrap* community detection methods to cover variations of graph partitioning methods on the Salt Lake City graph.
- Adding direct (elbow) and statistical (gap statistics) methods for deciding the optimal number of clusters on the city graph which is crucial for clustering algorithms.
- Studying the effect of four exemplar selection methods on approximate paths: a) highest traffic, b) highest reach, c) closeness centrality and d) random walk centrality.
- Studying the impact of the following additions on the overall performance of the framework.

3 Framework

The main idea behind scaling of the path planning process is to partition the city to smaller parts and get an exemplar for each cluster that can represent the nodes of the cluster. Then instead of planning a path from each source node to a destination node, we connect each node to one of the neighboring exemplars and find a path between the exemplars. The paths between exemplars are pre-computed for faster response in query time.

3.1 City and Edge Weights

The city is modelled as a directed graph consisting of a set of vertices, V, which represent road intersections and edges, E, that represent road segments between vertices. We consider the city graph to be planar (i.e., edges intersect only at their end points). If we consider the number of nodes in the planar graph as $|V|$ and the number of edges as $|E|$, the relationship between them is $|E| << |V|^2$ [1,22,27]. Associated with each edge of the graph is a travel cost used as the edge weight in our directed graph.

Edge weights are represented as a probability distribution of travel time rather than a fixed value. Travel time random variable is a tuple of mean and variance of the expected travel time on each edge. We assume travel time on edges are independent and follow Gaussian random variable shown in Eq. 1 [1,3,27]. The mean of a path is the sum of the means of all edges included in the path (Eq. 2) in which t is query time and δ is the time takes to reach to any edge from the query time. Equation 3 shows how to calculate the variance of the path. Since we assume edge weights are independent from each other, then $cov(X_i, X_j)=0$ for $i \neq j$ and Eq. 4 is the result. Based on Eq. 4, the variance of a path is the sum of variance of all edges included in the path as shown in Eq. 5 [22,27].

$$t_e \sim N(m_e, v_e) \tag{1}$$

$$m_{path}(t) = \sum_{e \in path} m_e(t + \delta) \tag{2}$$

$$var(\sum_{i=1}^{n} X_i) = E([\sum_{i=1}^{n} X_i]^2) - [E(\sum_{i=1}^{n} X_i)]^2 \tag{3}$$

$$var(\sum_{i=1}^{n} X_i) = \sum_{i=1}^{n} \sum_{j=1}^{n} cov(X_i, X_j) = \sum_{i=1}^{n} cov(X_i, X_j) = \sum_{i=1}^{n} var(X_i) \tag{4}$$

$$v_{path}(t) = \sum_{e \in path} v_e(t + \delta) \tag{5}$$

Stochastic dependency between adjacent edges can be modelled by adding extra edges between dependent edges. This new edge captures the correlation between the two correlated distributions, maintaining the property that the variance of a path is the sum of the variances of all the edges in the path. Suppose that adjacent edges X_i and X_j are dependent. Based on Eq. 6, if we want to sum the variance of X_i and X_j, $Cov(X_i, X_j)$ is non-zero as edges are dependent. Therefore, we add one edge with mean 0 and variance of $2 * Cov(X_i, X_j)$. The number of nodes and edges grows by one for each pair of correlation. In our model, we do not transform the graph, and the assumption is that the dependence between edges affects the variance of the consecutive edges. For example, if edge A, has a strong dependency with edge B and congestion on edge A causes congestion on edge B, then the variance on edge B is high enough to represent this dependence [2,8,21,22,27].

$$var(X_i + X_j) = var(X_i) + var(X_j) + 2 * Cov(X_i, X_j) \tag{6}$$

For finding the mean and variance of a path, a sliding time window is used to imply the cost of each edge in the path depends on the amount of time that took to reach it, not just the initial departure time. For example, if we look at the path at time a and take δ to reach the 4th edge, the cost of the 4th edge is considered at the time of $a + \delta$.

3.2   Traffic Data

Edge weights are based on mean and variance of the expected travel time on them. In order to extract edge weights, yearlong traffic data from Utah Department of Transportation (UDOT) [32] has been used which is logged in 10 min intervals for each day of a week on Salt Lake City, Utah.

3.3 Open Street Map

For building the city graph, we used Open Street Map data [12]. Open Street Map is a free editable geographic map of the city. Open street map data structure has three main components: a) *nodes* which is a single point defined by latitude and longitude, b) *ways* which is a list of nodes, and c) *relations* which relates two or more data elements like a route, turn restriction, traffic signal or an area. Open Street Map represents physical entities on the ground like buildings, roads, intersections, and bridges. The data structure it uses is based on entities and for each entity there are multiple tags describing the characteristics of that entity.

3.4 Agents

In this framework, agents are car drivers, capable of pursuing different goals. We can technically model any type of agents' goals and incorporate it in the path finding framework. We modelled two following goals as they have interesting characteristics in the path planning domain.

– Risk seeking agents: the agents who are open to take a riskier route if has the shortest en-route time. These agents are flexible in leaving time.
– Risk averse agents: agents who are not willing to take risk and look for the path with highest probability of reaching destination before a desired arrival time, even if travel time is increased.

To make these two goals clearer, one example is in the context of a package delivery system. Suppose that we guarantee the delivery of a package by 4 PM, otherwise the customer doesn't accept the delivery, and we pay the shipping costs. In that case, we are interested in picking a path that has the highest chance of reaching destination before the deadline to avoid losing the shipping cost. The other possible case is delivering perishable products. If the product needs to be kept hot or cold, we desire a path that has the shortest en-route time. We are flexible in leaving anytime, but need to have the shortest en-route path while still making the target delivery time.

3.5 City Graph Partitioning

In dealing with large scale graphs, one of the possible approaches is to reduce the node set. The reduction process happens through partitioning the graph to a group of nodes in a way that the group can be represented by one node. For this work, we investigated 1) unsupervised learning (clustering methods), and 2) community detection methods for partitioning the city. After partitioning phase, an exemplar for each partition is selected. One can argue that community detection is similar to clustering. Clustering is a machine learning unsupervised technique in which similar data points are grouped into the same cluster based on their attributes. So in networks, clustering is merely based on the position of the nodes. On the other side, community detection methods are focused on partitioning the graph based on edges as communities are a group of well-connected nodes that are more strongly connected among themselves than the others.

Unsupervised Learning. A cluster refers to a collection of data points aggregated together due to the certain similarities using unsupervised methods. Given a set of data points, clustering puts each data point into a specific group. In theory, data points that are in the same group should have similar properties, while data points in different groups should have highly dissimilar properties. There are various clustering methods to be used on graphs and in this work, we used *k-means* [19] and *meanshift* clustering methods [9]. In our clustering a node has the following attributes: a) latitude, b) longitude, and c) traffic profile which is historical traffic level on the node (low, medium and high).

Optimal Number of Clusters. Most of the common clustering methods including *k-means* and *meanshift* require the number of clusters (k) to be defined ahead of time. There are various methods for deciding the optimal number of clusters in data including direct and statistical methods. Direct methods like elbow method [19] usually optimize a criterion such as the within cluster sums of square distance. Statistical methods such as gap statistics [31] compare evidence against expectation under random sample of data under uniform distribution.

  Elbow method looks at the total within-cluster sum of square distances (WSS) as a function of the number of clusters. WSS is the sum of the squared deviations from each observation and the cluster centroid (Eq. 7).

$$\sum_{i=1}^{n} min(\|x_i - \mu_i\|) \tag{7}$$

In general, a cluster that has a small sum of squares is more compact than a cluster that has a large sum of squares. The number of clusters is increased until adding another cluster does not improve the total WSS significantly. Steps of elbow method are as follows:

- Run clustering algorithm on varying values of k.
- For each k, calculate WSS.
- Plot the curve of WSS against number of clusters k.
- The location of a bend (knee) in the plot is considered an indicator of the appropriate number of clusters.

  Gap statistic compares the total within intra-cluster variation (W_k) for different values of k and compare it with their expected values under null reference distribution of the data. Null reference distribution of data is the samples of data under uniform distribution which we consider to reject the null hypothesis. Null hypothesis here states that our clusters of the data is same as the clusters of a uniform distribution of the data. W_k is the within-cluster sum of squared distances from the cluster means and can be found using Eq. 8. D_r is the some of pairwise distances for all of the points in the cluster and $d_{ii'}$ represents the distance between every i and i' pairs.

$$W_k = \sum_{r=1}^{k} \frac{1}{2n_r} D_r \qquad (8)$$

$$D_r = \sum_{i,i' \in C_r} d_{ii'} \qquad (9)$$

The optimal number of clusters is the value of k that yields the largest gap statistic. The largest gap means that the clustering structure is far away from the random uniform distribution of points. For gap statistics, we first cluster the data by varying the number of k and compute the corresponding W_k. Then, we generate B reference data sets with uniform random distribution and cluster each of them with varying number of clusters. Compute the estimated gap statistic as the deviation of the observed W_k value from its expected value W_{kb}^* shown in Eq. 10. Afterward, we choose the number of clusters as the smallest value of k such that the gap statistic is within one standard deviation of the gap at k+1 using Eq. 11. In Eq. 11 where s_k is the simulation error calculated from standard deviation of B replicas and found using Eq. 12.

$$Gap(k) = \frac{1}{B} \sum_{1}^{B} log(W_{kb}^*) - log(W_k) \qquad (10)$$

$$Gap(k) \geq Gap(k) - s_{k+1} \qquad (11)$$

$$s_k = sd(k) + \sqrt{1 + \frac{1}{B}} \qquad (12)$$

K-means Clustering. *K-means* is a very popular clustering algorithm because it easily scales to large data sets, guarantees the convergence and easily adapts to the new data points. The *k-means* clustering aims to partition n observations into k clusters. Clusters are formed to minimize within cluster variance. The centroid (used as the exemplar) is the arithmetic mean position of all the points in the cluster. The *k-means* algorithm starts with a first group of randomly selected centroids, which are used as the beginning points for every cluster, and then performs iterative calculations to optimize the positions of the centroids. It ends when there is no change in the value of centroids or the defined number of iterations has been achieved. As k needs to be defined ahead of time, we use both elbow and gap statistics methods to get optimal number of clusters on the graph of Salt Lake City before using *k-means*. The optimal number of clusters using the elbow method is 157 and for gap statistics is 172. Therefore, we set the value of k as the average of these two and set the number of k as 162. Figure 1 (top) shows the distribution of 162 clusters and the visualization of the clusters on Salt Lake City. As distribution shows, the majority of clusters have 70 to 400 nodes and few large clusters with node size larger than 1000 nodes.

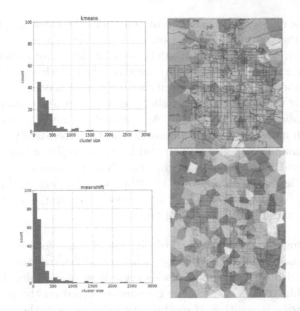

Fig. 1. Distribution of main nodes in each cluster and visualization of them on Salt Lake City. Each color represents one cluster. Top for *K-means* clustering and bottom for *MeanShift*. (Color figure online)

MeanShift. *Meanshift* [9] clustering is a non-parametric centroid-based algorithm, which works by updating candidates for centroids to be the mean of the points within a given region. Unlike other clustering algorithms which assigns the data points to the clusters iteratively, *meanshift* tends groups points towards the mode. Hence, it is also called a mode seeking algorithm. In the context of *meanshift*, mode is the highest density of data points in the region. *Meanshift* uses the concept of kernel density estimation (KDE) [23] which is a method to estimate the probability density function of the data. It works by applying a Gaussian kernel on each point in the data set. Adding up all of the individual kernels generates a probability surface example density function. *Meanshift* is a model free approach which doesn't assume any distribution of the data. It is robust to outliers as it uses kernel density functions. Similar to *k-means*, the number of clusters needs to be defined ahead of time. We run elbow method and gap statistics method on the graph of Salt Lake City with *meanshift* clustering. Elbow method provided 211 and gap statistics's optimal number of clusters were 247. Then we set the average as 229. Figure 1 (bottom) shows the distribution and the visualization of the clusters on Salt Lake City. It provided 229 clusters with majority of clusters had the size in the range of 50 to 700 and few large clusters.

Community Detection Methods. A community, with respect to graphs, is defined as a subset of nodes that are densely connected to each other and loosely connected to the nodes in the other communities in the same graph. Depending on the type of the community detection methods, the city graph can be partitioned differently. Major community detection methods are divided into three main categories: a) divisive methods, b) agglomerative methods and c) optimization based methods [30]. Divisive algorithms begin with a complete network and iteratively divide the network into smaller communities. An example of divisive methods is *Leading Eigenvector* [26]. Agglomerative based methods begin by considering each node as its own community and then iteratively combine nodes into larger communities. *Walktrap* [24] and label propagation [13] are the examples of agglomerative methods. Optimization based methods find the optimal set of communities based on an objective function. *Multilevel* [34] is an example of optimization based method. There are a few important definitions which is common in community detection algorithms:

- Modularity measures the strength of division of a network into communities and reflects the concentration of edges within modules compared with random distribution of links between all nodes regardless of modules. If the number of edges within groups exceeds the number expected on the basis of chance, then modularity is positive. If modularity value is zero, then edges are randomly distributed and negative value of modularity indicates the absence of a community in the graph.
- A random walk is a path between two nodes where each step is randomly chosen.
- Path lengths for walks between two nodes are the number of edges one would have to use to walk from one node to another.

Leading Eigenvector. *Leading Eigenvector* [26] is a divisive community detection approach which is built on maximizing modularity over possible divisions of the graph utilizing the properties of adjacency matrix of the city graph. Based on the adjacency matrix, the modularity matrix is defined. Modularity matrix is defined using the Eq. 13 where A_{ij} is adjacency matrix, k_i, k_j are degrees of the vertices and m is $\frac{1}{2} \sum_i^n k_i$.

$$B_{ij} = A_{ij} - \frac{k_i k_j}{2m} \qquad (13)$$

Then, the eigenvector corresponding to the *leading eignevector* of the modularity matrix is considered. Utilizing the signs of elements in this vector we decide the group. The elements of the *leading eigenvector* measure how firmly each vertex belongs to its assigned community. In the maximization process, the division of the graph with maximum modularity value is the best distribution of communities. We run the same algorithm over the newly formed communities and continue unless all the communities obtained are indivisible. Running *Leading Eigenvector* on the graph of Salt Lake City produces 21 communities with 48398 nodes in one community. The big community includes the main downtown area of the Salt Lake City.

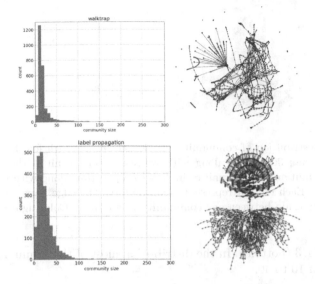

Fig. 2. Left: Distribution of communities in *Multilevel* approach and representation of them. Each red dot represent a community. (Color figure online)

Walktrap. *Walktrap* [24] method is an agglomerative method for community detection based on random walks in which distance between vertices are measured through random walks in the network. The basic intuition of the algorithm is that random walks on a graph gets trapped into densely connected parts corresponding to communities. *Walktrap* uses the result of random walks to iteratively merge separate communities in a bottom-up manner by minimizing the overall random walk distance between nodes and communities defined by random walks. The algorithm continues until no more merge is possible. Figure 3 (top) shows the results of Running *Walktrap* on Salt Lake City. *Walktrap* provided 2751 communities with majority in the range of 20 to 40 nodes and few large communities in the range of 3000 to 4000 nodes.

Label Propagation. The *Label Propagation* algorithm [13] is a another agglomerative algorithm which detects communities using network structure without a pre-defined objective function. The intuition behind the algorithm is that a single label quickly becomes dominant in a densely connected group of nodes as it get trapped inside a densely connected group of nodes. In the beginning, every node is initialized with a unique community label. Then, the labels propagate through the network and at every iteration of propagation, each node updates its label based on the maximum numbers of its neighbours' labels and the communities are formed this way. *Label Propagation* stops if he user-defined maximum number of iterations is achieved or algorithm converges. Convergence occurs when each node has the majority label of its neighbours or no merge happens in further iterations. Running *Label Propagation* on the graph of Salt Lake City provides 2007 communities with the distribution similar to truncated normal distribution

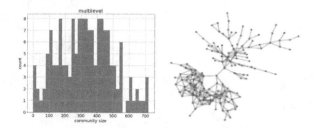

Fig. 3. Top: Distribution of communities in *Walktrap* approach for the clusters with node size less than 300 nodes along with representation of all of the communities. **Bottom**: Distribution of communities in *Label Propagation* along with representation of communities. Each red dot represent a community. The edge between communities shows the relationship between one community to another. (Color figure online)

depicted in Fig. 3 (bottom). In the distribution most of the community sizes are in the range of 10 to 40.

Multilevel. *Multilevel* [34] method is built on modularity optimization and creates communities in a way that the edges inside of the community are significantly denser than between communities. Multi-level is a two step iterative algorithm which stops when no improvement is gained. In step 1, every node is assigned to a random community, then in step 2 each node is removed from its own community and assigned to its neighboring community if the gain of modularity is positive. Applying *multilevel* community detection method on the city of Salt Lake City provides 157 communities on the graph of Salt Lake City which is shown in Fig. 2.

3.6   Exemplar Assignment

After partitioning the city, we need to find a node (termed the exemplar) that represents each partition of the graph. There are few possible ways of finding exemplars.

- The node with highest historical traffic. The idea is the node which historically has the highest traffic is the node that should represent the partition as historically lots of paths went through it.
- Node with highest reach. Reach is a concept introduced by Gutman et al. [15] and basically measures the use of a node. A node with higher reach is a node that appears the most in the shortest paths between pairs of the partition. For finding the node with highest reach, we run Floyd-Warshall [5,11] algorithm on all of the nodes of the partition which gives us shortest path for all pairs of vertices in the partition. The node that appears in the maximum number of paths is the exemplar of the partition.
- Center of the partition based on closeness centrality. Closeness centrality [28] of a node is calculated as the reciprocal of the sum of the lengths of

the shortest paths between the node and all other nodes in the partition. Thus, the more central a node is, the closer it is to all other nodes in that partition. Equation 14 shows the normalized value of closeness centrality as normalization allows comparisons of centrality value between nodes. In Eq. 14 $d(i,j)$ represents the distance between node i and j. Distance is defined based on shortest path between the pair of nodes.

$$C(i) = \frac{n-1}{\sum_{j \in nodes} d(j,i)} \tag{14}$$

- Center of the partition based on Random walk closeness centrality. Random walk closeness centrality also called Markov centrality is very similar to the closeness centrality but here closeness is measured by the expected length of a random walk rather than by the shortest path. A node is considered to be close to other nodes if the random walk process initiated from any node of the network arrives to this particular node in relatively few steps on average. The random walk closeness centrality of each node is the inverse of the average mean first passage time to that node. In order to calculate the centrality of each node, the inverse of the mean first passage time between every pair of nodes is taken. Nodes with higher centrality scores indicating that they occupy a more central position within the partition. The mean first-passage time (MFPT) defines an average timescale for a stochastic event to first occur. The mean first passage time from node i to node j is the expected number of steps it takes to reach node j from node i for the first time. Equation 15 shows how to calculate mean first passage time for each node. In Eq. 15, $P(i,j,r)$ denotes the probability that it takes exactly r steps to reach j from i for the first time.

$$MFP(i,j) = \sum_{r=1}^{n} rP(i,j,r) \tag{15}$$

3.7 Base Path Planning Framework

The goal of base path planning framework is to find paths align with agents' goals and deadline between every pair of nodes. The base path planning framework is extended from [4]. The first step is to find the candidate paths that can possibly satisfy the agents' goals. As it is computationally intractable to consider all of the paths between any pair of nodes. Then, among those candidates we select the one which has a minimum cost and matches the agents' goals.

Finding Candidate Paths. Considering all of the paths between any source, destination pair is computationally intractable; hence a primary step is needed to reduce the number of paths to the ones that have the highest similarity to the query. The goal of the pruning is to reduce the number of candidate paths to only explore the paths that meet the agent's goals and query deadline. For finding the candidate paths between nodes (n_1 and n_2), we start from n_1 and explore the successor nodes (*expanding*) until we reach n_2. When exploring each node, the heuristic estimates a path from that node to destination and if the expected estimated arrival time when using the heuristic path is greater than the provided deadline, the node is not expanded (pruned). Figure 4 (left) shows the pruning step.

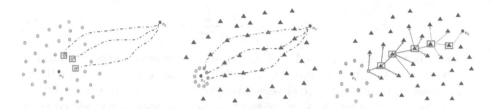

Fig. 4. Left: For finding a path from n_1 to n_2, successor nodes of n_1 (orange circles) are explored. Among the successor, the marked ones meet the deadline and rest are discarded. Dotted paths are heuristics paths from the successor nodes to n_2 and they are used as a pruning criteria for the successor nodes of n_1. **Middle**: Finding the heuristic path from m (a middle node in expansion shown as green circles) to n_2 uses $A*$ algorithm through exemplars of graph (green triangles). **Right**: From current exemplar to the neighboring exemplar the one with with the least $g(n)+h(n)$ is selected (green triangle). Figure shows the selected exemplar in each step of A^* on exemplars for heuristic path. (Color figure online)

The heuristic path from a node m (a middle node in expansion) to node n_2 is obtained by running A^* [16] on the exemplars instead of all the nodes of the graph (Fig. 4 (middle)). In each step of A^*, the next exemplar is picked based on the smallest $g(n) + h(n)$ value, where $g(n)$ is the shortest-length path from current node to the connecting exemplar and $h(n)$ is the direct distance heuristic from the connecting exemplar to n_2. Shortest-length paths between nodes and their exemplars and also the adjacent exemplars are pre-computed and they are retrieved to build the heuristic path. Figure 4 (right) shows the approach.

Paths Cost Definition and Selecting Best Path. The goal of the path planning is to pick a path with minimum cost which matches the agents' goals among the candidate paths. Expected cost of a path can be found using Eq. 16. In 16, t_{path} is the expected arrival time of the path and d is the deadline the agent has to make.

$$expected\ cost = Cost(t_{path}, d) * f_{path}(t_{path}|m, \delta^2_{path})$$
$$= \int_{-\infty}^{+\infty} u(t - d) f_{path}(t_{path}) dt_{path} = \int_{d}^{+\infty} f_{path}(t_{path}) dt_{path} \quad (16)$$

Path cost is modelled using a step cost function, but generally any type of cost function can be used in Eq. 16. The step cost function only penalizes the agent if it reaches the destination after the deadline. Based on Eq. 16, the whole cost is equal to the Cumulative Density Function (CDF) of Standard Normal Distribution. CDF generates a probability of the random variable (travel time in this case) when distribution is normal to be less than a specific value which is d (deadline) here. Then, maximizing the Θ value (Eq. 17), ultimately results in having a path that maximizes the probability of reaching the destination before deadline which matches the first agent goal.

$$\Theta(path) = \frac{deadline - m_{path}}{\sqrt{v_{path}}} \tag{17}$$

The second type of agent goal seeks the path with shortest en-route time that can make the deadline while they are flexible on departure time. We can modify Eq. 17 to Eq. 18 by replacing deadline as the difference of desired arrival time and departure time. Deadline is the amount of time the agent needs to reach the destination from query time. In this case, desired arrival time is fixed but departure time is flexible. In Eq. 18, ϕ is the argument of Gaussian CDF that makes the CDF equal to the probability of making the trip before deadline which in our case is 90%.

$$desired\ arrival\ time - departure\ time = m_{path} + \Phi(path) * \sqrt{v_{path}}$$
$$if\ departure\_time \subset [\tau 1, \tau 2] \tag{18}$$

To find the best departure time, the first step is to find what is the latest possible departure time (τ_2) to make the trip before the deadline. Then, considering the query time as the earliest possible departure time as τ_1, the interval of $[\tau_1, \tau_2]$ is the time frame that includes the best departure time. Divide the interval into 10-min segments. For each segment, the path that minimizes the trip duration (Eq. 18) is selected. Afterward, we pick the "time segment" which has the minimum cost path (based on Eq. 18) in comparison to other time segments. The found minimum cost path with this approach, is the path that has the least en-route time.

3.8 Pre-processing: Building Distance Oracles

In city scale path planning, the volume of path finding requests is high and, hence, calculating a path which satisfies the agents' goals and abides the deadline at query time is not a practical approach. Techniques such as pre-processing and approximation help in expediting the path finding process. For a graph of n vertices, one way is to simply store an n × n-distance matrix for a n-vertex graph. In that case, each query can be answered in constant time, but the space requirement is large and updating the n × n-distance matrix is very time consuming. Approximation is a way of making distance oracles more compact. Their aim is to find solutions which are not exact but clearly close. For example, in our case we don't need to store an n × n-distance matrix, but we can store the paths between exemplars in our city graph which helps in reducing the path finding time. Distance oracles store the best path between every two exemplars for each agent goal for different time slots of each day of week. Time slots are every 10 min of every day of the week. Building distance oracles is an offline task and distance oracles are updated weekly to reflect recent traffic patterns on the edges of the city. In each update, the traffic data for the preceding year is used. Stored paths between exemplars help us to quickly answering the path finding requests by connecting the source-destination pair to their respective exemplars and provide the path. Details of the approximate path finding is explained in Sect. 3.9). The solution is space and time efficient.

3.9 Scalable Algorithm

Each path finding query contains source, destination, agent's goal and deadline. The first step is to connect the source and destination to their respective exemplar. Each node may have up to nine exemplars around it, one candidate is the exemplar of the region it is located and the others are the exemplars of neighboring regions. For selecting the right exemplars, a hypothetical direct path between source and destination is considered and the exemplars with the most similarity to the direction of the hypothetical path are selected. The connecting paths that connects the source, destination to the exemplars are calculated based on shortest length path. Then, the path between exemplars that matches the agent's goals in the query is retrieved from distance oracles. Afterward, connecting paths are added to the retrieved path from distance oracle and the final path is constructed and sent as the result of the query. The path between exemplars does not necessarily need to go through other exemplars. Figure 5 illustrates a path between source and destination.

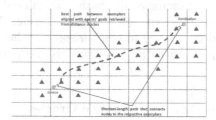

Fig. 5. Red rectangles are exemplars of each region. Green circles are the typical source and destination. (Color figure online)

4 Experiments and Results

We experimented multiple methods of city graph partitioning. Each partitioning method provided various partitions. The key question is, "How many partitions are needed to represent Salt Lake City with reasonable approximation?" This question is answered in Sect. 4.1. We discuss which community and clustering approach is picked for partitioning the city in Sect. 4.2. In Sect. 4.3 we show which node in each partition should be used as exemplar to represent all of the nodes in the partition. We run exact and approximate path finding algorithms to compare the approximate paths to exact paths in Sect. 4.4. Lastly, we analyze the space and time complexity of our proposed framework in Sect. 4.5.

4.1 How Many Partitions Are Needed to Represent the City Graph?

City partitioning is used to reduce the large scale city graph to the set of exemplars. We ran multiple clustering and community detection approaches on the city graph and discussed the provided distribution of each in Sect. 3.5. It is obvious that, the more the partitions the more approximate paths get closer to the exact paths as we increase the number of partitions. However, our goal is to reduce the number of nodes of city graph as it impacts the storage required by distance oracles. Also, we want to keep the accuracy of approximate paths in the acceptable range. Accuracy is measured based on the deviation of travel time of generated approximate paths from exact path for each source and destination for the 5000 source destination samples in various time slots of different days of a week. Travel time basically tells us how much longer the paths will be due to approximation. For picking the right number of partitions, we divide the city based on a variety of partition numbers and look at the percentage of travel time deviation of approximate paths from exact paths for both of the agents' goals. If the point of inflection on the curve is seen, then it is a good indication that the underlying number of partitions fits best at that point. For measuring the deviation, grid-based city partitioning is used as baseline of the city partitioning in approximate path planning. Grid based partitioning is a simple method to partition the city in a grid.

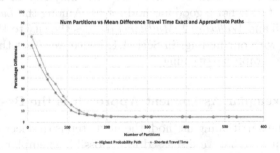

Fig. 6. Number of partitions vs the mean difference of travel time of exact and approximate path.

Figure 6 shows the percentage deviation of travel time of exact and approximate paths for the both agents' goals for variation of partitions. As it shows, the more the partitions the more accurate the paths are. However, having more partitions increases the node size which leads to more storage and time to update distance oracles. Based on Fig. 6, having 150 to 170 partitions looks reasonable with the mean difference of travel time of exact and approximate paths around 7%. Inspired by the findings of Fig. 6, we defined a grid based partitioning which partitions Salt Lake City to 150 partitions to be used as the baseline of the other experiments.

4.2   Which Partitioning Method We Picked?

Clustering. For the clustering approach, we tried *k-means* and *meanshift* methods. *K-means* provided 162 clusters and *meanshift* produced 229 clusters. Both of the methods provides clusters in the accepted range of number of partitions. Hence, we need to look at the quality of clusters in order to pick best choice. One widely used metric for measuring the quality of clustering algorithms is Silhouette Index [25]. This metric uses concepts of cohesion and separation to evaluate clusters, using the distance between nodes to measure their similarity found using Eq. 19.

$$S(C_i) = \frac{\sum_{v \in C_i} S_v}{|C_i|} \quad where \quad S_v = \frac{b_v - a_v}{max(a_v, b_v)} \tag{19}$$

where a_v is the average distance between vertex v and all the other vertices in the same cluster and b_v is the average distance between v and all the vertices in the nearest cluster. The silhouette index for a given cluster is the average value of silhouette for all its member vertices. Comparing silhouette index of *k-means* and *meanshift* shows that *k-means* has a better index, therefore we picked *k-means* as our clustering algorithm.

Community Detection. Among the community detection methods that we used, *Leading Eigenvector* provided 21 partitions with majority of the area in one partition. Hence, this is not a good method for us. Among the *Label Propagation* 3.5, *Multilevel* 3.5 and *Walktrap* 2, *Multilevel* divides the city to 157 communities which is aligned with our findings in Sect. 4.1, hence we select this approach for community-based graph partitioning.

4.3   Which Exemplar Assignment Approach Is the Best?

After selecting the partitioning method, the next step is to select the exemplar of each partition. In Sect. 3.6 we discussed four possible exemplar selection methods: a) highest traffic, b) highest reach, c) closeness centrality and d) random walk centrality. To determine which is best, we picked 5000 source destination pairs in various time slots of different days of a week. We use grid based city partitioning as a baseline. Then we find approximate paths for the 5000 source destination pairs each time with one exemplar selection method for each agents' goal. Then, we look at the percent of times the approximate path planning approach has the closest (mean, variance) of travel time to the exact path. Then the

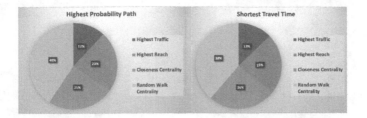

Fig. 7. Comparison of four methods of exemplar selection a) highest traffic, b) highest reach, c) closeness centrality and d)random walk centrality.

method with highest number of similarity is selected as the exemplar selection method.

As Figure 7 shows, random walk centrality provides a better representation of exemplars in comparison to the other three methods for the both agent goals as the paths using random walk centrality are more similar to exact paths.

4.4   How Is the Quality of Approximate Paths?

For the purpose of experiments, we choose 5000 source, destination pairs randomly among all of the possible source-destination pairs to represent the path planning universe. Path planning queries are distributed across the traffic profiles at different time slots of weekdays. Each path planning query has the following inputs: a) source, b) destination, c) time of query, d) deadline and e) agent's goal. Then, for all of the queries we compare the approximate path generated from our proposed algorithm and the exact path.

Highest Probability Path. In order to compare the quality of our proposed approximate paths, we considered the relative difference of mean and variance of travel time of paths between exact and approximate path. For partitioning part of the approximate paths we used community detection (multi-level method), clustering (*k-means*) and grid based. Grid based is used as a baseline as it doesn't have an intelligent way of partitioning the city graph and it is only based on a grid. Gird-based method help us to compare the effectiveness of community and clustering method. Figure 8 shows the relative difference of mean and variance of travel time of paths between exact and approximate path planning approaches for rush and non-rush hours.

Here are the finding from Fig. 8:

- Multi-level approach has the least relative difference to exact paths in comparison to clustering and grid-based method partitioning.
- The relative difference of travel time of all of the approximate methods is more significant in rush hour in comparison to non-rush hour. As in non-rush hour, the traffic is not high, hence both approximate and exact approach are almost the same.
- The mean of travel time of community approach is 5% longer than the exact path in rush hour and this percentage is 3% longer in non-rush hour.

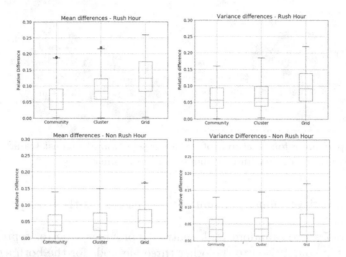

Fig. 8. Y axis is the relative difference percentage of mean and variance of travel time of paths for exact and approximate approach for peak and non-peak hours for the agent's goal of highest probability path.

- The variance of travel time of community approach is 8% longer than the exact path in rush hour and this percentage is 4% longer in non-rush hour.
- in both rush and non-rush hour community and clustering method outperform grid-based method and this shows the impact of an intelligent graph partitioning on the quality of approximate paths.

After looking at the relative difference of travel time of community, clustering and grid based approximate paths, now we want to see among the 5000 source, destination samples of the experiment, what is the ratio of each method in terms of having the closest mean, variance of travel time to exact paths. Figure 9 shows this ratio and based on it in rush hour, 54% of the closest paths to the exact were from the community approach with 37% clustering and a small fraction of grid approach (8%). In non-rush hour traffic the differences are less but still the pattern is the same. This emphasizes the fact that having an accurate graph clustering approach is more important during high traffic.

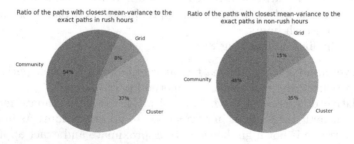

Fig. 9. Ratio of paths with the closest mean-variance to the exact path in peak and non-peak hour for the agent's goal of highest probability path.

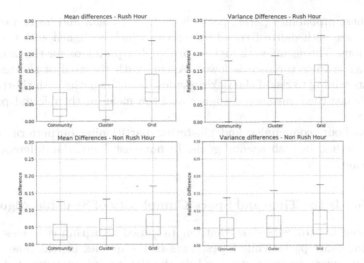

Fig. 10. Relative difference of travel time of mean and variance of paths for exact and approximate approach for rush and non-rush hours for the agent's goal of shortest en-route time.

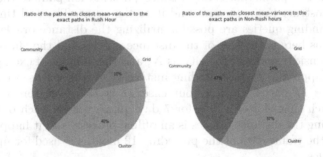

Fig. 11. Ratio of paths with the closest mean-variance to the exact path for the agent's goal of shortest en-route time.

Shortest Travel Time. In this section we repeat the experiments in Sect. 4.4 for the agent goal of shortest en-route time. Figure 10 and Fig. 11 illustrates the results.

Here are the findings from Fig. 10 and Fig. 11 and also the comparison of the results with Sect. 4.4.

- Similar to the previous section, community method outperforms other approximate approaches in terms of closeness of relative difference from approximate and exact paths.
- Approximate path planning methods in rush hour have larger travel time difference than non-rush time and in rush hour the mean of community method is 4% and its variance is 9% higher than the exact path.

- In highest probability paths, paths have higher mean and lower variance in comparison with shortest travel time paths which is aligned with their goals' definitions. The agents with highest probability path look for the most secure path hence their variance is lower. Agents with the goal of shortest travel time are willing to risk if the risk provides them the paths with shorter travel time, hence their variance is higher and the mean of their found paths are shorter.
- In rush hour, community and clustering partitioning outperform the grid based method in both agents' goals. In non-rush hour, the difference is less significant.

4.5   What Is the Time and Space Complexity of Scalable Algorithm?

The previous experiments show that our proposed algorithm is at least 95% as good as the exact paths while it responds to the queries in real time. When a path finding query comes, source and destination nodes are connected to their respective exemplars. Then, the stored path between exemplars for that time of the day, day of the week and type of agents' goal is retrieved. The retrieved path along with the sub-paths that connect source, destination pairs to the respective exemplars construct the path and send it to the agent. The real time response to the path finding queries are possible utilizing the distance oracles. Now one of the concerns here is the size of the distance oracles and the effort to update them. If we consider nodes of the city as N, and the number of exemplars as M, utilizing the approximate path finding instead of $N * N$ paths, we are storing $N * M + M * M$ paths which in our case M is 157. We store one distance oracles for each time slot of a day, for 7 days of a week for each of the agent's goals. Updating the distance oracles is an offline process, and it happens weekly. Every week, the traffic data of the preceding 12 months is used for updating the distance oracles.

5   Conclusion and Future Work

This paper introduces a practical scalable path planning framework in the city scale framework while agents have the capability of pursuing different goals. Some agents look for the most secure path and others seek the path with the shortest en-route time while it might have some degrees of risks involved in it. Each path is evaluated by the amount of cost associated with it and cost of the paths are estimated mainly based on the travel time of the path leveraging cost functions. Each agent finds a path with minimum cost which stratifies its goal. Since city scale path planning involves with lots of path requests at the same time, we need to expedite the path planning process. For this reason, the city is partitioned to smaller parts and each partition is represented with an exemplar. Multiple method of exemplar assignment has been studied and random walk centrality is picked as the proper method of exemplar assignment. For partitioning the city graph, we used community detection and clustering methods. Clustering focuses on partitioning the graph based on similarity of nodes, while community detection methods are focused on finding communities based on richness of edges in the community.

In the time of a path planning requests, source and destination nodes are connected to their corresponding exemplars. This connection is based on the direction of hypothetical direct path between source and destination and the final path is created by adding the connecting path to the retrieved path between exemplars. In the pre-computation step, the path between exemplars are computed and stored in distance oracles based on the preceding year data at the time of update and the oracles are updated every week to reflect the recent changes on the network. In this framework, graph partitioning reduces the graph size; pre-computation helps in answering the queries in real time and approximation helps in reducing the space needed for storing the paths. Our results show that community-based approaches produce closer results to exact path planning approach in comparison to clustering method and approximation provides paths with mean and variance which are not exact but close to the exact path, while the solution is space and time efficient. There are few directions to be considered as a future work. Since we are modelling a real world domain, adding new agents goals to the domain increases the complexity and hence the goal directed path planning is scale is more crucial. Also, we can consider traffic data prediction to enhance the decision-making process which is currently based on historical data.

References

1. Ahmadi, K.: Intelligent traffic management: from practical stochastic path planning to reinforcement learning based city-wide traffic optimization. Ph.D. Dissertation, All Graduate Theses and Dissertations, Utah State University (2021). https://doi.org/10.26076/a68e-ef6a
2. Ahmadi, K., Allan, V.H.: Stochastic path finding under congestion. In: International Conference on Computational Science and Computational Intelligence (CSCI), pp. 135–140. IEEE (2017). https://doi.org/10.1109/CSCI.2017.22
3. Ahmadi, K., Allan, V.H.: Congestion-aware stochastic path planning and its applications in real world navigation. In: Proceedings of the 13th International Conference on Agents and Artificial Intelligence, ICAART 2021, pp. 947–956. SCITEPRESS (2021). https://doi.org/10.5220/0010267009470956
4. Ahmadi, K., Allan, V.H.: Scalable stochastic path planning under congestion. In: Proceedings of the 13th International Conference on Agents and Artificial Intelligence, pp. 454–463. SCITEPRESS (2021). https://doi.org/10.5220/0010394104540463
5. Ahmadi, K., Allan, V.H.: Smart city: application of multi-agent reinforcement learning systems in adaptive traffic management. In: 2021 IEEE International Smart Cities Conference (ISC2), pp. 1–7 (2021). https://doi.org/10.1109/ISC253183.2021.9562951
6. Bauer, R., Columbus, T., Rutter, I., Wagner, D.: Search-space size in contraction hierarchies. Theoret. Comput. Sci. **645** (2016). https://doi.org/10.1016/j.tcs.2016.07.003

7. Büchel, B., Corman, F.: Review on statistical modeling of travel time variability for road-based public transport. Front. Built Environ. **6**, 70 (2020). https://doi.org/10.3389/fbuil.2020.00070
8. Chen, Y., et al.: A multiobjective optimization for clearance in Walmart brick-and-mortar stores. INFORMS J. Appl. Anal. **51**(1), 76–89 (2021). https://doi.org/10.1287/inte.2020.1065
9. Cheng, Y.: Mean shift, mode seeking, and clustering. IEEE Trans. Pattern Anal. Mach. Intell. **17**(8), 790–799 (1995). https://doi.org/10.1109/34.400568
10. Fan, Y., Nie, Y.: Optimal routing for maximizing the travel time reliability. Netw. Spat. Econ. **6**(3), 333–344 (2006). https://doi.org/10.1007/s11067-006-9287-6
11. Floyd, R.W.: Algorithm 97: shortest path. Commun. ACM **5**(6), 345 (1962). https://doi.org/10.1145/367766.368168
12. Lardinois, S.C.F., Topf, J.: OpenStreetMap. UIT Cambridge, Cambridge (2011)
13. Garza, S.E., Schaeffer, S.E.: Community detection with the label propagation algorithm: a survey. Phys. A: Stat. Mech. Appl. **534**, 122058 (2019). https://doi.org/10.1016/j.physa.2019.122058
14. Geisberger, R., Sanders, P., Schultes, D., Vetter, C.: Exact routing in large road networks using contraction hierarchies. Transp. Sci. **46**(3), 388–404 (2012). https://doi.org/10.1287/trsc.1110.0401
15. Gutman, R.: Reach-Based Routing: A New Approach to Shortest Path Algorithms Optimized for Road Networks, pp. 100–111, January 2004
16. Hart, P.E., Nilsson, N.J., Raphael, B.: A formal basis for the heuristic determination of minimum cost paths. IEEE Trans. Syst. Sci. Cybern. **4**(2), 100–107 (1968)
17. Hu, J., Guo, C., Yang, B., Jensen, C.S.: Stochastic weight completion for road networks using graph convolutional networks. In: 2019 IEEE 35th International Conference on Data Engineering (ICDE), pp. 1274–1285 (2019). https://doi.org/10.1109/ICDE.2019.00116
18. Loder, A., Ambühl, L., Menendez, M., Axhausen, K.W.: Understanding traffic capacity of urban networks. Sci. Rep. **9**(1), 1–10 (2019)
19. Macqueen, J.: Some methods for classification and analysis of multivariate observations. In: In 5-th Berkeley Symposium on Mathematical Statistics and Probability, pp. 281–297 (1967)
20. Nie, Y.M., Wu, X.: Shortest path problem considering on-time arrival probability. Transp. Res. Part B: Methodol. **43**(6), 597–613 (2009). https://doi.org/10.1016/j.trb.2009.01.008
21. Niknami, M., Samaranayake, S.: Tractable pathfinding for the stochastic on-time arrival problem. In: Goldberg, A.V., Kulikov, A.S. (eds.) SEA 2016. LNCS, vol. 9685, pp. 231–245. Springer, Cham (2016). https://doi.org/10.1007/978-3-319-38851-9_16
22. Nikolova, E.: Approximation algorithms for reliable stochastic combinatorial optimization. In: Serna, M., Shaltiel, R., Jansen, K., Rolim, J. (eds.) APPROX/RANDOM -2010. LNCS, vol. 6302, pp. 338–351. Springer, Heidelberg (2010). https://doi.org/10.1007/978-3-642-15369-3_26
23. Parzen, E.: On estimation of a probability density function and mode. Ann. Math. Stat. **33**(3), 1065–1076 (1962). https://doi.org/10.1214/aoms/1177704472
24. Pons, P., Latapy, M.: Computing communities in large networks using random walks. J. Graph Algorithms Appl. 191–218 (2006)
25. Rousseeuw, P.J.: Silhouettes: a graphical aid to the interpretation and validation of cluster analysis. J. Comput. Appl. Math. **20**, 53–65 (1987). https://doi.org/10.1016/0377-0427(87)90125-7

26. Ruaridh Clark, M.M.: Eigenvector-based community detection for identifying information hubs in neuronal networks—bioRxiv (2018). https://www.biorxiv.org/content/10.1101/457143v1
27. Rus, D., Lim, S., Balakrishnan, H., Gifford, D.K., Madden, S.R.: Method and apparatus for traffic-aware stochastic routing and navigation (2020). https://patents.google.com/patent/US10535256B1/en
28. Sabidussi, G.: The centrality index of a graph. Psychometrika **31**, 581–603 (1966)
29. Samaranayake, S., Blandin, S., Bayen, A.M.: Speedup Techniques for the Stochastic on-time Arrival Problem. In: ATMOS (2012). https://doi.org/10.4230/OASIcs.ATMOS.2012.83
30. Smith, N.R., Zivich, P.N., Frerichs, L.M., Moody, J., Aiello, A.E.: A guide for choosing community detection algorithms in social network studies: the question alignment approach. Am. J. Prevent. Med. **59**(4), 597–605 (2020). https://doi.org/10.1016/j.amepre.2020.04.015
31. Tibshirani, R., Walther, G., Hastie, T.: Estimating the number of clusters in a dataset via the gap statistic **63**, 411–423 (2000)
32. Utah Traffic: UDOT: Utah Department of Transportation (2020). www.udot.utah.gov/main/f?p=100:6:0::::V,T:1
33. Yang, B., Dai, J., Guo, C., Jensen, C.S., Hu, J.: *PACE*: a *PAth-CEntric* paradigm for stochastic path finding. VLDB J. **27**(2), 153–178 (2017). https://doi.org/10.1007/s00778-017-0491-4
34. Yang, Z., Algesheimer, R., Tessone, C.: A comparative analysis of community detection algorithms on artificial networks. Sci. Rep. **6** (2016). https://doi.org/10.1038/srep30750

Author Index

Printed in the United States
by Baker & Taylor Publisher Services